Human Health and Ecological Integrity

The connection between environment and health has been well studied and documented, particularly by the World Health Organization. It is now being included in some legal instruments, although for the most part case law does not explicitly make that connection. Neither the right to life nor the rights to health and to normal development are actually cited in the resolution of cases and in judges' decisions.

This volume makes the connection explicit in a broad review of human rights and legal issues associated with public health and the environment. It will be particularly useful as many legal instruments emphasize the right to 'development' without fully discussing the necessary safety and public health aspects, and the respect for the ecology of any area where such 'development' (often unwanted by local or indigenous communities) is to be located. Climate change is another pressing variable that is considered, and several chapters address the interface between human health and ecological conditions. Overall, the book integrates perspectives from a wide range of disciplines, including ethics, ecology, public health and epidemiology, and human rights and law.

Laura Westra is Professor Emerita (Philosophy) at the University of Windsor, Ontario, Canada, and Sessional Instructor in the Faculty of Law both at the University of Windsor and the University of Milano (Bicocca), Italy.

Colin L. Soskolne is Professor of Epidemiology in the School of Public Health, University of Alberta, Canada.

Donald W. Spady is an Adjunct Associate Professor of Pediatrics in the Faculty of Medicine & Dentistry and an Adjunct Associate Professor of Public Health in the School of Public Health, both at the University of Alberta, Canada.

Human Health and Ecological Integrity

Ethics, law and human rights

Edited by Laura Westra, Colin L. Soskolne and Donald W. Spady

Routledge
Taylor & Francis Group
LONDON AND NEW YORK

First published 2012 by Routledge
2 Park Square, Milton Park, Abingdon, Oxon OX14 4RN

Simultaneously published in the USA and Canada by Routledge
711 Third Avenue, New York, NY 10017

Routledge is an imprint of the Taylor & Francis Group, an informa business

British Library Cataloguing in Publication Data
A catalogue record for this book is available from the British Library

Library of Congress Cataloging in Publication Data
Human health and ecological integrity : ethics, law and human rights / edited by Laura Westra, Colin L. Soskolne
and Donald Spady.
p. cm.
Includes bibliographical references and index.
1. Public health laws, International. 2. Public health laws. 3. Environmental law, International. 4. Human ecology–Government policy. I. Westra, Laura. II. Soskolne, Colin L. (Colin Lionel) III. Spady, Donald.
K3570.H86 2012
179'.1–dc23
2011052218

ISBN 13: 978-0-415-50427-0 (hbk)
ISBN 13: 978-0-203-12840-4 (ebk)

Typeset in Baskerville
by Saxon Graphics Ltd, Derby

MIX
Paper from responsible sources
FSC® C013604

Printed and bound by CPI Group (UK) Ltd, Croydon, CR0 4YY

Dedication

To my son Peter Christopher Westra – Laura Westra

To all the children of the world – Colin L. Soskolne

To my children and grandchildren – Donald W. Spady

and to Václav Havel (1936–2011) in memoriam

Contents

Contributors

Christian Baatz, MA
Country of affiliation: Germany
PhD Candidate
University of Greifswald
Department of Philosophy
christian.baatz@uni-greifswald.de

Vladimír Bencko, MD, PhD
Country of affiliation: Czech Republic
Professor
Charles University in Prague
First Faculty of Medicine
Institute of Hygiene and Epidemiology
vladimir.bencko@lf1.cuni.cz

Donald A. Brown
Country of affiliation: United States
Associate Professor
Environmental Ethics, Science, and Law
Penn State University

Roger Brownsword, LLB
Country of affiliation: United Kingdom
Professor
King's College London
Roger.brownsword@kcl.ac.uk

Paul Carrick, MA, PhD (Philosophy)
Country of affiliation: United States
Professor of Philosophy and Humanities
Gettysburg College
Harrisburg Area Community College
pcarrick@gettysburg.edu

Brunetto Anton Chiarelli
Country of affiliation: Italy
Professor (Anthropology)
University of Florence
Faculty of Natural Sciences
Web: www.iihs.it E-mail: antropos@unifi.it

Pavel Cudlín, Doc RNDr, CSc
Country of affiliation: Czech Republic
Associate Professor, Researcher, Lecturer
J. E. Purkyne University in Usti nad Labem,
Mendel University in Brno
Global Change Research Centre, Academy of Sciences, Czech Republic
www.czechglobe.cz
cudlin.p@czechglobe.cz

Antonio D'Aloia
Country of affiliation: Italy
Full Professor (Constitutional Law)
University of Parma, Department of Law
antonio.daloia@unipr.it

Joseph W. Dellapenna, BBA (Michigan), JD (Detroit College of Law), LLM (International and Comparative Law) (George Washington), LLM (Environmental Law) (Columbia)
Country of affiliation: United States
Professor of Law
Villanova University School of Law
dellapen@law.villanova.edu
www.law.villanova.edu/Our%20Faculty/Faculty%20Profiles/Joseph%20W%20Dellapenna.aspx

Karolína Dobiášová, Mgr (Public Policy)
Country of affiliation: Czech Republic
Assistant Professor
Charles University, Institute of Public Health and Medical Law
karolinad@seznam.cz

J. Ronald Engel, AB., BD., MA, PhD
Country of affiliation: United States
Professor Emeritus
Meadville/Lombard Theological School (University of Chicago affiliate)
jronengel@comcast.net

Geoffrey Garver, JD, LLM
Countries of affiliation: Canada and United States
PhD Candidate (Geography)
McGill University
gginmont@sympatico.ca

Lawrence O. Gostin
Country of affiliation: United States
University Professor and Director of the O'Neill Institute for National and Global Health Law
Georgetown University Law Center
www.law.georgetown.edu/oneillinstitute
www.law.georgetown.edu/faculty/gostin.html

Franz-Theo Gottwald, Professor, Dr
Country of affiliation: Germany
Professor (Environmental Ethics)
Director of Schweisfurth Foundation
www.schweisfurth-stiftung.de
info@schweisfurth.de

Helena Hnilicová, PhD, PhD (Social Medicine)
Country of affiliation: Czech Republic
Assistant Professor
Charles University, Institute of Public Health and Medical Law
hhnil@lf1.cuni.cz

Kathryn Kintzele, JD
Country of affiliation: United States
Director, Global Responsibilities Program
Center for Humans and Nature
Deputy Chair, Ethics Specialist Group
IUCN Commission on Environmental Law
kathrynkintzele@humansandnature.org

Louis J. Kotzé, BComm, LLB, LLM (cum laude), LLD
Country of affiliation: South Africa
Professor
Professor of Law, North-West University, South Africa
Louis.kotze@nwu.ac.za

Yuliya Lyamzina, PhD, MBA
Country of affiliation: Czech Republic
PhD in Public Health, Master in Business Administration
Department of Preventive Medicine, Masaryk University, Brno, Czech Republic.
lyamzina@yahoo.com
www.linkedin.com/pub/yuliya-lyamzina-phd-mba/3/705/313

Owen McIntyre, BA, LLB, PhD
Country of affiliation: Ireland
Senior Lecturer
Faculty of Law
University College Cork
National University of Ireland
o.mcintyre@ucc.ie

Kathleen Mahoney, FRSC, LLB, LLM, Dip. Int'l Human Rights
Country of affiliation: Canada
Professor of Law
Barrister and Solicitor
University of Calgary
kmahoney@ucalgary.ca

Jack P. Manno, PhD
Country of affiliation: United States
Associate Professor and Graduate Studies Coordinator
SUNY College of Environmental Science and Forestry, Department of Environmental Studies
jpmanno@esf.edu

Megan J. M. Mitchell, LLM
Country of affiliation: New Zealand
Postgraduate Student, Faculties of Law and Philosophy
University of Waikato
mjmm2@waikato.ac.nz

William Onzivu, MR, Master of Laws (LLM)
Countries of affiliation: United Kingdom, Uganda
Lecturer in Law (tenured)
Bradford University Law School, University of Bradford, West Yorkshire (United Kingdom)
Web: www.brad.ac.uk/management/people/profile/?name=wonzivu
Email: w.onzivu@bradford.ac.uk

Konrad Ott, Professor, Dr
Country of affiliation: Germany
Professor of Environmental Ethics
University of Greifswald
Institute of Botany and Landscape Ecology
ott@uni-greifswald.de

Jan Pokorný, Doc RNDr, CSc
Country of affiliation: Czech Republic
Assoc. Professor, Director ENKI, o.p.s.
Lecturer: Charles University Prague, Czech University of Life Sciences Prague
ENKI, o.p.s. Třeboň, Czech Republic
www.enki.cz
pokorny@enki.cz

John Michael Quinn V, MPH
Countries of affiliation: United States, Czech Republic
MD/PhD candidate
Charles University in Prague, First Faculty of Medicine
John.quinn@lf1.cuni.cz

Kathleen Ruff, MA
Country of affiliation: Canada
Senior Human Rights Adviser, Rideau Institute
Founder & director, RightOnCanada.ca
Rideau Institute; RightOnCanada.ca
www.rightoncanada.ca; kruff@bulkley.net

Josef Seják, Doc Ing, CSc
Country of affiliation: Czech Republic
Associate Professor (Landscape Management and Protection)
J. E. Purkyne University in Usti nad Labem
Lecturer and researcher, Faculty of Environment
http://fzp.ujep.cz, sejak@seznam.cz

Colin L. Soskolne, PhD (Epidemiology)
Country of affiliation: Canada
Professor
Fellowships: American College of Epidemiology; Collegium Ramazzini
University of Alberta, School of Public Health
Web: www.colinsoskolne.com
E-mail: colin.soskolne@ualberta.ca

Donald W. Spady, MD, MSc, FRCP(C)
Country of affiliation: Canada
Adjunct: Departments of Pediatrics and Public Health Sciences, Faculty of Medicine and Dentistry, School of Public Health
University of Alberta
dspady@ualberta.ca

Prue Taylor, LLB, LLM, LLM
Country of affiliation: New Zealand
Senior Lecturer
University of Auckland
Prue.taylor@auckland.ac.nz

Valentina Vadi, PhD
Countries of affiliation: The Netherlands, Italy
Marie Curie Postdoctoral Fellow
Maastricht University
www.maastrichtuniversity.nl/web/Faculteiten/FdR/Thema/OverDeFaculteit/Medewerkers/MedewerkersAbc/VadiV.S..htm
v.vadi@maastrichtuniversity.nl

Laura Westra, PhD, PhD (Law)
Countries of affiliation: Canada, Italy
Professor Emerita (Philosophy)
University of Windsor
Sessional Instructor, Faculty of Law
Web Address: www.ecointegrity.net
GEIG: www.globalecointegrity.net
University of Milano (Bicocca) Faculty of Law

Tomáš Zelený
Country of affiliation: Czech Republic
Institute of Economic Studies, Charles University
Zeleny.t@gmail.com

Abbreviations

ACL	Asbestos Corporation Ltd
AOSIS	Association of Small Island States
ATCA	Alien Torts Claims Act
BC	British Columbia
BDI	Beck Depression Inventory
BSE	bovine spongiform encephalopathy
BVM	biotope valuation method
CAI	Canadian Asbestos Institute
CDR	carbon dioxide removal
CE	climate ethics
CESCR	Committee on Economic, Social and Cultural Rights
CH	common heritage of mankind
CO2-eq	carbon dioxide equivalent
COP	Conference of the Parties
CRB	Commodity Research Bureau
CVD	cardiovascular disease
DM	diabetes mellitus type II
EA	efficiency approach
EC	European Commission
ECFR	European Charter of Fundamental Rights
ECHR	European Court of Human Rights
EESC	European Economic and Social Committee
EIA	environmental impact assessment
ELC	European Landscape Convention
EROEI	energy returned on energy invested
ETR	energy–transport–reaction
EU	European Union
EVW	energy–water–vegetation
FAO	Food and Agriculture Organization of the United Nations
FCTC	Framework Convention on Tobacco Control
FDI	foreign direct investment
FFPI	FAO Food Price Index
GEIG	Global Ecological Integrity Group

GHG	greenhouse gas
GMO	genetically modified organism
GMT	global mean temperature
GPI	Genuine Progress Indicator
GSCI	Goldman Sachs Commodity Index
HPV	human papilloma virus
HSCL-25	Hopkins Symptom Checklist-25
IAASTD	International Assessment of Agricultural Knowledge, Science and Technology for Development
ICA	International Chrysotile Association
ICCPR	International Covenant on Civil and Political Rights
ICESCR	International Covenant on Economic, Social and Cultural Rights
ICJ	International Court of Justice
IDP	internally displaced person
IPCC	Intergovernmental Panel on Climate Change
ISA	International Seabed Authority
ISEW	Index of Sustainable Economic Welfare
IUCN	International Union for Conservation of Nature
JALI	Joint Action and Learning Initiative
LDC	least-developed country
LOS	Law of the Sea Convention
LRTAP	Convention on Long-range Transboundary Air Pollution
MEA	multilateral environmental agreement
MPRDA	Minerals and Petroleum Resources Development Act (South Africa)
NAFTA	North American Free Trade Agreement
OHCHR	Office of the High Commission of Human Rights
OMVS	L'Organization Pour la Mise en Valeur du Fleuve Senegal
PAP	Publications Assistance Program (Canada)
PDS	Post-traumatic Stress Diagnostic Scale
ppmv	parts per million by volume
PPP	purchasing power parity
PTSD	post-traumatic stress disorder
PVC	polyvinyl chloride
QBCRA	Quebec Business Concerns Records Act
REACH	Registration, Evaluation and Authorisation and Restriction of Chemicals
SCC	Supreme Court of Canada
SPA	standard price approach
SRM	solar radiation management
STD	sexually transmitted disease
TB	tuberculosis
TMDL	total maximum daily loads
TOE	ton of oil equivalent

UNCHR	United Nations Commission on Human Rights
UNDP	United Nations Development Programme
UNDRIP	United Nations Declaration on the Rights of Indigenous Peoples
UNEP	United Nations Environment Programme
UNFCCC	United Nations Framework Convention on Climate Change
UNGA	United Nations General Assembly
UNHRC	United Nations Human Rights Committee
WCB	Workers' Compensation Board (Canada)
WHA	World Health Assembly
WHC	World Heritage Convention
WHO	World Health Organization
WROEI	welfare returned on energy invested

Foreword

Public health, environment and human rights: a two-stage approach

Roger Brownsword

Introduction

For liberal societies in the developed world, the legitimation of public health policy demands a creative accommodation of, on the one hand, the interest that individuals have in deciding how to lead their own lives, and, on the other, the collective interest in maintaining the conditions for good health and well-being. In such societies, the sponsors of public health programmes will encounter resistance if their interventions are perceived to be 'paternalistic' – at once, accusations of a resurgence of the 'nanny state' will be made. One much-discussed strategy for overcoming this difficulty centres on the acceptability (even to liberals) of default settings that 'nudge' individuals towards acts that are conducive to health (Thaler and Sunstein, 2008); and another attempted accommodation draws on the state's stewardship responsibilities (Nuffield Council on Bioethics, 2007). While there is much to be debated about the coherence and adequacy of these approaches, the fact that they are largely proposed and piloted within well-resourced communities means that they are of limited relevance. Accordingly, in this foreword to an exceptionally timely volume on public health, human rights and the environment, I want to sketch a radically different two-stage approach – an approach that is more discomforting than accommodating.

Briefly, the first stage of this approach turns on the idea of an essential infrastructure for human health and well-being. To secure such an infrastructure, there needs to be a *global* strategy. Moreover, even if the infrastructural requirements were to be thinly specified, such a strategy would have massive redistributive implications. With the infrastructure secured, we get to the second stage, which is where we reconnect with the public health debates that are ongoing in the developed world. The question for such societies is how far they wish to prioritize public health (over and above the essential infrastructural conditions).

The first stage: the essential infrastructure

The general idea of an infrastructure as the underlying foundation for a system is reasonably settled; and the conventional wisdom is that infrastructures in this sense are found in transportation and communication systems, as well as being constituted by basic public services such as sewers, water and energy (Frischmann, 2005). However, the infrastructure that is central to the first stage is one that is *generic*, in the sense that it is essential for any human activity (rather than being specific to particular activities). For example, while the track and signalling infrastructure is necessary for a railway transport system, it is not generic. It is not even generic in the context of transport systems because waterways and road traffic, for example, can function perfectly well in the absence of a railway infrastructure; and it is certainly not generic in the broader sense of being essential for any kind of agency to be viable. What, then, might be candidates for the generic infrastructure in this broader and most fundamental sense?

As Laura Westra has tirelessly pointed out, one thing that humans must have before they are capable of acting, transacting or interacting in the purposive (goal-directed) way that we associate with agency is a minimal level of health and well-being. For humans whose basic health and well-being is under threat, there is little prospect of actualizing their agency—it is akin to the train system being paralysed by damage to the tracks. Although there will be different views as to the details of the generic conditions, we surely share a rough sense of what it means to say that a human enjoys basic health and well-being, such that we can readily identify the kind of factors that are antithetical to the enjoyment of such a condition. For example, we can point to problems with food security and clean water, to environmental pollution and to the prevalence of disease. Sadly, chronic deficiencies of this kind can be found in many parts of the world and, following a natural disaster, we will often see some of them in an acute form.

Even if the most egregious examples of an infrastructural failure can be rectified, there needs to be a debate about whether the essential conditions are static. Arguably, in a world of rapid technological development (particularly bearing in mind the development of global information and communication technologies), we need to review the basic needs of agency. On this view, it is not so much that a digital divide represents another kind of global injustice; rather, it is that humans who are not connected cannot exercise their agency in an increasingly networked world.

If a generic infrastructure is to be secured, there will need to be an unprecedented degree of international coordination and shared responsibility. Moreover, because politics tends to operate with short-term horizons and local interests, it implies not only that the infrastructural stewards have some independence from the political branch, but also that they should actively employ precautionary reasoning in defence of the infrastructure (Beyleveld and Brownsword, 2009: 175).

The second stage: beyond the infrastructure

To return to our wealthier developed societies, there are many public health initiatives that agitate liberals. For example, while prohibitions on smoking in closed public buildings can be justified (on the ground that smoking causes harm to others), it is much less clear how smoking bans in open spaces can be justified; and, while there are good paternalistic reasons for addressing obesity in children, it is less acceptable to tell adults that, as Inez de Beaufort has colourfully put it, they should cut out 'queen of puddings, sticky toffee puddings, and knickerbocker glories'.[1] What is more, the development of large-scale public health biobanks raises concerns about how the anticipated findings might be applied. For example, if a range of key genetic markers is identified, will it be proposed that any human embryos that carry a relevant marker should not be used? We should recall that such screening already takes place for markers associated with a predisposition to cancer; so why not also for markers associated with, say, obesity or addiction? Or, what if a similar approach is taken to pre-natal testing, so that a foetus with the relevant marker is recommended (or required) to be aborted? In short, how far, in a liberal community, will it be accepted that the state can not only set the stage in the right (health-promoting) way, but may also act as gatekeeper for who is admitted to the community, and then as a monitor of individual lifestyles?

In my view, the most defensible version of liberalism is one that focuses on the protection of the generic rights of agents. In practice, this overlaps very substantially with a human rights view, as well as being perfectly congruent with the first-stage requirement that the essential infrastructure for agency should be secured. The default rules for a political community of this kind are:

- that no political decision or policy should impinge on the generic rights of citizens unless the right in question has been universally waived;
- that political decisions should be transparent and should be based on inclusive public engagement; and
- that routine political decisions and policies should reflect the preferences of citizens.

These defaults might be modified but, in the paradigmatic case, a general preference for enhanced public health measures (such as no smoking bans in public parks or terminating foetuses with unhealthy genetic profiles) may be legitimately pursued so long as they do not impinge on the generic rights of any agents in the polity. Equally, if agents prefer to consume high-calorie foods, they may resist public health advocates who want to remind them, as they peruse the menu, that there are healthier options. In this way, the public health profile may vary from one community to another; but in no community should the profile fall short relative to the essential infrastructural requirements.

Conclusion

So long as millions of people are threatened by diseases that are virtually ignored by major programmes of research and development, so long as they lack clean water, and so long as they subsist on no more than the equivalent of a dollar a day, the first stage of the public health project has a long way to go. If and when the essential infrastructure has been put in place worldwide, local communities can legitimately debate their preferences for the enhancement of public health. In liberal communities, there will be debates of the kind that we already have. However, liberals should not direct all their anger at the 'public health police' who seem to want to discipline their lifestyles; rather they should spare some of their ire for the developed world's insouciant neglect of the global conditions for the basic needs of agents.

Note

1 'Whose potbelly is it anyway?', public lecture, hosted by the Nuffield Council on Bioethics, delivered at the Royal Society, London, 26 April 2010.

References

Beyleveld, D. and Brownsword, R. (2009) 'Complex technology, complex calculations: uses and abuses of precautionary reasoning in law' in M. Duwell and P. Sollie (eds), *Evaluating New Technologies: Methodological Problems for the Ethical Assessment of Technological Developments*, Springer, Berlin, p175

Frischmann, B. M. (2005) 'An economic theory of infrastructure and commons management', *Minnesota Law Review*, vol 89, pp917, 923 et seq.

Nuffield Council on Bioethics (2007) *Public Health: Ethical Issues*, Nuffield Council on Bioethics, London

Thaler, R. H. and Sunstein, C. R. (2008) *Nudge: Improving Decisions about Health, Wealth, and Happiness*, Yale University Press, New Haven, NJ

Prologue

Ecological integrity, human health and the Czech democratic tradition: from Jan Hus to Josef Vavroušek

J. Ronald Engel

One reason why the meeting of the Global Ecological Integrity Group (GEIG) in Prague, Czech Republic, was such a special event is that it was held in a nation that is one of the healthiest in the world (by standards of infant mortality), enjoys one of the highest standards of human development – ranking 28th in the 2010 United Nations Development Programme (UNDP) index of 'very high development' nations – held the first summit of European Ministers of the Environment in 1991, and ranks ahead of the United States (and only slightly behind Germany) on the 2010 Democracy Index of 'full democracies'.

Equally pertinent to the concerns of this volume, the meeting permitted members of GEIG to make personal contact with the remarkable company of Czech citizens and public intellectuals who have fought valiantly and contributed greatly to our common struggle for global ecological integrity, human rights, and the health of persons and communities – in a word, to the vision of Earth Democracy. Those who attended the conference this year at Charles University had the privilege of engaging members of this community, and readers of this volume will have a similar opportunity in the pages that follow.

Prague has many symbolic reminders of the radiant history that Czech dissenters and visionaries have made over the centuries. At the centre of it all is the statue of Jan Hus in the Old Town square, graced by his memorable words, 'The truth shall prevail', and Bethlehem Chapel nearby, where he told the poor the truth about the immorality of the imperial regime of his time, a heresy that contributed to his death at the stake in 1415. Other symbols remind us of how the testament of Hus has lived on through the twentieth century: the bronze relief of hands raised in appeal for justice at 16 Narodni Trida, commemorating the night of 17 November 1989, when 50,000 students bravely stood their ground and ignited the Velvet revolution; or the Metronome overlooking the Vltava River, marking the minutes since the rebirth of the Republic in 1991. And then the castle, where two of the wisest democratic philosopher kings of the world have held court – Tomáš Mazaryk, founder and first president of the republic, 1918–1936, and Václav Havel, president, 1990–2003.

Such symbolic memorials of courage and sacrifice on behalf of human liberty, equality and solidarity are not restricted to Prague. They are found throughout the Czech Republic; for example, in Tabor, where late one starless night my wife and I literally bumped by accident into the stone altar table that the followers of Hus set in the town square; and as far away as the University of Chicago, where for forty years I regularly passed by the great statue of the Blanik Knight on horseback at the east end of the Midway Plaisance, dedicated to the memory of Tomáš Masaryk.

We all recognize that the history we are discussing is not identical with the history of Czechoslovakia or the Czech Republic. The Czechoslovak peoples have known human cruelty and betrayal – at their own hands and, most brutally, at the hands of others – as well as what Czech philosopher Erazim Kohák calls the great 'naught' of contemporary postmodern culture. The social repression, ecological ruin and loss of human life that marked the German invasion and the years of communist rule were recent chapters in a long and tragic story. Neither, unfortunately, are we speaking of the primary trajectory of Czech governance since the mid-1990s when, by many accounts, concern for the environment and its impact on public health have fallen into neglect, dominated as these years have been by the neoliberal economic politics and philosophy of Václav Klaus (Tickle and Welsh, 1998, pp1–29).

We are rather speaking of those persons and groups who have stepped forward throughout Czech history and sought to call their fellow citizens and their oppressors to the better angels of their nature. We are speaking of those who – often at great personal cost – have prophetically denounced all totalitarian ideologies – whether theocratic, imperial, fascist, communist or capitalist. These are the persons Kohák names 'pilgrims through time'. We are speaking of those who have tried to set forth an alternative interpretation of historical meaning: one that finds in shared democratic responsibility for the flourishing of Earthly life the commanding ethical imperative and metanarrative of human existence. By building this vision, and seeking to live by it, they effectively influenced, even if they did not ever fully govern, the actual course of events.

Josef Vavroušek

There is no better way to set the stage for this volume and pay tribute to our hosts in the Czech Republic than to speak of Josef Vavroušek, and through the prism of his life, to identify the elements of the inspiring Czech tradition of social and ecological commitment in which he stood. Josef Vavroušek was the minister of environment of the Czechoslovak Republic in the first years of the presidency of Václav Havel (1990–1992). I was privileged to know Josef in the years immediately following his ministry.

Born in 1944 in Prague, Josef developed an interest in ecological systems theory through his studies at the Czech Technical University. In January,

1968, at the age of 24, as the heavy hand of communist rule was being temporarily eased, Josef joined an expedition to truck medical supplies to Albert Schweitzer's bush hospital at Lambarene in Gabon, west Africa. This was a life-determining experience, and Josef often referred to it in conversations and essays. As he later wrote:

> Traveling through fourteen African countries, I realized for the first time what grinding poverty was, what the exhaustion of a landscape turned to desert by overuse looked like ... We returned in the autumn, after the Russian tanks. We learned of the invasion from French dockers at Marseilles, but we went back home all the same because we felt that we should be there to fight the totalitarian regime from within, with the people. (Vavroušek, 1993, p87)

Josef's experience in Africa in 1968 is a grand paradigm for the Czech history we are celebrating, and for the subject of the 2011 GEIG conference. It vividly displays how interdependent are the quality of human health and the quality of the environment, and how our concerns for one lead inevitably to our concerns for the other. It also shows how important it is for each of us to understand the plight of persons and ecologies in other parts of the world if we are to grasp the full moral and political significance of each of our particular national struggles, and the critical importance in these struggles of solidarity with our fellow citizens, both globally and domestically. As Donella Meadows (n.d.) wrote in tribute to Vavroušek in a piece titled 'The global citizen: the Czech environmental testament': 'he was one of the few people who felt responsible for the whole planet ... a positive role model for action on behalf of health and the environment'.

Missing the Prague Spring had one important benefit for Vavroušek. It meant that while his dissident friends were being driven from their jobs, he was not pestered. So, for the twenty dark years from 1968 to 1988, Josef was able to work as a scientist and keep in touch through underground universities with colleagues like Meadows at Cornell University in the outside world. As a member of the Czech and Slovak Association of the Club of Rome, he was responsible for translating Meadows *et al.*'s (1972) *Limits to Growth* into Czech.

Vavroušek's growing awareness of the urgency of environmental issues, and their inseparable connection to communist state dictatorship, led to his increasing political radicalization, and in 1989 he co-founded an illegal protest group called the Independent Intellectuals Circle. He also became actively involved in the Co-ordination Centre of the Citizens Forum, the core leadership of the Velvet Revolution, authoring its first political manifesto, 'What we Want'.

With the election of Václav Havel to the presidency, Vavroušek was appointed federal minister for the environment and, in the two short years in which he served in that capacity, he established himself as one of the world's leading environmental statesmen. He organized and led the first meeting of European ministers for the environment, called 'Environment for Europe', at Dobříš Castle, Czech Republic, in 1991.

After the separation of Slovakia from the Czech Republic in 1992, Josef was appointed to the Faculty of Social Sciences at Charles University, where he taught human ecology and biopolitics. That same year, he founded and served as first president of the Society for Sustainable Living, whose purposes sound virtually the same as those of GEIG (Vavroušek, n.d.).

In 1995, after helping to organize the first post-Cold War international conference linking Ecology and Democracy in České Budějovice (Hanousková *et al.*, 1994), Josef took his daughter, Petra, then nineteen and a student at Charles University, on a ski vacation to the Tatra mountains in Slovakia. Josef was an ardent mountaineer; he and his daughter loved to climb high mountains together. Tragically, an avalanche took both of their lives.

Josef Vavroušek's biography provides a clear understanding of the ideas and motivations that governed his life. Let me further explicate these by drawing upon his writings and the work of three other notable twentieth century Czech public intellectuals – Tomáš Masaryk, Václav Havel and Erazim Kohák – who shared Vavroušek's commitment to Earth Democracy. Masaryk, Havel and Kohák are all authors of a substantial body of published work that is available in English, as well as Czech. Kohák, author of the environmental classic, *The Embers and the Stars* (1984), left Czechoslovakia with his family of political refugees in 1948, and lived in the United States until 1990, when he returned to his homeland to teach at Charles University.

Vavroušek's comprehensive ethical and spiritual vision

Václav Havel wrote in tribute to Vavroušek:

> It was primarily the awareness of oneness with nature, respect for life in all its forms and for nature as a whole, as well as humility in the face of the 'order of being' and respect for the free will of man, which gave hope and life to [Vavroušek's] conception of 'sustainable living'. (Havel, 1998)

At a time when those of us in North America were only beginning to integrate social ethics and environmental ethics under the banners of 'environmental justice' and 'ecojustice', Czech environmental leaders such as Vavroušek were articulating a strong ethic of human responsibility for the well-being of people and the land together, and doing so within a comprehensive ethical vision that Vavroušek described in 1994, when he joined Laura Westra and me to speak at our Buenos Aires World Conservation Congress workshop on Ethics and Law, as 'the search for harmony between man and nature, society and environment, so that we reach the ideals of humanism and respect for life and nature and its forms in all time horizons' (Vavroušek, 1994).

What we find in the Czech philosophical tradition, from Masaryk to Vavroušek and his late twentieth century contemporaries, is a unique form of ethical and spiritual naturalism; an updating, if you will, of classical natural law theory in keeping with the modern empirical sciences. In contradistinction to Carnap and the Vienna circle of positivists nearby, the Czech tradition has found meaning and value no less given in human experience, and no less available to human reason, than mathematical relations or physical principles. Ethics is therefore as much a concern of the scientist as the philosopher, and no less the fruit of scientific investigation as the measurable physical facts of the situation, an epistemological postulate many members of GEIG find congenial.

Vavroušek always started his speeches with values and facts together because he believed value structures are as much built into objective reality as physical and biological structures; indeed, they are two sides of the one reality of nature. The significant contrast is between rational and irrational understandings of facts and values. The aim of the scientist–ethicist is to empirically and reflectively discover ways to maintain and augment those facts and values that are healthy and sustainable for life. And so Vavroušek threw himself intensely into the work of discerning what facts and values were currently directing the course of human societies, and how they might be redirected so as to simultaneously fulfil the actual value potential of our species and be 'harmonious', 'compatible' and 'mutually fulfilling' of our host, the world of nature.

The second observation we need to make about Vavroušek's vision has to do with its distinctively spiritual dimension. Josef's trip to Schweitzer's hospital at Lambarene made a lasting impact on his life. He joined the expedition because of his profound respect for Schweitzer's ethic of reverence for the life of all living beings. Vavroušek shared Schweitzer's view that humankind had reached a stage in its world evolution such that the spiritual dimension of human consciousness needed to break free of the confines of our inherited religious institutions, however indebted we may be to the wisdom these institutions still bear, and reach out to embrace the whole of humanity and the whole of living beings on Earth, for only life itself could now be an object truly worthy of our love, respect and reverence.

Note that life so perceived as worthy of reverence and sacred is an empirical datum. We are not speaking of a 'Wholly Other' apart from the world, above the world, at the beginning of the world, at the end of the world, but of the heart of existence itself, the world as we encounter it.

Tomáš Masaryk frequently spoke of this transcendent reality as life lived *sub specie aeternitatis* – under the aspect of eternity. Václav Havel regularly referred to it as the 'something in the order of being which exceeds all our competence ... the absolute horizon of our existence' (1986, p153). I have always felt great kinship with this naturalistic Czech religious philosophy because it seems so convergent with my own American transcendentalist forbears, who also found spirit immanent in nature. 'I see, smell, taste, hear, feel, that everlasting Something to which we are allied,' Henry Thoreau wrote, 'at once our maker, our abode, our destiny, our very Selves … the actual glory of the universe' (1983, p173).

It is our misfortune, however, that we know this glory not only – or even most commonly – in our high mountaintop moments, as when Schweitzer saw four hippopotamuses and their young plodding along a sandbank in Africa (Schweitzer, 1923; cited in Kohák, 2000); or when Masaryk on a winter train ride looked out of the window into a forest and saw a group of trees still green with leaves despite the wintertime, and had the 'feeling of something eternal, strong, living, ruled by order' (Polák, 2000); or when Kohák, living in exile in America, contemplated the stars above his cabin clearing in the forest of a New Hampshire hillside; or when Vavroušek and Petra went skiing in their beloved Tatra mountains. Too often we know this glory by its violation. To our great regret, it is by the negation of the will to live that the supreme rightness of the will to live is revealed to us, along with the recognition that it is we humans who, more often than not, are responsible for that violation and therefore matters could be otherwise – the religious foundation of our moral sense of responsibility. Havel gives us a striking example of this kind of experience in his essay, 'Politics and conscience':

> As a boy … I used to walk to school in a nearby village … and on the way see on the horizon a huge smokestack of some hurriedly built factory … It spewed dense brown smoke and scattered it across the sky. Each time I saw it, I had an intense sense of something profoundly wrong, of humans soiling the heavens. (Havel, 1986, p136)

Vavroušek had this experience as he drove the truck laden with medical supplies across Africa and 'realised for the first time what grinding poverty was, what the exhaustion of a landscape turned to desert by overuse looked like'. He was drawn to Africa by the lure of Schweitzer's example of reverence for life, but found it most memorably present in the experience of its absence.

No wonder that Josef's presentation at Buenos Aires was a set of sharp contrasts – the world's cultural values and facts as they now pertain versus the world's values and facts as they could and should be if we are to live in harmony with ourselves and the rest of nature – an expression of his religious consciousness that something else – something more real, true, beautiful and good – may be (ought to be) the case.

Vavroušek's democratic faith

The Czech philosophers, writers, poets, artists and musicians who sought to establish a universal humanistic foundation for their nation in the late eighteenth and early nineteenth centuries were known as the 'awakeners'. When Václav Havel assumed the presidency in 1990, he spoke of 'coming to our senses', and wore a parka about the castle with the word 'awakenings' across the back. Vavroušek was another one of the great 'awakeners' of the Czech people, awakening them to what it means to 'live in the truth'.

There is a high view of citizenship in the Czech progressive democratic tradition that I am tracing. There are two reasons for this. First, the Czech democratic ideal of self-governing citizens and human rights is deeply rooted in the comprehensive ethical and spiritual vision I have been describing. Masaryk concluded his book on Marxism with the statement: 'Democracy must broaden into an all-embracing world view. The politics of such a democracy will be a genuine politics of life as well as the world – a political *sub specie aeternitatis*' (Masaryk, 1972). Second, there have been a number of dramatic events that have created and renewed that vision over the centuries. I have noted the seminal witness and martyrdom of Jan Hus. Accidentally bumping into the stone altar table on the plaza at Tabor was a memorable experience for Joan and me because followers of Hus took the radical democratic step of moving the altar table from the church into the plaza so that everyone could partake of the full sacrament of the Eucharist, the wine and bread of our health and salvation. Hence the saying that the Czech people are 'people of the chalice'.

During the presidency of Ronald Reagan (1980–1988), my students were profoundly discouraged about the prospects for serious democratic citizenship in the United States. The one author whom they took seriously, however, was Václav Havel. In his essay 'The power of the powerless', they heard the voice of someone who could credibly testify to the power of citizens with a conscience to carve out a parallel polis of democratic freedom, equality and community 'from below' in keeping with the inherent self-organizing powers of life (Havel, 1986, pp36–122). Earlier generations of Czechs, Europeans and Americans, familiar with the daring leadership of Masaryk during the First World War, heard a similar voice. They believed him when he shared his faith that people are capable of growing to the maturity of rational freedom and responsible citizenship (Warren, 1941).

Building on this history, Kohák argues that there is a common posture which constitutes a normative conception of what it means to claim a Czech cultural identity. This posture is to be found in:

> the Enlightenment ideal for which freedom is not just an absence of constraint but an achievement and a fulfillment of our humanity. To grow to freedom here means to outgrow the need for tutelage, to be capable of self-direction, but not just that. It also implies a basic self-respect, a sense of human dignity … Humans confident of their own worth, of their own dignity, can live at peace with themselves even in privation and hardship … There is a profound sense of equality ingrained in such freedom. None is master who could look down on his

> fellow, none serf having to submit to the arrogance of another. Such freedom is both the most basic possibility and the noblest achievement of being human. (Kohák, 2008, p219)

Vavroušek's prescriptions for sustainable living were firmly based on the faith that citizens of free democratic societies could grow into sufficient moral maturity to exercise self-control over their proclivities for aggrandizement at the expense of others and the environment, and to cooperate for the common good. Following Masaryk's view that democracy is a protest against the claim anyone can own the life and work of another, and on behalf of the conviction that persons become free through democratic work together, he trusted that worker-owned and worker-managed organizations would offer a third way for the sustainable economic development of the country.

Vavroušek's democratic faith was more than an aspiration, however; it had its foundations in his experience organizing independent ecological organizations in the 1980s, the very kind of 'parallel polis' that Havel extolled in 'The power of the powerless'. Furthermore, as he began to take active political leadership in the 1990s, he was encouraged by the fact that a common concern for the environment and public health served as a catalyst for people to come together and create new institutions of democratic governance, and, in the process, to engage in public deliberation, debate and reasoned argument. For Masaryk, 'democracy is discussion', and so too it was for Vavroušek. By such means 'truth shall prevail'.

Vavroušek's courage to speak truth to power

'Awakening' our fellow citizens to their potential for moral maturity, and to the reverence for life on which it is grounded, often requires saying unpopular things in the town square and making fateful, life-risking decisions. Voluntarily returning to Czechoslovakia in 1968 was such a decision for Josef Vavroušek.

In 1977, Czechoslovakia's communist rulers incorporated into Czechoslovak law the Helsinki Agreement, which pledged the signatories to observe the human rights of their subjects. A group of Czech dissenters took the regime at its word and, in Charter 77, called on the regime to honour its commitments. As a result, Václav Havel and others were sentenced to over four years in prison. Although Josef was not a signatory to Charter 77, he demonstrated integrity and courage in his authorship of the first sets of demands of the Civic Forum in 1989, which included the demand for the resignation of communist leaders who supported the Warsaw Pact invasion in 1968, and the release of political prisoners. He showed similar integrity and courage in his approach to the historic Dobříš Conference of European Environment Ministers in 1991. In his opening speech, he spelled out clearly the need to protect nature 'not only for the good of mankind, but mainly for its unique intrinsic value', and proclaimed that 'We must discover Albert Schweitzer's philosophy of reverence for life' (Vavroušek 1991, p4). He also invited Erazim Kohák as a keynote speaker, thus assuring that the challenge of a radical ecological ethic was foregrounded in the conference deliberations.

In retrospect, I can better understand why Josef's first words upon arriving in the convention hall in Buenos Aires in 1994 were: 'what's the plan?' How was this workshop on ethics and law going to speak truth to power and impact the General Assembly of the World Conservation Union? Josef was eager to contribute to the work of the World Conservation Union (IUCN) Ethics Working Group that organized the workshop, now led by GEIG members Klaus Bosselmann and Kathryn Kintzele. He saw this as a way of holding the IUCN leadership and members accountable to their espoused values. In Vavroušek's mind, as well as that of his countrymen Masaryk, Havel and Kohák, one of the greatest obstacles to moral progress is the lack of courage of persons in significant leadership positions, whether government or civil society, to use their political skills to promote their own convictions (Havel, 2005).

But it was on my home ground, at the University of Chicago later that year, when I hosted Vavroušek and arranged for a meeting with faculty identified with Milton Friedman's 'Chicago school of economics', that I experienced Josef's intellectual stamina and moral courage first hand. Much to my embarrassment, the Chicago faculty proved themselves to be as rude as they were ill-informed, repeatedly interrupting his presentation with questions about why we should be so concerned for the environment when accelerating economic growth through overseas investment was the issue at hand in eastern Europe. Vavroušek refused to be bullied and argued vociferously that the privatisation, marketisation, turn to tradable currencies and reduced social expenditure imposed by the World Bank and the International Monetary Fund had disastrous effects on the health of Czech society, its people and ecology, calling into question the economics profession as it was practiced in the West.

Vavroušek's rooted cosmopolitanism

An observation often made by Czechs about themselves is that circumstances have required them to develop a positive understanding of the relationship between the local and the global. There are obvious practical reasons for this. As Masaryk put it: 'We must always bear in mind that we are a small nation in an unfavourable geographical position' (1938, p209) – truly an understatement in light of the centuries of domination of the Czech and Slavic lands by foreign powers. But it is to the immense credit of Czech leaders such as Masaryk that the very practical need of the Czech people for protection of their territory and cultural integrity by means of international cooperation has gone far beyond considerations of realpolitik and resulted in a rich philosophy of the relationship between the local and the global, or what Kohák (2008) poetically names, in the title of his most recent book, *Hearth and Horizon: Cultural Identity and Global Humanity in Czech Philosophy.*

Josef Vavroušek was a model of the global citizen: struggling for cultural autonomy and responsible democratic self-government at home, while simultaneously promoting responsible democratic self-government for the world as a whole, by every avenue available to him – academic exchange, governmental negotiation and 'anti-political politics'. Vavroušek saw the old United Nations melting down, making necessary new platforms for future political reunification of world community. He not only proposed ambitious programmes of coordinated action on the environment and health for Europe, such as the European Environmental Protection and Restoration System, but set forth a blueprint at the 1992 Rio Summit for the reform of the United Nations that would move environmental governance to the centre of global concern by the formation of a UN World Environment Organization, a clear precursor to similar proposals now being considered for discussion at the 2012 Earth Summit (1993, pp87–111).

Yet Vavroušek was equally committed to the importance of the local in its living concreteness. As much as possible, he argued, we should set aside state political boundaries and concentrate on eco-cultural regions as the foundational units of sustainable global governance. At the conclusion of the Salzburg Seminar that he hosted in Prague in 1994, he wrote:

> But there is no absolute and single way towards a sustainable future. Quite the contrary. Each person, village or city, ethnic or religious group, nation, state, region or culture could and should search for its own way based on its own unique historical roots and specific natural conditions. Only with strong local roots can sustainability endure. It cannot be imposed. (Vavroušek 1995, p2)

The Czech democratic tradition has been a leader in advancing what we now call a relational or ecological world view. World community is not something that happens above the world in some realm called 'international' or 'universal', but is concretely constituted by complementary and mutually supportive relationships between widely diverse individuals, cultures, polities and ecosystems. This is the fundamental metaphor of Earth Democracy – individuality in community – and stands over and against all abstract systems of reason, politics, economics or culture that seek to repress the irrepressible diversity of life. The Earth is, and should be, a community of communities.

Vavroušek's witness to hope in hopeless times

We live today at a time of the dismantling of the public realm and the continuing deterioration of the integrity of the biosphere, with serious implications for the health of human populations the world over. In the early 1990s, flush with the hopes that were raised in Rio, Josef and I never expected the international community to fail so miserably to take up the challenge of environmental governance. If Josef were here now, I am confident that he would remind us that he and his countrymen lived through much darker times, and, as he once wrote, 'we learned during the Velvet Revolution that nothing is impossible' (Vavroušek 1993).

Observers of those years have commented on how quickly and unexpectedly the whole ideological edifice of Marxist–Leninism disappeared. The bitter experience of previous years had hollowed it out, made it apparent that it was a lie, and that everyone knew it was a lie – a lie now only kept alive by habit and the police, and the advantages it provided for select classes and individuals of the population. Havel and Vavroušek were clear that the lie Czechoslovakia lived from 1948 to 1989 was not substantively different from the lie that Western consumer society still lives. Like dialectical materialism, market ideology is the acme of unreason because it is not open to question, and its power is maintained by bribery, deception, propaganda and coercion. Surely not by democratic consent, and surely not by hope. Might it too not dissolve some night?

Josef Vavroušek's message to us, if he could give one last shout from the top of the Tatra mountains, where he experienced the exhilaration of personal and ecological health, would be that no matter how bad it becomes, we should never give up our grip on life, our reverence for life, our confidence in the truth of life, our efforts to 'live in the truth' of life, our conviction that 'the truth shall prevail', and the integrity of human and natural existence *sub specie aeternitatis* is greater than all the imagined virtual worlds we can ever conjure up – that the cosmos favours life, and therefore life will win over all our negations and blasphemies and stupidities, and that we should be ever thankful for it!

References

Hanousková, I., Lapka, M. and Cudlínová, E. (eds) (1994) *Ecology and Democracy: The Challenge of the 21st Century*, Proceedings of the First International Conference, NEBE s.r.o., České Budějovice, Czech Republic

Havel, V. (1986) *Living in the Truth*, Faber and Faber, Boston, MA

Havel, V. (1998) 'Foreword', in A. Tickle and Ian Welsh (eds) *Environment and Society in Eastern Europe*, Addison-Wesley Longman, Harlow, UK

Havel, V. (2005) 'The emperor has no clothes', *Journal of Democracy*, vol 16, no 4, pp8–10

Kohák, E. (1984) *The Embers and the Stars: A Philosophical Inquiry into the Moral Sense of Nature*, University of Chicago Press, Chicago, IL

Kohák, E. (2000) *The Green Halo: A Bird's Eye View of Ecological Ethics*, Open Court, Chicago, IL

Kohák, E. (2008) *Hearth and Horizon: Cultural Identity and Global Humanity in Czech Philosophy*, Filosofia, Prague, Czech Republic

Masaryk, T. G. (1938) *On Thought and Life: Conversations with Karel Capek*, George Allen and Unwin, London

Masaryk, T. G. (1972) *Masaryk on Marx: An Abridged Edition of The Social Question: Philosophical and Sociological Foundations of Marxism*, E. Kohak (tr.), Bucknell University Press, Lewisburg, PA, p377

Meadows, D. (n.d.) 'The global citizen: The Czech environmental testament', *The Donella Meadows Archive*, www.webcitation.org/61mNAm7x9, accessed 17 September 2011.

Meadows, D. H., Meadows, D. L., Randers, J. and Behrens III, W. W. (1972) *The Limits to Growth*, Universe Books, New York

Polák, S. (2000) 'Masaryk's personal religion', typewritten translation by C. Kovtun of 'Masarykovo náboženství' in *Masarykův Sborník* X 1996–1998, Masarykův ústav AV ČR, Prague, Czech Republic

Schweitzer, A. (1923) *Civilization and Ethics*, A. Nash (tr.), A. & C. Black, London

Thoreau, H. D. (1983) *The Illustrated A Week on the Concord and Merrimack Rivers*, C. F. Hovde, W. L. Howarth and E. H. Witherell (eds). Princeton University Press, Princeton, NJ

Tickle, A. and Welsh, I. (eds) (1998) *Environment and Society in Eastern Europe*, Addison-Wesley Longman, Essex, UK

Vavroušek, J. (1991) 'Vavroušek on ecological issues facing Europe', *Foreign Broadcast Information Service*, JPRS Report, 25 September

Vavroušek, J. (1993) 'Institutions for environmental security', in G. Prins (ed.) *Threats Without Enemies*, Earthscan, London

Vavroušek, J. (1994) 'Perspectives of the human values compatible with the sustainable ways of living', *Future Generations (Journal of the Global Network on Responsibilities towards Future Generations and their Environment)*, vol 13, no 1, p6

Vavroušek, J. (1995) 'Conclusions of the seminar', *Salzburg Seminar Sustainable Living Network Newsletter*, May, Salzburg

Vavroušek, J. (n.d.) 'The society for sustainable living', 6-page typescript, privately circulated, in possession of author

Warren, W. P. (1941) *Masaryk's Democracy: A Philosophy of Scientific and Moral Culture*, University of North Carolina Press, Chapel Hill, NC

Introduction

Laura Westra, Colin L. Soskolne and Donald W. Spady

For 20 years, Professor Laura Westra has been at the helm of the Global Ecological Integrity Group (GEIG). This group of nearly 300 members from all parts of the world is unique in its widely interdisciplinary composition, and its annual meetings reflect its eclectic nature.

Every year, about 50 members of the group convene somewhere in the world to participate in a cultural and historic conversation that stimulates thinking about global problems and solutions. Through engagement and interaction among its members, greater appreciation is achieved for the policy linkages that enable healthy societies through promoting the flourishing of all forms of life.

In 2008, Earthscan published the fifteenth anniversary collection, *Reconciling Human Existence with Ecological Integrity* (Westra *et al.*, 2008). At that time, by employing various perspectives, we explored how human existence could be reconciled with the need for ecological integrity, as defined by James Karr, Laura Westra and others in our 2000 collective work, *Ecological Integrity: Integrating Environmental Conservation and Health* (Pimentel *et al.*, 2000).

Each year, a book is launched that reflects a collection of papers presented at the previous year's meeting. These collections, which help to bring focus to the GEIG's selected theme for the meeting for that year, have been jointly edited by Professor Westra, along with the support of at least one or two of the group's members. The 2011 meeting of the group in Prague, Czech Republic, which followed our tradition of yearly meetings, has resulted in this volume, which reflects the broad interdisciplinary array of contributions presented in Prague.

Two of the co-editors for this book broadly reflect the disciplines of medicine, epidemiology and public health. These specialties are relevant to a book titled *Human Health and Ecological Integrity: ethics, law and human rights*. Indeed, as the GEIG has evolved over the past 20 years, it has become apparent that giving prominence to the *right to health* is an important way to focus on the issue that the group has been concerned with since its inception, namely that of ecological integrity.

Ecological integrity has been advanced in several of Westra's prior publications. Put simply, ecological integrity is defined as the ability of life-supporting ecosystems (in their production of fresh air, safe potable water and fertile soils) to withstand assaults or perturbations arising through the continued expansion of the human enterprise. Current trends indicate that all life on Earth is being over-stressed.

The current book is one that extends the public health focus that the Group addressed in 1998 at a formally structured World Health Organization (WHO) workshop under the auspices of the European Centre for Environment and Health based in Rome, Italy. This meeting resulted in 1999 in a groundbreaking discussion document entitled *Global Ecological Integrity and 'Sustainable Development': Cornerstones of Public Health* (Soskolne and Bertollini, 1999). It served a major advocacy role in bringing attention to the linkages between ecological integrity and health. This document demonstrated that, to ensure a sustainable future, we must pay attention to the biological integrity of life on Earth. It recognized that humans are the world's single largest disruptive force.

The widening range and accumulating gravity of environmental harms make it imperative to focus our efforts on the *right to health* as the most basic of all human rights in relation to the need to protect all forms of life. As a group, over the past 20 years we have brought attention to the escalating declines in all that sustains life. Now, the time of crisis is upon us, and our intent through this book is to reflect, using some case studies, on how the current declines might be arrested.

As intelligent and creative social beings, humans need to develop legal instruments and regulations to protect us from ourselves; we need both environmental and health protections in our governance regimes. This necessity inspired the decision to dedicate the Prague meeting of the GEIG to public health. In light of its strong philosophical and academic tradition as articulated so eruditely in the prologue by J. Ronald Engel, we accepted the invitation of the Charles University First Faculty of Medicine in Prague for our meeting.

The selected focus for the Prague meeting resulted in a harmonious collection of papers discussing law, human rights, the environment and other related topics, the main thrust being public health and global environmental hazards. This combination produced an exciting and novel programme for the meeting and – we hope – an equally interesting and innovative book.

In our foreword, Roger Brownsword acknowledges the limited role of international law regarding the multiple aspects of environmental harms, all of which ought to be contained and enforced through global governance, but are not. World Trade and other international economic legal regimes produce the most severe harms in the world, including those arising from climate change, with its related extreme weather events. The essential infrastructure of governance needs drastic revision to achieve a truly global strategy for a sustainable future.

This book is organized so as to bridge the connection between health and the environment. It starts, in Part I, with an examination of the problem followed by the principles by which life might be sustained. In Part II, the role of sovereign nations for protecting public health and how these roles can be influenced are discussed. In Part III, several issues are identified that reflect on governance. Questions relating to climate change and water are addressed in Part IV. The relevance and appropriateness of recognizing indigenous rights are addressed in Part V. The chapters comprising Part VI tackle the challenges of agriculture, food security, financial regimes and international law. The idea of *ecological law* is put forward as a possible way forward.

Several other chapters propose various innovative solutions for better ways to move forward than the present forms of global governance. Prue Taylor suggests a strengthening of the Principle of the Common Heritage of Mankind that might take the place of current, less effective regimes. Megan Mitchell proposes a revised approach to environmental laws, and Kathryn Kintzele and Antonio D'Aloia advocate further study of national constitutions taking a stronger position on environmental issues. Needed changes include continuity beyond immediate political time horizons, as well as greater effectiveness for their implementation in domestic legal frameworks.

Lawrence Gostin concludes, after acknowledging the grave harms engendered by climate change, arguing for the emergence of a 'Global Health Treaty' to cement the interface between public health issues, based on environmental hazards, and human rights. He notes that 'the post-MDG global health framework is yet to be developed'. Perhaps this time may represent a solid start, one that points to a better healthier future, at a time when even the World Health Assembly is considering far-reaching reforms.

References

Pimentel, D., Westra, L. and Noss, R. F. (2000) *Ecological Integrity: Integrating Environmental Conservation and Health*, Island Press, Washington, DC

Soskolne, C. L. and Bertollini, R. (1999) *Global Ecological Integrity and 'Sustainable Development': Cornerstones of Public Health: A Discussion Document.* World Health Organization, European Centre for Environment and Health, Rome, Italy, available at www.colinsoskolne.com/documents/WHO-1999_Discussion_Document.pdf

Westra, L., Klaus Bosselmann, K. and Westra, R. (eds) (2008) *Reconciling Human Existence with Ecological Integrity: Science, Ethics, Economics and Law*, Earthscan, London

Part I

Health and the Environment

Introduction

Laura Westra and Colin L. Soskolne

Foundational to the 2011 meeting of the Global Ecological Integrity Group (GEIG) in Prague – with its focus on public health – the first part of this book contains five chapters. Each chapter addresses the key elements that connect life, health and the environment. The right to health as embodied in supranational conventions and law is addressed throughout. The main focus is on the legal aspects of the interface between environment and health. The final chapter appeals to Aldo Leopold to remind the reader of the pivotal importance of ecological integrity, not only to the GEIG, but to anyone considering health and the environment, as Leopold himself did.

In Chapter 1, Westra discusses the flaws in present international legal regimes, and the denied connection between environment and the human right to health. These flaws emerge clearly in the paucity of jurisprudence dealing explicitly with that link, even when environmental causes and the resulting illnesses are the reason why a case is brought to the courts. Despite the presence of explicit appeals to the right to health and to a 'healthy environment' existing in various instruments, the link between that right and the environment is denied by omission in all case law.

In Chapter 2, Kintzele discusses the presence of environmental and public health clauses in numerous constitutions, in the states on all continents. She notes that biodiversity conservation is explicitly named in Article 38 of the Statute of the International Court of Justice. Thus, it is entirely appropriate for state statutes to adopt not only that principle, but also to support explicitly the connection between it and public health. This interconnection is clearly present in the constitutions of states from South Africa to Bahrain, from Somalia to Kenya, and from Bolivia and Ecuador to Sweden and France. Kintzele notes especially the importance of safety in food, brought to the attention of the world community in Europe with their resistance to genetically modified organisms (GMOs), and – even more recently – in Japan, as the impact of radiation on food was noted after the Fukushima disaster.

In Chapter 3, Mitchell attempts to trace an 'ecological interpretation of international law'. Her starting point is the necessity for change, a change that acknowledges ecological integrity as the basis of all possible instruments that attempt to connect public health and environment, and the right to life. What she proposes is an 'ecologically literate interpretation of the law', but she also hopes for more explicit declarations to emerge from the work of the UN Human Rights Committee.

Taylor turns to international law in Chapter 4, where she carefully examines the possibilities inherent in the principle of the Common Heritage of Mankind (CH), a well-respected principle of international law since its emergence in 1960. Taylor views that principle as a possible antidote to the ongoing 'final enclosure of the commons' (Westra), as she considers whether the CH could be used to 'overcome some of the traditional democratic deficit of international law', as she traces its history and present and earlier usage. Particularly important is the question she raises as to whether 'humanity' can now be considered a subject of international law, given the unique language of the CH.

Finally, in Chapter 5, Carrick examines the GEIG's starting point, in some sense; that is, the work of Aldo Leopold. Leopold had explicitly connected health and the environment, clarifying how the 'community health perspective', 'the holistic health perspective' and the 'perspective of legal moralism' combine to support and reinforce the emphasis on ecological and biological integrity. The latter have been the main platform of our group, and of this book.

The importance of including principles relating to human rights in soft- and hard-law instruments is revealed to be essential for protecting human health and, indeed, all life on Earth. Without these foundational governance instruments, the weight of argument for protecting the right to health will be less compelling and persuasive.

1 Life, health and the environment

The denied connection

Laura Westra

Introduction

This chapter is intended to explore the interface between human rights violations of human health and legal regimes intended for environmental protection. The time seems appropriate to explore this topic, on which a number of initiatives have converged over the last decade, and particularly over the last year. Examples include:

- the United Nations General Assembly (UNGA) Human Rights Council Resolution (16th Session) of 12 April 2011 on 'Human rights and the environment';
- preparatory meetings under way for the Rio+20 United Nations Conference on Sustainable Development in June 2012;
- the World Health Organization (WHO) work on the social determinants of health in 2008; and
- the United Nations Commission on Human Rights (UNCHR) Resolution 2002/31 (22 April 2002), addressing 'The right of everyone to the enjoyment of the highest attainable standard of physical and mental health'.

My concern is that, for the most part, the interface between human rights and environmental hazards is not well represented in legal regimes; in fact, most often the interface is deliberately misunderstood, with a view to protecting commercial interests and maintaining the status quo (Mattei and Nader 2009). In order to present a concise but inclusive summary of some of the problems we face in this regard, I briefly discuss the issue under the following four separate (but interconnected) topic areas:

- explicit denial of the interface in jurisprudence, from United States cases under the Alien Torts Claims Act (ATCA), to the European Court of Human Rights and the International Court of Justice;
- lack of explicit prohibitions on the part of the WHO regarding industrial chemical and agricultural processes, despite the abundant evidence

amassed by that UN body and available in medical journals regarding the human health consequences of those industrial activities, which today can be compared with the evidence gathered by the WHO before drafting their Framework Convention on Tobacco Control (WHO, 2003);

- ongoing denial of the egregious human rights violations that follow upon climate change, including glacial melts in the Arctic through drought and famine in sub-Saharan Africa, while the same Western practices continue to contribute to global warming, including the over-use of water and grains in industrial meat production with its resulting methane releases;
- insistence on the 'right' to 'sustainable development', without the right of Indigenous and other land-based communities to say 'no' when the development in question is unwanted, as it continues to impact gravely these peoples' very subsistence, as well as their health and survival, both as individuals and as peoples.

Hence, I begin with a summary survey of some of the existing material for the protection of health and the environment (without, however, disclosing any specific binding document defining the interface between the two). I then consider other issues mentioned in the list above, before finally arguing for the urgent need for reforms to the candidate most likely to propose enforceable legal instruments, without risking the 'veto' that often accompanies other attempts to propose resolutions in defence of human rights on the part of UN organs (Westra, 2012). As well, the WHO is particularly well positioned to offer guidelines and courses of action that are seen as being beyond dispute.

Health and the environment: the missing linkages

> In confronting the insalubrious ramifications of globalization, human rights scholars and activists have argued for greater national and international responsibility pursuant to the human right to health ... However, in pressing for the highest attainable standard for each individual, the right to health has been ineffective to address burgeoning inequalities in underlying determinants of health focusing on individual medical treatments at the expense of public health. (Meier, 2006, pp711–712)

The problem is not a lack of instruments, declarations and resolutions that extol the value of health, and even the universal right to it; rather, it is that such a right is universally non-enforceable and that the instruments that prescribe it are non-binding. The main problem is that the abundant scientific information available to connect health and environment is not, in practice, considered. In addition, public health refers to collective (universal) rights, or at least to community rights, while for medicine it is individual rights that are central, and most significant.

On the one hand, there are declarations and even instruments that enshrine the right to health (if not the right to life); on the other hand, there is the research undertaken by the WHO and by scores of independent scholars, whose findings link health, inescapably, to environmental conditions. Nor are there only human rights in many documents clearly intended for the protection of health (e.g. UN, 2000; WHO, 2008), but both UN documents and recent scholarly work point clearly to the interface between environment and health as they advocate for the right to both.

Nevertheless, neither regulatory regimes nor judgements when cases come to court reflect that interface. One reason may be that neither lawmakers nor judges are trained to understand that connection and make it explicit. The other is the pervasive influence of economic interests and of the institutions that support them. Particularly significant is the recent UNGA document entitled 'Harmony with nature' (UNGA, 2010). In 2009, resolution 64/196 (UNGA, 2009) was intended to promote life in harmony with nature; but the later document adds also the dubious notion of 'sustainable development' that is oriented to trade and economics instead.

Annex B of this document addresses various worldwide efforts towards 'sustainable development', intended to 'strengthen stewardship of the global commons' (UNGA, 2010, para. 67): they include new constitutional provisions in several countries in South America, including Argentina (forest preservation), Bolivia (Indigenous Peoples' vision/new constitution); Cuba (environmental protection law, 1 July 1997), Chile ('socioeconomic factors that promote a healthy life'), and several others. Other countries' reported efforts bypass entirely the human–nature connection, as they refer to 'the right to have the environment protected, while promoting justifiable economic and social development' (South Africa Constitution), or even the Marrakesh Task Force on Education for Sustainable Consumption (UNEP, 2010).

The United States' Executive Order 13514, requires 'federal agencies to improve energy efficiency ... mitigation of greenhouse gas emissions ... and recycling' (White House, 2009, para. 85); and the European Union is somewhat less inconclusive, as it explicitly recognizes that the natural resource base for human life and development is in great danger and that fundamental changes in the way societies produce and consume are vital for achieving sustainable development.

Yet even this ignores the necessity for degrowth (contraction and convergence), and the fact that, according to ecological footprint analysis (Rees, 2006, pp143–158), the present rates of consumption and economic 'development' are completely unsustainable, as they already exceed the capacity of the Earth to sustain present human populations. Hence, the only possible 'development' may be spiritual, intellectual or moral, as every other form of material development is already unsustainable.

It is understandable that 'Harmony with nature' (UNGA, 2010) would take such a position; a position of covert (if not explicit) support for globalized economics, given that it is based on the work of neoclassical economists (Stiglitz *et al.*, 2009). Essentially, all that the UNGA document proposes, despite its promising title, is a list of empty justifications and band-aid solutions that will – at best – slightly modify the status quo, without any recognition of the gravity of the ongoing human rights violations that globalization supports and defends (Mattei and Nader, 2009; Westra, 2011). Even the wonderful new constitutions of many South American countries (Ecuador, Colombia, Bolivia), with their spirited defence of nature (Pachamama), and of Indigenous Peoples and their traditional ways, remain no better than paper tigers; once individuals or communities harmed by 'development' and globalized trade regimes attempt to use them in their defence, they carry no weight. I will return to this subject later in this chapter).

Nonetheless, the 'Conclusion and recommendations' end on a more realistic note:

> Nature has been treated as a commodity that exists largely for the benefit of people, and all environmental problems as solvable with a technological fix. Loss of biodiversity, desertification, climate change and the disruption of a number of natural cycles are among the costs of our disregard for nature and the integrity of its ecosystems and life-supporting processes. (UNGA, 2010, para. 101)

In its support of this conclusion, the document cites a three-page article in *Nature* (Rockström *et al.*, 2009), ignoring the ample literature that exists on the necessity for ecological integrity and its relation to health for all life, including humans (Leopold, 1949; Westra, 1994; Daily 1997; Westra, 2006; Bosselmann 2008). The document also ignores the unmasking of 'sustainable development' as 'plunder' (Mattei and Nader, 2009), legitimized by the legal instruments and organizations that support it in today's 'lawless world' (Sands, 2005).

Environmental rights and the right to health in jurisprudence

> All peoples may, for their own ends, freely dispose of their natural wealth and resources without prejudice to any obligation arising out of economic international cooperation, based upon the principle of mutual benefit and international law. In no case may people be deprived of its means of subsistence. (ICCPR, 1966, article 1(2))

All corporate claims to be involved in 'development' projects (under free trade regimes?), and all government approvals of such plans, whether they occur in so-called 'developing countries' or in areas inhabited by Indigenous communities, would be evaluated according to their article. Space will not permit a thorough survey of the abundant available case law; a few examples will suffice.

The first example is of the Canadian case of Grassy Narrows and White Dog, where the Judge himself found the justice system so insufficient that he counselled arbitration and a settlement instead, in order to provide some timely relief to the people of the affected First Nations:

> … the settlement and the events leading up to it provide a striking example of the fragility of Canadians' environmental rights in the face of environmental wrongs. Access to justice has been difficult to achieve for victims of environmental catastrophes. The substantive, procedural and evidentiary rules in private environmental actions appear biased in favour of the polluter. (West, 1987, p132)

The Indigenous peoples in South America are not better protected by either their own courts (despite the excellent constitutions many such countries have recently enacted) or the United States court system, under ACTA. Little recourse is available to non-citizens who have been harmed in other countries by multinational corporations in extractive industries, with offices in the United States, who have a long history of imposing environmental and health harms with impunity.

Citizens of Peru and Ecuador brought class action suits alleging that the defendant, an oil company, polluted rainforests and rivers in their countries, causing environmental damage and personal injury (*Maria Aguinda and others including the Federation of the Yagua People of the Lower Amazon and Lower Napo v. Texaco*, 2002). This case is typical of this kind of jurisprudence and it has a long previous history that led to this unsuccessful appeal (*Aguinda v. Texaco, Inc.*, 1996; *Aguinda v. Texaco, Inc.*, 2001; *Jota v. Texaco, Inc.*, 1998). The plaintiffs brought a suit against Texaco in 1993, as the latter's activities had polluted the rainforest and rivers in both Ecuador and Peru, and those polluting and harmful activities were 'designed, controlled, conceived and directed … through its operation in the United States' (*Aguinda v. Texaco, Inc.*, 1996). The indigenous peoples sought to recover damages, citing negligence, public and private nuisance, strict liability, medical monitoring, trespass, civil conspiracy and violations of ATCA.

Finally, we can consider a major source of environmental harms to public health: climate change. A recent case, successfully argued in the United States in 2009, is the case of *State of Connecticut et al., v. America Electric Power Company, Inc. et al.* First, several 'trusts' (the Open Air Institute, Inc., Open Space Conservancy, Inc. and the Audubon Society of New Hampshire) joined with the states of Connecticut, New York, California, Iowa, New Jersey, Rhode Island, Vermont and Wisconsin, as well as the city of New York, against several electrical power companies. Second, these states and trusts jointly claimed 'the ongoing contributions to the public nuisance of global warming are causing and will continue to cause serious harms affecting human health and natural resources' (*Connecticut et al. v. American Electric Power Co. et al.*, 2009).

Third, although the defendants claimed the whole issue was a 'non-justiciable political question', for that they 'lack[ed] standing', or that they attempted to displace 'federal common law', the Court of Appeals rejected all these arguments. Fourth, the states itemized singly and collectively the harms of climate change, which will produce 'substantial adverse effects on their environments, residents, and property', and all of which will cost each state billions of dollars to respond. As an example, 'the reduction of California's mountain snowpack, the single largest freshwater source critical for sustained water to the State's 34 million residents during the half of each year, when there is nominal precipitation' (*Connecticut et al. v. American Electric Power Co. et al.*, 2009, p8).

In addition, in the fifth place, the states listed several significant cases of 'increased illnesses and deaths caused by prolonged heat waves', the harms from smog and poor air quality, and the impacts on 'property, ecology and public health' (*Connecticut et al. v. American Electric Power Co. et al.*, 2009, p9).

But despite this favourable judgement, which recognized the necessary connection between environmental harms and public health, using traditional principles and doctrines in a novel way, the Supreme Court of the United States reversed this earlier decision on 20 June 2011 (*American Electric Power Company Inc. et al. v. State of Connecticut et al.*, 2011). As expected, the court did not engage with the substantive issues involved, or with the connection between environmental causation and damages to public health. Instead, the judgment held that 'The Clean Air act and EPA action the Act authorizes displace any federal common-law right to seek abatement of carbon dioxide emissions from fossil fuel-fired power plants.'

The judgement further argued that 'the Clean Air act is no less an exercise of the Legislature's considered judgement concerning air pollution regulations because it permits emissions until EPA acts' (*American Electric Power Co. et al. v. Connecticut et al.*, 2011), and essentially stated that it should be left to the EPA to do such 'complex balancing', as 'the expert agency is surely better equipped to do the job than federal judges who lack the scientific, economic and technological resources an agency can utilize in coping with issues of this order' (*American Electric Power Co. et al. v. Connecticut et al.*, 2011).

Note especially the omission of 'public health' considerations, the main focus of the argument of the earlier case, and the addition of 'economic and technological' as significant areas of expertise on the part of the EPA, clearly intended to provide the solution to their understanding of the problem.

The 'denied connection' and a possible role for the WHO

> 26. In this new environment, a model characterized solely by donors and recipients of aid is no longer viable. In this place is a need to think about collective responsibility, shared vulnerabilities, and values, sustained solidarity, and health as a global public good. …
>
> 84. An overarching objective of reform is to capitalize more effectively on WHO's leadership position in global health, specifically to strengthen the role that WHO can play in line with its primary Constitutional function as 'directing and coordinating authority on international health work.' (WHO, 2011)

The WHO, with the cooperation of the World Health Assembly (WHA), appears to be the only international institution capable – at least in principle – of mandating and supporting the needed remedies for the situation briefly described above. That situation includes:

- lacunae in the clarity and specifically of the language of legal regimes;
- grave inadequacies in the education of lawyers and judges; and, perhaps the best area where the WHO may prevail;
- a clear indictment of products, practices and processes that are already proven to be hazardous to health; the latter should result in
- a new Framework Convention against such products and substances, particularly those that involve the chemicals that have already been indicted by the WHO's own publications (Tamburlini, 2002; Licari *et al.*, 2005; Grandjean and Landrigan, 2006).

It is urgent that the intimidation and outright bullying practiced by many multinational corporations, especially those connected with chemical and other extracting and mining industries worldwide, against weak national governments and the local and indigenous community areas that are most often the target of their operations, should not be allowed to continue with impunity, in order to eliminate the ongoing 'collateral damage' (Leader, 2004) they create.

It was not easy for the WHO to prevail against 'Big Tobacco', as they finally produced their Framework Convention on Tobacco Control (WHO, 2003). It would be harder, no doubt, for them to alienate most of the industrial conglomerates and the government officials that support them and are supported by them in turn. Consider, for instance, 'Big Oil' and its many corporate supporters who were involved in an ongoing battle to discredit climate change science, and to ignore the plight of those exposed to their toxic operations.

It is worth noting that even the reform agenda of the WHO does not, at this time, include any action in regard to the main problems and outlined as follows:

> The WHO reform agenda includes: (1) a proposal for a global stakeholder forum to help shape the global health agenda; (2) clearer articulation of WHO's unique role and functions; and (3) managerial reforms within the WHO to increase its accountability to Member states, improve organizational structure and revive its human resource strategy. (O'Neill Institute, 2011)

A framework convention on global health

> What is truly needed, and which richer countries instinctively (although not always adequately) do for their own citizens, is to meet what I call 'basic survival needs' ... Basic survival needs include sanitation and sewage, pest control, clean air and water, tobacco reduction, diet and nutrition, essential medicines and vaccines, and functioning health systems for the prevention, detection and mitigation of disease and premature death. (Gostin, 2008, p3)

The following are the two most important components of an instrument designed for the protection of human rights and are present in Gostin's proposal:

1 recognition of the environmental aspects of human health; and
2 understanding the right to health as being more than the right to medical care when ill, important though that is.

For the former, 'basic survival needs' include 'clean air and water' and 'nutrition'; for the latter, 'health systems for the prevention, detection and mitigation of disease and premature death'. In addition, rather than leaving these aspects of the right to health to the goodwill of individual states, Gostin also proposes that the WHO or a newly created institution could set ongoing standards, monitor progress and mediate disputes (Gostin, 2008, p3).

Such a Convention would go to the heart of the environmental justice issue – that is, to the blatant inequalities in life expectancy, and the incidence of infectious and chronic diseases in developing countries, on the one hand, compared with rich nations, on the other (Gostin, 2008; Hill, 2006, p161; Ruger and Hak-Ju, 2006, pp928–936; Westra, 2006):

> Chances of living merely to the age of five are low among the world's poor compared to the wealthy. The poorest 25% of children in the world are two and a half times more likely to die before age five than the wealthiest 25%. In fact, of the 10.8 million children under five who die each year, 10 million are from low-income countries – more than twice the number of children born annually in the United States and Canada combined ... The World Bank reports that, in one year alone, 14 million of the poorest people in the world died, while only four

> million would have died if this population had the same death rate as the global rich. (Gostin, 2008, p5; see also Gawtkin *et al.*, 1999)

These are just some of the statistics that indicate the ongoing injustice that has been viewed as criminal by some (Sachs, 2004; Westra, 2006). No one denies the pivotal importance of socioeconomic status in health statistics, and the conclusion is that the poorer and less powerful are the most affected, globally.

In fact, one could argue that the activities are kept deliberately from affecting the favoured, at the expense of minorities: 'Indigenous persons experience an 'epidemiological accumulation', whereby disease and disability are exacerbated due to unmet basic needs' (Gostin, 2008; see also Kunitz, 2000, p1531; Rojas, 2005).

The situation of local and Indigenous communities, as globalization and global change conspire to render their conditions non-liveable, demonstrates clearly why (i) the nations and corporate agents that contribute to the situation (or, at times, are directly causative of it) cannot and should not claim ignorance and avoid their responsibility; and (ii) most often, even after migration, the conditions of those individuals and communities remain equally hazardous.

Unlike other human rights concerns, health concerns are readily accepted, for the most part, by national infrastructures, and promoted to the public, although, in many cases, economy and trade might be affected. In other cases, however, powerful economic interest blocks obstruct the appropriate measures: the best example can be found by large chemical interests and their influence on preventative measures for cancer (Epstein, 1987) and the ongoing proliferation of untested chemicals, despite their documented effects (Grandjean and Landrigan, 2006; Westra, 2007).

> The WHO Constitution envisaged an agency that would use law and exercise power to proactively promote the attainment of 'the highest possible level of health'. But the agency has never met these key expectations. (Gostin, 2008: p26; see also Burci *et al.*, 2004)

Many scholars have criticized the WHO's passive/reactive position, and have advocated a much stronger involvement in the right to health on their part than what their past performance has demonstrated:

> WHO's advancement of national and international public health and supervisory institutions is critical to furthering the realization of the right to health. Encouraging countries to develop specific binding legal obligations with respect to the right to health, and publicizing their compliance and non-compliance with those obligations, can powerfully influence states to rethink priorities and redirect national resources to national health care. (Taylor, 1992, p302)

WHO's mandate of 'Health for All', declared in 1977, was intended to be achieved for all the world's citizens by 2000. Nevertheless, it is hard to find any appeals to science or health in the jurisprudence concerning Indigenous Peoples' rights. There appears to be a disconnect between the WHO health mandate, despite its position in the UN, and other documents, which, even if they address the question of health, do so in general terms and with no reference to the WHO, let alone to the possibility of binding regulations.

Yet the WHA has a power that could/should be exercised in addition to the technical recommendations it normally issues:

> WHA also enjoys authority to adopt regulations regarding sanitary and quarantine requirements to deter the international spread of disease, and standards for safety, purity and potency of biological and pharmaceutical products that move in international commerce, among other things. (Taylor, 1992:302)

Thus a precedent exists whereby an arm of the WHO (i.e. the WHA, its legislative organ) is empowered to limit trade, and also to limit freedom of action of individuals in the usual public health fashion, through sanitary regulations and quarantines.

Public health is the mandate and the duty of the WHO, internationally, and they do have a history of speaking for the most vulnerable (for instance for children's exposures and diseases): all the signatories of the Convention on the Rights of the Child (UNGA, 1989) are obliged to report periodically to Geneva on how their countries are integrating the mandates of that document in their own domestic laws (Westra, 2006, chapter 9 and appendix 2).

Essentially then, the right to health, guaranteed by the International Covenant on Economic, Social and Cultural Rights (ICESCR, 1966, Article 12), provides for 'the right of everyone to the enjoyment of the highest attainable standard of physical and mental health'.

Yet the WHO has recently achieved an important success, despite the powerful interests that have been deployed against it for far too long: the Framework Convention on Tobacco Control (WHO, 2003; see also Taylor and Leviriere, 2005). Gostin adds: 'The critical question, however, is whether the WHO can build on these recent achievements to deal with the most important and intractable health problems in the poorest regions of the world' (Gostin, 2008, p28).

Conclusion

The problems discussed in this chapter are global and grave. They reach to the very heart of legitimacy and legality of human rights regimes. The economic interests that militate against their recognition are equally global and powerful. Hence, it is only from a position of acknowledged authority that an organization like the WHA might be able to speak out with both scientific knowledge and the mantle of legitimacy provided by the UN, in order to initiate and even enforce the radical changes that are needed.

References

Bosselmann, K. (2008) *The Principle of Sustainability*, Ashgate, Aldershot, UK

Burci, G. L. and Vignes, C.-H. (2004) *World Health Organization*, Kluwer Law, The Hague, The Netherlands

Daily, G. (1997) *Nature's Services: Societal Dependence on Natural Ecosystems*, Island Press, Washington, DC

Epstein, S. (1987) *The Politics of Cancer*, Sierra Club, San Francisco, CA

Gawtkin, D. R., Guillot, M. and Heuveline, P. (1999) 'The burden of disease among the global poor', *The Lancet*, vol 354, no 9178, 14 August, pp586–589

Gostin, L. O. (2008) 'Meeting basic survival needs of the world's least healthy people: toward a framework convention on global health', *Georgetown Law Journal*, vol 96, January, p3

Grandjean, P. and Landrigan, P. (2006) 'Developmental neurotoxicity of industrial chemicals', *The Lancet*, vol 368, no 9553, 16 December, 2167–2178

Hill, K. (2006) 'Making deaths count', *Bulletin of the World Health Organization*, vol 84, p161

ICCPR (1966) 'International covenant on civil and political rights', adopted and opened for signature, ratification and accession by General Assembly resolution 2200A (XXI) of 16 December 1966, entry into force 23 March 1976, in accordance with Article 49, Office of the United Nations High Commissioner for Human Rights, Geneva, available at www2.ohchr.org/english/law/ccpr.htm

ICESCR (1966) 'International covenant on economic, social and cultural rights', adopted and opened for signature, ratification and accession by General Assembly resolution 2200A (XXI) of 16 December 1966, entry into force 3 January 1976, in accordance with article 27, Office of the United Nations High Commissioner for Human Rights, Geneva, available at http://www2.ohchr.org/english/law/cescr.htm

Kunitz, S. J. (2000) 'Globalization, states, and the health of indigenous peoples', *American Journal of Public Health*, vol 90, no 10, pp1531–1539

Leader, S. (2004) 'Collateralism', in R. Brownsword (ed.) *Global Governance and the Quest for Justice*, vol. IV, Hart Publishing, Oxford, UK

Leopold, A (1949) *A Sand County Almanac and Sketches Here and There*, Oxford University Press, New York, NY

Licari, L., Nevmer, L. and Tamburlini, G. (eds) (2005) *Children's Health and the Environment*, World Health Organization Regional Office for Europe, Copenhagen, Denmark

Mattei, U. and Nader, L. (2009) *Plunder*, Blackwell Publishing, Oxford, UK

Meier, B. M. (2006) 'Employing human rights for global justice: the promise of public health in response to insalubrious ramifications of globalization', *Cornell International Law Journal*, vol 39, pp711–752

O'Neill Institute (2011) 'The World Health Assembly: Reforming the WHO and Global governance for health', briefing paper, 11 May, O'Neill Institute for National and Global Health Law, Georgetown University, Washington, DC, available at https://www.law.georgetown.edu/oneillinstitute/documents/2011-05-11_O%27Neill%20Institute%20Briefing%20Paper.pdf

Rees, W. E. (2006) 'Ecological footprints and bio-capacity: essential elements in sustainability assessment', in J. Dewulf and H. Van Lagenhove (eds), *Renewables-based Technology: Sustainability Assessment*, John Wiley and Sons, Chichester, UK, pp143–158

Rockström, J., Steffen, W., Noone, K., Persson, Å. F., Chapin III, F. S., Lambin, E. F., Lenton, T. M., Scheffer, M., Folke, C., Schellnhuber, H. J., Nykvist, B., de Wit, C. A., Hughes, T., van der Leeuw, S., Rodhe, H., Sörlin, S., Snyder, P. K., Costanza, R., Svedin, U., Falkenmark, M., Karlberg, L., Corell, R. W., Fabry, V. J., Hansen, J., Walker, B., Liverman, D., Richardson, K., Crutzen, P. and Foley, J. A. (2009) 'A safe operating space for humanity', *Nature*, vol. 461, no. 7263, 24 September, pp472–475

Rojas, R. (2005) *Health Program of the Indigenous Peoples of the Americas: Action Plan 2005–2007*, Pan American Health Organization, Washington, DC

Ruger, J. and Hak-Ju, K. (2006) 'Global health inequalities: an international comparison', *Journal of Epidemiology and Community Health*, vol 60, pp928–936

Sachs, W. (2004) 'Climate change and human rights', in *Scripta Varia, vol 106: Interactions between Global Change and Human Health*, Pontifical Academy of Sciences, Vatican City, pp349–368

Sands, P. (2005) *A Lawless World*, Allen Lane (Penguin Books), London, UK

Stiglitz, J., Sen, A. and Fitouss, J.-P. (2009) *The Measurement of Economic Performance and Social Progress Revisited: Reflections and Overview*, 16 September, available at www.stiglitz-sen-fitoussi.fr/documents/overview-eng.pdf

Tamburlini, G. 2002, 'Children's special vulnerability to environmental health hazards', in G. Tamburlini, O. Von Ehrenstein and R. Bertollini (eds) *Children's Health and the Environment: A Review of the Evidence*, EEA report no 29, World Health Organization, Geneva, Switzerland

Taylor, A. L. (1992) 'Making the World Health Organization work: a legal framework for universal access to the conditions for health', *American Journal of Law and Medicine*, vol 18, pp301–346

Taylor, A. and Leviriere, J. (2005) 'Origins of the WHO Framework Convention on Tobacco Control', *American Journal of Public Health*, vol 95, p936

UN (2000) 'Substantive issues arising in the implementation of the International Covenant on Economic, Social and Cultural Rights', General Comment no. 14, UN Doc E/C12/2000/4 (General Comments), 11 August, United Nations Economic and Social Council, New York, available at www.unhchr.ch/tbs/doc.nsf/%28symbol%29/E.C.12.2000.4.En

UNEP (2010) *Here and Now! Education for Sustainable Consumption – Recommendations and Guidelines*, United Nations Environment Programme, Nairobi, Kenya, available at www.unep.org/pdf/Here_and_Now_English.pdf

UNGA (1989) 'Convention on the rights of the child', adopted and opened for signature, ratification and accession by General Assembly resolution 44/25 of 20 November 1989, entry into force 2 September 1990, in accordance with article 49, United Nations General Assembly, New York, available at www2.ohchr.org/english/law/crc.htm

UNGA (2009) 'Resolution adopted by the General Assembly [on the report of the Second Committee (A/64/420)] 64/196. Harmony with nature', Sixty-fourth session, Agenda item 53, UN Doc A/RES/64/196, 21 December, United Nations

General Assembly, New York, available at www.worldlii.org/int/other/UNGARsn/2009/184.pdf

UNGA (2010) 'Harmony with nature: Report of the Secretary-General', Sixty-fifth session, Item 20 (i) of the provisional agenda, UN Doc A/65/314, 19 August, United Nations General Assembly, New York, available at www.un.org/esa/dsd/resources/res_pdfs/res_ga65_unedited/SGReportHwNEnglish.pdf

West, L. (1987) 'Mediated settlement of environmental disputes: Grassy Narrows and White Dog revisited' *Environmental Law*, vol 18, pp131–150

Westra, L. (1994) *The Principles of Integrity*, Rowman Littlefield, Lanham, MD

Westra, L. (2006) *Environmental Justice and the Rights of Unborn and Future Generations*, Earthscan, London, UK

Westra, L. (2007) *Environmental Justice and the Rights of Indigenous Peoples*, Earthscan, London, UK

Westra, L. (2011) *Globalization, Violence and World Governance*, Brill, Leyden, The Netherlands

Westra, L. (2012) *'Faces' of State Terrorism*, Brill, Leyden, The Netherlands

White House (2009) 'Federal leadership in environmental, energy, and economic performance', Executive Order 13514, 5 October, Office of the Press Secretary, The White House, Washington, DC, available at www.whitehouse.gov/assets/documents/2009fedleader_eo_rel.pdf

WHO (2003) 'Framework convention on tobacco control', WHO Doc A56/VR/4, 21 May, World Health Organization, Geneva, Switzerland, adopted by the World Health Assembly 21 May 2003, into force 27 February 2005, available at www.who.int/gb/ebwha/pdf_files/WHA56/ea56rl.pdf

WHO (2008) *Closing the Gap in a Generation: Health Equity through Action on the Social Determinants of Health*, World Health Organization, Geneva, Switzerland, available at http://whqlibdoc.who.int/publications/2008/9789241563703_eng.pdf

WHO (2011) 'The future of financing for WHO: World Health Organization: reforms for a healthy future', report by the Director-General, Executive Summary, sixty-fourth World Health Assembly A64/4, 5 May, Provisional Agenda, World Health Organization, Geneva, Switzerland, available at http://apps.who.int/gb/ebwha/pdf_files/WHA64/A64_4-en.pdf

2 Keeping nature alive

Ethical principles on the environment and human health in state statutes

Kathryn Kintzele[1]

> 'Environment' as used in this Law refers to the total body of all natural elements and artificially transformed natural elements affecting human existence and development.[2]

Introduction

The roots of jurisprudence are ethical roots: fairness, equity, justice. Ethics asks us, as a society, what is right and wrong with a given or proposed action, and when does responsibility attach. This is the very essence of the development, implementation and enforcement of law.

The development of law by state statutes, or legislative and parliamentarian bodies of governments, is a foundational component of the governance of a nation state. For many states around the world, the environment has always had a role in their statutes, but what kind of role? Some states see the environment merely as a component of ownership, as evidenced in property law; others as a matter of responsibility for current and future generations, such as with natural resource management. Some states root environmental law in terms of trade and movement (commercial law), others for the purpose of international relations (public international law; e.g. transboundary resource rights and transboundary harm prevention). Today, most states have compartmentalized the environment as its own body of environmental law, incorporating preservation, conservation and regulation for purposes such as species protection, economic and sustainable development, quality of life, and even life itself. A state cannot protect its citizens without protecting the foundations of human health: air, water, food, shelter/land and democracy.

This chapter will therefore give a comparative analysis of the relationships that state statutes give to the environment and human health, and the ethical principles that those relationships entail.[3] It will follow the Keeping Nature Alive methodology of the Biosphere Ethics Initiative, a soft-law programme of the Commission on Environmental Law of the International Union for the Conservation of Nature. This methodology combines practical research in policy implementation (i.e. Relatos), with comparative ethical and legal analyses.[4]

The chapter will begin with a brief overview of ethical principles of biodiversity conservation found in international law. Then, through select examples of state statutes, it will demonstrate how states view the environment–human health connection, and some of the trends that are occurring. The aim of the chapter is to show that state responsibility for environmental protection is inextricably linked to state responsibility for the health of their citizenry, and that the protection of human health is a global environmental responsibility for every state. For the future of human health on this planet, for the future of life on this planet, what protections are being afforded, and what protections should be afforded?

Ethical principles of biodiversity conservation in international law

The comparative review of state law forms principles of international law and is considered a major source of international law under Article 38 of the Statute of the International Court of Justice. From past research in comparative constitutional law and comparative judicial opinions, several ethical principles have surfaced as principles of international law.[5] These include truth; democracy; justice and equity; and respect and love. Within truth is the acknowledgment of humanity's utter dependence on the environment. This would include explicit recognition of human health as dependent upon environmental health. Also, it recognizes the inaccuracy and danger of the three-pillars planning of most states; the scientific reality is not economy, society and environment, but that the environment is the foundation for all else. Truth also encompasses having humility with what is known and not known, and using caution in the face of scientific uncertainty. In law, this is also referred to as the precautionary principle (or cautionary principle). Another legal principle could be the non-regression principle, which states that environmental laws should not digress in their levels of protection, once afforded. Lastly, within truth there is the recognition of natural limits. This would include a critique of the current economic system and growth paradigm, and raise issues of population, production and consumption.

The second over-arching ethical principle, which is also a foundation for human health for purposes of this article, is democracy. This includes rights and responsibilities: the right of self-determination, the right to be informed and have access to information, justice and decision-making, the appreciation of cultural diversity and indigenous knowledge, the need to foster local and regional alliances to solve environmental problems, and the need to protect the vulnerable people and places.

The third ethical principle is justice and equity. This advocates for supporting universal human rights, including those associated with human health such as the human right to water, as well as for social, economic and environmental justice. It calls for just and sustainable forms of governance, and the reconciliation of past harms to humans and nature, in the name of humans and nature. For example, the removal of indigenous peoples from a protected area; or the prohibition of certain races to protected areas.

The final overarching ethical principle is respect and love. This includes the obligation to respect and the compassion to love as a basis of care for living beings, places and people. This also includes ecological integrity and the health of the entire system, the danger of the commodification of nature (or of life), and the legal principle of the duty not to harm. These ethical principles provide the foundation for the environmental health–human health relationship, as evidenced in the following state statutes.

The environment and human health in state statutes

Of course, the most preferable recognition by a state law of the inextricable link between environmental health and human health is explicit recognition; for example, in the Nigeria National Policy on the Environment, 'There is no sustainable development without health', and goals include to 'Improve environmental health … as a component of primary health care' and 'Place high priority on improving environmental services in support of public health programs'.[6] The Brazil National Environmental Policy 'has the aim of preserving, improving, and recovering the environmental quality conducive of a healthy life, with a view to ensuring the socio-economic development, the interests of national security of the protection of human life'. Its Primary Norm of Environmental Quality is:

> … establishing the minimum or maximum values for the concentrations and periods allowable of elements, compounds, substances, chemical or biologic derivatives, energies, radiation, vibrations, noise or a combination of them, whose presence or absence in the environment may constitute a risk for the population's life or health.[7]

Within the definition of 'environment' in the South Africa National Environmental Management Act is:

> (i) the land, water and atmosphere of the earth; (ii) microorganisms, plant and animal life; any part or combination of (i) and (ii) and the interrelationships among and between them; and the physical, chemical, aesthetic and cultural properties and conditions of the foregoing that influence human health and wellbeing.[8]

Colombia makes it clear that the environment is 'the common heritage of humanity and necessary for survival and economic and social development of peoples'.[9]

States also often refer to the environmental cornerstones of human health when providing legal protections to its citizens: air, water, food and shelter/land. Air emission standards and air pollution considerations are now a common occurrence in state law; for example, in Bolivia, 'it is the duty of the State and society to keep the atmosphere conditions that allow life and its development in an optimal state and health',[10] and in the Environment Code of France, 'Each individual has the right to information about air quality and its effects on health and the environment.'[11]

However, the current trend narrows human health impacts from air pollution to human health impacts from cigarette smoke, such as Bahrain's Law No. 8, 'on smoking and tobacco – ban on cultivation, manufacturing, producing, importing.' This is an important particularization because its legal defences can be transferred to other human-caused pollutants, an individual's duty not to harm, and the state's duty to protect the general welfare. Bolivia includes smoking provisions within its air pollution regulation:

> The State through appropriate agencies shall regulate and control the air discharge of any substance in the form of gases vapors, fumes, and dusts that may cause damage to health, the environment, inconvenience of the community or its inhabitants, and harm to public or private property.[12]

It continues, 'Smoking on school premises is established as wilful damage because there are children and people with low resistance to air pollution effects', and prohibits 'smoking in enclosed public areas and ... transport'. China's public ban on smoking went into effect in May 2011. As one-fifth of the world's population die from smoking, this human health–pollutant impact should be a concern for all states.[13]

The Holy Qu'ran states: **حققنا من الماء كل شيء حي** ('We made from water every living thing').[14] Water is the blood of our planet, an integral component to human life. Although some states are beginning to recognize access to safe and adequate fresh water as a human right, it is important to note that the relationship between water and human health is much broader than direct human consumption. Water is necessary to every aspect of human life, for the individual and the community: for national security, for agriculture and sanitation, for the integrity of food and for the prevention of disease. With limited fresh water on this planet there are also issues of fair distribution (for example, how does one defend water-intensive farming in a water-scarce region?), access for drinking, sanitation, food and recreation, and concerns over privatization. In addition to the substantive access to water, and the regulatory/procedural use of water, there are also refugee considerations due to desertification and drought. In 2011, African drought victims from Somalia led to the creation of the world's largest refugee camp in Kenya. The Horn of Africa is suffering from its worst drought in 60 years, putting about 12 million people at risk of starvation across the region.

Section 4.8 of the Nigeria National Policy on the Environment, on water resources management, states that 'Proper management through incorporation of environment concerns is essential to minimize supply shortages, pollution, land degradation, and associated health hazards.' Articles 38 and 39 of Bolivia Law 1333 – Environmental Law states that the 'State shall promote comprehensive planning and use of water for the benefit of the community in order to ensure continuous availability to ensure drinking water for the entire population', and that the 'State will regulate and control the discharge of any substance or liquid waste, solid, and gas that causes or may cause water pollution or degradation of the environment.' In Part 3, Chapter 9 of the Ordinance on Environmentally Hazardous Activities and Health Protection, Sweden addresses groundwater collection structures and states that they 'shall be established and used in such a way as to ensure that detriment is not caused to human health.'

One of the most extensive statutes relating to water is France's Environment Code: 'Water is part of the common heritage of the nation – its protection, enhancement, and development as a usable resource with due respect to natural equilibriums are of general interest.'[15] It continues:

> Balanced management must allow the following requirements to be satisfied or reconciled during various types of use, activities, or work: Public health, public safety, and provision of drinking water to the population; Requirements of biological life within receiving media; Requirements for conservation and free flow of water and protection against floods; Requirements of agriculture, fishing, and marine culture, freshwater, fishing, industry, energy production, and in particular to ensure the safety of the electricity system, transport, tourism, protection of sites, leisure activities, and water sports as well as any other human activities legally carried out.[16]

Although several state statutes address water as important to human health, more needs to be done to contemporize the laws with the current harms that water issues are causing to human health.

There are several important environment–human health considerations in law regarding food and the importance of the agricultural sector to human health. Section 4.7 of the Nigeria National Policy on the Environment states that the 'Viability of the agricultural sector is crucial to the growth and development of the nation', as it 'strongly impacts food, security, industrialization efforts, quality of life, economic growth, political stability, and to some extent a nation's position in international relations and trade.'

The integrity of the food product includes feed for animals, treatment of animals, the genetic manipulation of plants and animals, as well as disease and contamination prevention and control. For example, the 2011 nuclear accidents at the Fukushima power station led to specific EU legislation, 'imposing special conditions governing the import of feed and food originating in or consigned from Japan following the accident at the Fukushima nuclear power station'.[17] Sanitation for food products is covered in a Bahrain statute, Sanitary Requirements for Transporting Food, and can be particular to diseases, such as the statute from Spain, Sanitary Measures Regarding Bovine TB, Surveillance of Pigs and Salted Guts from Australia. In Argentina, there is a statute that concerns 'animal health during transit, export/import'.

Concern over the health of genetically modified organisms (GMOs) continues to be a source of state statutes, particularly in Europe. In Sweden, 'Investigation shall be carried out prior to the contained use and deliberate release of genetically modified organisms',[18] and 'Special attention shall be paid to ethical concerns in connection with the contained use and deliberate release of genetically modified organisms and the placing on the market of products containing or consisting of such organisms.'[19] The Environment Code of France states, 'Each individual has the right to be informed of the effects that ... genetically modified organisms may have on public health or environment'.[20] Food labelling is also generally addressed in the San Marino – Delegated Decree No. 55.

The integrity of food processing includes large agri-businesses, seafood farming and Combined Animal Feeding Operations, fertilizer and pesticide use, run-off and land use, as well as the transportation of all food products, from cradle to grave. In Article 30 of Bolivia Law 1333 – Environmental Law, the 'State shall regulate and control the production, introduction, and marketing of pharmaceuticals, pesticides, and other hazardous substances that are harmful to health and/or the environment'. The Nigeria National Policy on the Environment aims to 'Encourage and support efficient use of crop and livestock waste products; Regulate production, use, storage, transportation, marketing, sale, and disposal of agricultural chemicals, [offers] Safe Use pesticide guides; and [requires] the Monitor[ing] of pesticide and agro-chemicals; and Integrated pest management.' Agro-businesses were specifically targeted in the Chile Basic Environmental Law, which states that 'projects/activities susceptible of causing environmental impact and subject to the environmental impact assessment system' include nuclear reactors and facilities, and agroindustries.[21]

There have also been several responses to the food industry recognized at the state, regional and local levels, including geographic indicators, such as those in the Tuscan region of Italy, as well as local and organic food movements, as seen throughout the United States.

Due to climate change and rising sea levels, shelter no longer simply means a roof over one's head; it now also means a floor beneath one's feet. Coastal cities and small island nations have new and pressing concerns, yet few states are recognizing them in domestic law, and the international response has been limited. Some cities have taken policy measures on their own accord, creating climate change adaptation plans, but there needs to be national-level protection. Also, and as discussed earlier, desertification and drought are forcing the migration of people across state boundaries, so there must also be international responses.

Climate change is being seen with increased frequency in domestic laws around the world. For example, the State Environmental Policy of the Czech Republic states:

> The most important global problem is global warming, which is related to a range of anthropogenic processes (combustion of fossil fuels, industrial emissions, deforestation, intensification of agriculture, etc.). In application of the 'polluter pays' principle in this and similar cases, the international community follows the principle of common responsibility, where the individual countries must accept commitments corresponding to the size of their economies and historical contribution to global emissions of greenhouse gases and possibly other externalities acting in a global context.

France's Environment Code states that the 'Fight against intensification of the greenhouse effect and the prevention of risks linked to global warming are recognized as being national priorities',[22] whereas Sweden states that the impact on climate is one of the purposes for an environmental impact assessment.[23]

There are many legal considerations when looking at shelter/land, including land use planning, landscape management; infrastructure and dwelling at the urban and rural levels; and the protection of traditional cultures and their relationships with the land. The Nigeria National Policy on the Environment states that 'Human comfort and survival are at the centre of concerns for sustainable development as man strives to achieve a healthy and productive life in harmony with nature.'[24] They also state that housing is 'conducive for family development' and that it is advisable to 'Discourage overcrowding both with respect to the number of houses per unit area and dwellers per unit of housing.' Nigeria also aims to 'Develop sustainable agro-forestry techniques for prevention and remediation of erosion and checking desertification.'

Some state laws address specific development plans, such as Viet Nam's recent statute on nuclear development plans,[25] or Italy's Friuli-Venizia Giulia Regional Act No. 10, on restoration of non-cultivated abandoned land. Other states address specific risks to land, such as Luxembourg's statute on the management of flood risks.[26] Many states incorporate urban and rural planning in their domestic law. For example, the Environment Code of France states that 'Laws and regulations organize the individuals' right to a healthy environment and contribute to ensuring a harmonious balance between urban zones and rural zones.'[27] In the Environmental Protection Law of the People's Republic of China, 'The targets and tasks for protecting and improving the environment shall be defined in urban planning,' and 'In urban and rural construction, vegetation, waters, and natural landscape shall be protected and attention paid to the construction of gardens, green land, and historic sites, and scenic spots in the cities in light of special features of the local natural environment.'[28] Albania's Law No. 9843 is more narrow, and dictates urban planning and the demolition of waste objects.

The State Environmental Policy of the Czech Republic promotes 'programs connected with care for nature and the landscape; and relates programs for renewal of rural areas to implementation of Local Agendas 21'. They also provide for sustainable landscape management in forest, agriculture and tourism planning, and list the following aspirations:

> Make land accessible through the construction of field roads, bicycle routes, hiking routes, educational trails and thematic trails and support small eco-tourism and eco-agri-tourism business enterprises; support the 'green code' for operators of hotels and accommodation facilities; and support the renewal and maintenance of local railway lines and railway stations as potential centres for services in environmentally sound hiking and cyclo-tourism.[29]

The Czech Republic also provides for sustainable urban development, including public green areas and 'the creation and extension of green belts around cities'.[30]

Sweden also shows the importance of balancing recreation with development: 'special consideration shall be given to the interests of tourism and outdoor recreation, in particular outdoor exercise in connection with assessments of the permissibility of development projects or other environmental intrusion'.[31] The Kenya Environmental Management and Coordination Act states 'a clean and healthy environment includes the access by any person to the various public elements or segments of the environment for recreational, educational, health, spiritual, and cultural purposes.[32]

Protection of quiet areas is also a concern for states: the Environment Code of France seeks to 'Prevent, suppress, or limit the emission of propagation ... of noises or vibrations of such a nature that they present a hazard, cause excessive disturbance to people, are harmful to their health, or harm the environment'.[33] Nigeria's Section 6.4 on Noise Pollution states that, 'Reduction of noise levels and control of noise pollution are requisites for creation and maintenance of comfortable and healthy living environment.'

The final component to human health to be considered is democracy, which includes access to information and the right to be informed (including recognizing the limits to human knowledge), participation in decision-making, the rights of future generations, justice and equity (including unsustainable resource consumption), protecting the vulnerable, the duties of the state and of the individual in a community, and liberty. It is implicit in state law that humans have a right to be free from harm, as states have a duty not to harm. This freedom from harm is expanded to be free from contaminants and poisons, violence and the threat of violence, and the spread of disease. The health of the environment, and these principles inherent in democracy, are directly linked to the physical and mental integrity of the person: to personal autonomy, to self-determination and to citizenship.

One of the basic principles of environmental protection for the Czech Republic is increasing public consciousness of environmental issues as 'Only educated and informed citizens and their representatives are capable of making the right decisions.' The statute states:

> An increase in public consciousness of environmental matters leads the public, not only to greater understanding of the environmental connections of the economic and social life of society, but also to an increase in the quality of consumer decision-making, to an increase in the legal awareness of citizens and, as a consequence, also to improved quality of life.

To this end, they have adopted an environmental education regime that targets students, educators, elected officials, the media, businesses and farmers. In addition, the law promotes the dissemination of information on sustainable development, a citizen's right to information, environmentally sound behaviour and agriculture, a healthy lifestyle, GMOs, food products, etc.

Chile's Basic Environmental Law provides for environmental education as a 'permanent interdisciplinary process intended to help citizens to create values, understand certain concepts and to develop the necessary abilities and attitudes to live in harmony with other human beings, its culture and its bio-physic environment'.[34] Nigeria's National Policy on the Environment also addresses environmental education, but stresses community involvement, calling for 'Sustained dialogue in rural populations' to 'Raise community awareness through appropriate technology and local expertise.' Sweden also has a recent decree (Decree 2010: 1341) that governs community involvement in conservation. The South Africa National Environmental Management Act states that 'Community wellbeing and empowerment must be promoted through environmental education, the raising of environmental awareness, the sharing of knowledge and experience'.

The South Africa National Environmental Management Act also states that 'The participation of all interested and affected parties in environmental governance must be promoted, and all people must have the opportunity to develop the understanding, skills and capacity necessary for achieving equitable and effective participation', and 'Decisions must take into account the interests, needs and values of all interested and affected parties, and this includes recognising all forms of knowledge, including traditional and ordinary knowledge.'[35]

The Australia Environment Protection and Biodiversity Conservation Act 1999 states that principles of ecologically sustainable development include 'decision-making processes should effectively integrate both long-term and short-term economic, environmental, social and equitable considerations', as well as the principle of ecological integrity and the principle of intergenerational equity, 'that the present generation should ensure that the health, diversity and productivity of the environment is maintained or enhanced for the benefit of future generations'.[36]

One of the purposes of the Environmental Code of Colombia is as follows:

> Ensure the preservation and restoration of the environment and conservation, improvement, and rational use of renewable natural resources, according to criteria that ensure fairness and harmonious development of man and of those resources, continued availability to benefit the health and welfare of present and future generations.

The Environment Code of France offers similar protections:

> … protection, enhancement, restoration, rehabilitation, and management [of natural areas] are of general interest and contribute to the objective of sustainable development which aims to satisfy the development needs and protect the health of current generations without compromising the ability of future generations to meet their own needs.[37]

As the gap between rich and poor widens, and as wealth gains greater access to healthcare and resources, equity will continue to be a key component to human health. The South Africa National Environmental Management Act states that 'Environmental justice must be pursued so that adverse environmental impacts shall not be distributed in such a manner as to unfairly discriminate against any person', and 'Equitable access to environmental resources, benefits and services to meet basic human needs and ensure human wellbeing must be pursued and special measures may be taken to ensure access thereto by categories of persons disadvantaged by unfair discrimination.'

To address equity, a state should also address sustainable consumption and population. The Czech Republic highlights that:

> Mobility of the labour force and an increase in working productivity are often achieved at the expense of social and human resources (erosion of traditional social structures, lowered birth rates, disintegration of the family, asocial behaviour, etc.) and of a cultural relation to the environment.

Nigeria has several strategies outlined in their National Policy on the Environment, including, 'Address issues of population growth and resources consumption; Set quotas for stabilization of the national population at a sustainable level; and Integrate resource consumption and demographic goals.'

It is important to also protect the vulnerable. As highlighted above with regard to smoking, children are often a protected class for state laws. The Czech Republic states, 'The highest attention will be focused on environmental protection and prevention of children's diseases and injuries, on development of indicators to monitoring the linkages between the state of the environment and the state of health'. A recent statute from the EU (no. 432/2011, 4 May 2011) will only hear health claims on food if it concerns a reduction of disease risk to children's development and health.

The protection of environmental health and human health is the responsibility of both the state and the individual. As Bolivia's Environmental Law states, 'It is the duty of all individuals to take appropriate preventive measures, inform the competent authorities, to avoid damage to the health of the population, environment, and property', and 'It is the duty of the State and society for prevention and control of environmental problems arising from … human activities'.[38]

Conclusion

From this comparative analysis of state statutes, framed by key ethical considerations, it is evident that several states are laying the foundations for the right relationship between environmental health and human health. However, with permeating, global and urgent issues such as climate change on the forefront, it is now even more important that states strengthen and expand their existing state statutes. The foundations of human health, of human life, need to be protected, and not just for the mere survival of the human species, but for the flourishing of the human species. It is the legal responsibility of every state to protect its citizenry, for the health of the individual and for the health of the community. And it is the ethical responsibility of every state to expand that community to the entire community of life on this planet.

Notes

1 The author would like to thank Ashley Haws (JD Candidate, 2012) for her research assistance.

2 Environmental Protection Law of the People's Republic of China (1989), Chapter 1, Article 2.

3 This article gives excerpts of statutes from the EU and the following states: Albania, Australia, Bahrain, Bolivia, Brazil, Chile, China, Colombia, Czech Republic, France, Italy, Kenya, Luxembourg, Nigeria, South Africa, Sweden and Viet Nam.

4 Relatos are meetings of local and global leaders from across disciplines, government and non-government, that seek to highlight principles of environmental ethics in practice. At a single meeting may be scientists, educators, managers, politicians, lawyers, ethicists and activists. Each Relato has

two purposes: (i) to inform the global Evolving Biosphere Ethic; and (ii) to create its own local ethic, particular to that region, state or organization.

5 Westra, L., Bosselmann, K. and Soskolne, C. (2011) *Globalisation and Ecological Integrity in Science and International Law*, Cambridge Scholars Publishing, Newcastle upon Tyne, UK.
6 Nigeria National Policy on the Environment, Section 4.16: Health.
7 Brazil National Environmental Policy, Article 2 – National Environmental Policy.
8 South Africa National Environmental Management Act, available at www.environment.gov.za/polleg/legislation/natenvmgmtact/natenvmgmtact.htm.
9 Colombia, Article 2.
10 Bolivia Law 1333 – Environmental Law. Article 40.
11 Environment Code of France, Article L125-4.
12 Bolivia Law 1333 – Environmental Law Article 41.
13 World Health Organization, *WHO Report on the Global Tobacco Epidemic, 2011: Warning about the Dangers of Tobacco*, available at http://whqlibdoc.who.int/publications/2011/9789240687813_eng.pdf.
14 Qu'ran, 21:30
15 Environment Code of France, Book II, Title I, Article L210-1.
16 Environment Code of France, Book II, Title I, Article L211-1.
17 Commission Implementing Regulation (EU) No 297/2011 of 25 March 2011.
18 Swedish Environmental Code, Chapter 13, Genetic Engineering, Section 8.
19 Swedish Environmental Code, Chapter 13, Genetic Engineering, Section 10.
20 Environment Code of France, Article L125-3.
21 Chile Basic Environmental Law (Law 19300, 1994), Article 10.
22 Environment Code of France, Chapter 9, Article L229-1.
23 Swedish Environmental Code, Chapter 6, Environmental Impact Statements and other Decision Guidance Data, Section 3.
24 Nigeria National Policy on the Environment, Section 4.3: Housing and Human Settlements.
25 Viet Nam, Decision No. 906/QD-TTg, 17 June 2010.
26 Luxembourg, 30 December 2010, implementing EU Dir. 2007/60/EC.
27 Environment Code of France, Book 1, Article L110-2.
28 Environmental Protection Law of the People's Republic of China (1989), Chapter 3, Article 22, 23.
29 State Environmental Policy of the Czech Republic, 3.4.4 Sustainable landscape management
30 State Environmental Policy of the Czech Republic, 3.4.5 Sustainable urban development
31 Swedish Environmental Code, Chapter 4, Basic Provisions Concerning the Management of Land and Water Areas, Section 2.
32 Kenya Environmental Management and Coordination Act, Article 3.
33 Environment Code of France, Title VII: Prevention of acoustic and visual nuisances. Article 571-1.
34 Chile Basic Environmental Law (Law 19300, 1994).
35 Nigeria's National Policy on the Environment, (4)(f) and (g).
36 Australia Environment Protection and Biodiversity Conservation Act 1999, Act No. 91 of 1999 as amended, taking into account amendments up to Statute Law Revision Act 2011. An Act relating to the protection of the environment and the conservation of biodiversity, and for related purposes. Administered by Sustainability, Environment, Water, Population and Communities, 3A: Principles of Ecologically Sustainable Development.
37 Environment Code of France, Book 1, Article L110-1.
38 Bolivia Law 1333 – Environmental Law, Article 21–22.

3 Human rights, environmental duties

An ecological interpretation of international law

Megan J. M. Mitchell

Introduction

Environmental changes taking place today have direct and imminent consequences for all inhabitants of this planet, particularly humans. The nature of contemporary environmental issues (i.e. inter-related, transboundary and increasingly linked to unbalanced patterns of resource consumption) more and more forces us to reframe environmental problems as being ultimately *human* problems. Many of the major causes of contemporary human suffering have their roots in environmental transformations for which we are not biologically, technologically, or philosophically equipped to adequately address. Basic human rights concerns such as hunger, poverty, sickness, armed conflict and even domestic violence are all able to be traced back to environmental factors at some level.[1]

In this chapter, I explore the relationship between international human rights standards and the ecological conditions necessary for their achievement. I argue that many of the goals of international human rights law are being undermined by poor environmental management, and will ultimately be unachievable unless proper regard is given in law to the environmental preconditions of these universal foundations of human well-being. At the heart of my argument is the idea that human rights law has the potential to be used as a powerful tool of environmental protection. It is important to note, however, that this does not reduce the relationship to one of parasitism, or the smuggling in of an environmental agenda on the coattails of human rights concerns. On the contrary, unless international law is able to adequately address the environmental barriers to the achievement of human rights, rights-based goals will never be fully realized. Indeed, at the risk of trivializing the environmental cause, it is possible to view the achievement of ecological integrity as simply a necessary (and extremely welcome) means to what is ultimately a human rights end.

Why change is necessary

That human rights depend upon environmental conditions for their fulfilment seems so self-evident that it ought to need no explanation. And yet even a cursory glance at the key instruments of international human rights law reveals a staggering lack of legal recognition of this relationship. While it could be argued that most (or indeed all) legally enshrined human rights are in some way environmentally dependent, a brief examination of those rights most obviously affected demonstrates the poverty of the law with respect to environmental realities. Among the rights to food, water, health, and life, there exists a scant handful of direct references to environmental duties. The actual texts of the core human rights instruments – the International Covenant on Civil and Political Rights (ICCPR) and the International Covenant on Economic, Social and Cultural Rights (ICESCR) – contain few direct references to environmental conditions, while interpretative comments issued by the governing bodies of these agreements go only minimally further.

The right to food, embodied in Article 11 of the ICESCR, has one of the most comprehensive discussions of environmental duties attached to it . Yet even here we find little emphasis as to the fundamental nature of these duties in terms of achieving the right. In terms of formal duties under the right to food, state parties to the ICESCR are required only to 'improve methods of production' and 'develop or reform agrarian systems in such a way as to achieve the most efficient development and utilization of natural resources' (ICESCR; Art 11(1)). This hardly speaks to a pressing need to protect ecological integrity. The General Comments, issued by the governing body of the convention to act as an interpretative aid, are slightly more thorough, but still cripplingly vague. Here we find that the right is intended to require 'the adoption of appropriate … environmental policies', the accessibility of food 'in ways that are sustainable', and that 'care should be taken to ensure the most sustainable management and use of natural and other resources for food at the national, regional, local and household level' (E/C.12/1999/5). This is more or less the extent of the legally influential material linking the right to food with obligations towards the environment.[2]

In itself, the paucity of detail and depth in the duties described would not necessarily be a cause for concern. The framework of sustainability is set, and it is certainly open to States to interpret the right as requiring an entirely adequate standard of environmental care. However, state practice fails to approach even a semblance of compliance with principles of sustainability, and even as more and more land is harnessed for food production, the ranks of the hungry continue to swell (Bailey, 2011). More tellingly still, there is no instance of a case being brought to the Committee of the ICESCR alleging a violation of the right to food on environmental grounds, despite a veritable epidemic of flawed government policy leading to food resource loss.

The right to health provides a slightly more promising example, with several references scattered through the text and interpretative documents that make some limited environmental demands upon states. Chief among these are requirements of environmental hygiene and the prevention of disease, both of which logically presuppose the necessity of environmental conditions that do not *preclude* these goods. The General Comment is more generous still, recognizing the importance of 'the underlying determinants of health, such as … a healthy environment' (CESCR, E/C.12/2000/4.). In fact, the word 'environment' receives more treatment in this context than anywhere else in a founding human rights document. However, its use is largely confined to discussion of a negative right not to be made ill through environmental impediments to health, rather than a guarantee of positive environmental conditions: 'in the environmental context, the right to health essentially implies feasible protection from natural hazards and freedom from pollution' (OHCHR, Ksentini Report, 1994).

Significantly, we can find cases at a regional level that uphold a duty of environmental management regarding the above right. While not as legally compelling as a complaint under the convention, these cases show that it is possible to give teeth to environmental requirements under a right to health. In an instance of state-sanctioned environmental pollution in Nigeria, the African Commission on Human and Peoples Rights found a violation of the right to health as it is found in Article 16 of the African Social Charter (Communication 155/96, The Social and Economic Rights Action Center and the Center for Economic, and Social Rights). It was held that the regional instrument – almost identical in form to the ICESCR right[3] – must 'obligate governments to desist from directly threatening the health and the environment of their citizens. In addition, the State must take measures to prevent pollution and ecological degradation' (Coomans, 2003). In another example, the European Court of Human Rights found in the *Guerra* case a violation of the right to health contained within Article 2: the right to life provision of the European Convention. In this decision, Judge Jambrek held that 'the protection of health and physical integrity is … closely associated with the right to life', and the exposure of a group of Italian citizens to air pollution, in combination with the failure of the government to provide information on the risks of such exposure, amounted to a violation of these rights (*Guerra and Others v. Italy* (116/1996/735/932)). While the wording of 'physical integrity' differs from that used at the more international level, the intent to protect a right to health from environmental threats is clear.

The provisions surrounding the 'right to life' are where we might expect to find a clear articulation of the total dependence of humanity upon the environment in which human life takes place. Perhaps predictably, such an expectation is thwarted by the limited language used to articulate this right. While it is now well accepted that the right to life extends beyond a mere prohibition upon its deprivation,[4] there is nothing in the supporting documents that suggests that such deprivation can be found to have occurred through environmental means.[5] The law in itself thus fails to recognize the life–environment link almost entirely.

On the other hand, promising material is emerging out of the law in practice, with the International Court of Justice (ICJ) stating that 'the protection of the environment is likewise a vital part of contemporary human rights doctrine, for it is a *sine qua non* for numerous human rights such as the right to health and the right to life itself' (*Gabčíkovo-Nagymaros Project* ICJ Rep 7, 1997). The European Committee of Social Rights has also made strong statements in this regard, for example in *Oneryildiz v. Turkey*, in which a methane explosion at a dump was deemed to have violated the right to life under Article 2 of the regional convention. Here, the right to life was found to impose an 'obligation to take appropriate steps to safeguard the lives of those within their jurisdiction', including from environmental threats.[6] This was further supported by the case of *Budayeva and Others v. Russia*, where it was found that the state had failed to meet its obligations under the right to life by failing to take action to prevent or lessen the harm caused by mudslides (ECHR, Application No. 15339/02). While these advances are excellent steps in the right direction and are in no way trivial, they are nonetheless not likely to be of a collective weight sufficient to find that the right to life entails a justiciable right to environmental quality at the present time.[7]

That the present state of the law is unsatisfactory seems clear. While the connection between human well-being of the kind enshrined in human rights instruments is accepted as a fact of both logic and biology, the international legal community has failed to embrace this reality. It is imperative that change occurs, and quickly, to allow our human rights instruments to address the environmental barriers to the achievement of the rights they seek to establish; not to do so is to deny the essential truth that '[d]esirable standards of health and welfare will be impossible to sustain in an atmosphere depleted of life-giving and life-sustaining elements … without a sound environment it would not be possible to sustain an acceptable quality of life or even life itself' (Weiss, 1992). What is needed at this point in history is an ecologically literate interpretation of human rights law: '[m]odern society requires an universal ethical and legal discourse that can correlate human dignity and ecological justice, human rights and the integrity of nature, and the rights of the present generations and future generations' (Vorster, 2010). While there is increasing interest in the development of a stand-alone 'human right to the environment', there are a number of difficulties inherent to this approach;[8] as such, our focus must shift to the alternative tactic of working within the existing legal boundaries.

An ecologically literate interpretation of existing law

An ecologically literate path would require both the ICCPR and the ICESCR to adapt to include the requirement of meeting the ecological prerequisites of the rights originally agreed, a type of expansion consistent with the idea that human rights instruments must remain living documents (Robinson, 1998). This line of attack has many advantages, perhaps most significant of which is the fact that it would avoid the difficulties attendant to the drafting process of any new international agreement: 'recognition of environmental deprivations of existing rights does not require the creation of any new doctrine, but merely an ecologically literate reading of existing human rights' (Collins, 2007). The approach has also found favour with a recent High Level Expert Meeting convened by the United Nations (UN), which weighed the merits of both the creation of a stand-alone human right to the environment and the expansion of existing rights as viable options for future development. The meeting concluded that the latter approach

> ... may provide a quicker and easier path than developing a new human right, particularly given the disputes over the justiciability and definition of a substantive right ... The experts [also] noted that, given how much international law has already developed in this area, any process forward should concentrate on obligations that governments have already agreed to and address gaps in a consistent manner, rather than attempt to develop entirely new obligations. (UNEP, 2010)

Essentially, what such an approach requires is not the articulation of any new legal concept, but the further development of interpretative materials to explicitly recognize the obligations already inherent to the existing law. The strategy for achieving this is twofold: increase the availability of expert knowledge and opinion on the relationship between the environment and violations of human rights, and, most importantly, see cases of this kind brought to court. It is only once a sufficient body of case law has been amassed from a sufficient number of state parties, recognizing the violation of convention-based rights by environmental mismanagement, that an attempt could be made to legally compel to action those state parties who have failed to act to protect their environment, and thus, in turn, their people.

The ultimate goal, and the marker by which it could be said that this milestone had been achieved, would be a decision from the ICJ recognizing the existence of environmental duties within the human rights regime. As the highest judicial authority of the UN, such a decision would cement the rule in international customary law, a position ultimately more powerful than enshrining the principle in a treaty alone; customary law is, in some circumstances, able to compel even dissenting states.

As discussed above, achieving such a decision would require a finding of both strong state practice and 'soft law' support. Clearly, it is state practice that has the farthest distance to go before environmental cognizance can be said to be an international norm. However, there are a number of ways in which states can be compelled towards acting with greater environmental responsibility in respect of their human rights duties.

In the first instance, it would be highly desirable for the United Nations Human Rights Committee (UNHRC) to issue an over-arching declaration (in the nature of the 1990 Comment defining state parties obligations) establishing the duty of environmental management in relation to human rights. Such a document would need to acknowledge the centrality of the environment to the broader human rights scheme and, at the same time, set out the specific nature of the obligations under each right. It would need to define what the obligations consist of, from whom and to whom the obligation is owed, how such obligations can be said to have been met, and the procedures for both assistance and rebuke in cases of non-compliance. Because such a document would necessarily be quite wordy, it may be more expedient to split this into more wieldy pieces and instead issue a separate comment regarding the environmental obligations inherent to each right, additional to the existing interpretations.[9]

As an example of how this might work in practice, it has already been mentioned that current state obligations under the right to food are woefully inadequate with regard to the environmental determinants of that right. A logical expansion of those obligations would see a number of environmental management strategies adopted as duties of the state: for example, a duty to provide education on sustainable farming techniques such as crop rotation, a duty to reduce reliance on fossil fuel-based fertilizers, a duty to monitor soil ecology and pollinator health, a duty to monitor irrigation practices and enforce environmentally responsible pesticide use. Duties would also exist at a lower level, where individuals and corporations are seen as having a responsibility to adopt sustainable practices, if not at an optimal level of maximizing long-term food production, at least to the point where they may not act to the detriment of the land in terms of an ability to produce food in the future. These are simply environmental management tools that must become part of the repertoire of right to food, since without them the prospects for long-term food security are almost nil.

Other high-level institutions have important roles to play in establishing environmental management as a human rights norm. United Nations General Assembly resolutions, though not legally binding, are nevertheless strong statements of sentiment, and a resolution that declared the necessity of considering *and acting to prevent* environmental impediments to human rights goods would act as a further interpretive aid to any judge seeking to ascertain international opinion on these matters. The drafting process of any such resolution would itself assist in the progress of customary international law by forcing states to engage with the science behind this movement and actively consider the issue with regard to their own level of compliance. It is tempting to think that this alone could act as a motivating factor in changing behaviour, once the advantages to their citizens of a sustainable, productive environment becomes apparent, but at the very least it would permit a more accurate assessment of states' current positions on this issue. Even if the reception to such an idea is initially hostile, it would at least enable a dialogue to commence which might address the concerns of dissenting states.

The ICJ, described in its Statute as the 'principal judicial organ of the United Nations', has already been mentioned with regard to achieving a definitive judgement on this subject. Any such judgement would likely take the form of an advisory opinion, the outcome of a special procedure whereby certain organizational structures within the UN are able to ask for clarification of a point of international law. Such opinions are generally (as the name suggests) merely advisory, despite the fact that they 'carry great legal weight and moral authority' (ICJ, 2011); however, under certain circumstances these judgements can be issued to have a legally binding effect.[10] Whether it is realistic to expect that a judgement on the environmental elements of human rights duties would achieve such elevated status, even a theoretically 'non-binding' decision would effectively cement such a principle as customary law.

Besides advisory opinions, the Court's main duty is to preside over contentious cases, the process by which a state brings a complaint against another state. A contentious case brought under international human rights law that dealt with transboundary environmental harm would be a valuable tool in building the case for a customary law linking human rights and the environment. While no such case exists at present, it is surely only a matter of time before a state alleges the violation of its citizens' human rights by another state's action or inaction on environmental matters; the escalating debate surrounding the right to water is just one example where one country's actions can literally dictate the ability of states located 'downstream' to meet their human rights obligations. As such, there is a role for legal experts in building the case for an expanded concept of existing human rights: it is essential that states are aware of the ICJ as an avenue of redress for environmental harm which impacts upon the ability to meet human rights obligations, and assisted in bringing such claims before the Court.

Other international organizations may play a similarly vital role. Statements and reports by high-level institutions such as the Food and Agriculture Organization (FAO), the World Health Organization, the UN Environment Programme (UNEP), the UNHRC, the relevant Special Rapporteurs, as well as regional human rights bodies would help to build momentum for state behavioural change. It is therefore essential that the relevant reports are commissioned with sufficient resources devoted to enable practical guidelines to be developed regarding the specific content of the environmental obligations arising under each right. These organizations are best equipped with specialist knowledge and access to a wide source of ground-level information. It is thus essential that these agencies are able to take the lead in clarifying the precise ways in which the environment can help or hinder human rights efforts.

A final burden rests upon academic and political commentators, who will necessarily function as a foundational information source for those seeking to make decisions at a higher level. By presenting strong arguments accompanied by legitimate quantitative data, which make the link between environmental degradation and violations of human rights, this community has the potential to influence international opinion on the issue from the bottom up. History has shown that where a sufficient weight of expert evidence is accumulated, states can find it difficult to justify inaction even in the face of powerful interest groups: the Montreal Protocol on Substances that Deplete the Ozone Layer is one example of action at an international level that was precipitated by strong consensus among expert groups.

If all of the above institutions and groups could be mobilized to act in the ways discussed here, it would not be an exaggeration to say that the case for finding a justiciable, environmentally literate interpretation of existing human rights in customary international law would be greatly strengthened. A combined effort, from international institutions, individual state governments, and the wider academic community, may achieve what each alone could not:

> Where rights have been strengthened, the cause is not so much individual factors acting independently – whether in law, politics, technology, economics, or consciousness – but a complex interweaving of mutually reinforcing processes. What pulls human rights forward is not a series of separate, parallel cords, but a 'rope' of multiple, interwoven strands. (Cassel, 2001)

While the path towards an expanded conception of existing rights may thus appear frustratingly rambling, the resultant law will ultimately be the stronger for having the weight of societal saturation behind it, something that may not likewise accompany the faster process of drafting a new instrument, bypassing as it does the need for obtaining acceptance at every level of the global community.

Conclusion

To summarize, international human rights law at present exhibits some startling deficiencies in terms of an inability to compel states to address and prevent breaches of human rights caused by environmental degradation. The dire state of both the natural world and human well-being demonstrates the necessity of addressing this lacuna with all possible haste. It is to be hoped that an ongoing dialogue about these issues, such as can be found in this volume, will continue to provide us with valuable insights as to the exact nature of the environmental necessities required to achieve a universal realization of human rights. In the meantime, an awareness of the gaps within existing international law can only serve to motivate those passionate about the human rights cause to find ways of incorporating environmental concerns into their thinking.[11]

Notes

1 Material detailing the human impact of environmental problems abounds, but for an introduction see Schade, C. and Pimentel, D. (2010) 'Population crash: prospects for famine in the twenty-first century', *Environment Development Sustainability*, vol 12, pp245–262; Brown, L. (2010) 'Food: will there be enough?' in L. Mazur (ed.) *A Pivotal Moment*, Island Press, Washington, DC, pp 166–178; Blanco, E. and Razzaque, J. (2009)'Ecosystem services and human well-being in a globalized world: assessing the role of law', *Human Rights Quarterly*, vol 31, no 3, August, pp692–720; UK Faculty of Public Health (2010) *Great Outdoors: How Our Natural Health Service Uses Green Space To Improve Wellbeing*, Faculty of Public Health, London, UK.

2 Though as we move further down the legal 'food chain', it is possible to find strong statements regarding environmental prerequisites to the right to food from the FAO, various United Nations Special Rapporteurs, and innumerable scholarly commentators; whether these statements are legally compelling is questionable.

3 Compare the ASC's 'Every individual shall have the right to enjoy the best attainable state of physical and mental health' with the ICESCR's 'right of everyone to the enjoyment of the highest attainable standard of physical and mental health'. These similarities contribute to the weight that the African decisions may carry in influencing any future expansion of the international law.

4 As far back as 1982, the Committee explicitly recognized that the Right to Life 'is a right which should not be interpreted narrowly', and 'the expression "inherent right to life" cannot properly be understood in a restrictive manner, and the protection of this right requires that States adopt positive measures.' Office of the High Commissioner for Human Rights, General Comment No. 6: The right to life (art. 6): 04/30/1982.

5 It might be possible to interpret the requirement to take action upon infant mortality, malnutrition and epidemics as requiring in turn environmental management strategies, but this strikes me as being a difficult proposition without a supporting judgement affirming such a position.

6 'The Court found, considering the evidence, that the authorities knew the risk and needed to take preventative measures… to protect the individuals, which they failed to do' (Orellan *et al*, 2010).

7 '[E]ven though environmental harms have been widely recognized as threats to human life and health, international tribunals have been cautious in finding that such harms violate the right to life' (Asia Pacific Forum, 2007, p62)

8 I discuss the deficiencies of this approach in greater detail in a paper titled *Human Rights and the Environment: People, Planet and State*, available from the University of Waikato.

9 In this situation, both HRC and the CESCR would have responsibility for issuing comments as appropriate for each right.

10 From the official website of the ICJ: 'Contrary to judgements, and except in rare cases where it is stipulated beforehand that they shall have binding effect (for example, as in the Convention on the Privileges and Immunities of the specialized agencies of the United Nations, and the Headquarters Agreement between the United Nations and the United States), the Court's advisory opinions have no binding effect.'

11 I thank Professor Claire Breen of the University of Waikato for her valued assistance and encouragement in the development of this research.

References

Cases

Gabčíkovo-Nagymaros Project (Hung. v. Slovk.), 1997 ICJ Rep 7, 88 (25 September)
Guerra and Others v. Italy ECHR (116/1996/735/932) 19 February 1998
Budayeva and Others v. Russia ECHR (Application No. 15339/02) & Ors (20 March 2008)
Oneryildiz v. Turkey ECHR (Application No. 48939/99 (18 July 2002)
Centre for Minority Rights Development on behalf of Endorois Community v. Kenya, Comm. 276/2003, May 2009/ Communication 155/96, The Social and Economic Rights Action Center and the Center for Economic, and Social Rights / Nigeria. See www.cesr.org/text%20files/nigeria.PDF

United Nations documents

Statute of the International Court of Justice, available at www.icj-cij.org/documents/index.php?p1=4&p2=2&p3=0
Committee on Economic, Social and Cultural Rights, General Comment 12, The Right to Adequate Food: E/C.12/1999/5
Committee on Economic, Social and Cultural Rights, General Comment 14, The Right to Health: (2000) E/C.12/2000/4
Committee on Economic, Social and Cultural Rights, General Comment No. 15, The Right to Water: (2002) E/C.12/2002/11
Office of the High Commissioner for Human Rights, General Comment No. 6, The Right to Life: 04/30/1982
Office of the High Commissioner on Human Rights, Ksentini, F. *Report of the Special Rapporteur on Prevention of Discrimination and Protection of Minorities: Human Rights and the Environment* (1994) E/CN.4/Sub.2/1994/p46
UNEP Division of Environmental Law and Conventions, Holmes, C. 'The New Future of Human Rights and Environment: Moving the Global Agenda Forward – High Level Experts Meeting' in *MEA Bulletin* (2010)

Bibliography

Asia Pacific Forum (2007) *Human Rights and The Environment*, Reference Paper to the Asia Pacific Forum, September, available at www.asiapacificforum.net/support/issues/acj/references/right-to-environment
Bailey, R. (2011) *Growing a Better Future*, Oxfam International, Oxford, UK
Barker, J. C. (2002) 'Mechanisms to create and support conventions, treaties, and other responses' in *UNESCO Encyclopaedia of Life-Support Systems*, EoLss Publishers, Paris, France
Blanco, E. and Razzaque, J. (2009) 'Ecosystem services and human well-being in a globalized world: assessing the role of law' in *Human Rights Quarterly*, August, vol 31, pp692–720
Cassel, D. (2001) 'Does international law make a difference?', *Chicago Journal of International Law*, vol 2, pp121–135

Collins, L. (2007) 'Are we there yet? The right to environment in international and European law', *McGill International Journal of Sustainable Development Law and Policy*, vol 3, p127

Coomans, F. (2003) 'The Ogoni case before the African Commission on Human and Peoples' Rights', *International and Comparative Law Quarterly*, vol 52, July, pp749–760

Faculty of Public Health (2010) *Great Outdoors: How Our Natural Health Service Uses Green Space To Improve Wellbeing*, Faculty of Public Health, London, UK

Glazebrook, S. (2009) 'Human rights and the environment', *Victoria University of Wellington Law Review*, vol 40, p293

Goulet, R. (2009) 'Food Sovereignty: a step forward in the realisation of the right to food', *Law, Social Justice and Global Development Journal*, vol 1, no 13, April

ICJ (2011) International Court of Justice, *Advisory Jurisdiction*, available at www.icj-cij.org/jurisdiction/index.php?p1=5&p2=2

Orellan, M., Kothari, M. and Chaudry, S. (2010) *Climate Change in the Work of the Committee on Economic, Social and Cultural Rights*, May, available at www.fes-globalization.org/geneva/documents/CESCR%20Climate%20Change_May 2010.pdf

Project DIANA at Yale Law School (2005) *Draft Declaration of Principles on Human Rights and the Environment, 1994*, Project DIANA, Yale Law School, available at www.yale.edu/lawweb/avalon/diana/undocs/33198-11.html

Robinson, M. (1998) 'Welcoming the downtrodden', *Refugees Magazine*, no 111 (special issue on the Universal Declaration of Human Rights' 50th Anniversary)

Rodriguez-Rivera, L. (2001)'Is the human right to environment recognized under international law? It depends on the source', *Colorado Journal of International Environmental Law & Policy*, vol 12, pp1–45

Shelton, D. (2009) 'Human rights and environment: past, present and future linkages and the value of a declaration', background paper for High Level Expert Meeting of the New Future of Human Rights and Environment: Moving the Global Agenda Forward, UNEP and OHCHR project

Shelton, D. (1992) 'What happened in Rio to human rights?' *Yearbook of International Environmental Law*, vol 2, p75

Taylor, P. (1998) *An Ecological Approach to International Law: Responding to the Challenges of Climate Change*, Routledge, London, UK

Vorster, N. (2010) ''An ethical critique of Milton Friedman's doctrine on economics and freedom'', *Journal for the Study of Religions and Ideologies*, vol 9, p26

Weiss, E. (ed.) (1992) *Environmental Change and International Law: New Challenges and Dimensions*, United Nations University Press, Tokyo, Japan

4 The common heritage principle and public health

Honouring our legacy

Prue Taylor

Introduction

The 'common heritage of mankind' (CH) is best known as a concept or principle of international law. It emerged in the 1960s to guide the management of the international commons (i.e. areas of Earth and space), beyond the jurisdiction of states. Despite its acknowledged relevance for the protection of ecological systems, recent multilateral environmental treaties have not used it. Indeed, it attracts considerable controversy. Some commentators dismiss it, claiming that states have overwhelmingly rejected it for political reasons. Others view it as an aspirational slogan, a utopian goal. It is also seen as protecting the 'status quo' of international law, leaving ecological systems vulnerable to exploitation in the interests of states and corporations.

This chapter argues that CH is neither a mere slogan nor a conventional concept for managed exploitation. On the contrary, it is potentially a powerful principle of international environmental law. This is because, at its core, CH is an ethical concept that requires collective management of the interdependent commons, for the present and long-term benefit of all life (not states). Further, it can overcome some of the traditional democratic deficits of international law, to remedy the twin tragedies of 'fragmentation' and 'free access exploitation' (Hardin, 1968), and turn back the tide of the 'final enclosure' of the commons (Westra, 2011). Far from being a political liability, it is one of most extraordinary developments in recent intellectual history and one of the most radical legal concepts to have emerged in recent decades (Baslar, 1997).

The emerging ecological world view recognizes that human health and well-being (cultural, social and economic) are integral to and dependent upon the healthy functioning of Earth's major ecological systems and all species. Our understanding of what is required to provide for and protect public health is beginning to reflect this larger context. Public health is no longer a matter of ambient environmental quality; nor is it a matter of protecting individual human rights to a healthy quality of life or even to the right of life. The real challenges for global population health arise from the complex inter-relationship between declining social cohesion (poverty and inequity) and ecological degradation (McMichael and Butler, 2006). Climate change is helping us to understand the full extent of our dependency on Earth's ecological integrity, the prevalence of destructive behaviour and the collectives dimensions. Recent statements, that climate change poses a real and urgent threat to international 'peace and security', acknowledge the scale and reach of the public health risks. But even climate change must be connected to human transgression of other key planetary boundaries (Rockström *et al.*, 2009).

Our scientific understanding is advancing, but our governance responses are not. We urgently need to create a governance regime that embraces the whole biosphere and profoundly changes our relationship with nature and with each other. The 'common heritage' provides an ethical and legal basis for such a regime.

This chapter begins by outlining the legal history of the 'common heritage'. This provides the context for responding to some controversies and for elucidating its potential.

1967–1982: the start of a revolution?

On 1 November 1967, Arvid Pardo (a Maltese diplomat and international lawyer) stood before the United Nations (UN) and delivered an electrifying three-hour speech. He argued that the seabed and ocean floor, beyond the limits of national jurisdiction, should be considered the 'common heritage of mankind'. As such, it should be subject to an international management regime for its use and long-term environmental protection. Pardo's concern was that continued unmanaged use of the oceans could become a serious threat to international peace and security. This threat arose from the environmental impact of new technologies, the militarization of the seafloor and expanding state claims to jurisdiction over parts of the oceans. It also arose from the growing economic disparity between the peoples of developed and developing states. Developed states had a clear advantage in both claiming and exploiting the ocean's resources. Pardo's vision was that future mining on the ocean's seabed be internationalized with revenue providing an independent revenue source for the UN and a source of wealth for developing states (Pardo, 1967).

This proposal lead to a number of important legal developments (Declaration of Principles, 1970) and helped create the necessary international consensus for the negotiation of a very ambitious agreement – the 1982 Law of the Sea Convention (LOS). This is no ordinary legal convention. It was intended to be a 'constitution for the oceans', setting out a comprehensive and universal legal order, agreed to by consensus (Beesley, 2004, p108; Tuerk, 2010, p160).

Part XI of LOS is key to the legal implementation of CH. It defines the 'Area' as the 'seabed and ocean floor, and the subsoil thereof, beyond the limits of national jurisdiction'. The Area and its resources (only) are the 'common heritage of mankind', leaving other parts of the ocean system to be governed by other legal principles (Article 136). Part XI also provides that no claim or exercise of sovereignty or sovereign rights over any part of the Area (or its resources) or appropriation by any state, natural or juridical person, shall be recognized (Article 137). Article 140 vests all rights in the resources of the Area in 'mankind', with the International Seabed Authority (ISA) established to act on behalf of (and for the benefit of) mankind. The ISA must ensure the equitable sharing of financial and other economic benefits arising from activities (such as mining) conducted in the Area, taking into particular account the needs and interests of developing states, and others. Key tasks include promoting marine scientific research, transferring technology to developing states, and protecting the environment from harm – the latter task being considered one of the ISA's main functions (Articles 143–145). The States Parties are all members of the ISA and are regarded as having to act through it. The Enterprise is to directly carry out operational activities in the Area (Articles 158, 166, 170).

The combined effect of these articles was to create a unique commons regime, the main elements of which are explained below. However, this regime applied only to a small part of the oceans system, namely the 'Area' (i.e. the deep-sea bed) and its resources.

Despite this serious limitation, the CH regime proved so controversial that the United States initially refused to sign LOS (Beesley, 2004, p108). The reasons for this withdrawal of support included a difference of opinion on how to use the Area and its resources to benefit mankind as a whole. Developing states argued that the only way to ensure equitable distribution, taking into account their needs, was via a global entity with exclusive exploitation rights. Developed states viewed this as a forum of distributive justice which was hostile to commercial investment and contrary to market-orientated economic approaches (Tuerk, 2010, pp161, 165). LOS eventually came into force more than 10 years later, following the 1994 Implementation Agreement that substantially reduced the distributive justice elements of the mining regime, in favour of greater protection of commercial interests (Tuerk, 2010, p169).

By the end of negotiations in 1982, Pardo expressed grave disappointment in what had been achieved (Borgese, 2000). A combination of political and economic factors greatly restricted the scope of CH to resources on the deep-sea bed. While this history proved to be divisive and disappointing, it was not a failure for CH. As will be discussed below, special recognition of it within LOS (together with other considerations) contributes to CH's evolution, as a principle of law, beyond the history of LOS.

1979 Moon Treaty

This treaty was negotiated in parallel with LOS. LOS and the 1967 Outer Space Treaty, in which traces of CH appear, influenced it. Exploitation of lunar resources via an international regime was controversial, but a compromise enabled states to declare the moon and its natural resources the 'common heritage of mankind' (Article 11(1)). It has been used to reject 'idle' claims to property rights in lunar resources (Tuerk, 2010, p172).

1988–1992: a period of abandonment?

The negotiation of key multilateral environmental agreements (MEAs) between 1988 and 1992 was not beneficial for the recognition and use of CH. States rejected it as a concept to guide UN treaty regimes on climate change and conservation of biological diversity.

The 1992 UN Framework Convention on Climate Change refers to the *problem* of climate change as being the 'common *concern* of humankind' (Preamble). Drawing on Pardo's legacy, Malta originally proposed a treaty declaring 'conservation of the Earth's global climate system' an integral part of the CH, because it is fundamental to life on Earth. Its vital nature required an international approach that transcended state sovereignty (i.e. the unilateral decisions of states) in the interests of present and future generations. However, when it became clear that states would reject this, the less ambitious option of a treaty on the specific problem of climate change emerged. Nevertheless, in Malta's view, 'common *concern* of humankind' was a necessary corollary of the 'common heritage' principle. It acknowledges that the global climate system can be used by each state within its own territory, but a conservation strategy is required 'which can not be restricted by political boundaries and must necessarily have as its primary objective the common good of mankind' (Borg, 2009, p9). 'Common concern' was also intended to evoke intra-generational (obligations towards developing states) and intergenerational elements. Humankind, via civil society, should have a right to participate in decision-making (Borg, 2009).

During LOS negotiations, developing states were major supporters of CH as a means of establishing the new international economic order (Tuerk, 2010, p166). However, by 1992, the suggestion that Earth's biological diversity be declared the (or a part of) 'common heritage' was rejected. They perceived it as a potential threat to their sovereign rights to use and benefit from the biological resources within their own territories and were suspicious of interference in their social and economic development, under the guise of environmental protection or via the acquisition of intellectual property rights. As a result, the UN Convention on Biological Diversity uses the term 'common concern of humankind' (Preamble).

Controversies

This history provides some context against which the key controversies that inhibit greater recognition of CH can be considered.

State rejection

One of the most common criticisms of CH is that it is too political –states have rejected its use in recent treaty regimes. This objection is significant. It reflects the view that international law comprises only those norms or rules specifically agreed to by states, as an exercise of their free consent. This view of the sources of international law potentially leaves humanity at the mercy of national political and economic self-interest and creates a 'democratic deficit'. An alternative view is that the law is also comprised of a number of fundamental norms or principles, intended to harmonize human behaviour with the laws of nature. These norms express universal ethical concepts and values that have, over time, attained social legitimacy as legal norms from which states cannot derogate (*jus cogens*).

As noted above, legal discussion of CH normally begins in 1967 with LOS and focuses on its subsequent rejection by MEAs. The implication is that CH is merely a 'second-order' legal principle that states can adopt or reject at will. This overlooks the philosophical foundations of CH. It is a very old moral concept, which has only recently been translated into international law. A full account of this history is beyond the scope of this chapter; therefore a few examples will illustrate.

At the core of CH is the notion of sustaining the basis or foundations of life, for the benefit of all. This is common to many cultures, religions and spiritual traditions – it is part of 'global wisdom' (Weeramantry, 2011, pxv; Borgese, 1986). It expresses concern and responsibility for the 'other', which encompasses human interrelations and the human–nature relationship. It implicitly focuses on controlling *human behaviour* to secure the well-being of the 'other'. This is very important in the ecological context as we can only 'manage' human conduct. To think that we can manage ecological systems is hubris. The 'other' encompasses present and future generations. Many traditional peoples have concepts requiring respect for past, present and future generations embedded in their cultures. The world's great spiritual and religious traditions also embrace concepts of responsibility, trusteeship and the need to sustain the basis of all life. Some also express the unity between humanity and all life – if we damage other beings, we are damaging ourselves (Weeramantry, 2011). Our failure to act consistently with this global wisdom, over the last few centuries, can be described as the abnormal becoming normal.

One of the first recorded uses of the CH in international law arose in 1830. It was suggested that things that could not be held by any nation, without affecting the interests of other nations, were the 'indivisible common patrimony'. Certain areas of Earth should be set aside for the common use of all, and were not capable of claims of state sovereignty or ownership, but would be subject to defined common use rights. In 1927, a jurist proposed that the living resources of the seas be a 'heritage of mankind' (Tuerk, 2010, p157). In 1946, a plan was developed to establish an international authority, for the collective ownership and management of all existing nuclear resources (Borgese, 1999, p7).

In 1948/1949, a group of eminent people drafted a preliminary World Constitution. The first chapter is a 'declaration of duties and rights' (not solely rights), and states:

> The four elements of life – earth, water, air, energy – *are common property of the human race. The management and use* of such portions thereof as are vested in or assigned to particular ownership, ... *shall be subordinated in each and all cases to the inherent interest of the common good.* (World Beyond Borders, n.d.; emphasis added)

A concern was that international social justice and peace could not be secured using existing concepts of property: including rights to use and misuse. Thus the draft established a new legal order to protect the Earth and its resources as the common heritage and property of mankind. This may have been utopian at the time, but twenty years later, the seabed and moon had been declared the common heritage of mankind, to be managed, for the good of all, by an international authority established for that purpose (Borgese, 1999, p9).

Another significant event occurred in early 1967. The World Peace through Law Conference referred to the high seas as 'the common heritage of all mankind' and recommended that the seabed be subject to UN jurisdiction and control (Tuerk, 2010, p158).

It is against this more complete understanding of CH's ethical content and early legal references that we can consider its use in LOS. Here we see traces of an important argument – that CH has attained the highest degree of social legitimacy – as a type of non-derogable legal norm, similar to a *jus cogens* norm.

First, LOS has a kind of 'constitutional' status as a document representing international consensus, articulating agreed norms and binding all states (not just State Parties). In this context, CH was singled out for special treatment; states expressly agreed not to amend, or derogate from, the basic principle of the seabed being the CH (Article 311(6); Reaffirmed – 1994 Implementation Agreement). This grants CH a special status 'above treaty law' (or secondary rules) similar to a *jus cogens* norm (Wolfrum, 2008). Second, the prohibition against any sovereign claim or appropriation (Article 137) expressly prohibits the recognition of any such a claim. This is reinforced by the fact that Article 137 is expressed to bind all states (not just Parties) and private persons/corporate entities. Together, the legal effect is similar to that of *jus cogens* (Wolfrum, 2008).

In Tuerk's opinion, the Moon Treaty is also indicative of CH attaining the status of a fundamental principle of international law because it is intended to bind all states, not only State Parties. However, he stops short of claiming it to be a *jus cogens* principle (Tuerk, 2010).

Putting to one side the difficult question of the current legal status of CH, some important qualities flow from it being a special legal norm, similar to a *jus cogens.* First, it could bind all states, irrespective of their express consent. Second, it could not be amended or derogated from by other agreements, unlike second order rules. Third, it would bind all persons, natural and legal. This is important because it recognizes that transnational corporations are key actors and perpetrators of ecological harm. Taken together, these qualities respond to one of the primary 'democratic deficits' of state-centred international law. States (and other entities) would not be free to exploit the ecological commons, with no regard for the collective interests of humanity (and other life), according to legal regimes that prioritize their own interests. Further, states (and others) would owe an obligation to protect the common good (see below).

The claim that states have rejected CH also ignores evidence of growing support for it since 1994. Full discussion of this trend is beyond the scope of this chapter, but a recent literature survey identified 1,750 academic articles on CH. Regarding state practice, UNESCO has continuously supported CH through a number of initiatives. This stems, in part, from the 1972 Convention for Protection of Cultural and Natural Heritage: 'parts of the cultural or natural heritage ... need to be preserved as part of the world heritage of mankind as a whole' (Preamble). Although difficult to define, 'natural and cultural heritage' includes tangible and intangible elements, ranging from archaeological sites and historic monuments to cultural phenomena (language, customary practices) and natural systems (islands, biosphere reserves). This possible use of CH is significant because it extends CH to areas and resources (ecological systems) that are *within* state jurisdiction, unlike the deep-sea bed and the moon.

It may still be some time before states are prepared to give wider acknowledgement to CH in international legal regimes. However, international law is no longer the sole domain of states. Global civil society is playing an increasing role in developing international law through, advocacy of ethical concepts such as CH (Boda, 2003; Earth Charter, 2000). CH's expression of universal communitarian values links it to renewed interest in cosmopolitanism and global constitutionalism (Bosselmann and Engel, 2010, p239).

A new kind of regime in international law?

An issue surrounding CH is the kind of regime it creates. Does it create a common property regime, according to which nation states *own* the CH in common? Does it give states property rights, analogous to ownership? Or, does it create a regime that attempts to avoid the 'propertization' of ecological systems so as to recognize the critical interest of all life, in maintaining the resilience of these systems (common good)?

The answer to this question is very important because the creation of a 'common property regime' places priority on ecological systems as a storehouse of resources for human exploitation and utilization. As a result, resource management regimes emerge that have an economic and procedural focus. Their use of market mechanisms and property rights tends to eliminate or diminish the need to respect ecological systems as the basis of all life (Grinlinton and Taylor, 2011). Approaches that merely slow down exploitation misunderstand both the nature and gravity of the situation. What is important is viewing Earth not only as property, 'but to consider it as comprised of natural systems whose integrity and support is essential to our survival, present and future' (Westra, 2011, p162).

As noted above, the question of whether CH created a common property regime has been divisive and resulted in emphasis on CH as primarily an equitable utilization regime. This leaves CH vulnerable to the criticism that it is of limited use when the priority needs to be respectful treatment of ecological systems, long-term protection, restoration and enhancement (Westra, 2011).

States have focused on the supposed 'property' elements of CH, for their own purposes and consistent with their own economic paradigms. However, this was not intended. In 1970, Pardo said:

> We did not think it advisable to use the word 'property' – not because I had anything against property ... Property is a form of power. Property as we have it from the ancient Romans implies the *jus utendi et abutendi* (right of use and misuse). *Property implies and gives excessive emphasis to just one aspect: resource exploitation and benefit therefrom.* (Borgese, 2000, pxxvii; emphasis added).

Pardo used CH to address two problems of 'property'. First, in 1967 large parts of the oceans remained outside state jurisdiction (the high seas), but they were vulnerable to creeping sovereignty claims – a form of privatization (Taylor, 1998, pp118–121). It was his intention to stop creeping claims by clarifying that the seabed *belonged to humanity* and was therefore *not* capable of any form of subsequent appropriation or ownership by states or others. This non-appropriation element enabled the CH to be used by all, but owned by none (*res communes omnium*). However, this alone would not be enough. The *freedom of* the high seas regime also had to be replaced. As an open-access (*laissez-faire*) regime, it left the high seas vulnerable to the tragedy of the commons phenomenon (Hardin, 1968). What began as a doctrine suited to the needs of ships and maritime empires, became the 'right to overfish and a license to pollute' (Beesley, 2004, p105). Therefore, CH created a new regime requiring common management by states, for the positive benefit of all humanity (not states). This did not preclude use of seabed resources, but use had to be carefully managed according to a range of principles akin to what we would now term ecosystem management. It is this element of CH that has been referred to as the great genius of Pardo. It also links CH to the development of community management regimes for common resources (Ostrom *et al.*, 2002).

Pardo's concern to make seabed resources available to the peoples of developing states also meant that environmental protection was not an end in itself. It was to be an integral part of use of marine resources – not simply an add-on (Borgese, 2000, pxxxiii). This social equity aspect is critical and can be applied beyond resource utilization regimes.

'Humanity' as a subject of international law?

The traditional view is that nation states are the primary subjects of international law. Accordingly, only states can directly benefit from, acquire obligations under, and enforce international law. This creates another kind of democratic deficit – giving sovereign states a monopoly power to pursue national interests.

Some commentaries suggests that the CH principle creates 'humanity' as a new subject of international law (Fuse, 1998, p95). In the view of Tuerk: '[i]nternational administration of the commons and management of its resources *for the common good*' distinguished CH from the high seas as *res communis* (Tuerk, 2010, p159). Wolfrum rejects this argument because of state control of LOS administrative organs (ISA). However, he agrees that present and future generations of humanity are the 'ultimate point of reference' (Wolfrum, 2008, para 28).

To solve global problems that had a direct impact on humanity, Pardo saw the need to accept humanity as a subject of international law (Fuse, 1998, p95). In this sense, CH creates the opportunity to put the *demos* into international law. If states remain in sole control (as they do via the LOS management structure), they can continue to subjugate the common good of humanity to their own sovereign interests. To prevent this, institutional structures giving a direct voice to the interests of present and future generations are required. This would enable humanity to determine what management 'for the benefit of mankind' entails – to advocate in its own cause.

The issue of enforcement is also an important aspect of subject status. Some *jus cogens* principles create obligations owed to the whole international community (*erga omnes*). This enables any member of the international community to enforce such obligations, against any other state. As 'international community' generally means only states, this is of little use when states mutually agree not to enforce the law. Subject status for humanity would potentially enable enforcement against states, on humanity's behalf.

States as trustees for humanity

As noted above, the CH belongs to humanity as a whole. The combination of the terms 'mankind' and 'heritage' is interpreted as invoking the notion of the common patrimony of humanity, which must be carefully managed for the benefit of present and future generations. This is a further revolutionary element in international law. In the case of LOS, states, as members of the ISA, have to act through it as 'a kind of trustee on behalf of mankind' (Tuerk, 2010, p164).

Some important elements follow from states being trustees for humanity. First, trustees have fiduciary obligations or responsibilities towards their beneficiaries (present and future generations). This is significant both because it potentially changes the nature of territorial state sovereignty (discussed below), but also because it reduces the predominant 'rights' focus of international law. It is increasingly observed that legal systems that focus on rights, without accompanying duties or responsibilities, create a flawed or lopsided approach to social, economic and ecological problems. Rights approaches, whether in international and municipal legal systems, prioritize individual entitlement over concern for the common good. Without the balance of ecological responsibilities, concern for the 'other', including future generations, is lost. For this reason, efforts are being made to actively reintroduce a 'responsibility' focus into the law. Properly understood, 'responsibility' involves both a positive duty of care *and* restraining from doing harm. Examples exist for bringing responsibility for the common good into international legal frameworks (Bosselmann, 2008, pp162–174). The most difficult aspect is to ensure the necessary degree of compulsion. Nevertheless, CH is considered one of the most developed applications of trusteeship or fiduciary relationship in an environmental context, 'and in that sense it represents a significant precedent'(Birnie and Boyle, 2002, p144).

Another important aspect of states as trustees is that expressions of sovereignty are limited by obligations to administer in the interests and for the benefit of all. This could be defined in terms of ecosystem management. One of the least controversial elements of CH is that it implies environmental management based around the concept of sustainability (Wolfrum, 2008). Elements of prevention, precaution and polluter pays are all relevant, with the last two elements being recently affirmed. As degradation of the oceans (for example) increases in scale, the focus will need to shift from 'less harm' to 'more good' (i.e. the active restoration and enhancement of ecological integrity).

Reclaiming the commons?

A further criticism is that CH does not overcome the *status quo* according to which the ecological 'whole' is artificially carved up into distinct parts;

common areas and areas within national jurisdictions. This perpetuates the tragedy of ecological 'fragmentation' and does not protect the ecology of areas *within* national jurisdictions which remain at the mercy of state sovereignty. This was not the original intention behind the use of CH and it need not be applied in this way. Furthermore, as explained below, CH was intended to transform state sovereignty, as exercised *internally*.

Pardo understood the unity of all ocean space. CH was a governance principle that should apply to the whole of ocean space, recognizing the interactions between all areas and uses. The 1971 Draft Ocean Space Treaty (promoted by Malta) applied CH to all ocean space without regard to the pre-existing jurisdictional status of any particular area. However, CH would be applied differently to areas *within* national jurisdiction. States would have the legal power to control and regulate a defined area of ocean space adjacent to their coasts, but this would be subject to limitations designed to protect the interests of the international community. This was an attempt to reject unfettered sovereignty or (more radically) replace sovereignty and sovereign rights, with a concept of jurisdiction (Tuerk, 2010, p160; Borgese, 2000, pxxxvii).[1]

Two very important points follow from this historical understanding. First, CH does attempt to transform state sovereignty, as exercised both *internally* and *externally*, in respect of shared ecological systems. As discussed above, the trust aspect casts nation states in the role of trustees, with fiduciary obligations to protect ecological systems for the common good. CH is therefore very consistent with other attempts to transform the sovereign state. The public trust doctrine is one such example (Wood, 2009; Bosselmann, 2008). Many ideas exist for articulating the changing role of the state, both internally and externally. These include 'guardianship', 'custodianship' and 'stewardship'. Internationally, Malta has proposed that the UN Trusteeship Council be transformed to hold the principle of CH in sacred trust and 'act as the conscience of the United Nations and the guardian of future generations' (Borgese, 2000, p12).

The second important point relates to appropriation. It is often argued that CH cannot apply to spaces and resources *within* a state's national jurisdiction because this would be contrary to the principle of 'non-appropriation'. This principle was critical to protect what remained of the high seas from continuing enclosure (or privatization), but it is not a requirement in all circumstances. This is clear from Pardo's application of CH to the whole of ocean space and from his suggestion that the content of CH be applied pragmatically in relation to international needs. 'World resources', he said, should not be conceived in a static sense (Borgese, 2000, pxxvii).[2] The ability of CH to reach inside a nation's jurisdiction, is one of its most controversial and revolutionary aspects. It also leads to suggestions that CH be extended to rainforests, geostationary orbit, Antarctica, and a range of cultural heritage and genetic resources, including the human genome. Ultimately, in an ecological and generational context, it is possible to argue that Earth itself is a global commons shared by each generation. Therefore CH should extend to all natural and cultural resources, wherever located, that are internationally important for the well-being of future generations (Taylor, 1998, p299; Borg, 1998, p89).

Conclusion: honouring our legacy

Traditional international law, with its focus on state sovereignty and liberal economic freedoms, is fast reaching its limits. In CH, we have a normative principle for recognizing ourselves as members of a larger community of life and for a primary allegiance to this larger community (Berry, 1988, pp42–43). Using CH does not require searching for something new, but honouring what we already have and the visionaries who have championed it. Arvid Pardo and Elizabeth Mann Borgese were two such visionaries. They saw in CH an ethical and legal concept capable of transforming global governance. Solving the interrelated issues of ecological degradation *and* social inequality 'will require profound changes in the ways we deal with each other and with nature. Like life itself, the new order started in the deep ocean, which has been declared to be the "common heritage of mankind" and is expanding over the seas and oceans to the coastal zones, until it embraces the whole biosphere in "the majesty of the oceanic circle".' (Borgese, 2000, p1).

Notes

1 The 1967 proposal was intentionally limited to the seabed and resources to give CH a foothold within the UN system (Borgese, 2000, pxxviii).

2 CH is not inherently anthropocentric; see Taylor (1998) and Borg (1998, pp86–87).

References

Baslar, K. (1997) *The Concept of the Common Heritage of Mankind in International Law*, Kluwer Law International, The Hague, The Netherlands

Beesley, A. (2004) 'Grotius and the new law', in A. Chircop and M. McConnell (eds) *Ocean Yearbook 18*, International Ocean Institute, Halifax, Canada, pp98–116

Berry, T. (1988) *The Dream of the Earth*, Sierra Club Books, San Francisco, CA

Birnie, B. and Boyle, A. (2002) *International Law and the Environment*, Oxford University Press, Oxford, UK

Boda, Z. (2003) 'Global environmental commons and the need for ethics', *Society and Economy*, vol 25, no 2, pp213–224

Borg, S. F. (1998) 'The common heritage 1967–1997', in R. Rajagopalan (ed.) *Proceedings of Pacem in Maribus XXV*, International Ocean Institute, Foundation for International Studies, Valletta, Malta, pp85–91

Borg, S. (ed.) (2009) *Climate Change*, University of Malta, Valetta, Malta

Borgese, E. M. (1986) *The Future of the Oceans*, Harvest House, Montreal, Canada

Borgese, E. M. (1999) *The IOI Story*, Dreiviertelverlag, Hamburg, Germany

Borgese, E. M. (2000) 'Arvid Pardo (1914–1999): in memoriam', in E. M. Borgese, A. Chircop, M. L. McConnell, and J. R (eds), *Ocean Yearbook 14*, International Ocean Institute, Foundation for International Studies, Valletta, Malta, ppxix–xxxviii

Borgese, E. M. (2000) 'The oceanic circle', in E. M. Borgese, A. Chircop, M. L. McConnell, and J. R (eds), *Ocean Yearbook 14*, International Ocean Institute, Foundation for International Studies, Valletta, Malta, pp1–15)

Bosselmann, K. (2008) *The Principle of Sustainability*, Ashgate, Aldershot, UK

Bosselmann, K. and Engel J. R. (2010) *The Earth Charter*, KIT Publishers, Amsterdam, The Netherlands

Fuse, T. (1998) 'Common heritage of mankind in 21st century, in R. Rajagopalan (ed.) *Proceedings of Pacem in Maribus XXV*, International Ocean Institute, Foundation for International Studies, Valletta, Malta, pp93–105

Grinlinton, D. and Taylor, P. (eds) (2011) *Property Rights and Sustainability*, Martinus Nijhoff, Boston, MA

Hardin, G. (1968) 'The tragedy of the commons', *Science*, vol 162, pp1243–1248

McMichael, A. J. and Butler, C. (2006) 'Emerging health issues: the widening challenge for population health promotion', *Health Promotion International*, vol 21, suppl 1, pp15–24

Ostrom, E., Dietz, T., Dolšak, N., Stern, P. C., Stonich, S. and Weber, E. U. (2002) *The Drama of the Commons*, National Academy Press, Washington, DC

Pardo, A. (1967) 'Address to the 22nd session of the General Assembly of the United Nations', UN GAOR, 22nd sess., UN Doc. A/6695, 18 August, United Nations, New York, NY

Rockström, J., Steffen, W., Noone, K., Persson, Å. F., Chapin III, F. S., Lambin, E. F., Lenton, T. M., Scheffer, M., Folke, C., Schellnhuber, H. J., Nykvist, B., de Wit, C. A., Hughes, T., van der Leeuw, S., Rodhe, H., Sörlin, S., Snyder, P. K., Costanza, R., Svedin, U., Falkenmark, M., Karlberg, L., Corell, R. W., Fabry, V. J., Hansen, J., Walker, B., Liverman, D., Richardson, K., Crutzen, P. and Foley, J. A. (2009) 'Planetary boundaries: exploring the safe operating space for humanity' *Ecology and Society*, vol 14, no 2, p32, available at www.ecologyandsociety.org/vol14/iss2/art32 (accessed 23 January 2012).

Taylor, P. (1998) *An Ecological Approach to International Law*, Routledge, London, UK

Tuerk, H. (2010) 'The idea of common heritage of mankind', Martínez Gutiérrez (ed.), *Serving the Rule of International Maritime Law*, Routledge, Abingdon, UK, pp157–175

Weeramantry, C. (2011) 'Rights, Responsibilities, and Wisdom from Global Cultural Traditions' in D. Grinlinton and P. Taylor (eds) *Property Rights and Sustainability*, Martinus Nijhoff, Boston, MA, ppxv–xxii

Westra, L. (2011) *Human Rights: The 'Commons' and the Collective*, University of British Columbia Press, Vancouver, BC

Wolfrum, R. (2008) 'Common heritage of mankind', Max Planck Encyclopedia of Public International Law, available at www.mpepil.com (accessed 25 October 2011)

Wood, M. C. (2009) 'Advancing the sovereign trust of government to safeguard the environment for present and future generations (Part I)', *Environmental Law*, vol 39, pp43–89

World Beyond Borders (n.d.) *Preliminary Draft of a World Constitution (1947–1948)*, available at www.worldbeyondborders.org/chicagodraft.htm

5 Aldo Leopold's concept of land health

Implications for sound public health policy

Paul Carrick

Wilderness is the raw material out of which man has hammered the artifact called civilization.

Aldo Leopold (1887–1948)

Introduction

Aldo Leopold famously claimed that his land ethic involves individual responsibility for the health of the land. Having defined *land health* (Leopold, 1949, p221) as 'the capacity of the land for self-renewal', and *conservation* as 'our effort to understand and preserve this capacity', I set out to explore whether his land ethic and his related notion of land health, in particular, are sufficiently robust to support three essential elements of sound public health policy. These essential elements are:

- *the community health perspective*, which links the health or disease of individual citizens to the overall responsibility of the larger community within which he or she lives and works;
- *the holistic health perspective*, which recognizes that the quality of a community's sanitation, housing, potable drinking water, workplace safety, and so on, significantly impacts the health and welfare of individual citizens; and
- *the perspective of legal moralism*, which acknowledges the liberty-limiting authority of the state to impose sanctions on individuals or corporations designed to promote sound health and safety practices and discourage harmful habits and practices (Carrick, 2007, p19–21).

My overall argument is a speculative and interpretative one. But if I am right, then we will be in a better position to appreciate the broader implications of Leopold's ecocentric ethic not only for environmental ethics, but also for medical ethics and public health policy. At bottom, I argue that Leopold's land ethic requires us to affirm that if we aim to rescue people from disease and suffering, we must work within a global ethical framework that both respects the Earth's delicate ecological balance and also warns against the limits of harmful human over-consumption.

Leopold's holistic outlook

As background to my focus on Leopold's concept of land health, it is instructive to recall core claims embraced by Leopold's philosophy of nature. I begin with his ecocentric action-guiding environmental maxim:

> A thing is *right* when it tends to preserve the integrity, stability, and beauty of the biotic community. It is *wrong* when it tends otherwise. (Leopold, 1949, pp224–225)

Although it is true that Leopold does not mention land health specifically in the above maxim, I will argue that appreciating Leopold's public commitment to land health is a precondition to fully understanding the problem-solving, civic-minded and practical orientation to which his philosophical legacy is ideally suited. Moreover, it will be recalled that Leopold's holistic vision of man and nature further endorses at least seven additional philosophical tenets:

1. That ethics are *evolutionary* in character.
2. That the land ethic reflects a newly evolving *ecological conscience* evidenced by a growing awareness of duties to preserve and protect the overall health and stability of the land (i.e. the biotic community).
3. That the emerging ecological conscience reveals Homo sapiens to be but one member of the whole biotic community, not its privileged overlord or conqueror.
4. That the land has value in and of itself aesthetically and culturally (i.e. intrinsic value), which goes beyond merely economic and instrumental ways of human thinking and doing.
5. That this ecological framework entails that land is an interconnected biotic pyramid so intimately linked that any major disorder, disease or pollution occurring in one part of the ecosystem may cause deleterious effects in other parts.
6. That the land is not a mechanism or dead matter but a whole living organism, each part of which is worthy of our moral consideration *before* we act or impose our collective will on the land.
7. That while humans may sometimes need to exploit, use and disrupt the land for economic, practical and other reasons, this needs to be done sparingly, weighing carefully the possible harmful consequences to the health and stability of the land and ultimately to the biosphere (Leopold, 1949, p201–226).[1]

Furthermore, I concur with philosopher Laura Westra, a strong proponent of a version of Leopold's land ethic, who writes:

> It is reasonable to conceive of humanity as being morally responsible to protect the integrity of the whole ecosystem ... Insofar as such responsibility is justified as a protection of human life and health, breaches of environmental regulations deserve not just economic penalties but criminal ones. (Westra, 2005, p576)[2]

Elsewhere, she observes: 'Because of this global connection between health and integrity, and the right to life and to living, a true understanding of ecological integrity reconnects human life with the wild, and the rights of the latter with those of the former' (Westra, 2005, p577). In sum, in its fullest application Leopold's land ethic is no mere lofty philosophical abstraction: it possesses practical and persuasive moral force toward the development of sound public health policy, international law and intergovernmental cooperation.

What is land health?

How, then, are we to understand Leopold's notion of land health? And how is it that this notion can be shown to support the three key aforementioned elements of sound public health policy? To find out, we need to do some digging not only into his classic *A Sand County Almanac* but also into at least three other lesser-known essays that he wrote in the last decade of his life, which were not published until 1999.

To begin, Leopold had no unified theory of land health. He used the phrase 'land health' both metaphorically and heuristically with the aims of: (i) educating the general public, farmers, businessmen, conservationists and others about the complexities of soil erosion and resource renewal; and (ii) connecting the health of the land to the health of the broader biotic community, including human and non-human animals, plants, and related organic and inorganic matter (waters, soils, fungi, wind vectors, mountains, streams, solar energy chains, etc.) – all caught-up in the planetary web of life.

In his little-known essay, 'The land-Health Concept and Conservation', written in 1944 but published posthumously in 1999, 'Leopold presented the notion of land health as analogous to the sense of well-being associated with the proper functioning of a living organism' (Minteer, 2006, p137). For Leopold, symptoms of land sickness included, among other things, uncontrollable loss of species, accelerating infertility of the soil, and the spread of biological pests, all pointing to the declining health of the larger land system (Minteer, 2006, p136). In a related essay, 'Biotic land use', also written in the early 1940s, Leopold identified two 'yardsticks' for the measurement of the stability and health of the land: first, the diversity of flora and fauna; and, second, the fertility of the soil (Minteer, 2006, p137).[3] Even more important for my thesis – which links Leopold's environmental vision to concerns for both the health of the land and, by extension, the health of the human community – Ben Minteer (2006, pp138–139) has recently called attention to Leopold's 1941 essay, 'Planning for Wildlife'.[4] In it, Leopold expresses his conviction (also echoed in *Sand County*) that land health could be achieved only if owners of private property (private lands) adopted it as a personal ethical obligation to the land. Minteer elaborates:

> Leopold reiterated his belief that appeals to profit and the self-interest of the landowner would prove insufficient ... Only a sense of community welfare and a personal pride in the health or 'unity' of the land would motivate the landowner and the wider public. Good land use practices, he suggested, must be presented 'primarily as an obligation to the community, rather than an opportunity for profit'. (Minteer, 2006, p139)

Further, Leopold's other writings and speeches to civic, professional and community groups strongly imply that Leopold was referring chiefly to the human community here. In other words, Leopold saw land health as a core conservation goal. If so, this reading of Leopold demonstrates his *commitment to the common good – and to the wider public interest* (Minteer, 2006, p139).

This suggests, too, that Leopold may have flirted, towards the end of his life, with adopting an ecocentric ethic, investing intrinsic value to the things of nature; in fact, I find that he never quite gave up his more traditional human-centred, anthropomorphic ethic, investing intrinsic value to the things of man.[5] This creative tension in his thinking may be seen especially in his persistent concern for land health and its related impact on humanity and on nature. Arguably, Leopold – as forester, outdoorsman, community organizer, nature writer and professor of game management at the University of Wisconsin – was completely at home using the experimental approach of a pragmatic, progressive thinker. Consistent with this scientific, human-centred orientation in *Sand County*, he concludes: 'Wilderness, then, assumes unexpected importance as a laboratory for the study of land health' (Leopold, 1949, p196). Note that 'wilderness' is here cast as a laboratory *for human use* and *not* as a pristine temple of utopian worship.

Ethical and social implications for public health policy

In sum, the health of the land is inextricably bound to the health and welfare of the human community. What's more, Leopold's notion of land health – however unsophisticated compared with today's biometric indices favoured by agronomists and climate scientists – is decidedly more than a purely descriptive diagnostic tool used to measure the integrity and stability of various Earth systems. Significantly, his concept of land health also serves as a prescriptive, normative standard of practical interest to farmers, environmental activists and policy planners alike.

Given this, I conjecture that Leopold's concept of land health does double duty. First, it serves as an *evaluative deontological standard* by which wildlife conservation measures can be judged as 'good' or 'bad' for the overall stability and well-being of the biotic community. This dimension of land health accents the pre-eminence of man's *ethical duty* to be faithful stewards of the land community by bending our collective wills to Leopold's environmental maxim.[6] In addition, it serves as an *aspirational teleological standard* by which the actual results of any new programme of wildlife conservation or environmental health reform may be judged as 'worthwhile' or 'worthless'. Hence, this dimension of land health accents the ultimate, *consequentialist end-in-view* for Leopold and his followers: to strive daily to live in harmony with the biotic community.

We are now in the strategic position to cash out these preliminary analytical and historical antecedents heretofore explored. However, two questions remain

- First, what is commonly meant by public health, the public health movement, or public health policy?
- Second, how could Leopold's concept of land health, along with his related land ethic, be understood to endorse – or at least be logically compatible with – the three essential public health perspectives that I introduced at the beginning of this inquiry: namely, the community health, holistic health, and legal moralism perspectives? (To clarify, I am asserting that these are necessary conditions. Hence, in their absence no public health policy, national or international in scope, can with soundness go forward).

To the first question above, *public health* is defined by medical historian John Duffy as 'the collective action by a community or society to protect and promote the health and welfare of its members' (Duffy, 2004, p2206). It is sobering to recall that a bona fide government sponsored *public health movement* is only about 160 years old, starting in England with passage of the Public Health Act of 1848. This progressive law enforced sanitary conditions for housing, waste disposal, drinking water, and so on, while establishing boards of health in cities and towns to carry out enforcement (Carrick, 2007, p14). To be sure, concern for the health and general welfare of the public extends back at least 2,500 years to the Athens of Hippocrates, Pericles, and Socrates (Carrick, 2001, p21–35). Yet the actual systematic development and deployment of government funded *public health policy* is largely a twentieth-century phenomenon. In addition, physician and historian George Rosen observes that:

> ... the major problems of [public] health ... have been concerned with community life, for instance, the control of transmissible disease, the control and improvement of the physical environment (sanitation), the provision of water and food of good quality and in sufficient supply, the provision of medical care, and the relief of disability and destitution. (Rosen, 1958, p25)

Note that Rosen rightly cites 'community life' as the central focus of sound public health policy. In addition, *the community health perspective* states that the health or disease of individuals is the proper concern of the larger community or government within which one lives, works and plays.

To the second question above, I submit that Leopold's concept of land health, as explicated here, would be completely compatible with this community health perspective. For does not Leopold imply that the health of individuals (whether persons or non-human organisms) is directly or indirectly affected by the entire biotic community? (See tenet 5, p57). And, moreover, that humans are collectively obligated by the land ethic to be attentive to the condition of individual members of the land community? (Tenet 6).

Next, consider *the holistic health perspective*. This states that an individual's health properly concerns not simply personal factors like exercise, diet, or genetic heritage. It also involves much wider environmental factors and linkages such as clean air and water, adequate sanitation, sound habitat (housing) and the like. If so, holistically considered, these external, non-personal factors that contribute to an individual's overall health and hygiene are seen from the holistic health perspective as the community's or government's responsibility to both monitor and regulate. But, again, I submit: Leopold's concept of land health would certainly be completely compatible with this holistic health perspective. For is not Leopold's land ethic fundamentally predicated on a holistic view of nature, according to which the whole is greater than the sum of its parts? (Tenet 3, p57). Indeed, we observed that one of Leopold's specific tenets (tenet 2) implies that *the ecological conscience* will make us sufficiently aware to act in time to preserve and protect the overall health of the land community, thereby also protecting the health of individuals organisms (including humans).

Moral legalism and the ecological conscience

Lastly, what about *the perspective of moral legalism*? How does this perspective fit into Leopold's holistic philosophy of nature? To be sure, this is a liberty-limiting philosophical principle. It is linked historically to John Stuart Mill's democratic defence of the limits of personal freedom and self-determination in his now-classic *On Liberty* (1859). Furthermore, this third perspective of legal moralism is easily the most controversial of this trio. To wit, it asserts that there is a moral duty on the part of governments to enact laws that would prohibit *objectionable behaviour* on the part of individuals or corporations, especially behaviour that, if left unchecked, would pollute, harm, destabilize or otherwise sicken the larger community. Obviously, this ambitious modus operandi carries challenging legal and moral overtones. For example, who or what agency ought to have the *authority* to decide what behaviours are objectionable, sickening, polluting? And by what *criterion* will such judgements be rendered?

Environmental education and enforcement

In brief, for Leopold, given the record of his own outstanding government service as a forester, regulator, policy analyst, civic leader and environmental educator, it is safe to say that one should invest this diagnostic and enforcement authority with a democratically run and scientifically oriented governmental body of some sort (whether on the regional, state, national or international level).[7] Granted, Leopold did acknowledge, in *Sand County Almanac,* that there were limits to what government could accomplish in introducing and enforcing progressive, healthy farming or conservation practices. Nevertheless, he still insisted that such efforts, backed by sound environmental education campaigns, had a legitimate civic role to play in fostering a kinder, gentler, more harmonious relationship with the biotic community (Leopold, 1949, pp207–214). If so, when it comes to deciding what specific individual or corporate behaviour is harming the environment, does not his concept of land health – which casts the land community as an interconnected biotic pyramid of energy chains – also obligate us to be caring physicians and stewards of the earth? The short answer is yes.

In my view, tenets 5, 6 and 7 of Leopold's ecocentric ethic together define *the working criterion* of land health. This it does by binding citizens of ecological conscience to its uncompromising ethical demands. But what exactly are these demands?

First, the imperative that we give moral consideration to the land before we act to exploit it (see tenet 6). Second, the imperative that we remain vigilant to the scientific evidence that any major disorder, disease, or pollution occurring in one part of the ecosystem may cause destabilizing or sickening effects in other parts (see tenet 5). And finally, the imperative that, while acknowledging the fact that humanity will almost certainly continue to exploit, use, and disrupt the land for economic, practical, competitive and other sometimes frivolous purposes – and that this unfortunate behaviour cannot always be prohibited within the relatively free market system of democratic societies – there yet remains a powerful, over-riding obligation. This obligation exhorts us to use the land thoughtfully and sparingly. It reminds us to weigh options carefully and then act decisively to reduce the harmful consequences that may result from the sometimes irrational felt needs and impulsive pressures of a consumer-driven marketplace (see tenet 7). In essence, this 'weighing', this 'vigilance', and the embodied moral courage of an enlightened human community to act in concert to prevent disease, derangement and suffering, galvanizes the theoretical and practical elements of Leopold's unalloyed notion of land health. Indeed, a philosophical, scientific and ethical commitment to land health, *coupled with direct action*, constitutes a powerful tool for national and international environmental protection.

Leopold's unifying humanitarian vision

Leopold asserted: 'A land ethic, then, reflects the existence of an ecological conscience, and this in turn reflects a conviction of *individual responsibility* for the health of the land' (Leopold, 1949, p221; emphasis added). If my conjectures are correct, we have seen that the fullest expression of Leopold's ecological conscience involves (i) not only an ethical duty to preserve and protect the health of the land, but (ii) an ethical duty to establish progressive policies of both public health *and* environmental health that, taken together, complement and strengthen each other. Moreover, I find that Leopold's land ethic, wedded to his concept of land health, inspires us to imagine a more promising future, one in which all citizens accept some personal responsibility toward achieving the following difficult goals:

1 Reversing or significantly limiting human overconsumption.
2 Respecting the Earth's ecological balance via both national and international vigilance and enforceable legal sanctions.
3 Taking direct action to educate the public about salient scientific links between environmental health and human health (e.g. see www.gatesfoundation.org/global-health/Pages/overview.aspx).
4 Promoting intergovernmental cooperation to secure more stable (and less toxic) human and planetary measures of land health – reducing thereby the suffering of all sentient creatures, while continuing to protect other vital and sustaining forms of life.

In conclusion, only if citizens risk direct action by daily practising the imperatives of their ecological consciences – at home, at work, at play, in their communities – will Leopold's dream of living in harmony with nature be fully realized on a truly humanitarian and global scale.

Notes

1 Hence, Leopold would probably be sympathetic to the precautionary principle: it is prudent to resist any likely serious harmful activity or substance from despoiling the biotic community even if, at present, we lack conclusive scientific proof of the alleged harm.
2 For an interesting contrary view of this oft-repeated ecocentric claim of human responsibility for protecting the health and welfare of the planet, see Stephen Jay Gould (2001) 'The golden rule – a proper scale for our environmental

crisis', in Louis Pojman (ed.) *Environmental Ethics: Readings in Theory and Application*, third edition, Wadsworth, Belmont, CA, pp214–218. Gould declares (p217): 'Such views ... are rooted in the old sin of pride and exaggerated self-importance. We are among billions of species, *stewards of nothing*.'

3 See also Leopold, A. (1999) *For the Health of the Land: Previously Unpublished Essays and Other Writings*, J. B. Callicott and E. T. Freyfogle (eds), Island Press, Washington, DC.

4 See also Flader, S. L. and Callicott, J. B. (eds) (1991) *The River of the Mother of God and other Essays by Aldo Leopold*, University of Wisconsin Press, Madison, WI.

5 For more on this meta-ethical, interpretative controversy, see Minteer (2006, pp128–132). While Baird Callicott insists that Leopold is fundamentally ecocentric (non-anthropocentric) in his ontology of man and nature, Bryan Norton finds in Leopold a civic-minded pragmatic orientation – allowing for a more or less anthropocentric approach to ethics. My view is that there is plenty of evidence in Leopold's writings to warrant both perspectives. In fact, for rhetorical purposes, Leopold may have equivocated between these positions depending on his audience. See also Norton, B. G. (1991) *Toward Unity among Environmentalists*, Oxford University Press, Oxford, UK; and Callicott, J.B. (1987) 'The conceptual foundations of the land ethic', in J. B. Callicott (ed.) *A Companion to A Sand County Almanac*, University of Wisconsin Press, Madison, WI.

6 For Leopold's 'environmental maxim', see p60 of this chapter.

7 If there is any real doubt about Leopold's cosmopolitan, international scale of thinking, recall that in the last year of his life, he accepted a position as 'conservation advisor' to the United Nations, the first such international appointment of its kind.

References and further reading

Beauchamp, D. (2004) 'Public health law: legal moralism and public health', in S. G. Post (ed.) *Encyclopedia of Bioethics*, third edition, vol 4, Macmillan, New York, NY, pp2231–2234

Callicott, J. B. (1987) 'The conceptual foundations of the land ethic', in J. B. Callicott (ed.) *A Companion to A Sand County Almanac*, University of Wisconsin Press, Madison, WI

Carrick, P. (2001) *Medical Ethics in the Ancient World*, Georgetown University Press, Washington, DC

Carrick, P. (2007) 'The public funding of health care: a brief historical overview of principles, practices, and motives', in N. Maclean (ed.) *Distributing Health Care*, Academic Imprint, Exeter, UK

Chesworth, J. (1996) (ed.) *The Ecology of Health: Identifying Issues and Alternatives*, Sage Press, Thousand Oaks, CA

Duffy, J. (2004) 'Public health: history', in S. G. Post (ed.) *Encyclopedia of Bioethics*, third edition, vol 4, Macmillan, New York, NY, pp2206–2211

Flader, S. L. and Callicott, J. B. (eds) (1991) *The River of the Mother of God and other Essays by Aldo Leopold*, University of Wisconsin Press, Madison, WI

Gould, S. J. (2001) 'The golden rule – a proper scale for our environmental crisis', in Louis Pojman (ed.) *Environmental Ethics: Readings in Theory and Application*, third edition, Wadsworth, Belmont, CA, pp214–218

Leopold, A. (1949) *A Sound County Almanac*, Oxford University Press, Oxford, UK

Leopold, A. (1999) *For the Health of the Land: Previously Unpublished Essays and Other Writings*, J. B. Callicott and E. T. Freyfogle (eds), Island Press, Washington, DC

Minteer, B. A. (2006) *The Landscape of reform: Civic Pragmatism and Environmental Thought in America*, MIT Press, Cambridge, MA

Norton, B. G. (1991) *Toward Unity among Environmentalists*, Oxford University Press, Oxford, UK

Pierce, J. and Jameton, A. (2004) *The Ethics of Environmentally Responsible Health Care*, Oxford University Press, New York, NY

Porter, R. (1999) *The Greatest Benefit to Mankind: A Medical History of Humanity*, W. W. Norton, New York, NY

Rosen, G. (1958) *A History of Public Health*, MD Publications, New York, NY

Westra, L. (2005) 'Ecological integrity', in C. Mitcham (ed.) *Encyclopedia of Science, Technology, and Ethics*, vol 2, Macmillan Reference, Detroit, MI, pp574–578

Part II

Ecosystem Services and State Responsibility for Public Health

Introduction

Donald W. Spady and Colin L. Soskolne

Maintaining one's health and recovering from illness have both individual and social components. A person's genetic heritage is one example of the individual component. However, we often forget, or do not realize, that most other factors, while they may have individual action as a 'final common pathway' to maintaining or restoring health, are influenced largely by environmental, economic, and societal factors which are under much less personal control. Thus, our smoking and drinking habits, or what we eat, or the illnesses that we acquire and whether or not they are treated, are influenced by where, with whom and under what conditions we live and work. This section of the book explores some of these factors and how they affect the health of the public, and the ability of a country's health service delivery model to meet society's needs.

In Chapter 6, Seják and co-authors explore how an appropriately scoped and total economic valuation of the natural landscape of a country demonstrates the benefits provided to society by intact ecosystems. They expose the dangers inherent in considering nature only as a source of resources rather than as the primary sustainer of all life. Some may argue that economically valuing nature's benefits inadequately enumerates those benefits, but economics is the *lingua franca* of politicians and planners. Using that metric, Seják and co-authors estimate that, in 2006, natural landscapes provided services to the Czech Republic that were valued at 50 times the annual GDP of the Czech Republic. Pursuing the current paradigm of unbridled economic growth and material accumulation is unsustainable, and thus ultimately incompatible with a healthy human society.

One important ecosystem service is that of provisioning, and an important provision for humanity over the last two centuries has been energy from fossil fuels. In Chapter 7, Manno describes how this cheap, compact and abundant energy enabled substantial and unprecedented human progress and population growth. However, we now realize that using fossil fuels, with their consequent pollution and energy-enabled over-consumption, seriously threatens Earth's biosphere and its biocapacity. We must move from our current industrial society – with its paradigm of energy-driven economic growth – towards a life-sustaining civilization where optimal energy use is valued and celebrated. Such a transition is imperative, and fraught with worry, but, if done well and equitably, could lead to a sustainable global human civilization.

Government actions affect public health, locally and globally, by creating public policy and also through the actions of its agents, such as national or local public health services. In doing so, epidemiology plays a key role by helping to develop healthy public policy by providing scientific evidence of the benefits or dangers associated with various agents or circumstances. This assumes that rational public policy in the public interest is the goal; however, this is not always the case. In Chapter 8, Soskolne and Ruff describe how a ruthless industry, in collusion with the Canadian and Quebec governments (and fully cognizant of the dangers of asbestos in causing fatal lung disease), promotes its international sale and use. They show how these agencies, for apparent reasons of money and power, use politics, law and weasel words to promote the sale of asbestos to countries where they know that it will probably be handled by workers with no protection, condemning many to a slow, painful death. Not only do such actions obstruct their right to health, but also their human rights.

In Chapter 9, Bencko and Quinn emphasize the strengths of primary prevention, an approach based on epidemiological research and practice to promote public health. They argue that the current allocation of resources is seriously over-balanced in favour of treatment-oriented healthcare relative to the demonstrably cost-effective provision of primary prevention services. They express frustration that the efforts, and the beneficial effects, of public health are often unnoticed. The persistent underfunding of primary prevention will pose steadily growing problems over the ensuing decades as we face the problems of overpopulation, resource depletion and climate change. The approach engendered in the maxim … *an ounce of prevention is worth a pound of cure* … is more likely to result in sustainable healthcare delivery and healthier populations.

Our fundamental dependence on the ecosystems within which we are embedded are revealed in these four different perspectives. This section of the book illustrates some of the factors and circumstances that affect the health of societies. Although public health services often function in the background, it is the environment within which we live and the associated ecosystem services to which we are indebted that form the seamless fabric upon which the tapestry of health is painted. The persistent decline of ecological integrity is society's greatest threat. The role of influence and the lust for power need to be constrained in the public interest, especially if future generations are to inherit a sustainable world.

6 Valuation of ecosystem services as an instrument for implementation of the European landscape convention

Josef Seják, Pavel Cudlín and Jan Pokorný

Introduction

The European Landscape Convention (ELC) aims to promote protection, management and planning of the European landscape. It is designed to organize European cooperation around landscapes to achieve sustainable development based on a balanced and harmonious relationship between social needs, economic activity and the environment (ELC, 2000). The ELC was adopted in 2000, ratified by 33 member states of the Council of Europe, and came into force on 1 March 2004. It is the first international treaty to be exclusively concerned with all dimensions of the European landscape in aiming to increase awareness among civil society, private organizations and public authorities on the *value of landscapes* (Article 6).

One of the main problems of neoclassical economic theory is that by 'scarce resources' it understands only those natural resources with direct benefits for users (owners). Within the utilitarian tradition of industrial societies, the natural landscape started to be viewed by economic agents as the domain for producing profit. Under the euphemism of 'land development', mostly the destruction of natural vegetation and the creation of impermeable surfaces can be found. During the last hundred years, an expanding human population and its insatiable self-interested striving for material wealth have resulted in natural landscapes that have been transformed; globally, half of the most important of the world's ecosystems have been destroyed.

Only at the end of the twentieth century did humans start to realize that they are critically dependent on the robust and flourishing existence of natural landscapes. These are essential to support life for people everywhere and serve as the most efficient producer and controller of the basic life-supporting services found in nature. Recently, some economic values have been ascribed to natural ecosystems (Costanza *et al.*, 1997), but these have not been implemented into the decision-making processes on land use. With southern Europe facing growing shortages of water, and with central Europe threatened by growing numbers of intense floods and windstorms, there is growing interest in and pressure to assign economic value to all of nature's services.

After thousands of years of a utilitarian approach to landscapes ('God entrusted the earth to human beings'), European countries ratified the ELC in its attempt to incorporate ecological and cultural values of landscapes into human decision-making.

The behaviour of ecosystems and of humans

From ecological sciences, thermodynamic laws and thermal gradients, we know that, through self-regulating processes, natural vegetation tends to maximize the efficiency of incoming solar energy. Natural vegetation also most efficiently regulates temperature extremes, and retains water inside ecosystems (Ripl, 2003).

Over the past centuries, humans have reduced natural vegetation through expansionist so-called development. Former civilizations collapsed after they had destroyed their forests with the resulting loss of wood and water. Today, with economic globalization, profit motives and accumulation of material wealth, humans, for the first time, have endangered natural ecosystems worldwide.

Humans, as a heterotrophic species, depend on healthy autotrophic ecosystems to provide food, fresh water, wood, fibre and fuel (*provisioning services*). We depend on ecosystems to provide fertile soil, cycle and purify air and water (*supporting services*). We depend on these same ecosystems to protect us against harmful cosmic radiation. They control specific atmospheric structures by producing oxygen. And, by latent heat changes of water, they mitigate climate temperature extremes, produce biomass, purify air and water, maintain biodiversity, control diseases, and decompose organic waste (*regulating services*). Finally, providing *cultural services*, ecosystems are sources of aesthetic, spiritual, educational, and recreational value (MEA, 2005).

Without humans, continents would again be covered by natural vegetation, which in Europe within the interglacial period is represented by forests, and in central Europe by mixed deciduous leafy forests. These forests help optimize the level of delivered life-supporting ecosystem services needed for human health and well-being. Human species could evolve only in an oxygenated atmosphere, with enough water and fertile soil on the continents. These life-supporting ecosystem services can be sustained only by sufficiently massive networks of natural vegetation.

Of the four service categories, only *provisioning services* are marketed and valued by humans. Along with a more intense environmental education, as articulated in the ELC, humans must start with monetary ecosystem service valuations and incorporate these values into decision-making processes.

Insufficiency of utilitarian demand-side valuations and the urgent need to reform economics

People traditionally value only those parts of nature that provide them some personal benefits (utility). Anthropocentric utilitarian approaches to economic valuation of natural resources (as sources of direct utility) were elaborated in the first half of the nineteenth century (Faustmann, 1849). In all cases, values were derived as sums of future net benefit from their utilization. In the second half of the twentieth century, under utilitarianism, scientists started to develop hypothetical markets for valuation (non-market valuations) of supporting, regulating and cultural services of ecosystems, asking people (consumers) what amount they would be willing to pay for such services.

All of these utilitarian, demand-curve approaches (like contingent valuation, travel cost and hedonic methods) suffer from one substantial defect: valuations are done by consumers who are far from integrating such hidden 'intermediary' ecosystem services into their value systems.

> Market economy is incompatible with ecological sustainability. There is a basic conflict between self-organizing principles of markets and the self-organizing principles of ecosystems. (Gowdy, 1994)

Such an incompatibility can be, at least partly, bridged by introducing the more realistic economic valuations of both, namely the costs and the benefits that natural ecosystems continuously provide for society.

Cost-based, supply-side methods

Under the replacement cost approach, we consider the cost of providing a substitute service that would perform a similar function as an ecosystem (for example, the flood protection service of a wetland may be valued on the basis of the cost of building man-made flood defences).

Taking into consideration that major, essential, life-supporting ecosystem services have not yet entered into the value system of humans, the replacement cost approach and the values derived seem to provide a more efficient way of revealing the decisive existential importance of ecosystem services for human species.

As Costanza *et al.* write:

> In fact, one additional way to think about the value of ecosystem services is to determine what it would cost to replicate them in a technologically produced, artificial biosphere. (Costanza *et al.*, 1997, p255)

Emergy valuations

The third important approach to ecosystem valuation is the 'emergy analysis' (i.e. the analysis of energy embodied in ecosystems). *Emergy* (embodied energy; *energy* is the ability to produce work) measures both the work of nature and that of humans in generating goods and services. Emergy is defined as available energy of one kind previously required directly and indirectly to make a service or product; its units are emjoules.

Emergy theory is rooted in the axiom that all of the real wealth of the environment comes from the work of the geo-biosphere (Odum, 1996, p35). The sun, the tides and the heat sources deep underground are the three main energy sources, each of a different energy form (sunlight insolation, 42%; tidal energy, 15%; deep heat underground, 43%). Emergy analysis identifies full energy inputs and reflects the supply-curve approach, and is broader than the labour theory of value.

From deeper studies on the theory of economic value, it has been derived that neither the utilitarian demand-side approach nor the cost-based supply-side approach is enough to reveal the real economic value of some goods or services. It has been known since the end of the nineteenth century that only with respect given to both aspects can real economic value be revealed. As Marshall wrote, 'We might as reasonably dispute whether it is the upper or the under blade of a pair of scissors that cuts a piece of paper, as whether value is governed by utility or cost of production' (Marshall, 1997 [1890], p164); and Daly added, 'Value has psychic roots in want satisfaction, as well as physical roots in entropy' (Daly, 2011, p70).

Applying the 'scissors approach' to review modern methods of non-market valuations of nature, we can see that they predominantly rely on the demand-side only, reflecting different aspects of human preferences. One of the main goals of our research has been to explicate the supply-side for revealing the real economic value of non-market services of ecosystems.

The first, well-known example of ecosystem service monetary valuation at the global level is from Costanza *et al.* (1997). It is an example of utilitarian, demand-side valuation that derives ecosystem values on the basis of people's willingness to pay for their services. These authors estimated the total value of 17 annual services of 16 world biomes in the range of US$16–54 trillion, with an average of US$33 trillion per year, which was approximately double (1.8-fold) the annual world GDP (US$18 trillion).

But if we put the question of how familiar ordinary consumers are with individual ecosystem services, we reveal that the level of such knowledge is very low, if not negligible. So it is clear that asking people about such unknown services produces a high underestimation of the real importance of life-supporting services upon which human existence depends. The majority of experts on ecosystem valuation argue that, without the services of ecological life-support systems, our economies and our lives would grind to a halt. Thus, in one sense, the total monetary value for the economy and for humans is infinite (Costanza *et al.*, 1997, p253; Toman, 1998).

Because of this, we have posed the question about the economic valuation of nature from the opposite end of the problem, namely the supply-side. If the Biosphere 2 experiment (Hawken *et al.*, 1999) needed a US$200 million investment for eight people, then the natural capital of the global ecosystem could roughly be estimated to have a value of US$165 quadrillion ($165 \times 10^{15}$). By using a 5 per cent discount rate, we achieve annual ecosystem services of US$8 quadrillion ($8 \times 10^{15}$), which is 500-fold greater than the annual global GDP. This estimate provides approximately an upper limit for the results from newer methods for the systemic valuing of the non-market services of nature.

Two methods for the systemic valuation of biotopes and ecosystem services in the Czech Republic

After the political change in 1989, the Czech Republic started to establish a basic legislative framework for environmental protection. All of the main environmental laws were passed in the first half and implemented during the second half of the 1990s. Consequently, emissions of basic pollutants were reduced tenfold.

Biotope valuation method

In 2001, our research team was contracted to elaborate the so-called Hessian valuation method of biotopes in a three-year project. The biotope valuation method (BVM) derives from the EU White Paper on environmental liability (COM (2000) 66 final, 9 February 2000). It corresponds to the needs of the EU NATURA 2000 system, and presents biotope monetary values. BVM is a systematic method for establishing a list of national biotopes and for ranking them according to their capacity as specific environments for living plants with animal species (including NATURA 2000). Each biotope type was valued by an interdisciplinary team of ecologists and economists from different scientific backgrounds using a six-point scale (1–6), according to eight ecological characteristics (matureness, naturalness, diversity of plant species, diversity of animal species, rareness of biotope, rareness of species, vulnerability, and threat to existence). A complete list of biotope values is available at http://fzp.ujep.cz/projekty/bvm/bvm.pdf.

Biotope point values are derived from the relative ecological significance of the respective biotope and are converted into monetary terms by the average national cost of restoration measures necessary for a one-point increase (i.e. for maintaining and improving the biotopes as environments for healthy ecosystems; Seják *et al.*, 2003).

The cost analysis covers 136 completed restoration projects in total. They were implemented over the last several years in different parts of the Czech

Republic and brought about increases in the point-values of these areas. A financial value of one point was calculated for one revitalization project as the sum of its cost divided by the sum of a single point increase expected in the long-term. Future values were discounted with a zero discount rate. Finally, the national average cost per one point increase was calculated as a weighted arithmetic mean. Presently, the average value of one point in the Czech Republic is set at €0.49 (e.g. in monetary terms, the most valuable Czech biotope – T3.3 Narrow-leaved dry grasslands – is valued at €41 m^{-2} = 84 points × €0.49).

The stock values of biotope types range from zero (chemically contaminated land, impermeable surfaces) to €41 per square metre. The size of biotope values shows the average costs that society has to pay to maintain the ecological quality of a landscape and its variable biotopes.

Applying the BVM at the national level through the CORINE Land-cover class, we estimated the national natural capital of biotopes in the Czech Republic and its development over time.

In Table 6.1 on pages 76–77, the total monetary value of biotope natural capital in the Czech Republic is presented, estimated by the biotope valuation method. This grew from €712 billion in 1990 to €727 billion in 2000, and then to €740 billion in 2006. Compared with the GDP of the Czech Republic (in constant prices), the stock value of national natural capital was 28 times higher in 1990, while in 2006 it was approximately 22 times higher than GDP in 2006. In 2006, the average value of $1m^2$ in the Czech Republic amounted to €9.40.

Biotope natural capital valuations, performed by the BVM, show the minimal 'cost' level of the biotopes and are easily implementable as an instrument for macro-economic environmental accounting. At the micro-economic level, they are mainly targeted at the valuation of environmental damage caused by legal and illegal anthropogenic activities that intervene in nature, inclusive of damages covered by the EU Directive on environmental liability (2004/35/EC). The BVM values biotopes as habitats for specific living species; at the same time, they are environments for provisioning specific ecosystem functions.

A limitation of the BVM is that it is not able to estimate the real benefits that humans permanently derive and consume in the form of ecosystem services. While ecosystem functions are physical, chemical and biological processes or attributes that contribute to the self-maintenance of an ecosystem, ecosystem services are the beneficial outcomes for people that result from ecosystem functions. Provisioning services can be identified with the functional group of a natural resource base; cultural services with the landscape and amenity resources; and supporting and regulating services can be identified with the life-supporting functions of ecosystems (Turner, 1994, p17).

Energy–water–vegetation-based method for the valuation of ecosystem services

In the period 2007–2009, our research team was given a new opportunity to further develop the second dimension of ecological values for the Czech landscape; namely the values for ecosystem services. Energy–water–vegetation-based (EWV) environmental accounting represents an ecological approach to estimate the non-market value of ecosystem services. This approach draws on the energy–transport–reaction (ETR) model (Ripl, 1995, 2003) and estimates the main forms of benefits that nature and her autotrophic ecosystems provide by way of delivering ecosystem services for society (e.g. climate regulation, water retention, oxygen production and habitat provision).

By the substitute cost method (sometimes also called replacement costs, or avoided costs), in combination with the BVM, we obtained minimal values for annual ecosystem services for selected natural ecosystems that have not previously been valued. As seen below, and from the viewpoint of thermodynamics, the dominant influence is that of ecosystem climate regulation and water retention services that, within the ecosystem self-regulating processes and, according to real monitored data of energy–material flows, tend to be maximized with climax vegetation.

For a deciduous forest ecosystem saturated with water, the pilot estimations of services (estimated by the replacement value approach and BVM) are as follows:

1 *Habitat provision:* Hardwood forests of lowland rivers are valued according to the BVM at 66 points per $1m^2$, which for 1ha means 660,000 points × CZK12.36 per point = CZK8,157,600 of stock value (€1 = CZK25). With a 5% discount rate, this means annual service at the level €16,320.
2 *Estimation of forest oxygen production:* In the temperate zone, 1ha of deciduous forest produces annually around 10 tons of biomass (expressed in dry mass). This corresponds to the release of 10.6 tons of oxygen (calculated from the fundamental equation of photosynthesis where formation of one molecule of 6-carbon sugar is associated with the release of 6 molecules of oxygen, i.e. the formation of 180 grams of sugar – cellulose etc. – is associated with the release of 192 grams of oxygen). According to Avogadro's law, one gram-molecule of gas under normal atmospheric pressure and at a temperature of 20°C has a volume of 22.4 litres (i.e. 32 grams of oxygen take up 22.4 litres). Thus, the mass of 1 litre of oxygen is 1.429g, or 1kg of oxygen has a volume of 700 litres:

   10,600kg/ha × 700 litres = 7.42 million litres × €0.02 per litre (oxygen price) = €148,400.

Table 6.1 Estimation of the biotope natural capital in the Czech Republic in 1990, 2000 and 2006 (through the BVM)

	1990					2000			2006		
LAND COVER 1:100,000	*Point value* ($point.m^{-2}$)	*Monetary value* ($€.m^{-2}$)	*Polygon count*	*Area* (km^2)	*Monetary value* (*bln €*)	*Polygon count*	*Area* (km^2)	*Monetary value* (*bln €*)	*Polygon count*	*Area* (km^2)	*Monetary value* (*bln €*)
1.1.1. Continuous urban fabric	2.39	1.18	14	15	0.02	14	15	0.02	19	16	0.02
1.1.2. Discontinuous urban fabric	10.22	5.06	5,417	3,578	18.09	5,424	3626	18.33	5,698	3774	19.08
1.2.1. Industrial or commercial units	2.95	1.46	828	521	0.76	845	548	0.80	893	599	0.87
1.2.2. Road and rail networks and associated land	8.23	4.07	87	48	0.20	99	53	0.22	118	63	0.26
1.2.3. Port areas	8.27	4.09	3	2	0.01	3	2	0.01	2	1	0.00
1.2.4. Airports	11.94	5.90	31	56	0.33	31	56	0.33	30	56	0.33
1.3.1. Mineral extraction sites	13.40	6.63	174	181	1.20	171	171	1.13	158	162	1.07
1.3.2. Dump sites	7.87	3.89	105	155	0.60	95	139	0.54	91	95	0.37
1.3.3. Construction sites	7.12	3.52	34	21	0.08	19	9	0.03	45	18	0.06
1.4.1. Green urban areas	19.27	9.53	120	65	0.62	121	66	0.62	116	66	0.63
1.4.2. Sport and leisure facilities	18.77	9.28	257	118	1.09	264	127	1.18	338	156	1.44
2.1.1. Non-irrigated arable land	11.18	5.53	5256	35541	196.4	4713	32622	180.3	5371	30109	166.4
2.2.1. Vineyards	15.25	7.54	161	111	0.84	169	119	0.90	190	158	1.19
2.2.2. Fruit trees and berry plantations	14.15	7.00	472	328	2.30	451	326	2.28	428	306	2.14

	1990					2000			2006		
LAND COVER 1:100,000	*Point value (point.m^{-2})*	*Monetary value (€.m^{-2})*	*Polygon count*	*Area (km^2)*	*Monetary value (bln €)*	*Polygon count*	*Area (km^2)*	*Monetary value (bln €)*	*Polygon count*	*Area (km^2)*	*Monetary value (bln €)*
2.3.1. Pastures	20.79	10.28	3969	2528	25.98	5415	5317	54.64	6968	7008	72.02
2.4.2. Complex cultivation	14.08	6.96	818	415	2.89	834	430	2.99	1033	474	3.30
2.4.3. Land with agricultural and natural vegetation	21.51	10.63	7816	6736	71.63	7844	6748	71.75	8248	7067	75.14
3.1.1. Broad-leaved forest	39.99	19.77	2057	2495	49.34	2054	2527	49.97	2120	2782	55.02
3.1.2. Coniferous forest	26.18	12.94	5999	16552	214.2	5649	16993	219.9	5144	17220	222.8
3.1.3. Mixed forest	28.48	14.08	5000	5855	82.44	5036	6042	85.08	5167	6170	86.88
3.2.1. Natural grassland	33.02	16.32	256	405	6.60	252	392	6.40	222	271	4.42
3.2.2. Moors and heathland	52.99	26.20	22	27	0.70	21	27	0.72	9	18	0.48
3.2.4. Transitional woodland shrub	23.51	11.62	3907	2487	28.90	2554	1870	21.73	2108	1604	18.64
3.3.2. Bare rock	39.79	19.67	7	2	0.04	7	2	0.04	5	1	0.03
3.3.3. Sparsely vegetated areas	61.65	30.48	0	0	0.00	0	0	0.00	4	1	0.04
3.3.4. Burnt areas	32.48	16.06	2	1	0.02	0	0	0.00	0	0	0.00
4.1.1. Inland marshes	33.47	16.55	64	54	0.88	66	53	0.88	82	61	1.02
4.1.2. Peatbogs	53.29	26.34	41	37	0.99	41	37	0.98	52	42	1.11
5.1.1. Water courses	23.14	11.44	14	43	0.49	14	43	0.49	18	46	0.53
5.1.2. Water bodies	18.67	9.23	535	493	4.55	548	510	4.70	561	520	4.80
Total Czech Republic	n/a	n/a	43466	78869	712.2	42754	78869	727	45238	78867	740.2

bln = billion (i.e. 1,000,000,000).

3 *Forest climate regulation service:* In the temperate zone, 1ha of deciduous forest evapotranspires around 700 litres of water from $1m^2$ during the vegetation season. Whereas photosynthesis (biomass production) uses less than 1 per cent of the incoming solar energy, by evapotranspiration (latent heat) around 80 per cent can be used in water saturated vegetation. The latent heat of 1 litre of water is equal to roughly 0.7kWh. The double air-conditioning effect of evapotranspiration exists: first, a tree cools itself and its environment by evaporation of water (solar energy is used as latent heat); second, water vapour condenses on cool surfaces (or in cool air) and releases latent heat. Considering the double air-conditioning effect (cooling during evapotranspiration and warming during water vapour condensation), annual climatizing service of 1ha can thus be estimated:

700l × 1.4kWh (0.7kWh cooling, 0.7kWh warming) × 10,000 × €0.08 (electricity cost price) = €784,000.

4 *Support of short water cycles and water retention services:* evapotranspiration of 600 litres/m^2 brings an annual service:

(600 litres/m^2) × €0.114 (distilled water price) × 10,000m^2 = €684,000.

Total annual services from 1ha forest = €1,632,720.

If a natural landscape is drained, as the following account of *drained foothill pasture* (channel straightening and recessing) shows, its ecosystem services substantially decline:

1 *Habitat provision:* Intensively managed or degraded mesic meadows × T.3 are valued (Seják *et* al., 2003) at 13 points per $1m^2$; per 1ha this means 130,000 points × €0.4944/point = €64,272 of capital value; with a 5 per cent discount rate, the value of annual services is €3,200.
2 *Oxygen production:* 2.8 million litres O_2 × CZK0.25–0.73 per litre (CZK0.50 = €0.02) = €56,000.
3 *Climate regulation services:* Around 300 litres of evapotranspired water from $1m^2$ during vegetation season. Annual climatizing service of 1ha can thus be estimated:

300 × 1.4kWh (0.7kWh cooling, 0.7kWh warming) × 10,000 × €0.08 (electricity cost price) = €336,000.

4 *Support of short water cycles and water retention services:* evapotraspiration of 30 m^3 of water per 1 ha on a sunny day brings an annual service:

(300 litres/m^2) × €0.114 (distilled water price) × 10,000m^2 = €342,000.

Total annual services from 1ha of drained pasture = €737,200.

Note that not only does a drained landscape waste the precipitated water; it usually also demands external inputs of energy for the production of biomass.

For the nationwide estimations of ecosystem functions and services, the four financially most important services were summarized: biodiversity service based on the BVM annual values; production of oxygen; climate regulation service; and short water cycling. The value map follows.

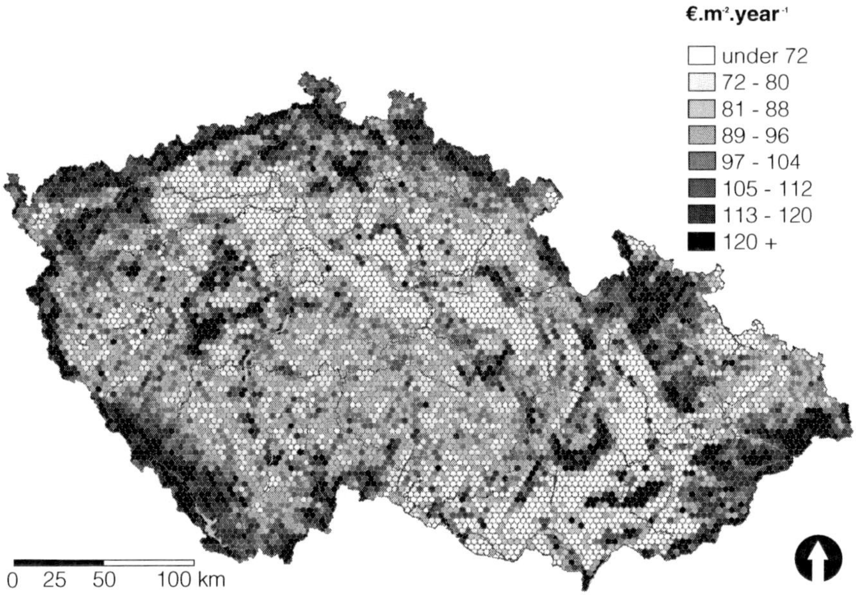

Figure 6.1 Map of total annual monetary values of four ecosystem services (climate regulation service, short water cycle, oxygen production, habitat provision) in euros per square metre per year (based on CLC 2000 in the Czech Republic)

Table 6.2 presents an overview of biotope, ecosystem service and economic capital values for the Czech Republic. Note the contradictions in how people value the territory (economic values, pushed up by draining the surfaces) and how ecosystems (working in synergy of solar energy fluxes, vegetation and water cycles) escalate the values of biotopes (BVM), and, mainly, values of life-supporting services (ecosystem service values), when left to develop naturally on their own, gradually become saturated by water and vegetation.

According to our estimates, the total amount for annual ecosystem services in the Czech Republic is about CZK182 trillion (182×10^{12}). Compared with the annual GDP in 2008 (3689×10^{9}), ecosystem services are 50 times greater each year.

Table 6.2 Biotope capital values, ecosystem service (ES) annual values, ecosystem service capital values and economic capital values of one square metre of territories of the Czech Republic

LAND COVER 1:100,000	*Biotope values*	*Annual ES values*	*ES capital values*	*Official prices*	*Notes*
1.1.1. Continuous urban fabric	0–1.20	27	535	1.4–90	acc. to urban size
1.1.2. Discontinuous urban fabric	5.04	78	1,557	1.4–90	acc. to urban size
1.2.1. Industrial or commercial units	0–1.32	32	638	1.4–90	acc. to urban size
1.2.2. Road and rail networks and associated land	4.00	58	1,156	1.4–90	acc. to urban size
1.2.3. Port areas	3.92	70	1,398	1.4–90	acc. to urban size
1.2.4. Airports	5.92	80	1,591	1.4–90	acc. to urban size
1.3.1. Mineral extraction sites	6.64	43	864	1.4–90	acc. to urban size
1.3.2. Dump sites	3.88	99	1,981	0.04	
1.3.3. Construction sites	3.52	42	844	1.4–90	acc. to urban size
1.4.1. Green urban areas	9.52	106	2,127	1.4–33	
1.4.2. Sport and leisure facilities	9.28	79	1,589	0.4–0.6	
2.1.1. Non-irrigated arable land	5.12	62	1,242	0.04–0.7	acc. to soil quality
2.2.1. Vineyards	7.52	88	1,769	0.04–6.4	
2.2.2. Fruit trees and berry plantations	7.00	88	1,764	0.04–4	
2.3.1. Pastures	10.28	102	2,050	0.04–0.4	Drain ann. ES €75/m²
2.4.2. Complex cultivation	6.96	85	1,696	0.04–0.4	acc. to soil quality
2.4.3. Land with agricultural and natural vegetation	10.64	100	1,996	0.04–0.4	acc. to soil quality
3.1.1. Broad-leaved forest	20.12	156	3,118	0.1–4.4	
3.1.2. Coniferous forest	12.96	124	2,490	0.1–4.4	
3.1.3. Mixed forest	14.08	131	2,616	0.1–4.4	
3.2.1. Natural grassland	16.32	109	2,177	0.04	
3.2.2. Moors and heathland	26.20	129	2,576	0.04	
3.2.4. Transitional woodland shrub	11.64	106	2,128	0.04	
3.3.2. Bare rock	19.68	107	2,144	0.04	
4.1.1. Inland marshes	16.56	159	3,174	0.04	
4.1.2. Peatbogs	26.36	168	3,361	0.04	
5.1.1. Water courses	11.44	139	2,776	0.3	
5.1.2. Water bodies	9.24	148	2,962	0.3	

Note: * Exchange rate: €1 = CZK25. Biotope capital values estimated by the BVM, ecosystem services capital value by a 5% discount rate, economic capital values ordered by the Czech Ministry of Finance in Decree no. 3/2008. Values in €/m².

Conclusion

The ELC promotes all dimensions of European landscape ecology and increases awareness of its multiple values. Since it is the natural (and not cultural, or human-made) landscape that most efficiently delivers the main ecosystem life-supporting services, it could only be helpful in educating the public and policy-makers if we were to routinely provide economic valuations of these declining services.

Based on the utilitarian, demand-side, willingness to pay (WTP) methods, Costanza *et al.* (1997) estimated the world's annual ecosystem services as 1.8-fold greater than the annual world GDP (US$18 trillion). Our pilot estimation of annual ecosystem service values in the Czech Republic, based on replacement-cost methods, assessed that annual ecosystem services are at least 50 times greater than the Czech Republic's annual GDP (Seják *et al.*, 2010).

It is not the replacement cost method that tends to overestimate the actual values of supporting and regulating services of ecosystems, but rather the utilitarian preference methods that underestimate the primary services of nature. Damage to life-supporting ecosystem services must be properly internalized (at least at the level of biotope values) in order to help motivate through a mechanism for informing the public discourse about the need to restore the basic environmental conditions for human health.

Putting a proper value on nature at the heart of human decision-making is only the first step to sustainability. The dominant welfare economic paradigm must be reformed, as the profit motive and accumulation of material wealth is not compatible with a sustainable future. The profit motive is globally failing (Lux, 2003). The pursuit of money and material wealth impedes the fulfilment of higher human needs (mainly the need of self-realization).

Today, capital hires labour. In sustainable economies, cooperating labour should hire capital at constantly low interest rates. Economic theory and economic activities should be organized, not driven by the profit motive, but rather to encourage human dignity and open up space for the development of creative human needs and self-realized people capable of inspiration and vision. A critical question remains: how to pass or evolve peacefully into this sustainable human order?

References

Costanza, R., D'Arge, R., De Groot, R., Farber, S., Grasso, M., Hannon, B., Naeem, S., Limburg, K., Paruelo, J., O'Neil, R. V., Raskin, R., Sutton, P. and Van den Belt, M. (1997) 'The value of the world's ecosystem services and natural capital', *Nature*, vol 387, pp253–260

Daly, H. and Farley, J. (2011) *Ecological Economics: Principles and Applications*, 2nd edn, Island Press, Washington, DC

ELC (2000) "European landscape convention", Council of Europe, Florence, 20 October, available at www.cidce.org/pdf/Landscape%20Convention.pdf (accessed 23 October 2011)

Faustmann, M. (1849) 'On the determination of the value which forest land and immature stands possess for forestry', in M. Gane (ed.) *Martin Faustmann and the Evolution of Discounted Cash Flow* (1968), Commonwealth Forestry Institute Paper No. 42, University of Oxford, Oxford, UK

Gowdy, J. (1994) *Coevolutionary Economics: The Economy, Society and the Environment*, Kluwer Academic Publishers, The Hague, The Netherlands

Hawken, P., Lovins, A., Lovins, L. H. (1999) *Natural Capitalism: Creating the Next Industrial Revolution*, Little, Brown & Company, New York, NY

Lux, K. (2003) 'The failure of the profit motive', *Ecological Economics*, vol 44, issue 1, pp1–9

Marshall, A. (1997) [1890] *Principles of Economics*, Prometheus Books, Amherst, NY

MEA (2005) *Ecosystems and Human Well-Being: Synthesis*, available at www.millennium assessment.org/documents/document.356.aspx.pdf

Odum, H. T. (1996) *Environmental Accounting, Energy and Environmental Decision Making*, John Wiley & Sons, Inc., New York, NY

Ripl, W. (1995) 'Management of water cycle and energy flow for ecosystem control: the energy-transport-reaction (ETR) model', *Ecological Modelling*, vol 78, pp61–76

Ripl, W. (2003) 'Water: the bloodstream of the biosphere', *Philosophical Transactions of the Royal Society B*, vol 358, pp1921–1934

Seják, J., Dejmal, I., Petricek, V., Cudlin, P., Michal, I., Cerny, K., Kucera, T., Vyskot, I., Strejcek, J., Cudlinova, E., Cabrnoch, J., Sindlar, M., Prokopova, M., Kovar, J., Kupka, M., Scasny, M., Safarik, M., Rousarova, S., Stejskal, V., Zapletal, J. (2003) *Valuation and Pricing Biotopes of the Czech Republic* (in Czech), Czech Environmental Institute, Prague, Czech Republic, English summary available at http://fzp.ujep.cz/projekty/bvm/bvm.pdf

Seják, J., Cudlin, P., Pokorny, J., Zapletal, M., Petricek, V., Guth, J., Chuman, T., Romportl, D., Skorepova, I., Vacek, V., Vyskot, I., Cerny, K., Hesslerova, P., Buresova, R., Prokopova, M., Plch, R., Engstova, B., Stara, L. (2010) *Valuing Functions and Services of Ecosystems in the Czech Republic* (in Czech), Faculty of Environment, J. E. Purkyne University, Ústí nad Labem, Czech Republic, English summary available at http://fzp.ujep.cz/projekty/valuingecosystemservices.pdf

Toman, M. (1998) 'Why not to calculate the value of the world's ecosystem services and natural capital', *Ecological Economics*, vol 25, pp57–60

Turner, R. K., Pearce, D., Bateman, I. (1994) *Environmental Economics*, Harvester Wheatsheaf, Hemel Hempstead, UK

7 Less energy, better health?

Jack P. Manno

Human health is directly tied to the availability of energy, be it the solar energy captured in the food we eat (calories), the cooking fire we need for safe consumption, the hearth for keeping warm and dry, the muscle power of grazers harnessed to work the land or the oil and gas that fuel the hospitals, pharmaceutical industry and doctor's offices. For the vast majority of our existence on Earth, humans have depended on solar energy captured by the plants and animals. Today, in the modern industrial world, we are no less dependent on solar energy than were our distant ancestors; it is just that we've come to expect instantly available energy, mainly from fossil fuels, the concentrated solar energy of eons ago.

The industrial revolution, made possible by the discovery and application of concentrated forms of usable energy, created the conditions for economic flourishing, for dramatic increases in population (Hall *et al.*, 2003), and for increasing dependence on highly commoditized goods and services to meet human needs and wants (Manno, 2000). The health of our economies and the health of our bodies have come to depend on ever-growing supplies of cheap energy.

The relation between energy and health is complex. This chapter explores this relation through the following argument: declining trends in environmental conditions combined with declines in energy returned on energy invested (EROEI) suggest a future constrained by energy scarcity; and, while most analysts focus on the potential negative effects on economic and human health of declining energy availability, it is possible that, as the title suggests, less energy in the future could mean better health, especially if we lay the groundwork now for new forms of energy-efficient and energy-conserving economic and social organization.

At the end of the first decade of the twenty-first century, a consensus began to emerge; we have come to a decisive turning point, a great transition. The transition has many dimensions: economic, social, environmental and cultural. The weight of evidence suggests that the steady growth of energy and material consumption associated with the consumer societies that have spread around the world cannot continue. Given that several billion people have access to less energy and material resources than are required to meet basic needs and support a decent standard of living, the amount of reduction in consumption (i.e. contraction in its demand for energy) required by the 'developed' world is substantial. And, if we believe that ever-widening disparities are socially unfair and potentially very damaging to the very fabric of civilization regionally and globally, then convergence between those who consume and those who do not is needed. Hence the appeal to 'contraction and convergence'. In a period of time when the suggestion of a slowdown in economic growth triggers panic, the expectation that the wealthier world will greatly reduce energy and material consumption, and that it will be good for us, may be seen as being too hopeful and a stretch, but it's a stretch that is both possible and necessary. The intent of this chapter is to argue why the transition to a lower energy intensive economy can be a positive thing for human health.

The implications of declining EROEI for human well-being

In this chapter, I focus on declining EROEI rather than the related phenomenon of 'peak oil'. The discourse of peak oil often leads to erroneous conclusions about the quantity of fossil fuels below Earth's surface, while the discourse of EROEI focuses on energy quality. The important issue is not the end of oil, but the end of cheap energy. EROEI represents a simple ratio; the amount of energy obtained from any energy-producing source/activity divided by the energy used to make that amount of energy available for productive activities.

EROEI is a ratio. A related term, net energy, refers to the remainder from subtracting energy input from energy output. Total net energy represents the 'productive energy': the energy available for all of the economic, social, cultural and other activities of daily life. Fossil fuels represent dense, convenient concentrations of energy available to apply to modern economic activity (industry?). These qualities are captured mathematically in higher EROEI values for fossil fuels compared to other energy sources. The EROEI of most alternatives does not come close to producing the net energy of fossil fuels – in particular, petroleum, and especially the petroleum recovered in the early years of the age of oil. Petroleum has been, by far, the dominant source of energy in the modern industrial age because of its special qualities, most important of them being its very high energy density (the amount of energy produced when burned) and its transportability (Cleveland, 2005).

The EROEI of fossil fuels has been in steady decline for at least the past 50 years. For example, Hall *et al.* (2008) calculate that the EROEI of domestic United States oil in the 1930s was approximately 100:1, meaning that the energy equivalent of one barrel of oil had to be invested in discovery, drilling, recovery, transportation and so on for every 100 barrels made available at the point of use. By 1970 the EROEI of oil produced in the United States had declined to between 40:1 and 20:1;[1] at present it may be as low as 5:1 or less.

Coal stands at 50–85:1, and would be considerably less if the energy costs of dealing with air and water pollution and its health effects were added. While steadily increasing, the EROEI of alternative and renewable energy sources such as wind and solar remain below 20:1 and, for biodiesel, EROEI slips into negative territory, meaning it takes more energy to grow the fuel crops and produce the biofuel than the resulting fuel yields. Again, depending on how you calculate energy costs, some analysts also place nuclear in negative territory, especially when adding the potential energy costs of storing high-level nuclear wastes and adequately responding to potential and real accidents. Equally pitiful negative EROEI numbers have been attributed to oil produced from tar sands. An additional value of EROEI numbers for a society trying to make rational energy decisions is that, unlike financial profitability, the energy costs of government subsidies and publicly provided infrastructure development are typically included in EROEI analyses.

The decline in EROEI and net energy of fossil fuels results from the fact that most of the readily available high quality fossil fuel reservoirs are already in production. This is simply the common result of the familiar 'best first' principle. As Hall *et al.* (2008, p118) describe it: 'the characteristics of humans to use the highest quality resources first, be they timber, fish, soil, copper ore or, of relevance here, fossil fuels'. The easiest to get at, the oil fields near the surface under high pressure, have all been discovered and many remain the sources of most of the continuing sources of supply. The peak in new oil discovery in the United States was reached in the 1930s; in the world it was in the 1960s. Newer discoveries tend to be in deep water, in remote and hostile surroundings, at great depths, bound in shale or sand, or otherwise in conditions requiring considerably more energy to bring to market than had been the norm during the first half of the age of oil. In addition to the increasing energy needed to obtain new oil, EROEI also declines when the quality of available fuels is poorer and therefore burns with less intensity. The documented decline in EROEI means the end of cheap fossil fuels; no longer cheap to extract, no longer cheap to process and distribute, no longer cheap (indeed, virtually free) to dispose of the greenhouse gas byproducts. It is this rise in energy costs rather than decline in supplies per se that will lead to (or already has led to) a peak in oil production worldwide.

Average EROEI of all energy sources is declining despite increasing EROEI of alternatives (wind, photovoltaics, etc.) because of the minuscule portion they make up in total energy consumption. This decline in total average EROEI must also necessarily lead to reductions in that portion of national income available for discretionary consumption and investment. More energy has to be used simply to obtain energy and therefore less is available for everything else a nation produces or invests in. This will have social consequences. The negative consequences are foreseeable as economic decline of various sorts. Some of the consequences of reduced energy availability, however, might be positive.

The implications of declining EROEI for human health and well-being are complex and open to interpretation. Consider the relation between energy and economy. Most journalists, financial analysts, business people and economists focus on markets, the flow of goods and services, income and employment, and financial valuation, including rates of change in prices with particular emphasis on finding the right recipe, the right mix of conditions to create and sustain economic growth. It's useful to remember that each dollar or any other unit of currency represents a claim on access to a certain amount of energy and material resources. While the relation between energy and GDP is not static and an economy can become more or less efficient in producing economic value per unit of energy consumption, the underlying relation remains: the more goods and services produced, the more energy required.

Thus, declining EROEI poses an especially thorny problem for energy-intense economies. As EROEI declines we must allocate more and more energy just to obtain energy. Therefore, just to produce the same amount of goods and services requires more energy and thus a greater portion of available capital. But investment in energy grows riskier even as energy prices rise. The increasing costs of ever deeper, more remote, riskier conditions for obtaining new sources of liquid fuels combine with the lack of consumer demand reduced by having to spend increasing portions of personal, corporate and national income just on securing supplies. The result is that society's discretionary spending is likely to decline substantially as more and more of society's output is required to maintain necessary inputs. Economic growth may stall and long-term stagnation may result.

But considering that a significant (if not readily quantified) portion of the energy consumed in modern industrial societies powers activities that are destructive to human well-being and the environment, choices might be made that direct available energy towards what is sometimes referred to as downshifting (Schor, 1998). There are many reasons why frugal living and an energy diet could be beneficial. A shift of emphasis towards increasing the amount of wellbeing or welfare derived per unit of energy used or invested (welfare returned on energy invested, or WROEI) would make it possible to imagine and plan for a prosperous way down (Odum and Odum, 2001) or what the European advocates of décroissance (Degrowth.net, 2010) have defined as 'an equitable downscaling of production and consumption that increases human well-being and enhances ecological conditions at the local and global level, in the short and long term'. (Schneider *et al.*, 2010) It also is in agreement with the nascent movement in the United States for a 'steady state economy' (Daly, 2005; see also http://steadystate.org).

A threshold hypothesis for the relation between energy consumption and human well-being

In one of the early issues of *Ecological Economics* journal, the Chilean economist Manfred Max-Neef offered a threshold hypothesis. He argued that:

> For every society there seems to be a period in which economic growth (as conventionally measured) brings about an improvement in the quality of life, but only up to a point – the threshold point – beyond which, if there is more economic growth, quality of life may begin to deteriorate. (Max-Neef, 1995)

Niccolucci *et al.* (2007) reviewed data on the Index of Sustainable Economic Welfare (ISEW) and the Genuine Progress Indicator (GPI), two indicators proposed as supplements to GDP as a measure a nation's progress. Analysing the relation between GDP and a nation's ecological footprint, the authors concluded that 'increase in economic wealth often results in worse, not better, conditions for people because the welfare related to a given GDP is 'polluted' and diminished by environmental stress and social pressures'. This is consistent with Herman Daly's (2005) concept of 'uneconomic growth' when environmental and social costs are greater than the benefits of production. Given the tight correlation and logical link between economic growth and total energy use, a similar 'inverted U' curve holds for the relation between increased energy use and a number of measures of wellbeing. The United Nations Development Programme (UNDP, 2005) estimates that it requires one ton of oil equivalent (TOE) per capita to reach a fairly high state of national health and development. Energy consumption beyond that buys little additional benefit. Energy analyst Vaclav Smil (2003) has estimated that consumption of 1.194–1.672 TOE of commercial energy per person is enough to meet essential physical needs plus high quality education and social services. On average, in 2005 the world's population consumed 1.778 TOE per capita annually (WRI, 2010). The world's energy glutton, Qatar, consumed over 19,000 TOE per capita, while in the United States and Canada annual consumption hovers around 8,000 TOE per capita. In general, as annual per capita energy use increases, measures of quality of life increase in step, up to a point after which increases in quality of life are no longer evident. As Smil concluded, 'Higher energy use does not guarantee anything except greater environmental burdens' (Smil, 2003, p386). Measures of WROEI would probably demonstrate a significant decline at the margins beyond the modest levels of energy consumption associated with frugal and energy efficient lifestyles.

Similarly, self-reported levels of happiness among the poor tend to rise with increased income while levels of emotional depression decline. The relation between self-reported state of happiness and personal income, however, largely disappears beyond moderate levels of income (Lane, 2000). Up to a point, one can buy at least a chance at happiness, but that point may be well below what is taken for granted in affluent societies. None of this is surprising. Too much energy introduced into a system can overwhelm it. By way of analogy, consider the problem of eutrophication of a lake or pond. An overabundance of fertilizing nutrients entering the water stimulates the growth of plankton, and thus excessive photosynthesis and a decline in oxygen that leads to rapidly degrading conditions for most fish. The shore becomes awash in rotting algae and dead fish. Think Lake Erie in the 1970s. Consider also how a starving person rapidly improves by increasing caloric intake. However, the average North American, who presently takes in 3,600 calories a day (world average is 2,700 calories), is not well served by adding another pound of steak to his daily diet. Consider that the energy that goes into producing, processing, storing, transporting and preparing the average American meat-eating diet emits 8,800 pounds of CO_2 per day, just less than the average United States car (Goodland, 1997). The WROEI beyond these points turns rapidly negative.

Many of the means we have to reduce energy use are also steps towards improving one's health. Walk, ride bikes, drive less. Eat more fruits and vegetables, preferably organic and locally grown. The Worldwatch Institute (2004), in its *State of the World* report, points out how our isolated, lonely lives expand our energy consumption: 'A one person household in the United States uses 17% more energy per person than a two person household.' Friendship and sharing meals, tools, conversation, skill-sharing and other community-building activities go a long way towards reducing our dependence on individual consumption to achieve satisfaction and maintain health, while significantly reducing ecological footprints.

The positive consequences of declining EROEI may be less obvious than the negatives, but when one looks at the range of inverted U relations between energy consumption and human well-being, the notion begins to dawn that society should be guided by the concept of an optimal level of energy consumption rather than by the push to maximize economic activity and thus energy. It is completely possible and, to some, obvious that wealthy industrial societies have exceeded a sustainable optimum, in particular those nations that can be considered energy gluttons. For those societies on the upward slope of the energy and well-being U curve, more available energy should lead to more social and individual well-being, and increasing WROEI. For modern industrial societies that appear to be on the downward slope where the marginal cost of energy use exceeds the marginal benefit (thus declining WROEI), an energy diet would be beneficial. Like most addicts, people in modern industrial societies are unlikely to voluntarily choose to live less energy intense lifestyles, despite the best persuasive efforts to encourage simpler living. But facing less availability and higher prices associated with declining EROEI, less energy is what we will have.

Alternative future scenarios: not just societal collapse

Two recent efforts have formalized alternative scenarios related to limits to growth: the Tellus Institute's Global Scenarios for the Century Ahead: Searching for Sustainability (Raskin *et al.*, 2010) and the scenarios developed for the Millennium Ecosystem Assessment (MEA, 2005). The similarity between these scenarios and others suggests that, while the future may be unknowable, given energy and environment trends, plausible scenarios are not unlimited. Each project posited four scenarios they considered most plausible. Each referred to similar uncertainties: a wide range of possible climate change feedbacks and ecosystem responses, whether and how human values may change, the potential for global cooperation or conflict and many other potential feedback loops that could seriously alter any given scenario. Both seriously question the sustainability of the 'business as usual' scenario and suggest social change will happen; the question is, towards what end?

It is not surprising that plausible scenarios would generally follow along the lines of business-as-usual, utopian and dystopian futures. There will be, as there always is, a struggle for the future among competing perspectives on justice, fairness, righteousness and faith. Energy analysis and social

Table 7.1 Future global scenarios from the Tellus Institute and the Millennium Ecosystem Assessment

Tellus Institute		
Conventional worlds	*Alternative visions*	*Millennium Ecosystem Assessment*
Market forces Business as usual; global incomes, GDP and population grow; profound inequalities; conflicts over scarce resources; collapse	**Fortress world** Authoritarian order imposed; elites retreat to protected enclaves; environmental degradation exacerbated	**Global orchestration** Economic cooperation, global growth, trickle-down benefits for environment and other public goods **Techno-garden** Ecological engineering and biotechnology follow adoption of reforms based on natural capitalism, profits from mimicking efficiencies of natural processes
Policy reform Government directed reforms towards sustainability objectives; serious reduction in GHG emissions; internationally agreed poverty-reduction strategies	**Great transition** Values shift to a just, sustainable world; human solidarity and environmental stewardship; reduction in consumption through frugal lifestyles; voluntarily reduced population pressures	**Adapting mosaic** Managing socio-ecological systems through adaptive management; free flow of information, more restricted flow of trade goods and services; great regional variation; Local/regional co-management **Order from strength** Breakdown of global cooperation, authoritarian responses to social and environmental crises

theories can inform what is possible, but not necessarily what is likely. Dystopian and utopian tendencies will emerge together and the outcome may be a mix of both for a long time to come. While the state of economic disparity, global climate, biodiversity, water, and so on all tend towards the dystopian, social movements are growing to bring about what the Tellus scenarios call the 'great transition', and what author and organizer Joanna Macy (2011) refers to as the 'great turning', 'the essential adventure of our time: the shift from the industrial growth society to a life-sustaining civilization.' Social change activism to bring the great turning about groups into six forms of social change activism:

- Softening the blow. On-the-ground work to protect and restore the most vulnerable and endangered ecosystems and people, whether through seed banks or food banks, preserves or shelters.
- Institutional and economic reform. Co-housing, web-based sharing networks, and larger institutional reforms including community and earth-based stakeholder representation on corporate boards, environmental financial and tax reforms, payments for the provisioning of ecosystem services and many more policy reforms with an eye to improving well-being while minimizing energy and material throughput and waste. Other policies will be needed that help communities to adjust to lower levels of energy consumption. These include: reduced working hours, parental leave, benefit packages for part time work, regulation of advertising; tying corporate charters to achievement of social and environmental objectives, innovative models of local-living economies, sustainable communities and transition towns, and many more.
- Developing new tools and technology. The crafts of a less energy-intense lifestyle will bring back the small-scale engineer who develops tools specific to crop, hydrology and other local ecosystem-based phenomena. These will include a range of green technologies, permaculture, ecological engineering and the like.
- Developing a theory base. Intellectual work to explain how overconsumption of resources has led to environmental destruction. The field of environmental studies is crucial here. The development of a biophysical social theory based on thorough analysis of networks of energy and material flows could make significant contributions. Comparison of alternative patterns of energy and material use in terms of wellbeing generated per unit of energy invested would be valuable.
- Cultural work. The era of cheap energy helped market-based connectedness overwhelm the importance and awareness of culture-based and earth-based connectedness. The building and symbolizing of these 'lost' connections is an essential role for art, music and poetry.

- Interpersonal and psychological work. Culture alone may not be enough to bring about a new ecological consciousness. As Clive Hamilton (2010) has written, it 'will depend not so much on a change of beliefs and attitudes but on the emergence of a new sense of self and the relationship of that self to the natural environment. In the first instance, we therefore need to understand how people construct their sense of self, that is, how they form their personal identity and how they act out those identities in their behaviour.' Can renewed forms of culture-based and earth-based connectedness help people handle the stress, fear, anger and other powerful emotions likely to be stimulated during times of major social and cultural transition? Healing from the effects of broken connections between people and the earth may be crucial throughout the transition. Self-identities formed in the age of the consumer will need to be reconstructed as people newly identify themselves as active inhabitants and participants of an ecosystem and engaged citizens in a social system. Declining EROEI has the potential to reverse the emphasis back to production from consumption, to actors rather than consumers.

In summary, the negative effects of the end of cheap energy are likely to predominate unless a strong movement for social change can explain broadly what is happening and why it is happening.

Note

1 EROEI estimates can differ considerably depending on accounting method; especially what energy costs are included. For example, should the energy used to provide the food for oil workers be counted? How about a portion of the energy to power the offices of the companies providing drilling insurance? While we can leave the accounting to the experts, what matters are the clear and indisputable trends towards decline.

References

Cleveland, C. J. (2005) 'Net energy from the extraction of oil and gas in the United States', *Energy: The International Journal*, vol 30, no 5, pp769–782

Daly, H. (2005) 'Economics in a full world', *Scientific American*, vol 293, no 3, pp100–107

DeGrowth.net (2010) 'Degrowth Declaration of the Paris 2008 conference', *Journal of Cleaner Production*, vol 18, pp523–524

Goodland, R. (1997) 'Environmental sustainability in agriculture: Diet matters', *Ecological Economics*, vol 23, pp189–200

Hall, C. A. S., Tharakan, P., Hallock, J., Cleveland, C. and Jefferson, M. (2003) 'Hydrocarbons and the evolution of human culture', *Nature*, vol 426, no 6964, pp318–322

Hall, C. Powers, R., and Schoenberg, W. (2008) 'Peak oil, EROI, investments and the economy in an uncertain future', in D. Pimentel (ed.) *Renewable Energy Systems: Environmental and Energetic Issues*, Elsevier, London, pp113–136

Hall, C. A. S. and Day, J. W., Jr. (2009) 'Revisiting the limits to growth after peak oil', *American Scientist*, vol 97, pp230–237

Hamilton, C. (2010) 'Consumerism, self-creation and prospects for a new ecological consciousness', *Journal of Cleaner Production*, vol 18, pp571–575

Lane, R. E. (2000) *The Loss of Happiness in Market Democracies*, Yale University Press, New Haven, CT

Macy, J. (2011) 'The great turning', available at www.joannamacy.net/thegreatturning.html (accessed 30 September 2011)

Max-Neef, M. (1995) 'Economic growth and quality of life: a threshold hypothesis', *Ecological Economics*, vol 15, no 1, pp115–118

MEA (2005) 'Scenario assessment', Millennium Ecosystem Assessment Scenarios Working Group, available at www.maweb.org/en/Scenarios.aspx (accessed 15 December 2010)

Niccolucci, V., Pulselli, F. M. and Tiezzi, E. (2007) 'Strengthening the threshold hypothesis: Economic and biophysical limits to growth', *Ecological Economics*, vol 60, pp667–672

Odum, H. T. and Odum, E. C. (2001) *A Prosperous Way Down*, University Press of Colorado, Boulder, CO

Raskin, P. D., Electris, C. and Rosen, R. A. (2010) 'The century ahead: searching for sustainability', *Sustainability*, vol 2, pp2626–2651, doi:10.3390/su2082626

Schneider, F., Kallis, G. and Martinez-Alier, J. (2010) 'Crisis or opportunity? Economic degrowth for social equity and ecological sustainability', *Journal of Cleaner Production*, vol 18, p511

Schor, J. B. (1998) *The Overspent American: Upscaling, Downshifting, and the New Consumer*. Basic Books, New York, NY

Smil, V. (2003) *Energy at the Crossroads Global Perspectives and Uncertainties*, The MIT Press, Cambridge, MA

UNDP (2005) *International Cooperation at a Crossroads: Aid, Trade and Security in an Unequal World*, UN Development Report 2005, United Nations Development Programme, New York, NY, available at http://hdr.undp.org/en/reports/global/hdr2005 (accessed 23 October 2010)

Worldwatch Institute (2004) *State of the World 2004*, Worldwatch Institute, Washington, DC

WRI (2010) *Earth Trends: The Environmental Information Portal*, World Resources Institute, Washington, DC, http://earthtrends.wri.org (accessed 17 December 2010)

8 Canada's 'rogue nation' position on asbestos

Colin L. Soskolne and Kathleen Ruff

Introduction

The authors use a current case study analysing Canada's role in the extraction of and international trade in asbestos. We show that the bridging of the disciplines of epidemiology and human rights can reveal useful knowledge to inform public policy, locally and globally.

Being the discipline that provides the scientific basis (i.e. the evidence) for public health policy formulation, the focus of epidemiology is on prevention. To achieve its prevention goals, epidemiology is the study of the distribution (i.e. the 'where' and 'when') and determinants (i.e. the 'what' and 'why') of disease in populations and its application to the control of health problems. This paper focuses on prevention at the policy level (i.e. primordial prevention; Beaglehole *et al.*, 1993).

All the work that is done in epidemiology is undertaken in a context of legal and ethical norms that include considerations of human rights. Being an applied science, epidemiology in public health is context-bound in which normative standards apply. Where standards may be inconsistent with practice norms, the role of the epidemiologist is to inform both the public and policy-maker alike with a view to influencing a change in norms (e.g. laws) that better serve the public interest.

The task of the epidemiologist thus is to inform policy with a view to reducing harm by preventing disease and premature mortality at the community level. Consistent with the mission of those working in public health, the role of the epidemiologist is to maintain, enhance, and promote health in communities worldwide. Thus, epidemiologists work to protect the public health interest above any other interest. But what is the epidemiologist to do when there is a clash between evidence and political decisions driven by government ideology and related policies? The overlap between public health and human rights enquiry can be instructive in addressing this question.

When political decisions clash with evidence it is typically due to the distorting influence of powerful special interests. The greater the imbalance of power, the greater the danger that public health decisions, instead of being grounded in objective evidence, will be shaped by dominant political and economic vested interests.

Human rights imperatives run exactly counter to that distortion. They require that decisions be grounded in the principle that all human beings, by virtue of their humanity, are entitled to equal dignity and equal rights. Decisions must be made transparently on the basis of evidence and, rather than serving the interests of the powerful, special attention must be paid to ensure that the rights of the most vulnerable are protected.

A case study of asbestos: facts versus politics

Case studies can be revealing and thus can serve as useful teaching tools. We first present the facts, followed by the ethical dimensions, and then the political and legal dimensions of the case.

Facts (evidence)

What is asbestos?

Asbestos is a natural mineral with unusual qualities. It is strong enough to resist high temperatures, chemical attack and wear. It has high tensile strength. Asbestos can be spun into yarn, woven into cloth or braided into rope. Asbestos can also be added to materials as diverse as cotton and cement. This combination of properties gives asbestos a role as an ingredient in such products as asbestos-cement roofing sheets, water pipes and brake pads.

What has asbestos been used for?

Asbestos has been used over the past 4,500 years. The ancient Greeks wove it into oil lamp wicks, funeral shrouds and ceremonial tablecloths. During the late 1800s, it insulated the hot engines, boilers and piping that powered the Industrial Revolution. Until the 1980s, asbestos was used for a variety of purposes in industrial nations: in buildings, transportation (in shipbuilding), and electrical systems. In some developing countries, it is used in asbestos-cement materials such as roofing, pipes and water storage tanks.

Asbestos types and associated fibres

Asbestos minerals are divided into two main groups, based on their fibre structure: serpentine (which includes only chrysotile asbestos) and amphibole (which includes amosite, crocidolite, anthophyllite, tremolite and actinolite). Chrysotile asbestos accounts for approximately 95 per cent of all asbestos used in the twentieth century and is the only type still being traded internationally.

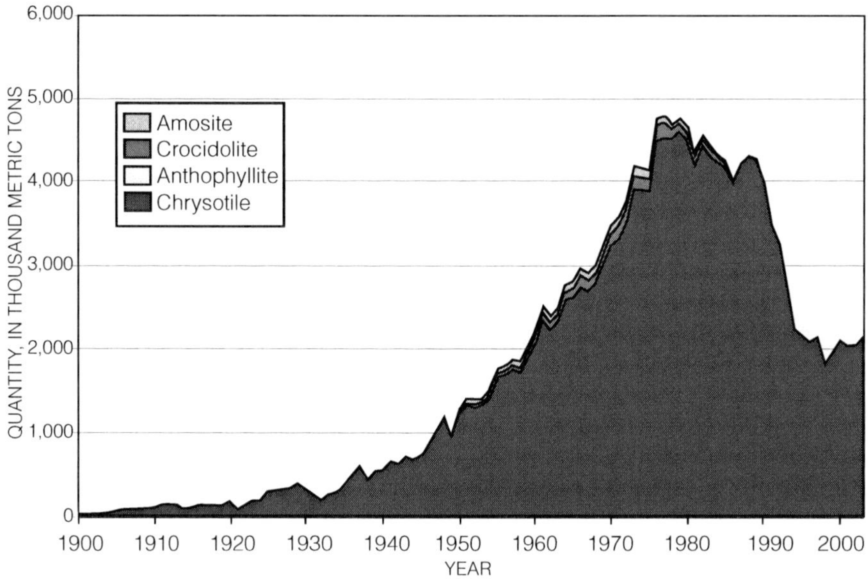

Figure 8.1 World production of asbestos by type from 1900 to 2003
Source: based on data from Virta (2005)

Producing nations

In 2006, 2.3 million tonnes of chrysotile asbestos were mined worldwide, with Russia, China, Kazakhstan, Canada and Brazil producing 93 per cent of this total. In the past, other countries also have been in the business of mining and exporting asbestos. Today, more than 50 countries have seen fit to ban asbestos.

Of all asbestos produced for the past century, 95 per cent was chrysotile and, for more than 25 years, it represents the only form of asbestos traded in the world. See Figure 8.1 for the world production of asbestos, by type. From 1900 to 2003, about 173 million metric tons (Mt) of chrysotile, 3.92 Mt of crocidolite, 2.81 Mt of amosite and 460,000 Mt of anthophyllite were produced (Virta, 2005).

History of health concerns

Over the past 100 years, evidence has implicated all types of asbestos in the causation of asbestosis, various cancers and mesothelioma. The World Health Organization (WHO), the International Labour Organization (ILO), health and labour organizations have called for use of asbestos to stop. In Canada, there is virtually no use of asbestos, but the country chooses to mine and export it.

Ethics

From the field of applied ethics, the four governing principles that constitute the framework for ethical analysis pertaining mainly to medical practice and health research (bioethics) are:

1 respect for autonomy (the right to self-determination);
2 beneficence (do good);
3 non-maleficence (do no harm); and
4 justice (the fair and equitable allocation of resources, risks, and benefits to all without discrimination).

This framework is extended to public health because, unlike the context of the physician–patient relationship in medicine (where the physician advocates on behalf of his/her patients), professionals in public health advocate on behalf of entire communities.

Thus, under justice from bioethics, in public health we include the principle of environmental justice. Under this principle, before taking an action, we need to ask about who is taking the risks while who is deriving the benefits? Also, the polluter pays principle is one that helps to incentivize the internalization of costs in the pricing of products so that the burden of costs associated with harms caused is not borne by others than those responsible for their production and use. Particularly relevant in this case study are the principles of solidarity and accountability. The former requires consideration of (international) norms, while the latter requires taking responsibility for the local and global impacts of our actions.

Canada stands alone among developed nations in maintaining the double-standard of exporting asbestos while not using it at home. In this chapter, we explore Canada's intransigence in denying the scientific evidence and maintaining this double-standard.

At time of writing, the government of Canada essentially claims that asbestos can be used safely in developing countries. The data, however, show the exact opposite.

Principle- and virtue-based ethical analysis: a question of professional and moral integrity

In 1983, Clayson and Halpern noted that 'Industry's offensive against the regulation of health and safety hazards uses academics to downplay or deny the seriousness of the hazards'. While refutation is essential to scientific progress, timeliness is of the essence when the evidence warrants action in the public interest.

To complement the principle-based approach to ethical analysis, virtue ethics (Weed and McKeown, 1998) is helpful for examining how some experts adhere to ideological interpretations that support the status quo.

Table 8.1 shows what constitutes virtuous traits of character among professionals.

The combination of virtue- and principle-based approaches to professional endeavours makes for a professional with integrity. Yet, in practice we do not always find professionals acting with integrity. Indeed, two recent textbooks have drawn attention to the 'doubt industry', designed to foment uncertainty in order to defend powerful vested interests. This industry started in the 1950s with tobacco, and then moved to asbestos and other hazardous products.

David Michaels (2008) reveals how the tobacco industry's duplicitous tactics spawned a multimillion dollar industry that is dismantling public health safeguards. Product defence consultants, he argues, have increasingly skewed the scientific literature, manufactured and magnified scientific uncertainty, and influenced policy decisions to the advantage of polluters and the manufacturers of dangerous products. To keep the public confused about the hazards posed by global warming, second-hand smoke, asbestos, lead, plastics and other toxic materials, industry executives have hired unscrupulous scientists and lobbyists to dispute scientific evidence about health risks. In doing so, they have not only served to delay action on specific hazards, but they have constructed barriers to make it harder for lawmakers, government agencies, and courts to respond to future threats.

The Orwellian strategy, according to Michaels, of dismissing research conducted by the scientific community as 'junk science' and elevating science conducted by product defence specialists to 'sound science' status also creates confusion about the very nature of scientific inquiry, and undermines the public's confidence in science's ability to address public health and environmental concerns. Michaels (2008) demonstrates that the regulatory system in the United States has been broken. He offers concrete, workable suggestions to take the politics out of science and ensure that concern for public safety, rather than private profits, guides regulatory policy.

Table 8.1 Virtues of professionals

Humility	Respect the input and opinions of others/self-effacement
Fidelity	Honour one's commitments/promote trust
Justice	Act fairly
Patience	Take time to hear others' viewpoints
Industry	Do your level best/excel
Veracity	Tell the truth/be honest
Compassion	Empathise
Integrity	Demonstrate good moral character
Serve	Protect the most vulnerable/serve the public interest
Prudence	Err on the side of caution/demonstrate good judgment

Source: adapted from Weed and McKeown (1998)

In Devra Davis's book (2007), the abundant documentation – much of it obtained from industry's own secret archives – substantiates that millions of cancers from tobacco, asbestos, polyvinyl chloride (PVC) manufacture, dioxin, oestrogen-laced personal care products and hundreds of other known carcinogens were preventable. Davis proves that scientific evidence of harm was available, and that both industry and government leaders knew it. She reveals what was known by 2008 about cell phones, diagnostic radiation exposure, aspartame and Ritalin, as well as industry and governmental efforts to suppress and distort the evidence.

Indeed, Davis reveals how government and industry leaders used familiar methods that have served them well for decades: create doubt, claim proprietary trade secrets, stage character assassinations, manipulate public perception, and intimidate. These strategies have quashed dissent and criticism, destroyed careers, kept workers ill protected and blocked victim compensation.

In Mallinder's (2011) recent and directly relevant exposé on the history of Canada's role in asbestos malfeasance, she reveals a systemic bias in support of powerful, moneyed asbestos interests since the mid-1940s. While it is true that industry's support for occupational health research, in general, including research into the health effects of asbestos among workers, has been significant, at the same time it is morbidly clear that the industry exercised its influence in suppressing vital knowledge to the detriment of worker health. Reliance on industry funding severely compromised the ability of worker health and safety, particularly among Quebec asbestos miners.

The two books (Michaels, 2008; Davis, 2007) and the historical review article on asbestos (Mallinder, 2011) demonstrate how malfeasance operates in practice. They specifically document how the asbestos lobby has undermined the ability of governments to serve the public interest. Evidence of continuing support of the asbestos industry in Canada reinforces this same trend today.

How can such malfeasance be exposed and yet Canadian policy in support of asbestos continues? One answer is the seduction that substantial rewards provide to contest the evidence in support of industrial interests, seeding doubt and uncertainty about the harms of asbestos. Because epidemiology is a 'soft', applied science, its ability for inferring causation is less direct than in the 'basic' or hard sciences. There is, therefore, more opportunity to contest the interpretation of applied (soft) sciences.

There are scientists with the professional integrity to resist pressures to tow the line of industrial interests, thereby ensuring that the public interest trumps vested interests. The classical approach by powerful interests is to apply the 'four Ds': the pressures of *denial*, *delay*, *division* and *discredit*. And, as recognized by Mallinder (2011), powerful interests may buy the services of the scientist so as to more directly control the direction of their work to foment uncertainty. Despite this, the ethical health researcher can rely on Hill (1965), who reminds us that:

> All Scientific work is incomplete – whether it be observational or experimental. All scientific work is liable to be upset or modified by advancing knowledge. That does not confer upon us a freedom to ignore the knowledge we already have, or to postpone the action that it appears to demand at a given time.

A recent example of apparent malfeasance

On 4 July 2011, in the criminal trial in Turin, Italy, against the asbestos multinational Eternit, public prosecutor Raffaele Guariniello called for 20 years in jail for asbestos magnates Stephan Schmidheiny and Belgian Baron Jean Louis Marie Ghislain De Cartier de Marchienne. Guariniello called the conduct of Eternit 'an appalling disaster' and requested to increase the jail sentences to be imposed on the accused in light of 'the incredible seriousness of the damages caused' and the serious degree of wilful and direct intent.

It is alleged that even though the accused were aware of the foreseeable risk of asbestos exposure, they chose not to take the preventative actions needed to safeguard the health of employees and local people. In this trial, not yet concluded at the time of writing, Swiss billionaire, Schmidheiny, is estimated to be spending 10 million euros a year on legal defense and public relations services and, in December 2011, he offered the town of Casale Monferrato 18.3 million euros to withdraw from the civil case against him. This illustrates the extreme measures that powerful interests undertake to defend their positions.

Politics

Public health policy, instead of being grounded in rational, objective evidence, can be shaped by dominant, systemic, political and economic interests. An example of gross political malfeasance is Canada's role in the 2011 United Nations Rotterdam Convention deliberations on listing chrysotile asbestos as a hazardous substance.

The Rotterdam Convention

Adopted in 1998, and effective in 2004, the Rotterdam Convention is a process that requires of all current 143 member countries:

- a scientific review panel to assess whether chemical substances should be listed under the Convention; and
- at a two-yearly Conference of the Parties (COP) to the Convention, consensus decisions on recommendations from the scientific panel (the Chemical Review Committee).

If listed, the only requirement is for member countries that export listed chemicals to secure prior informed consent from importing countries, and to provide instructions on 'safe use'.

An analysis of Canada's behaviour through the COP

Those who hold positions of power are accountable for the decisions they take. The more serious the consequences of the decision, the higher the level of accountability and transparency required. This is the foundation of human rights and democratic freedoms. When those who hold high positions of public trust take decisions that will cause loss of life and refuse to provide any reason for their action, this constitutes a serious violation of human rights and democratic accountability.

In fact, the government of Canada has repeatedly been the lead country in blocking the listing of chrysotile asbestos on the Rotterdam Convention's list of hazardous substances, even though a Canadian scientist, nominated by the Canadian government, has sat on the Chemical Review Committee that has consistently recommended that chrysotile asbestos be listed, and even though Health Canada, the government's health agency, recommended listing. The government refused to give any reason for its stance to the Canadian public, in whose name it acts, or to the Convention delegates. This is a disturbing example of how a country that claims to be democratic is demonstrating shameful disregard for human rights and democratic accountability.

The right to prior informed consent with regard to hazardous substances, provided by the Convention, is a critical public health tool. It is a right that Canadians enjoy. And, through Canada's 2011 blocking of the listing of chrysotile under the Convention, asbestos continues to be exported without formal warning and without its safe use ever being possible.

The refusal of the government of Canada to allow developing countries to have that right is an unethical double-standard where those who are the most vulnerable, instead of being afforded the greatest protection from harm, are denied even basic protection.

According to McKnight (2011), this latest decision, in sabotaging the Rotterdam Convention, is characteristic of the Canadian government's 'defense of asbestos and, more generally, of their hostility toward science and truth'. McKnight adds:

> The Conservative Party's stance on asbestos - which drew worldwide condemnation - is just the latest example of the federal government's embrace of an alternate reality bereft of scientific evidence and morality. (McKnight, 2011)

According to Leuprecht (2011), Professor of Public International Law, former Director of the Montreal Institute of International Studies, former

Dean of the Law Faculty of McGill University, and former Director of Human Rights and Deputy Secretary-General of the Council of Europe, from an ethical point of view, exporting a dangerous substance that is no longer accepted at home to other, mostly poor countries where it will sow death, cannot possibly be justified. The export of asbestos threatens the human rights of people in the receiving countries, particularly the most fundamental human right: the right to life and the right to health.

Human rights can be – and are being – violated not only by states, but also by non-state actors such as individuals, groups and corporations. In particular, Leuprecht notes:

> The producers of asbestos, asbestos product-manufacturing companies, and the scientists, lobbyists, and financial interests supporting them, do not accept the scientific evidence. They are operating a massive, Orwellian 'denial machine' ... The Canadian Broadcasting Corporation (CBC) program documented how powerful interests are trying to deny global warming, supported by scientists—or rather pseudo-scientists—some of whom had previously worked for 'Big Tobacco' and received donations from coal and oil companies. The parallel is striking: In the same way that some have attempted to deny the human health dangers of tobacco and the dramatic consequences of global warming, the producers and supporters of asbestos are trying to make us believe that it is not dangerous or that there are possibilities of its 'controlled' and 'safe' use. Once again, we see science pitted against spin. (Leuprecht, 2011)

Corporate interference in public health policy through political influence

The registered lobby group for the Canadian asbestos industry, the Asbestos Institute (now renamed the Chrysotile Institute) was modelled on the strategy employed by the tobacco industry. While claiming to be a scientific organization, it suppresses independent, reputable science. As documented by Castleman (2005), for decades, it has undermined efforts, at both the national and international levels, to protect public health by ending the use of asbestos.

The Canadian Chrysotile Institute is the nexus of a shadowy and unaccountable global asbestos lobby. The deleterious role played by this lobby can currently be seen playing out in Malaysia, where the Department of Occupational Safety and Health has proposed a ban on asbestos. According to human rights and epidemiology principles, this public health question should be decided transparently and ethically on the basis of scientific evidence and the Malaysian public interest.

However, the decision-making process was distorted by powerful vested interests, when APCO Worldwide, headquartered in Washington, DC, intervened in June 2011 to oppose the ban. APCO cut its teeth working for the tobacco industry. It was hired by Philip Morris in 1993 to set up a front group, the Advancement of Sound Science Coalition, to block public health initiatives to protect people from second-hand tobacco smoke. Now, it is rendering similar services to the asbestos industry.

APCO refused to identify who paid it to intervene in the internal Malaysian public health process. It was discovered, however, that their client was the International Chrysotile Association. The expert witness hired by APCO to defeat the ban was David Bernstein, whose work is funded by the asbestos industry and who, previously, for eighteen years, carried out research for the tobacco industry.

Who is the International Chrysotile Association (ICA)? In spite of its impressive name and the resources it enjoys to hire APCO, it is difficult to obtain information as to who the ICA is, who funds it, or what its activities are. A search reveals that, in 1997, the Asbestos International Association was incorporated in Quebec and was lodged with the Canadian Asbestos Institute (CAI) in Montreal. In 2005, in a joint public relations move, both replaced the word 'Asbestos' with the word 'Chrysotile' in their names. The ICA now has its office in the small Quebec town of Thetford Mines, the location of Canada's last asbestos mine. The ICA refuses to provide information, referring queries to Bob Pigg, a long-time United States lobbyist for the asbestos industry. Pigg also refuses to provide information.

A search of Quebec's corporate directory shows Chrysotile Institute president, Clément Godbout, as being the lead administrator of the ICA. The list of other administrators is a who's who of the global asbestos lobby, with lobbyists from Indonesia, Bolivia, Peru, United Arab Emirates, Mexico, Vietnam, Brazil, Iran, Kazakhstan, Russia, China, India and Senegal. Thus, Canada, once again, plays a pivotal role in servicing the global asbestos lobby and in impeding public health progress to end preventable asbestos-related illness and premature death.

Manipulation, legal challenges and legal liability

For most of the past century, the Quebec asbestos mines were owned by multinational corporations such as Johns Manville and Turner Newall. After being sued by victims, these companies went through bankruptcy proceedings and extricated themselves from the asbestos business. For a brief period, the Quebec government nationalized the asbestos mines, but then sold them to private Quebec investors in the 1980s.

Paradoxically, the fact that Quebec companies, and not foreign multinationals, now own the asbestos mines, may make the industry less accountable to victims. The reason is that Quebec asbestos mining companies are hijacking the Quebec Business Concerns Records Act (QBCRA), a 'blocking' law intended for antitrust cases, as a shield to refuse to disclose documents to courts outside Quebec when victims file cases for compensation.

In 1993, the Supreme Court of Canada (SCC) ruled that it was unconstitutional for Quebec asbestos companies to use the QBCRA to refuse to provide company documents in the case of a British Columbia (BC) electrician, George Hunt, and other workers who sought compensation for mesothelioma after being exposed to asbestos from Quebec. Hunt alleged 'negligent manufacture, negligent failure to warn against dangerous effects of the fibres, and conspiracy to hide the dangers of asbestos from the public'.

In its landmark decision, the SCC ruled that the Quebec asbestos companies had violated minimum standards of order and fairness. The BC Supreme Court awarded Hunt approximately $130,000 in damages (http://canlii.ca/en/bc/bcsc/doc/1990/1990canlii434/1990canlii434.html). The case against the Quebec asbestos companies was to enable the Workers' Compensation Board (WCB) to recuperate these funds and for Hunt to obtain additional compensation.

The SCC ruling did not apply to victims outside Canada, but the foreign companies who owned Quebec mines could not use the QBCRA to shield documents held at their head offices outside Quebec. However, the Quebec company, Asbestos Corporation Ltd (ACL), the major owner of Quebec asbestos mines, is using the QBCRA to refuse to provide documents in a United States case brought against it by the family of Mark Buttitta, who died of mesothelioma in 2002. ACL has no headquarters outside Quebec and thus it is attempting to use the QBCRA to provide a total shield for its documents.

The New Jersey Superior court reprimanded ACL for 'wrongful conduct' for seven times violating the order of the court to produce documents in the Buttitta case. The court went further and imposed a sanction on ACL to prevent it 'from benefiting from its wrongful conduct'.

In 2010, the New Jersey Appeal Court stated that ACL was misusing the QBCRA, pointing out: 'Moreover, the policy behind the QBCRA, namely to protect Canadian businesses against the application of United States and other foreign countries' antitrust laws, is outweighed by the interest of the United States in protecting our citizens from hazardous exposure to asbestos.'

As if the QBCRA were not sufficient an obstacle to prevent asbestos victims from obtaining redress for harm suffered, in its 2010 Annual Report, when speaking of the numerous legal cases filed against it by victims, ACL points out further legal obstacles available to the company:

> However, according to the opinion of legal advisers consulted, even if a default judgment was rendered against the Company, such judgment could not be enforced against the Company prior to its verification or recognition by a competent court in the Province of Quebec. (Société Asbestos Limitée, 2010)

Apparently, no such case for verification has ever been brought forward in Quebec. If victims in the United States face such an exhausting barricade of legal obstacles, what chance will victims in India or Bangladesh have?

In May 2011, the Quebec government approved a $58 million loan guarantee for a consortium of investors who wish to reopen a Quebec asbestos mine and export millions of tonnes of asbestos to developing countries for decades to come. According to the government, a financial analysis, carried out by the accounting company KPMG, concluded that the project would be financially profitable.

One of the factors contributing to this anticipated profitability is the fact that complex legal barriers, described above, grant Quebec asbestos companies a special degree of impunity for harm caused to victims.

It is noteworthy that the president of ACL, prominent Quebec business leader, John LeBoutillier, was a member of the 2002 Canadian Democracy and Corporate Accountability Commission. This Commission held hearings across Canada and issued a report with 24 recommendations.

In his presentation to the Mining Association of Canada in 2002, LeBoutillier emphasized the Commission's recommendations that companies:

- should re-establish basic values such as integrity, honesty and ethics;
- should act with more transparency and greater accountability;
- should consider the consequences of corporate decisions on the lives of citizens of others countries;
- should disclose their approach to corporate social responsibility;
- should add a chapter on corporate social responsibility issues to their annual report; and
- should show commitment to corporate social responsibility at the highest corporate level.

LeBoutillier has not put his recommendations into practice in his own company. There is nothing in ACL's 2010 Annual Report about corporate social responsibility and no concern shown about the impact of the company's asbestos on the lives of impoverished, vulnerable people in developing countries, where awareness and safety protections regarding the hazards of asbestos are lacking.

When asked by a journalist about the Buttitta case, in which the company refused seven times to obey a court order to produce documents, and where the judge reprimanded ACL for its 'wrongful conduct', LeBoutillier claimed to know nothing about the case; hardly an example of corporate social responsibility (Montreal Gazette, 2010).

Discussion and conclusions

Just like the tobacco industry, the asbestos industry has succeeded in undermining public health policy and blocking action to end the use of asbestos as the only effective means of preventing a continuing epidemic of asbestos-related illness and death. The reason for this failure of public health policy is the lobbying power of the asbestos industry.

Recognizing that little progress could be made in the face of the tobacco lobby's power, the WHO included a landmark provision in its Framework Convention on Tobacco Control (FCTC) to block subversion of public health policy by the tobacco lobby.

The WHO states that the FCTC is 'the first treaty negotiated under the auspices of the World Health Organization ... The FCTC is an evidence-based treaty that reaffirms the right of all people to the highest standard of health'. The Convention includes a legally binding provision to ensure that corporate spin does not trump evidence. Article 5.3 states:

> In setting and implementing their public health policies with respect to tobacco control, Parties shall act to protect these policies from commercial and other vested interests of the tobacco industry in accordance with national law. (WHO, 2003)

Detailed guidelines spell out the strategies employed by the tobacco industry to undermine health policy, the legal obligation governments now have, and the practical measures they should implement to block these strategies. The FCTC, now ratified by 174 countries, is already proving an effective tool in blocking efforts of the tobacco industry to infiltrate and undermine public health policy in Canada and globally.

Meanwhile, the global asbestos lobby continues to subvert public health policy, both nationally and internationally. It has succeeded in preventing chrysotile asbestos from being put on the Rotterdam Convention's list of hazardous substances since 2004. And it intervenes in developing countries to prevent action on asbestos. Clearly, a similar Convention to the FCTC is needed to stop the asbestos lobby from undermining global public health.

In our globalized world, Canada is at the heart of the global asbestos lobby. It displays its disrespect for the principle of solidarity, demonstrating profound arrogance. Canada's conduct reflects a double-standard, which violates the human right to health and life under international law – hence the label 'rogue nation' for Canada.

References

Beaglehole, R., Bonita, R. and Kjellstrom, T. (1993) *Basic Epidemiology*, WHO, Geneva, Switzerland

Castleman, B. I. (2005) *Asbestos: Medical and Legal Aspects*, 5th edition, Aspen Publishers Inc, New York, NY

Clayson, Z. E. and Halpern, J. L. (1983) 'Changes in the workplace: implications for occupational safety and health', *Journal of Public Health Policy*, vol 4, no 3, pp279–297

Davis, D. (2007) *The Secret History of the War on Cancer*, Basic Books, New York, NY

Hill, A. B. (1965) 'The environment and disease: association or causation?' *Proceedings of the Royal Society of Medicine*, 14 January, pp295–300

LeBoutillier, J. (2002) 'Canadian democracy and Corporate Accountability Commission', presentation to the Mining Association of Canada, Fort McMurray, 18 June

Leuprecht, P. (2011) 'Stop Canadian death export of asbestos', editorial, *International Journal of Occupational and Environmental Health*, vol 17, no 3, pp285–286, available at www.ijoeh.com/index.php/ijoeh/article/view/1843/1178

Mallinder, L. (2011) 'Deadly secret', *Canada's History*, April–May, pp32–38

McKnight, P. (2011) 'A deadly disdain for science', *Vancouver Sun*, 9 July, available at www.vancouversun.com/health/deadly+disdain+science/5077717/story.html #ixzz1RcpOdt30

Michaels, D. (2008) *Doubt is Their Product: How Industry's Assault on Science Threatens Your Health*, Oxford University Press, Inc., New York, NY

Montreal Gazette (2010) Asbestos: silky, strong – deadly, May 15, available at http://www2.canada.com/montrealgazette/news/saturdayextra/story.html?id=01de621f-aa24-43ab-84c1-1603a2d498ac&p=5

Société Asbestos Limitée (2010) *Annual Report*, Société Asbestos Limitée, available at www.sedar.com/DisplayCompanyDocuments.do?lang=EN&issuerNo=0000 1326

Virta, R. L. (2005) 'Mineral commodity profiles: asbestos', *United States Geological Survey Circular*, 1255–KK

Weed, D. L. and McKeown, R. E. (1998) 'Epidemiology and virtue ethics', *International Journal of Epidemiology*, vol 27, no 3, pp343–348

WHO (2003) 'Framework convention on tobacco control', WHO Doc A56/VR/4, 21 May, World Health Organization, Geneva, Switzerland, adopted by the World Health Assembly 21 May 2003, into force 27 February 2005, available at www.who.int/gb/ebwha/pdf_files/WHA56/ea56rl.pdf

9 Public health and primary prevention

Past and present opportunities and barriers

Vladimír Bencko and John Quinn

Introduction

Key challenges in contemporary medicine include the rapidly growing financial demands placed on health policy. Escalating costs are driven, in part, by pressures to use best practices to deliver optimal health outcomes at both the individual and population levels. In addition, the need to ensure access to primary healthcare physicians and medical specialists increases costs. The effectiveness of investments in healthcare is seen in the observed extension of life and the generally improved quality of life over the past century, the relative containment of infectious diseases, and the education of the general public in healthy life skills. Most of these achievements are, however, also due to 'primary prevention' – the prevention of disease before it occurs.

This chapter highlights the strengths of primary prevention in promoting public health locally, nationally, and globally. We argue that the current allocation of resources between those needed for treatment-oriented healthcare and those needed for the purposes of primary prevention must be reconsidered. This argument is driven by the observation that health policies, practices, and allocated resources that promote the goals of primary prevention are losing out in competition with treatment-oriented healthcare policies and practices, particularly with in excess of 90 per cent of healthcare budgets globally being allocated to care, and less than 10 per cent being allocated to prevention. Our argument is made even more compelling by the observation that all aspects of healthcare face the common problems of increasing financial and resource constraint (Rechal *et al.*, 2011; Woolf, 2011) at a time when demand is likely only to rise.

The cost-effectiveness of primary prevention in providing healthcare and improving subsequent human health and quality of life is clear (Goetzel, 2009; Pickett, 1983; Roper, 1992; Walls *et al.*, 2008; Wong *et al.*, 2009). Therefore, we argue that global investment in primary prevention must increase dramatically to assure continued improvement in overall public health and quality of life.

The need for a 'rebalancing' is urgent. In today's circumstances of increasing global population, rising human material expectations, and significant, rapid and generally negative global changes in climate, biocapacity and resource availability, the promotion and maintenance of health through primary prevention is obligatory.

The economic rationale and justification for 'rebalancing'

With investments in primary prevention nowhere near the levels that they need to be, the focus is moved from preventing disease to treating diseases with the greatest social and political impact. This is a policy decision that tends to promote inequity in care, and does not necessarily address the most pressing health needs of a society. In essence, primary prevention is cheap and applicable to population groups with disparate economic and social status; therapeutic medicine is expensive and largely available only to those who can pay. Powerful interests are heavily invested in maintaining the status quo.

Even though primary prevention is the most cost-effective form of healthcare, globally, the resources and finances necessary for primary prevention are difficult to obtain and maintain. This paradox will likely worsen as governmental and healthcare budgets tighten and they direct their focus increasingly to acute care services. Reasons for this shift include an aging population in the developed world, a growing population in the developing world, the high costs of treating common and commonly preventable chronic illnesses, and the negative health effects related to environmental, geopolitical, social and economic upheaval.

Treating the sick or injured (i.e. being reactive) is a far more obvious action than is the much cheaper act of preventing illness or injury (i.e. being proactive), where no noticeable event – or, more importantly, the improvement of health – is the desired outcome. The effectiveness of investments in primary prevention may not be seen for decades (such as increased longevity, decreased infant mortality, and hence reduced demand on healthcare services). Unfortunately, policy-makers often have a much shorter time horizon. Except when epidemics or disasters occur, prevention offers few immediately obvious benefits, and often has little immediate political benefit. This conundrum is a major obstacle to support for prevention programmes.

The next decades will pose unique challenges to healthcare, manifesting initially as recurring financial and resource crises. Global change is increasingly obvious and destructive to countries and to economies. Our growing global population of 7 billion has steadily rising expectations, but the necessary physical resources, especially fossil fuels, necessary for trade and commerce, are at their limits. Consequently, the financial and physical resources to provide acute healthcare may be unable to satisfy demand. We argue that, while therapeutic medicine will always be important, primary prevention is the best investment to ensure the public's health, and every healthcare system should place a high priority on implementing this inexpensive and effective approach.

Primary prevention, hygiene, epidemiology and public health

Hygiene and epidemiology, the disciplines that address the primary prevention of disease and illness, developed in response to epidemics like the black death, tuberculosis, food and water-borne illnesses, AIDS, and various chronic and preventable illnesses (Little, 2007). Many serious diseases have been suppressed, even eradicated, as understanding improved regarding disease origins and how simple human actions, such as washing hands, could reduce disease spread. Vaccination is one of the most successful public health initiatives, improving population health by preventing vaccine-preventable diseases (CDC, 1999; Stern and Markel, 2005; Orenstein *et al.*, 2005). The development of vaccines has led to the global elimination of smallpox, and newer vaccines have decimated other infectious diseases such as poliomyelitis (polio) and measles. The inexpensive and low-risk prevention of these illnesses is much less than the finances and resources required to treat individuals who would be otherwise afflicted. These are prime examples of cheap, effective, preventive healthcare that have saved millions of lives from premature death and disability.

Other preventive healthcare achievements include providing safe drinking water, public health education programmes, embedding in many societies a culture of health, food and water quality standards and immunization programmes. These programmes are virtually universal among developed countries, and most developing countries are also working to adopt them. These activities have led to dramatic reductions in human premature morbidity and mortality, and enabled economic stability and development in countries implementing them.

Primary prevention reduces disease and injury incidence by avoiding (sometimes also removing) the cause of a disease; it prevents the disease or injury before it occurs (Wallace, 2008). Examples of primary prevention include preventing environmental exposure by maintaining safe drinking water and reduced atmospheric pollution, using immunization to improve resistance to specific diseases, and developing public education programmes regarding healthy lifestyles, such as developing good activity patterns and eating habits, practicing safer sex and legislating the use of seat-belts (Mayes and McKenna, 2011). Thus, by developing illness prevention strategies, primary prevention needs to play an active role in developing healthy public policy to prevent disease and premature mortality.

Many of these activities are carried out on the institutional or administrative level, such as food laws or vehicle restraint laws. Some activities, such as promoting healthy lifestyle practices, use advertising directed to population groups, and healthcare practitioners reinforce these messages at an individual patient level. Primary care also performs many secondary prevention activities such as screening for and treating common diseases such as diabetes and hypertension (Bencko, 2011a).

Indeed, secondary prevention is a logical 'next step'. It attempts to identify and mitigate diseases within an individual that are not yet evident. Most common health screening procedures are examples of secondary prevention (such as breast self-examination for early indicators of cancer). Secondary prevention also screens for clinically evident, but undetected conditions, such as clinical depression or other mental illnesses (Wallace, 2008). A third level of prevention, tertiary prevention, seeks to minimize the extent to which the disease spreads, causes disability, or recurs (Jones, 2005). Finally, under global ecological change, primordial prevention is critical for its focus on upstream policy interventions (Beaglehole *et al.*, 2006).

In the Czech Republic, the expanding market economy and the privatization and reorganization of government services, has led to major health and political reforms. Unfortunately, this has created an uncertain environment for health services (Holcik and Koupilova, 2000; Bencko, 2007). Some changes have created opportunities for public health policy formation and implementation, but significant public health issues and diseases, such as HIV/AIDS and obesity, pose major challenges. An increasingly important challenge is the growing importance of antibiotic resistance and hospital-acquired infections that cause significant morbidly and mortality. These issues are important because they are largely due to human-induced changes in microbial ecology.

Prevention versus precaution

The precautionary principle relates to preventive actions warranted in the face of uncertainty. It is a fundamental tenet of public health goals and policy formulation. It asserts that the burden of proof for potentially harmful actions rests on the assurance of safety by the agent proposing the change (e.g. industry) and, where there are threats of serious damage, scientific uncertainty must be resolved in favour of prevention (Goldstein, 2001). This concept is crucial in public health and primary prevention and its implementation can increase public participation in decision-making (Kriebel and Tickner, 2001). Using available data, exploring alternatives to possibly harmful actions, and applying the precautionary principle within a risk assessment framework provides a complementary approach to addressing public health (Bencko, 2011a).

The steady increase in the prevalence of preventable illness and non-communicable disease is evidence of the negative health consequences of poor lifestyles and inappropriate health behaviours. Thus, behaviours such as smoking and obesity, are closely associated with hypertension, diabetes mellitus type II (DM) and the eventual development of cardiovascular disease (CVD); these are all major causes of death in developed countries. Unfortunately, while these diseases can largely be prevented, most funding, research and public awareness, remain directed to treatment.

Obesity is a major precursor of DM, CVD and several other serious diseases. Although obesity should be preventable through public education and behaviour modification (Klein *et al.*, 2007), current efforts have not been successful and the prevalence of obesity is rising globally. Obesity is associated with many modifiable risk factors including over-consumption of food, inactivity and a sedentary lifestyle. Public health intervention programmes include public education campaigns, community and medical programmes focused on physical activity and healthier lifestyles, and industry-supported changes in food supply and eating patterns (Apovian, 2010). Treatment, often initially successful, is centered on improving or reducing current or future obesity-related co-morbid conditions, lifestyle changes and, when indicated, pharmacotherapy and surgery (Eckel, 2008; Thompson *et al.*, 2007; Kushner, 2010; Flier and Maratos-Flier, 2010). Maintaining a sustained weight loss is uncommon.

An essential public health task in preventing obesity is public education regarding the need for regular physical activity. This message has been discussed *ad nauseum* at all levels of public health programming and policy creation, and reflects a fundamental problem for many public health endeavours. The problem is one of implementing lifestyle change, and doing so at a population level remains a major obstacle – everywhere – to the success of population health programmes. While obesity may be a useful example of the importance of behaviour and lifestyle in determining health, many other health problems, such as cancer and injury, have similar components; however, space precludes discussion here.

Current difficulties in primary prevention funding and policy

A key pitfall in the current market-oriented diagnosis and treatment-oriented approach to medical problems lies in the rapidly growing financial demands of this kind of medicine. Diagnosis and therapy have high demands in terms of money and resources, as does medical research, but the benefits are self-evident. The effectiveness of acute-care medicine is reflected, in part, in rising life expectancies seen in most countries. In the Czech Republic, this is especially obvious over the past two decades, mainly due to the use of modern methods of interventional cardiology and the introduction of a wide spectrum of chemotherapy in clinical practice (Bencko, 2011b). However, these approaches to maintaining population health are costly and unsustainable, yet reasonable and effective primary prevention efforts are not funded at appropriate levels. Why is this?

A key reason is likely that the 'costs now, benefits later' structure of preventive medicine requires economic foresight and a philosophy of risk mitigation that does not entail an expectation of immediate, obvious effect (Garrison *et al.*, 2011); this is in contrast to the immediate effects seen with most medical therapy. Said differently, vaccines can save many lives, but can also be greatly undervalued and unnoticed by the general public and policy-makers.

Healthcare economics is the discipline that oversees the economic aspects of all facets of healthcare; it involves both private and public agencies and organizations. Research in healthcare economics helps dictate where healthcare resources are placed to optimize medical outcomes at the best cost while ensuring the lowest risk to patients. Resolving the observed increase in chronic disease and illness is most cost-effective when tackled through primary prevention (Booth *et al.*, 2000), which is the potential frontline for mitigating healthcare expenditures for healthcare systems that manage population healthcare delivery. A primary prevention programme can alleviate the spiralling costs of acute and chronic healthcare expenditure by detecting disease early. Investment in primary prevention is clearly desirable. But this investment must be based on evidence of effectiveness.

Three economic concepts are applied to healthcare interventions in primary prevention: cost–benefit analysis, cost-effectiveness analysis and cost–utility analysis (Meltzer, 2011). These act to reconcile budgetary constraints and public health needs; their application drives health policy at many levels.

Cost–benefit analysis includes all costs and benefits associated with, for example, a vaccination campaign, and is helpful when comparing vaccine costs with the costs of treating the disease once infected. Cost-effectiveness analysis assesses the costs and savings associated with a medical intervention, as it relates to lives saved or to the number of people who do not become infected with, for example, measles, after being innoculated. Cost–utility analysis assesses health outcomes in terms of survival and quality of life. A major shortcoming is that these analyses save money, not necessarily lives. One can argue that a vaccine campaign may be insufficiently effective for use in a given community. But the argument may not consider the health and quality of life of anyone who acquires a vaccine-preventable disease. Unless otherwise noted, public health proponents usually endorse vaccination programs for any endemic disease that is effectively preventable through safe vaccination.

Cost–benefit analysis in immunization programmes, or in screening for various diseases, drives much public health policy. Such programmes are considered money well-spent for the betterment of health and society. But other policy-makers may disagree, and argue against some primary prevention programmes. This is more common when stakeholders or their representatives are poorly educated about vaccines and their benefits, or they subscribe to baseless myths associated with a vaccine. The use of the human papilloma virus (HPV) vaccine in adolescents (both males and females) is an example. Lifetime HPV prevalence ranges from 5 per cent to 40 per cent of the population (Dunne *et al.*, 2007; Dinh *et al.*, 2008; Parkin, 2006). It is known that some common subtypes of HPV can lead to cervical cancer in women and penile cancer in men (ACS, 2011). HPV vaccine will reduce the likelihood of developing these cancers, and at a small fraction of the financial, familial and personal costs for someone with cervical or penile cancer. But many policy-makers, and a good proportion of the public, do not accept that the HPV vaccine can help to prevent cancer, and thus may refuse immunization for themselves or, more importantly, their children (Haber *et al.*, 2007; Casper and Carpenter, 2008).

Primary prevention must also respond to emergencies; it must have plans in place to act effectively and in a fiscally responsible manner. Doing so can be difficult, and is always expensive. In an emergency or epidemic situation, rapid assistance and support are key to successful outcomes. This type of emergency response requires significant human and material resources and finances to address the logistics, staffing, expertise and provisioning of medical supplies to meet the anticipated need. Most public agencies will spend any funds available to meet this demand. The resources needed usually must be manufactured.

Commonly, limited supply leads to rising prices. Thus, manufacturers of essential medicines or other materials can benefit significantly from the emergency. An example was the stockpiling and use of Tamiflu (oseltamivir) to treat the Mexican or 'swine' flu epidemic in spring 2009. Huge amounts of money were spent to treat an illness whose severity was uncertain, resulting in public scepticism. Later analysis of data showed that the risk of death was similar to a previous seasonal flu and depended largely on the socio-economic situation and level of healthcare that patients experienced in their society. But, at the time, there was real fear. This is clearly illustrated by the 18-fold difference in swine flu mortality levels seen in Mexico (72 deaths; 3,648 cases) relative to the United States (6 deaths; 5,469 cases) early in the epidemic. Clearly, living circumstances and access to medical care and to medicine were significant determining factors of mortality. However, the early fears about the flu, and hence the 'need' to stockpile Tamiflu, were fed by the high mortality rate in Mexico.

No doubt, in the swine flu epidemic, some level of hysteria, and possibly questionable public health risk communication policies, were factors in responding to the epidemic. In addition, other factors, such as an inordinate concern regarding the risks of genetic mutation of the virus into a more dangerous variant for humans, also played a role. Viral mutations do happen, and some mutations may increase viral virulence. Ideally, a serious and sober risk assessment of any danger is necessary before decisions are made. Unfortunately, epidemics do not permit prolonged second-guessing; critical decisions must be made in the face of pressure from the media, the pharmaceutical industry, healthcare workers, the public, and from politicians. This is a clear example where pre-planning is essential. It must occur continually, and consider many possible health threats. This will not eliminate misadventure, but should reduce it.

One may worry about poor or even counter-productive outcomes of 'emergency' vaccination campaigns, which can happen when facing an imminent or existing epidemic. These campaigns may reduce vaccination compliance, especially in a suspicious/skeptical population. This poor compliance is seen in many developing countries where vaccines are refused because of cultural or religious attitudes holding that vaccines harm the recipients. This is seen even with highly effective and safe vaccines like measles and polio vaccine, and is seen in all countries of the world.

Of course, no medical intervention is devoid of risk, and vaccines are no different. The potential for flu-like symptoms and other minor medical side-effects are real. But, the chance of becoming severely ill or dying from measles, polio or tetanus is much greater for the unimmunized child. This is seen today in both developed and developing countries where there is decreased herd immunity for diseases like measles or whooping cough because of poor uptake. There are presently many outbreaks of measles in sub-Saharan Africa, Asia and even on college campuses in North America.

Evidenced-based medicine and primary prevention

Evidence-based medical practice refers to the integration of clinical experience and best available medical evidence to best serve patients (Sackett *et al.*, 1996). The consensus in settings practicing evidence-based medicine is that clinical decision-making must reflect the integration of clinical experience combined with data obtained from peer-reviewed literature and appropriate clinical research. This uncompromising and demanding requirement of contemporary evidence-based medicine also applies to public health practice, policy formulation, and implementation. It sets a high standard, but the aim and primary goal of evidence-based medicine is to maximize medical outcomes and encourage best practices in medicine, public health practice and primary prevention. Proposed projects and/or prevention programs must be based on the results of biomedical research and public health experience, confirmed in clinical practice. With advances in the biomedical, societal, economic and public policy fields, evidence-based practice in public health is a well-justified requirement.

Since the mid-twentieth century, many public health and medical professionals have paid heed to the negative impact of various environmental factors within the social and environmental context, trying to determine causal relationships between the quality of the environment and related risk factors and their effects on public health. These factors include climate change, water access, food security and rising sea levels. For many globally, these factors are pervasive, they have health effects of their own, and, by becoming part of the tapestry of illness that some pundits have referred to as 'diseases of civilization', they add to a growing degree of social stress experienced by much of society. As a last resort, and if evidence-based practices in public health are insufficient to help guide policy-makers to support primary prevention, contemporary problems in post-modern society can be, at the very least, paraphrased as moral obligations. The Nobel laureate Konrad Lorenz warns us:

> If the human race will destroy itself, it does not need to happen necessarily by suffocation from lack of oxygen, destruction of marine algae and rain forests, and not because it exposes itself to progressively increasing dangers of radioactivity. Mankind extinguishment suffices quite enough when the modern man gets rid of all moral values. We must warn before that danger so strongly as before the fundamental threats of our environment encompassing us as a result of our civilization. (Lorenz, 1987)

In summary, evidenced-based practice in public health and primary prevention must rely on solid data about the ecological integrity of the planet and how it affects public health across populations. The present evidence in the literature overwhelmingly supports the hypothesis that neglected ecological integrity and the consequent environmental degradation lead to deterioration in population health (Soskolne and Bertolini, 1999; Ladd and Soskolne, 2008). Primary prevention must focus on the impact of a degrading environment on human health and how human action is leading to environmental degradation, presenting a serious danger for the right to health of unborn and future generations (Westra, 2006).

Conclusions

A strategic challenge of twenty-first century medicine is the prevention of illness and the promotion and maintenance of health in an increasingly vulnerable global population. Primary prevention is the best vehicle to achieve this. It is a major contributor to reducing healthcare costs, maximizing healthcare outcomes with limited resources, and to improving the quality of life. The main contribution of public health policy with respect to human health has been in preventing and eliminating disease and premature mortality. Economic principles applied to public health policy seek to engender a culture of maximizing healthcare outcomes most cost-effectively with the greatest community benefit. The precautionary principle must be followed in some public policy instances when seeking public health policies that will offer optimal outcomes in the public interest.

Primary prevention in public health is fundamental to the success and progression of societies, globally. For primary prevention regimes to effectively reduce preventable disease and promote health, public health must be provided with adequate financial and physical resources, along with political and policy-based support to meet the challenge.

Both public healthcare and therapeutic medicine are complementary components to maintain human health, thus they should not have to compete for resources. However, we are facing a resource and fiscal crunch, and competition is inevitable. Even though the evidence is clear that primary prevention is the most cost-effective healthcare process to ensure population health, it is hard to compete with the dramatic and immediate effects of therapeutic medicine. This is especially so when policy-makers and stakeholders focus almost exclusively on short-term political and social goals. The true economic benefits and health successes of primary prevention are hard to document when 'nothing happens' (for instance, when pandemics and major disease burdens are averted). A concerted emphasis on primary prevention is needed for all public health policy to succeed in the long-term in support of sustainable health.

References

ACS (2011) *Cancer Facts and Figures 2011*, American Cancer Society, Atlanta, GA, available at www.cancer.org/Research/CancerFactsFigures/CancerFactsFigures/cancer-facts-figures-2011

Apovian, C. (2010) 'The causes, prevalence, and treatment of obesity revisited in 2009: what have we learned so far?' *American Journal of Clinical Nutrition*, vol 91, pp277S–279S

Beaglehole, R., Bonita, R. and Kjellstrom, T. (2006) *Basic Epidemiology*, 2nd edn, WHO, Geneva, Switzerland, available at http://whqlibdoc.who.int/publications/2006/9241547073_eng.pdf

Bencko, V. (2007) 'Environmental epidemiology, present changes and challenges for future', *Central European Journal of Public Health*, vol 15 (suppl.), ppS6–S8

Bencko, V. (2011a) 'Use of epidemiological data for cancer risk assessment: approaches, concepts and issues', *The Open Epidemiology Journal*, vol 4, pp94–98

Bencko, V. (2011b) 'Primary prevention of diseases: current challenges and opportunities', (Original in the Czech language) *Prakticky Lékar*, vol 91, no 3, pp127–130

Booth, F., Gordon, S.E., Carlson, C. J. and Hamilton, M. T. (2000) 'Waging war on modern chronic diseases: primary prevention through exercise biology', *Journal of Applied Physiology*, 1 February, vol 88, no 2, pp774–787

Casper, M. J. and Carpenter, L. M. (2008) 'Sex, drugs, and politics: the HPV vaccine for cervical cancer', *Sociology of Health and Illness*, vol 30, no 6, September, pp886–899

CDC (1999) 'Impact of vaccines universally recommended for children–United States, 1990-1998', *Morbidity and Mortality Weekly Report*, 2 April, vol 48, no 12, pp243–248

Dinh, T. H., Sternberg, M., Dunne, E. F. and Markowitz, L. E. (2008) 'Genital warts among 18- to 59-year-olds in the United States, National Health and Nutrition Examination Survey, 1999–2004', *Sexually Transmitted Diseases*, vol 35, no 4, p357

Dunne, E. F., Unger, E. R., Sternberg, M., McQuillan, G., Swan, D. C., Patel, S. S. and Markowitz, L. E. (2007) 'Prevalence of HPV infection among females in the United States', *Journal of the American Medical Association*, vol 297, no 8, pp813–819

Eckel, R. H. (2008) 'Clinical practice: nonsurgical management of obesity in adults', *New England Journal of Medicine*, vol 358, p1941

Flier, J. and Maratos-Flier, E. (2010) 'Biology of obesity', chapter 74 in *Harrison's Principles of Internal Medicine*, 17th edn, McGraw-Hill, New York, NY

Garrison, L. P., Bauch, C. T., Bresnahan, B. W., Hazlet, T. K., Kadiyala, S. and Veenstra, D. L. (2011) 'Using cost-effectiveness analysis to support research and development portfolio prioritization for product innovations in measles vaccination', *Journal of Infectious Disease*, July, vol 204 (suppl. 1), ppS124–S132

Goetzel, R. (2009) 'Do prevention of treatment services save money? The wrong debate', *Health Affairs*, January/February, vol 1, pp37–41

Goldstein, B. (2001) 'The precautionary principle also applies to public health actions', *American Journal of Public Health*, September, vol 91, no 9, pp1358–1361

Haber, G., Malow, R. M. and Zimet, G. D. (2007) 'The HPV vaccine mandate controversy', *Journal of Pediatric and Adolescent Gynecology*, vol 20, no 6, pp325–331

Holcik, J. and Koupilova, I. (2000) 'Primary health care in the Czech Republic: brief history and current issues', *International Journal of Integrated Care*, October–December, vol 1, pe06

Klein, S., Allison, D. B., Heymsfield, S. B., Kelley, D. E., Leibel, R. L., Nonas, C. and Kahn, R. (2007) 'Waist circumference and cardiometabolic risk: a consensus statement from Shaping America's Health: Association for Weight Management and Obesity Prevention; NAASO, The Obesity Society; the American Society for Nutrition; and the American Diabetes Association', *American Journal of Clinical Nutrition*, vol 85, no 5, pp1197–1202

Kriebel, D. and Tickner, J. (2001) 'Reenergizing public health through precaution', *American Journal of Public Health*, September 2001, vol 91, no 9

Kushner, R. F. (2010) 'Evaluation and management of obesity', chapter 75 in *Harrison's Principles of Internal Medicine*, 17th edition, McGraw-Hill, New York, NY

Ladd, B. and Soskolne, C. (2008) 'A toolkit for ecoepidemiological enquiry under global ecological change', *Sustaining Life on Earth: Environmental and Human Health through Global Governance*, Lexington Books, Plymouth, UK

Little, L. K. (2007). 'Life and afterlife of the first plague pandemic', in L. K. Little (ed.) *Plague and the End of Antiquity: The Pandemic of 541–750*, Cambridge University Press, Cambridge, UK

Lorenz, K. (1987) *The Waning of Humaneness*, translated from German by Robert Warren Kickert, Little, Brown, Boston, MA

Mayes, R. and McKenna, S. (2011) 'Public Health and Primary Care: struggling to "Win friends and influence people"', *Journal of Primary Care and Community Health*, January, vol 2, no 1, pp65–68

Meltzer, M. I. (2001) 'Introduction to health economics for physicians', *Lancet*, 22 September, vol 358, no 9286, pp993–998

Orenstein, W. A., Douglas, R. G., Rodewald, L. E. and Hinman, A. R. (2005) 'Immunizations in the United States: success, structure, and stress', *Health Affairs (Millwood)*, May–June, vol 24, no 3, pp599–610

Parkin, D. M. (2006) 'The global health burden of infection-associated cancers in the year 2002', *International Journal of Cancer*, vol 118, no 12, pp3030–3044

Pickett, G. (1983) 'Prevention in a free society', *The Journal of Primary Prevention*, vol 3, no 4, pp215–223

Rechal, B., Suchrcke, M., Tsolova, S., Suk, J., Desai, M., McKee, M., Stuckler, D., Abubaker, I., Hunter, P., Senak, M. and Semenza, J., (2011) 'Economic Crisis and communicable disease control in Europe: a scoping study among national experts.' *Health Policy*, December, vol 103, no 2–3, pp168–175

Roper, W. (1992) 'A framework for assessing the effectiveness of disease and injury prevention', *Morbidity and Mortality Weekly Report*, vol 41, pRR-3

Sackett, D., Rosenberg, W., Muir Gray, J., Haynes, R. and Richardson, S. (1996) 'Evidence based medicine: what it is and what it isn't', *British Medical Journal*, vol 312, p71

Soskolne, C. and Bertollini, R. (1999) 'Global ecological integrity and sustainable development: Cornerstone of public health', available at http://www.colinsoskolne.com/documents/WHO-1999_Discussion_Document.pdf

Stern, A. M. and Markel, H. (2005) 'The history of vaccines and immunization: familiar patterns, new challenges', *Health Affairs (Millwood)*, May–Jun, vol 24, no 3, pp611–621

Thompson, W. G., Cook, D. A., Clark, M. M., Bardia, A. and Levine, J. A. (2007) 'Treatment of obesity', *Mayo Clinical Proceedings*, vol 82, p93

Wallace, R. (ed.) (2008). *Maxcy–Rosenau–Last Public Health and Preventive Medicine*, 15th edn, Appleton and Lange, Norwalk, CT, pp4–5

Walls, H. L., Peeters, A., Reid, C. M., Liew, D. and McNeil, J. J.(2008), 'Predicting the effectiveness of prevention: a role for epidemiological modeling', *The Journal of Primary Prevention*, July, vol 29, no 4, pp295–305

Westra, L. (2006) *Environmental Justice and the Rights of Unborn and Future Generations: Law, Environmental Harm and the Right to Health*, Earthscan, London

Wong, J. B., Mulrow, C. and Sox, H. H. (2009) 'Health policy and cost-effectiveness analysis: yes we can, yes we must', *Annals of Internal Medicine*, 17 February, vol 150, no 4, pp274–275

Woolf, S. H. (2011) 'Public health implications of government spending reductions', *Journal of the American Medical Association*, vol 305, no 18, pp1902–1903

Part III

Public Health Issues

Introduction

Donald W. Spady and Colin L. Soskolne

A common pathway to human health lies in the provision of effective public health services. The environment within which these services are delivered includes biological, political, cultural, economic and social components. The chapters in this part of the book largely address the human-derived environment. But, as one reads them, it becomes apparent that the natural environment, along with its limits, and the consequences of a disordered natural environment, are ever-present with a variety of pressing and vexing challenges and constraints.

In Chapter 10, Spady discusses some public health implications of a transition from today's high-energy globalized society to one consuming much less energy, and more dependent on locally and regionally derived resources. He emphasizes that this new society must live in a right relationship with nature. He argues that resources for both treatment-based healthcare and public health services will be significantly constrained relative to today. Indeed, treating illnesses or injury may be inordinately expensive at a time of fiscal constraints, and the necessary resources to do so may be hard or impossible to obtain unless one is affluent. To most effectively use what is available, emphasis should be placed on primary prevention. To this end, Spady advocates embedding the concepts and practices of public health into local society in order to promote healthy living and reduce the incidence of preventable illness and injury.

A more immediate problem, one of access to healthcare for migrants, is detailed by Hnilicová and Dobiášová in Chapter 11. Although their analysis is confined to the Czech Republic, over the coming years, access to healthcare will manifest as a potentially intractable global problem as the consequences of climate change and environmental disasters unfold, creating multitudes of migrants as environmental refugees. The real problems that this chapter addresses are not so much access, but rather who will pay, how insurance agencies use legalese and chicanery to avoid their mandated responsibility (largely to the detriment of the most vulnerable), and how a government with modest means tries to respond fairly and humanely. This case study exposes questions of justice and human rights, typically needing to be addressed in many countries.

War and insurrection are common sources of migrants and refugees. Among the most vulnerable are those who, just because they are women, are targets for violence and indifference, whether for cultural or political reasons, or simply to instil terror. In Chapter 12, Lyamzina presents original research documenting the effects of violence arising from civil war on the mental health of women. This research, conducted in seven countries where civil insurrection was common, found that women in these countries were often exposed to high levels of violence and that significant mental illness commonly resulted. Equally concerning is the fact that, when addressing the global burden of disease, mental illness is not a priority, and when considering the need (especially in developing countries) for human capital to make economic, social and environmental contributions, neither are women. This reality does not auger well for the future health and well-being of these societies.

Original research describing the expenditure trends of three well-developed healthcare systems (United States, Japan and France) is reported by Zelený in Chapter 12. He demonstrates that, if current trends persist, all three systems are financially unsustainable. Two plausible reasons for this are:

1 unrealistic expectations of what treatment-oriented medical care can and should be expected to do; and
2 too little regard and insufficient financial resources allocated to illness prevention and health promotion.

These reasons reflect underlying public policy that may have arisen because of the easy availability of resources in the past and the marvels of medical progress. How policy will evolve in a time of increasing fiscal and resource constraints remains to be seen, but increasing hardship is likely.

With widening disparities in the world, the polarization of approaches to resolving problems is likely to worsen, becoming even more extreme. There are lessons to be learned from the case studies presented in these chapters. We ignore their ramifications at our collective peril.

10 Public healthcare in the time of transition

The need to revert to basics

Donald W. Spady

Introduction

In this chapter, I discuss how public health services may be provided over the next few decades as society experiences a transition[1] from current unsustainable lifestyles, to lifestyles characterized by sustainable living within a mutually beneficial relationship with the environment. Providing basic public health services to a community, engaging the community to consider health dimensions in all aspects of living, and advocating for what are commonly called the 'social determinants of health' will be critical to maintaining the health of a community. This is due, in part, to the fact that a person's health is determined more by the broad environment within which they live than by the availability of a doctor or hospital. In addition, the technological complexities, high resource use, and excessive costs associated with the acute healthcare system render it vulnerable in a time of transition and it may well be unable to meet healthcare demand. Consequently, a key aim must be to maintain population health; this is the role of public health. I address the issue from the perspective of an individual living in a well-developed country.

Currently, maintaining public health assumes a 'business as usual' economy and lifestyle, with necessary resources available to perform our tasks, a growth economy and rising living standards. Due to the serious social and biophysical consequences of resource depletion and global change, however, these assumptions are dubious (Spady, 2011). Evidence of change is obvious. For example, 2010 was a record-breaking year for climate associated disasters (Romm, 2010), and climate change costs for Canada are estimated to be $21–43 billion per year by 2050, and even higher beyond that if we do not quickly reduce carbon emissions (NRTEE, 2011). Much of the world is already being shaken by economic uncertainty and added annual costs such as these are clearly unsustainable. In addition, the Fukushima nuclear disaster illustrates the fragility of a highly complex society as it faces the consequences of a natural disaster combined with human error. Fukushima also illustrates how our assumptions regarding natural disasters, regulatory compliance, and disaster preparedness can underestimate reality.

If the welfare of society is to be given serious consideration, a public health service must work together with the society it serves to weave a successful transition, a journey from today's unsustainable way of living to a new lifestyle where living is more local, sustainable, and in harmony with the natural world. When we start a journey, we usually have some idea of its nature and duration; in this instance, our journey – 'our' journey, because we will all take it – will be characterized by a constant process of reacting to the consequences of our exploitation of nature that we considered necessary to meet our demands as we created a world bent on 'progress'. This journey will be hindered by resource scarcity, significant economic, social and political change, plus dramatic global change. We will have to feel our way and muddle through, and the public health profession will be among those muddling.

As is characteristic of all human history, and of evolution more generally, there is no end; the journey just changes. There is a direction, however; and our direction should follow the idea expressed by Thomas Berry in *The Great Work*: 'to carry out the transition from a period of human devastation of the Earth to a period when humans would be present to the planet in a mutually beneficial manner' (T. Berry, 1999, p3).

We are bringing a lot of baggage with us. Some of it is 'bad' baggage, especially our demonstrably ecocidal attitudes towards the natural world. But we also bring the 'good' baggage of philosophy, theology, science, culture, art, music, literature, ethics and our experience: 'in all our attempts to renew or correct ourselves, to shake off despair and have hope, our starting place is always and only our experience' (W. Berry, 2000). This is what we bring and can use on our journey.

We also bring with us the critical elements of collective human wisdom, intelligence, adaptability and the hope that that these elements enable. Hope is important. Wendell Berry wrote:

> If we find the consequences of our arrogant ignorance to be humbling, and we are humbled, then we have at hand the first fact of hope: We can change ourselves. and If the ability to change oneself is the first fact of hope, then the second surely must be an honest assessment of the badness of our situation. (W. Berry, 2008)

But are we humbled, and do we really want to know the badness of our situation? There is today a collective societal denial that a problem exists. With clear evidence of increasing economic, political, biological and ecological fragility, we are in overshoot. Yet we refuse to accept this reality. In conversations, you sometimes hear 'we need a major climate change disaster to wake us up.' But nearly all of the leading powers in the world have already experienced at least one such disaster, and still nothing is being done to change course. Our very survival depends on accepting that dangerous global change is happening now, and it will only worsen.

Regardless of what we do, transition will come, but the chances of a successful transition would be better if we had some influence in how it proceeds.

This chapter is a disaster plan, but unlike most disasters, the timeframe is longer and external help less certain. Surplus resources will be scarce and communities may have to resolve issues on their own. Health professionals must consider whatever short-term disasters or other events may occur, plus develop and maintain the basic infrastructure of public health as life becomes more local, resources and finances deplete, and climate change wreaks havoc.

We start from the strength of an existing infrastructure – at least in developed countries – that permits a full programme of public health activities. Unlike the medical care system, which uses highly specialized and dedicated equipment, buildings and laboratories, much of the infrastructure used by public health is similar to civil infrastructure everywhere: buildings, bridges, roads, transport, computers, communication, the electric power grid, and water and sewage facilities. While some specialized physical infrastructure is used, such as public health laboratories, much of the uniquely 'public health' infrastructure lies in the knowledge and professionalism of those who carry it out. Both forms are at risk and both forms will change to something simpler, sparing and uncertain. During this transition, key process roles for public health will be:

- to identify those aspects of existing physical infrastructure and public health practice that can still be used;
- identify and develop effective and sustainable alternative structures, processes, and methods that still work when money and resources are considerably diminished; and
- set priorities as to what programs to keep, constrain or cut.

This is already happening; numerous newspaper and other reports exist documenting budget cuts to public health programmes, and the frustration with which these cuts are received. In response to current economic conditions, national and state governments are exploring how reductions of 5 to 10 per cent or more in financial support will affect public health programmes. As resources decline, especially fossil fuels, and as global changes intensify and economies contract, these reductions will deepen. Yet, for the same reasons, the social demands for government help will rise.

Much of our existing physical infrastructure needs expensive repair or replacement (Mirza, 2006; Thompson *et al.*, 2008). This requires both physical and fiscal resources, which are already scarce and in time will be even more so. Hence, any long-term dependence on physical infrastructure is problematic. But, as long as infrastructure lasts and is functional and cost-effective for useful purposes, it should be used because it contains embedded energy and resources, and, if it can be maintained, it eliminates the need to spend resources and energy to replace it. However, infrastructure eventually fails and it must be disposed of, with all useful components being salvaged where possible. When new infrastructure is proposed – for any reason, not just public health – consideration must be given to the costs and resource demands for construction, for function and the opportunity costs foregone. Longevity, maintenance and multipurpose use should be closely examined. Location should be based less on opportunity, beauty, or business, but rather with consideration as to who will use it and what kinds of transport will be needed to access it. Public health clinics, hospitals and doctor's offices should be sited where there is easy public transportation.

Infrastructure can also relate to the services that the physical structures enable, such as transport services, communication, information storage and retrieval, and also the materials to carry out tasks. These components are closely interrelated and commonly depend on other components. Thus, failure in a key area can have significant downstream effects.

Virtually all forms of infrastructure depend on abundant, affordable energy in order to function. However, fossil fuels are the most common form of energy, and they face imminent decline. Oil production, for example, has peaked and now is in decline. By 2020, this will be apparent in all countries of the world. Gas and coal are not that far behind. In 2004, fossil fuels provided 80 per cent of the world's energy supply (IEA, 2004); however, by 2050 the absolute amount of energy used from fossil fuels will be considerably lower and, by 2100, lower still (Rosen *et al.*, 2010). This reduction is not because the resource is exhausted, but because of the high fiscal and energy costs of extraction. This is bad, because our economy is driven by energy. But it is also good, because climate change is due substantially to the release of carbon dioxide from burning fossil fuel. In the future, energy will come mainly from renewable sources; thus, how the future will evolve depends to a large extent on what type of energy is available, and how much of it there will be.

One answer comes from David MacKay, who estimated that, in the UK, about 15 per cent of the energy we currently use could likely be replaced by renewable forms (MacKay, 2009). Other authors have different estimates, but all agree that energy availability and consumption will be significantly lower than today (Heinberg and Mander, 2009). It seems reasonable (but frightening) to estimate that energy production in 2050 will be about a quarter of that used today in the United States, even in the face of population growth and associated demand; this figure is slightly higher than today's global per capita energy consumption. This decline in energy supply will affect all aspects of our lives: how we live, work, obtain food, shelter, heat and clothing, and maintain our culture and our health. Tax revenues will drop, hindering the ability of governments to function, and demand for government services may rise. A typical public health system will be faced with repeated fiscal cuts, and service may become sharply limited, just when demand for public health services rises.

In summary, while infrastructure today is reasonably good, much of it requires urgent repair. New infrastructure is expensive and resource intensive, and resources are declining. Thus, any new infrastructure must be demonstrably essential, and close consideration given as to purpose, location, support and maintenance. Many people today would deride this perspective and say that technology will solve our problems. However, while technology can be exceptionally useful, it also reflects Greer's 'logic of abundance' in that we create new technology and use it afterwards often just because we can (Greer, 2009). That logic is treacherous; most technology depends on electricity, such as in computers, which may not be consistently available anywhere, and not available at all in some areas. Our technology may end up at the level of the slide rule rather than the computer. The slide rule, the book of logs and simple calculators were used to a large degree to build much of the major physical infrastructure up to the first seven decades of the twentieth century. They represent intermediate technology that is cheap and adequate and which can often be built and repaired locally using local resources and skills.

One fragile technology is electronic information storage. Two common examples from the health area are electronic medical records and the replacement by academic libraries of scientific journals and books by electronic media. Today, these technologies are very convenient and effective. But they depend on an intact power grid, computers, and a functioning and accessible Internet, each of which has other dependencies. The possibility of failure is real, the consequences disastrous; yet, denial prevails (Hecker, 2007). Books are a classic form of intermediate technology that can be maintained indefinitely. The library is the classic repository, and is commonly an important community gathering point. We need libraries.

This is not to dismiss all technology, but our attitude towards technology should be 'not necessarily technology, but technology if necessary and practicable'. The second qualifier is important; we can always visualize a necessity, but we must be realistic in its implementation. In the past, much technology was developed to save on labour, which in the future may be cheap, and the labourers thankful for the opportunity to work.

A critical and resilient, but unconventional, type of infrastructure is the human mind, especially our imagination and our creativity. We have used our intellect and our imagination not only to create civilizations and to conquer the world, but also to damage nature and make our own survival precarious. We can use the same intellect and creativity and acquired knowledge to learn from our mistakes and to live within Earth's limits. This idea is not new; for millennia, philosophers, theologians and environmentalists have urged human society to learn to live within nature rather than apart from it, or eventually face the consequences. Repeatedly, society has repulsed the idea. The consequences are arriving in force, however, and our survival depends first on living through their effects and simultaneously learning how to live in harmony with nature. Exactly what form this takes is up to society, but public health not only will have to act to promote and maintain human health, but also play an extended role ensuring that achieving health does not, at the same time, destroy Earth's ecological integrity upon which humans depend. The only infrastructure we can be sure of is within ourselves, within our spirit, our intellect, our imagination and our community.

The role of public health

Public health's primary task will be to preserve and promote population health so that society can maintain its ability to respond to challenges. It will work to create, deliver and maintain an environment with clean air and water, and safe, adequate and affordable food, shelter and warm clothing; an environment that is stable and secure, and in which people are sufficiently educated to be productively employed and to live in relatively happy relationships with each other and the community, and to have a world view that lets them see their place in the community and the cosmos.

Many public health professionals may see this as too broad a role, one that extends into the roles and responsibilities of other social institutions; however, in a time of uncertain transition with likely considerable biological, physical and social disruption, all institutions will have to integrate their skills and resources and work together to ensure the survival and health of everyone. This integration of public health into the community will help ensure that health becomes a 'way of thinking' in the community. In addition, by being an integrated local institution, the face of public health is ever-present, and it also allows public health professionals to advocate for and support issues not typically viewed as public health issues, such as the need for full employment in a community, for cultural development, for libraries, for appropriate schools, for adequate wages, and for other important social determinants of health.

What kind of health do we need?

Maintaining the health of the public is far more cost-effective than treating their illnesses. Thus, encouraging community members to consider the health implications of their actions and also embedding public health practices within a community, may be the most equitable, socially acceptable and cost-effective way to maintain public health. Hence, the role of public health in promoting and maintaining the health of the population is paramount. The kind of health necessary is less like the World Health Organization definition of health – 'a state of complete mental, physical, and social well-being, and not merely the absence of disease' (WHO, 2006) – and more like Aldo Leopold's definition of health as 'the capacity [of the land] for self-renewal' (Leopold, 1970). While Leopold addresses land, the concept is easily transposed to humans in that it relates to the human qualities of renewal and resilience. Leopold's definition reflects an absolute requirement for any human society as it develops and uses the characteristics of resilience and adaptability to respond to change and challenge. If the society cannot deal successfully with the problems it faces, it will die.

Last defines public health, in part, as 'a way of thinking, a set of disciplines, an institution of society, and a manner of practice'(Last, 2007). Two of these 'a way of thinking' and 'an institution of society' – are particularly relevant. They do not necessarily require extensive professional knowledge to be effective, although obviously it is desirable. Nor do they require many resources or much money. The first component reflects the importance of individual and societal education and behaviour regarding health promotion and maintenance. It also reflects the need to develop within society an understanding about our current predicament. If people understand the reasons for the problems, the events, and the disasters that they are likely to experience, then perhaps they can anticipate problems and develop appropriate adaptive solutions, and understand why we must change our attitudes towards the natural world.

The second component reflects the requirement of the public health system to become embedded within the community so as to create an effective environment within which public health is seen as a valued and respected institution that actively and completely interacts with and advocates for the society it serves. Critically, in addition to its usual tasks, it will need to be a forceful advocate for the development and maintenance of the physical and social determinants of health. Its aim is to try to create a society that promotes the health of individuals both consciously, using its traditional tools, and unconsciously, using the tools of political persuasion, advertising, and advocacy. In so doing, it will use fewer resources, less technology and less money than traditional healthcare. It will not prevent all illness and will not be ideal; there will be glitches and mistakes, but it may be the best resource available in an uncertain, changing world.

For the remaining two components, the first: the 'set of disciplines', may be hard to maintain because a community, or a region, may lack the necessary educational facilities and resources for appropriate professional development; the second: the 'manner of practice', will vary by local needs, resources, and abilities. Just how these two components can be effectively maintained (as living becomes simpler) should become priorities for schools of public health everywhere.

Public health may well be the most important factor in ensuring the long-term survival of a society, and all of the above components are critical to its success. Medical care clearly is essential, but as resources decline, it is unlikely to be able to respond to a heavy burden of disease. Thus, illness prevention and health promotion must predominate. Public health must prevent illnesses from occurring and work to create those conditions of living that promote health.

A scenario

To gain some idea of what might happen, let us explore one plausible scenario. Consider a time-frame of 40 years, until 2050 – approximately the professional lifetime of today's graduates. They will experience the initial shocks and issues of a world undergoing profound change. This may cause considerable angst by virtue of the fact that they grew up with today's paradigm of consumption and hence they may reflect on what life was like while simultaneously experiencing what life is becoming. As adults, we generally view our current lifestyles as better than when we were children; today's graduates will have the opposite experience, at least in material matters. But, unlike the more recent generations who knew there were problems rising (but ignored them), today's generation is stuck. They have to deal with it.

This scenario differs from most other disaster plans in that the 'disaster' extends over many years and any assumption of support from 'outside' is unrealistic. Apart from the Sun there is no outside physical support for Earth, and, in the current predicament, all of Earth is affected; hence, we are on our own. Such a global perspective is not too useful from a public health perspective, so let us consider a more local situation. This is relevant because, over time, transportation will become increasingly limited, our lives and communities will also become much more independent, or isolated, and we will have to depend on local resources and abilities to meet local demand. For example, today shipping goods from one side of the world to the other is commonplace; later this century, such transportation will be extremely expensive, even if possible. Indeed, shipping goods across a country may become inordinately expensive and challenging and likely take longer. Personal travel will be similarly constrained.

Since this scenario presents a 'slow disaster', it will not happen overnight; the rate of change is uncertain, but the trend is unequivocal. It is also a cumulative disaster; one crisis and challenge piling onto another. It will be driven by steadily diminishing supplies of energy and other resources, as well as the need to attend to the consequences of climate change, such as flooding, drought, severe storms, sea-level rise and food insecurity. All of these are real problems happening right now; in time, they will spread to where we live. Although some communities and regions will have more resources than others, let us assume that only the most fundamental public health facilities and services are present, with only a few health 'professionals' having basic supplies. This could apply even in large cities, which are often formed of smaller communities and, as government revenues drop, services will diminish and public health services may end up being provided at the community level. Local health workers, even in cities, may be trained to manage minor health problems and also to act as the eyes and ears of public health, also teaching health issues to the public. Standards may slip, but they need not fall precipitously.

The detailed structure and function of any given public health system will be dictated largely by local demands and the local resources available to meet those demands. Local resources form some of the critical elements of infrastructure. Thus, what is useful in London may be useless in Lagos. Each community has different resources, strengths, weaknesses, cultures, health needs and demands, and the health system must reflect these. Clearly, fundamentals exist, such as clean water, good sewage, safe housing and adequate, affordable food; these are requirements for all societies, but they are met locally. Each community must write its own book. The long-term goal is to make a public health service that can function more or less independently of external sources of support. Although fortunately not today's situation, it will be the situation for a society with decreased and costly energy, especially transport energy. While world commerce today is characterized by globalization, this is unlikely to last. Global trade depends on long, complex supply systems, plus reliable, inexpensive transportation. Over time, global trade will diminish because the fiscal and physical resources needed to maintain them and to respond to global change will be depleted (Curtis, 2009). The logistics of supply will change, and 'just-in-time' delivery of materials may become unrealistic; local storage may be necessary, as will the need to find closer sources, particularly local ones, and to look for alternatives. This will improve local resilience and, while it is likely that, over time, some communities will fail, and even die, the diversity of local responses may enhance humanity's overall likelihood of survival.

While stable external support systems and effective levels of government exist today, the events and circumstances likely to occur over the next decades raise the prospect that external supervision and support systems will become increasingly tenuous and unstructured. Ultimately, any given public health system may have to do without. This independence means that a community has to depend more on itself and the ability and willingness of its members to respond to disasters. If Town A is hit by a disaster, it may take a long time for Towns B, C and D to arrive with help, or even be aware of it, or do something about it, if they can. This problem already exists in many communities, but it will become significantly greater over the coming decades.

The public health system during transition must be resilient and, while it probably will be under some form of higher supervision, it will need a high level of local independence. It has to be able and competent, but humble, not omnipotent. It cannot do everything, and it must be aware of and defend its limits. It has to be sustainable and integrated with other local institutions to share tasks and resources. It has to be assertive, but non-competitive, and based not on the logic of abundance, but on the logic of constraint. During this time of transition and uncertainty, it must meet the needs of the present, but work towards a time when we will live on what is available locally, what is renewable and what is ecologically sustainable. It should salvage the useful products and materials that it can. It should not plan on securing newer, or fancier, or more energy-intensive goods and services; nor should such goods and services be considered acceptable. It should set its priorities, determine its resources and define its choices.

Today, whether we recognize it or not, we are entering the period of transition. It is a time to learn, to accept, to educate and to adapt. It is a time of dropping and retaining, and exchanging ideas and thoughts in moving to products more suitable to our needs and abilities. It is a move from high technology to intermediate technology, to low technology. It is also moving from throw-away to durability. Some might say this describes a plan for decline, not for growth. It does describe a decline in our material way of living, we have no choice. But, at the same time, this plan says nothing about decline in the critical aspects of humanity: in our relationships with others, our chance to reconnect with our neighbours and families, our philosophies, our old myths and legends and the new ideas and cultures that will arise; indeed, of enriching our lives both individually and collectively. As we rekindle our relationship with nature, with our community, and with each other, and develop the non-material aspects of our lives, these elements of humanity will become enriched.

Most importantly, the transition will, with some luck, bring us back to Earth; to the realization that we are a part of the cosmos, that every component of that cosmos has a relationship with every other part, and that each is essential. We have been gifted with unsurpassed intellect, imagination and creativity, on a minuscule planet in a minuscule part of the universe. We have fully explored our globe; we cannot move to another planet and start over. We have played with the fire and nearly burned the house down. We must use what we have now to survive, thrive and rebuild our new world on Earth.

Note

1 An excellent website devoted to transition is: http://transitionculture.org.

References

Berry, T. (1999) *The Great Work: Our Way Into the Future*, Bell Tower, New York, NY

Berry, W. (2000) *Life Is a Miracle: An Essay Against Modern Superstition*, Counterpoint, Washington, DC

Berry, W. (2008) 'The way of ignorance', in B. Vitek and W. Jackson (eds) *The Virtues of Ignorance: Complexity, Sustainability, and the Limits of Knowledge*, The University Press of Kentucky, Lexington, KY

Curtis, F. (2009) 'Peak globalization: Climate change, oil depletion and global trade', *Ecological Economics*, vol 69, pp427–434

Greer, J. M. 'The economics of decline', *The Archdruid Report*, 20 May, available at www.energybulletin.net/node/48971

Hecker, T. E. (2007) 'The post-petroleum future of academic libraries', *Journal of Scholarly Publishing*, vol 38, no 4, pp183–199

Heinberg, R. and Mander, J. (2009) *Searching For a Miracle: 'Net Energy' Limits and the Fate of Industrial Society*, False Solution Series no 4, The Post Carbon Institute, San Francisco, CA

IEA (2004) *World Energy Outlook, 2004*, International Energy Agency, Paris, France

Last, J. M. (2007) *A Dictionary of Public Health*, Oxford University Press, Inc, New York, NY

Leopold, A. (1970) 'The land ethic', in *A Sand County Almanac, With Essays on Conservation From Round River*, Ballantine Books, New York, NY, pp237–261

MacKay, D. J. C. (2009) *Sustainable Energy – Without the Hot Air*, UIT Cambridge Ltd, Cambridge, UK

Mirza, S. (2006) 'Durability and sustainability of infrastructure – a state-of-the-art report', *Canadian Journal of Civil Engineering*, vol 33, no 6, pp639–649

NRTEE (2011) *Paying the Price: The Economic Impacts of Climate Change for Canada*, National Round Table on the Environment and the Economy, Ottawa, Canada

Romm, J. (2010) 'The year of living dangerously. Masters: "The stunning extremes we witnessed gives me concern that our climate is showing the early signs of instability"', *Climate Progress*, 23 December, available at http://thinkprogress.org/romm/2010/12/23/207216/the-year-of-living-dangerously-masters-weather-extremes-climate-change (accessed 24 January 2012)

Rosen, R., Electris, C. and Raskin, P. D. (2010) *Global Scenarios for the Century Ahead: Searching for Sustainability*, Tellus Institute, Boston, MA

Spady, D. W. (2011) 'Public health in a time of resource depletion and ecological disintegrity', in L. Westra, K. Bosselmann and C. Soskolne *Globalization and Ecological Integrity in Science and International Law*, Cambridge Scholars Publishing, Newcastle upon Tyne, UK, pp392–411

Thompson, C., Cullian, J., Bloomsbury, A. and Englebretson, R. (2008) *The Problem is More than Money: Global Infrastructure Crisis*, Deloitte LLP, available at www.deloitte.com/assets/Dcom-UnitedStates/Local%20Assets/Documents/us_consulting_globalinfrastructurecrisis_0708.pdf (accessed 24 January 2012)

WHO (2006) *Constitution of the World Health Organization*, World Health Organization Basic Documents, 45th Edition, Supplement, World Health Organization, Geneva, Switzerland, pp1–18

11 Migrants' access to healthcare in the Czech Republic

Ethical challenges

Helena Hnilicová and Karolína Dobiášová

Introduction

Migrants everywhere are considered a vulnerable group with specific health needs (Tulchinsky and Varavikova, 2009). Discrimination, language and cultural barriers, and working in low-paying positions in high-risk sectors and marginal living conditions on the edge of poverty are important factors affecting their health (Ingleby *et al.*, 2005). Owing to increasing numbers of immigrants, the issue of health and migration is becoming a recognized issue in public health and health policy, particularly in developed countries (Mladovsky, 2009). Ensuring accessibility and quality healthcare to migrants, as well as public health protection within the host country are considered urgent migration-related policy targets (Ingleby *et al.*, 2005; Mladovsky, 2007).

Addressing the health needs of migrants has been discussed within the European Union (EU) in the context of its fundamental rights agenda. The European Economic and Social Committee (EESC), an advisory body of the European Commission (EC), considers that the EC should strengthen its fundamental rights culture at the EU level. Proposed ways to do this include monitoring legislative proposals and the whole legislative process, plus assuring their full compliance with the Charter of Fundamental Human Rights of the European Union in all Member States.

Democracy in the European multicultural environment in the twenty-first century can be improved through better participation of residents from non-EU countries, whose right of participation are, in some member states, more or less restricted. To encourage integration of immigrants, the EESC proposes that Europe's municipal and regional authorities set up migration-related forums and platforms, the purpose of which is to enable civil society organizations focusing on migration to participate in, and to be consulted on, integration policies that can address all forms of discrimination and inequity (EESC, 2011).

The Czech Republic belongs among those Member States whose healthcare integration policy is discriminatory. Although the Czech Republic entered the EU in 2004, the current Czech migrant-related health legislation still includes certain enactments which create real barriers in access to needed healthcare by legally resident, but non-EU migrants. This chapter focuses on the impacts of existing legislation on healthcare accessibility to selected groups of migrants in the Czech Republic and reflects on its ethical consequences.

Immigration in the Czech Republic

Immigration and its accompanying social processes are significant new phenomena in the predominantly homogeneous Czech post-war environment. Over the past 20 years, the Czech Republic has had rapid population growth due to migration. Between 1990 and 2006, the number of foreigners in the Czech Republic increased almost tenfold (Czech Statistical Office, 2009, 2010, 2011). Even despite a drop in the number of legal and long-term resident foreigners in the Czech Republic, caused by the economic crisis, more than 420,000 foreigners were living legally in the Czech Republic in mid-2010; this is about 4 per cent of the population (Czech Statistical Office, 2011).

As in other developed countries, there is an unknown number of illegal migrants residing in the country. About 60 per cent of migrants in the Czech Republic are male. For a long time, the composition of migrants by nationality has remained unchanged. The largest groups include Ukrainians 32 per cent, Slovaks 18 per cent, Vietnamese 14 per cent, Russians 7 per cent and Poles 6 per cent. Most migrants are economic migrants, and thus mostly of working age; thus, 77 per cent of migrants are between 20 and 65 years of age. People aged over 65 make up only 3 per cent of the population (Czech Statistical Office, 2011). Young people (those under 19 years of age) make up 20 per cent and, in the past few years, the number of children born to foreigners has gradually risen. All migrants are potential consumers of healthcare, thus ensuring its availability is important not only for them, but also to protect the public health of the general population (Hnilicová and Dobiášová, 2010).

In terms of accessibility to healthcare in the Czech Republic, migrants are not a homogeneous group. There is a range of subcategories of 'migrants', based on the type of migration: students, economic migrants and their families, asylum seekers, refugees and illegal migrants (Mladovsky, 2009; Spallek *et al.*, 2010). This chapter focuses on economic migrants and their families legally residing for the long term in the Czech Republic. The other categories of migrants are not the subject of this study and will be mentioned only incidentally as needed.

The health of migrants in the Czech Republic

There are two basic sources of information that describe the health of migrants in the Czech Republic. The first consists of routine statistical data and the second are data obtained from specific research and survey samples

(Dobiášová and Vyskočilová, 2004; Dobiášová *et al.*, 2006). In summary, existing knowledge is not comprehensive enough and does not cover all groups of foreigners equally. Because of this, the available data provide an incomplete picture of health, healthcare needs, and factors affecting the health of migrants.

Access to routine statistics to describe the health of migrants who live and work in the Czech territory as a whole is very limited, because most of the statistics on mortality and morbidity lack data on ethnic origin. Nevertheless, some data do exist. These mainly concern tuberculosis (TB), sexually transmitted diseases (STDs) and HIV/AIDS. There is also mandatory reporting of work-related injuries and whether or not the injured person is a foreigner.

Since 2000, the Czech Statistical Office has monitored various data describing healthcare utilization by foreigners ('foreigners' is a term used in all official Czech statistics and documents related to migrants). However, while interpreting these data, several limitations must be considered. Only hospitalization data and only those foreigners who are not insured in the public health insurance framework are monitored; however, three-quarters of economically active foreigners in the Czech Republic participate in public health insurance, thus any picture of health utilization is incomplete (General Health Insurance Company of the Czech Republic, 2010). It can be improved by using the results of several research projects carried out in the last two decades in the Czech Republic; these provide supplementary data on the health and healthcare needs of migrants (Nesvadbová *et al.*, 1998; Dobiášová and Vyskočilová, 2004; Dobiášová *et al.*, 2006; Tóthová *et al.*, 2010).

Migrants' health, health determinants and healthcare utilization

Very specific and detailed information on migrants' health in general is available from the surveys described above that investigated migrants' health and healthcare utilization patterns. Although not strictly representative, these studies may provide useful insights into health and health-related issues for some migrant groups. Most of the studies focused on legal migrants from the former USSR and who comprise 40 per cent of all migrants in the Czech Republic. Valid and reliable data were provided by a comparative study on subjective perceptions of health and health determinants, as well as estimates of healthcare utilization made in 2004 (Dobiášová and Vyskočilová, 2004).

Equal numbers of migrants and comparable Czechs were balanced according to gender and age (n = 1,062, migrants and Czechs). Significant differences were identified between migrants from the Former Soviet Union and the sample of Czechs. The results showed a large working load as well as very risky working conditions for the workers from the Former Soviet Union. Migrants usually worked more hours per day and many regularly worked six days per week. As a consequence, the occurrence of work-related injuries was three times higher than that of the Czechs. Additionally, the lifestyles and health-related behaviour of migrants appeared to be more risky. There were significantly more smokers, and heavy smokers, among them than among the Czech group. They also consumed more alcoholic beverages.

On the other hand, both genders of migrants from the Former Soviet Union indicated better subjective health, fewer chronic diseases, and reported fewer health problems and pain. This phenomenon, called 'the healthy migrant effect' (Mladovsky, 2009; Kristiansen *et al.*, 2007; McDonald and Kennedy, 2004), was confirmed also for migrants in the Czech Republic. Compared to the Czechs, migrants used healthcare services substantially less. Consequently, migrants also had significantly less sick leave than did the Czechs.

The health of migrants and the health risks they face can also be explored using routinely collected statistics. These statistics are mandatory, and deal mainly with work injuries and infectious diseases. The data shows that one of the most common health risks in the migrant community is injury, which is also the most common reason for hospitalization (Czech Statistical Office, 2009, 2010, 2011). Analysis of the statistics of the National Work Inspectorate shows that the rate of work-related injury among migrants has been growing in recent years (Hnilicová and Dobiášová, 2009). This may be related to the fact that 60 per cent of migrants are employed in higher-risk sectors such as construction and industry (Czech Statistical Office, 2010) Except for the above-mentioned extensive workload, another important contributing factor is the failure to follow health and safety rules because of poor language skills (Hnilicová and Dobiášová, 2009).

With respect to infectious diseases, the Czech epidemiological situation is stable and generally well-managed. However, a disquieting growth of some infectious diseases has been recorded in recent years. This is not due to TB. Despite the growing number of foreigners in the Czech Republic, the incidence of TB has been very low and is declining (Institute of Health Information and Statistics of the Czech Republic, 2011). However, foreigners pose a problem in that 20 per cent of the TB occurs among foreigners; this figure is significantly higher than what would be expected given the proportion of foreigners in the Czech population. The epidemiological situation in the Czech Republic is thus beginning to resemble the situation found in developed EU countries where the prevalence of TB among migrants is much higher than in the domestic population. More worrisome is the situation regarding HIV/AIDS and some sexually transmitted diseases. Although HIV/AIDS in the Czech Republic is still relatively uncommon, growing numbers of HIV positive individuals have been recorded in recent years. In the past few years, about 25 per cent of newly registered patients are migrants, most frequently from eastern Europe and sub-Saharan Africa (National Institute of Public Health,

2009, 2010, 2011). In this context, there is no doubt that efforts to provide all necessary healthcare to all migrants as well as relevant public health protection policy should be a priority for migration-related health policy.

Entitlement to healthcare among migrants in the Czech Republic

Healthcare is understood to be one of the basic human rights of Czech citizens, and accessibility to healthcare is a crucial aspect of the integration of migrants into the host country (Ingleby *et al.*, 2005). For Czech citizens, healthcare is guaranteed by the Czech Constitution, with the Charter of Fundamental Rights and Basic Freedoms as an integral part of the Constitution. Implementation of this right and the provision of necessary healthcare are assured by public health insurance based on the principle of solidarity. The health insurance premium is financed by a payroll tax divided between employees and employers (one-third to two-thirds). Children, mothers on maternity leave, pensioners, students (up to 26 years of age), the unemployed, poor people living below the poverty line and some other groups of citizens are exempt from paying the contributions; their health insurance is covered by the State (Ministry of Health of the Czech Republic, 1997).

As for migrants, there are some differences between EU citizens and non-EU citizens in their legal entitlement to Czech public health insurance. EU citizens residing in the Czech territory have the same access to public health insurance as Czechs. Public health insurance is also available for all regular migrants permanently residing in the Czech Republic, and to all migrants from the EU staying in the Czech territory for more than 90 days (long-term stay).

Migrants from non-EU countries can participate in public health insurance as long as a company or institution registered in the Czech Republic employs them. In addition, by law, all foreigners staying in the Czech Republic on a long-term basis are legally obliged to participate in some health insurance plan throughout their stay. Meeting this condition is required immediately after entering the country; entry to the country may be refused if a foreigner is unable to prove that he or she has adequate health insurance coverage (Ministry of the Interior of the Czech Republic, 1999). Foreigners may meet this requirement via public or commercial health insurance offered by several Czech commercial insurance bodies. They include the following migrant groups: all self-employed persons, all children up to 18, parents and partners of non-EU migrants (if they are not EU citizens or they have not secured permanent resident permits), students not covered by international agreements, and some others. The total number of all these migrants is estimated at 100,000–120,000 persons, representing about one-quarter of the total number of migrants in the Czech Republic (General Health Insurance Company of the Czech Republic, 2010; Czech Statistical Office, 2011).

Migrants' commercial health insurance versus Czech public health insurance

In comparison with public health insurance, conditions of commercial health insurance are significantly worse for migrants; this insurance is not generally in their interest. Like any other insurance product, it is based on market principles and the scope of the care covered is not well regulated by law. Current legislation provides only a very vague framework and is not concerned with the consumer's (i.e. the client's) protection. In accordance with EU regulations, it is only required to cover medical expenses amounting to a minimum of €60,000 (Ministry of the Interior of the Czech Republic, 1999). According to market principles, the health risks of the insured individual dictate the specific insurance contract and premium paid.

Although commercial health insurance is mandatory for defined groups of migrants, a commercial insurance company is not legally obligated to accept any application for insurance. Also, with commercial insurance there are frequent exclusions and limits to the extent of coverage. Thus, some risky applicants will be refused and will remain uninsured; this includes people with higher health risks, children born prematurely or born with congenital defects or with chronic diseases (Dobiášová *et al.*, 2006; Hnilicová *et al.*, 2010; Hnilicová and Dobiášová, 2009).

Commercial health insurance is particularly inadequate in cases of serious illness. For example, it does not include insulin-dependent diabetes, chronic renal insufficiency and haemodialysis, congenital defects, most psychiatric care, hepatitis, plus some other diseases. A further problem, especially for migrants, is that the insurance policy is usually written in rather complicated legalese, so it is difficult to understand its details for people without legal education or fluent language skills or good knowledge of the Czech healthcare system. There is a maximum limit to any payout, the premium increases as the insured person ages, and people over 70 are usually not insurable for an affordable price. Insurance premiums are paid in advance and as a lump sum for the whole insured period (up to two years). This creates a great financial burden, particularly for migrant families with children.

It is odd that some serious diseases, for which there is mandatory treatment in the Czech Republic, are explicitly excluded from all available kinds of commercial insurance. This concerns illnesses where the sick patient may be not only dangerous to himself/herself, but to those around him/her and, therefore, his/her hospitalization and treatment are necessary. These are primarily psychiatric illnesses, but also include mental disorders connected with drug and alcohol abuse. Also excluded are sexually transmitted diseases including HIV/AIDS, the treatment of which is mandatory according to Act No. 258/2000 on the Protection of Public Health.

As a result of these limits, exclusions, and high costs, the commercial health insurance for a large number of foreigners in the Czech Republic presents many serious problems regarding the provision of necessary healthcare. Prematurely born children and children born disabled or with congenital defects are considered most vulnerable, since they remain uninsured even when they urgently require intensive neonatal care. Despite this fact, in practice, necessary intensive care is fully provided for such children. Legally, as well as ethically, Czech physicians are obliged to provide all care required to such children. Not only under medical law, but also for common ethical reasons, it is not acceptable in Czech culture to leave any human being affected by a serious health threat without help and necessary care. Practically speaking, however, the critical issue is that in many cases nobody pays for such care. It is a fact that a part of necessary care provided to migrants remains financially unaddressed (Czech Statistical Office, 2009, 2010, 2011; Hnilicová and Dobiášová, 2011).

Discussion

Health policy dealing with migrants or with migration issues as applied in practice is not being fully implemented in accordance with Czech integration policy and as declared in official government documents (Government of the Czech Republic, 2011). The Czech political community is aware of this problem. Elimination of existing inequalities between migrants from EU member states and migrants from non-EU countries regarding access to public health insurance has been a priority of Czech government migration policy for several years.

More recently, the Czech Parliament adopted an amendment to the Immigration Act which responds to some of these problems. For example, commercial insurance companies will no longer be able to apply certain exclusions from insurance coverage (e.g. necessary treatment in a situation of self-inflicted harm or injury, such as a suicide attempt, or a sports injury). The financial ceiling for healthcare coverage was also increased to €60,000; for many years, it was only €30,000. The amount of insurance coverage must be greater than that needed for emergency care to preserve and extend life.

The above-mentioned changes certainly are improvements in the health insurance situation for migrants. Nevertheless, the analysis of insurance conditions shows that none of the available products of commercial insurance in the Czech Republic provide a sufficient guarantee that the necessary healthcare costs will be reimbursed to foreigners. In practice, neither foreigners nor healthcare institutions can be certain that the healthcare provided will be reimbursed. Aside from the ethical and humanitarian reasons concerning foreigners' equal right to healthcare, the purpose of foreigners' statutory duty to be insured is to ensure that, in accordance with the public interest, the enforceable (with difficulty) claims of healthcare institutions do not arise. These claims rise from healthcare which was provided, but not paid.

Equal rights to healthcare for foreigners would mean also that physicians will have reasonable assurance that they will be paid for the healthcare services they provide to persons legally living in the Czech Republic. Research shows that the fear of no reimbursement affects a physician's decisions when providing healthcare to foreigners. Together with the administrative difficulties of commercial healthcare, this creates barriers and discriminatory conditions which are ethically unacceptable (Dobiášová and Hnilicová, 2011). The current products of the Czech commercial health insurance companies, however, do not meet the needs of migrants, nor do they satisfy the public interest as there are too many exceptions and the possibility to refuse an applicant is high. At the same time, in the case of life-saving healthcare that must be provided ethically or for public health protection reasons, such as mandatory treatment, medical institutions or physicians cannot take the limits and exceptions into consideration and must provide the needed care in all such cases.

Conclusions

Not only is it unjustifiable to discriminate between access to healthcare by foreigners coming from EU countries and those coming from elsewhere, it is also unethical. In the case of children, such discrimination is also not in accord with the Convention on the Rights of the Child (OHCHR, 1989), which was adopted by the Czech Republic in 1993. Article 24 of this agreement guarantees needed healthcare to all children within the territory of the state without exception. The fact that a significant number of foreigners from non-EU countries who legally reside in the Czech Republic must rely on commercial healthcare is very unusual compared with the rest of the EU (Mighealthnet, 2007). In most EU countries, foreigners with a long-term residence permit are basically entitled to the same rights and commitments as nationals of the state in question (Mighealthnet, 2007).

The most urgent problem of Czech health policy in relation to migrants remains the inadequate guarantee of a legal entitlement to healthcare. This concerns a large group of migrants with long-term residence, since the current legal regulation discriminates against migrants coming from countries outside the EU. Despite long-standing efforts of NGOs working for migrants (e.g. the Multicultural Centre in Prague and the Counselling Centre for Citizenship and Human Rights) and the additional efforts of some academic institutions (e.g. the Institute of Public Health and Medical Law at First Faculty of Medicine, Charles University) under the auspices of the Czech Republic Government Council for Human Rights to solve the current situation, no change has been made. The inclusion of foreigners from outside the EU in the public health insurance scheme has not yet been achieved. Amendments to the relevant legal act have been repeatedly refused, most recently in August 2011. Failure of the legislative process to make the needed changes might have been influenced through lobbying by the commercial insurance companies whose objections, raised through the Commercial Chamber, were eventually accepted by the government.

References

Czech Statistical Office (2009) *Foreigners in the Czech Republic 2008*, Czech Statistical Office, Prague, Czech Republic

Czech Statistical Office (2010) *Foreigners in the Czech Republic 2009*, Czech Statistical Office, Prague, Czech Republic

Czech Statistical Office (2011) *Foreigners in the Czech Republic 2010*, Czech Statistical Office, Prague, Czech Republic

Dobiášová, K. and Hnilicová, H. (2011) 'Migrants and health care from the perspective of practice in the Czech Republic', *Praktický lékař*, vol 91, no10, pp590–595

Dobiášová, K. and Vyskočilová, O. (2004) 'Potřeba a spotřeba zdravotní péče imigrantů', *Zdravotnictví v ČR*, no 1, pp32–39

Dobiášová, K., Křečková, N. and Angelovská, O. (2006) *Zdravotní péče o děti cizinců. Realita a zkušenost*, Institute of Health Policy and Economics, Kostelec nad Černými lesy, Czech Republic

EESC (2011) 'EESC opinion: cooperation in integrating immigrants', CESE 1174/2011 – SOC/411, European Economic and Social Committee, available at www.eesc.europa.eu/?i=portal.en.eesc-opinions-highlights&page=2

General Health Insurance Company of the Czech Republic (2010) 'Výroční zpráva VZP za rok 2009', Prague, Czech Republic, available at www.vzp.cz/uploads/document/PDF/vyrocni_zprava_2009.pdf

Government of the Czech Republic (2011) 'Aktualizovaná Koncepce integrace cizinců. Společné soužití', Government of the Czech Republic, Prague, Czech Republic, available at www.cizinci.cz/files/clanky/741/Usneseni_vlady_ 090220 11.pdf

Hnilicová, H. and Dobiášová, K. (2009) 'State of art. Version 1', available at www.mighealth.net/cz/index.php/State_of_Art_Czech_Republic._Version_1

Hnilicová, H. and Dobiášová, K. (2010) 'Migranti a veřejné zdraví ve světle výzkumů', in *Přínos a potenciál výzkumu v oblasti migrace*, Ministry of the Interior of the Czech Republic, Prague, Czech Republic

Hnilicová, H. and Dobiášová, K. (2011) 'Migrants' health and access to health care in the Czech Republic', *Central European Journal of Public Health*, vol 19, no 3, pp134–138

Hnilicová, H., Dobiášová, K. and Čižinský, P. (2010) 'Komerční zdravotní pojištění cizinců', Multicultural Centre Prague, Prague, Czech Republic, available at www.migraceonline.cz/e-knihovna/?x=2219641

Ingleby, D., Chimienti, M., Ormond, M., De Freitas, C. and Hatziprokopiou, P. (2005) 'Social integration and mobility: education, housing and health. IMISCOE Cluster B5 State of the art report', in L. Fonseca and J. Malheiros (eds) *Study on Regional and Urban Planning No. 67,* Centre of Geographical Studies, Lisbon, Portugal

Institute of Health Information and Statistics of the Czech Republic (2011) 'Tuberculosis and respiratory disease in 2010', Institute of Health Information and Statistics of the Czech Republic, Prague, Czech Republic, available at www.uzis.cz/en/publications/tuberculosis-and-respiratory-diseases-2010

Kristiansen, M, Mygind, A. and Krasnik, A. (2007) 'Health effects of migration', *Danish Medical Bulletin*, vol 54, no 1, pp46–47

McDonald, J. T. and Kennedy, S. (2004) 'Insights into the "healthy immigrant effect": health status and health service use of immigrants to Canada', *Social Science and Medicine*, vol 59, no 8, pp1613–1627

Mighealthnet (2007) 'State of the Art Reports', Mighealthnet project, available at www.mighealth.net/index.php/State_of_the_Art_Reports

Ministry of Health of the Czech Republic (1997) 'On public health insurance and on revisions of some relevant acts', Act No. 48/1997 Coll. as subsequently amended, Ministry of Health of the Czech Republic, Prague, Czech Republic

Ministry of the Interior of the Czech Republic (1999) 'On the residence of foreign nationals in the Czech Republic', Act No. 326/1999 Coll. as subsequently amended, Ministry of the Interior of the Czech Republic, Prague, Czech Republic

Mladovsky, P. (2007) 'Migrant health in EU', *Eurohealth*, vol 13, no 1, pp9–11

Mladovsky, P. (2009) 'A framework for analysing migrant health policies in Europe', *Health Policy*, vol. 93, no 1, pp55–63

National Institute of Public Health (2009) 'Zpráva o výskytu a šíření HIV/AIDS za rok 2008', National Institute of Public Health, Prague, Czech Republic, available at www.szu.cz/tema/prevence/zprava-o-vyskytu-a-sireni-hiv-aids-za-rok-2009

National Institute of Public Health (2010) 'Zpráva o výskytu a šíření HIV/AIDS za rok 2009', National Institute of Public Health, Prague, Czech Republic, available at www.szu.cz/tema/prevence/zprava-o-vyskytu-a-sireni-hiv-aids-za-rok-2009

National Institute of Public Health (2011) 'Zpráva o výskytu a šíření HIV/AIDS za rok 2010', National Institute of Public Health, Prague, Czech Republic, available at www.szu.cz/tema/prevence/zprava-o-vyskytu-a-sireni-hiv-aids-za-rok-2010

Nesvadbová, L., Rutsch, J., Kroupa, A., Vajnarová, J. and Sojka, S. (1998) *Zdravotní, psychologické a sociální aspekty migrace*, Ministry of Health Czech Republic, Prague, Czech Republic

OHCHR (1989) 'Convention on the rights of the child', Office of the United Nations High Commissioner for Human Rights, available at www2.ohchr.org/english/law/crc.htm

Spallek, J., Zeeb, H. and Razum, O. (2010) 'Prevention among immigrants: the example of Germany ', *BMC Public Health*, vol 92, no 10, pp1–6

Tóthová, V. *et al.* (2010) *Zabezpečení efektivní ošetřovatelské péče o vietnamskou a čínskou minoritu*, Triton, Prague, Czech Republic

Tulchinsky, T. H. and Varavikova, E. A. (2009) *The New Public Health*, Elsevier Academic Press, San Diego, CA

12 Gender, violation of human rights and mental health

Yuliya Lyamzina

Introduction

The World Health Assembly in its 1996 resolution WHA 49.25 (WHA, 1996) declared violence a leading public health problem. While in parts of the world today there is significant progress in lifestyle, social status and the rights of women, this progress is uneven. According to the Director General of the World Health Organization (WHO), Dr Margaret Chan:

> ... not everyone can benefit from this progress and many women and girls are still unable to reach their full potential because of persistent health, social and gender inequalities and health systems inadequacies. (WHO, 2009)

Women's health is becoming an urgent priority because of persisting armed conflicts all over the world. In the foreword to the study on *Women, Peace and Security*, the then UN Secretary-General, Kofi A. Annan, pointed out one critical, tragic feature, apart from poverty, of all conflicts taking place:

> [T]he struggle for scarce resources and violations of human rights and its disproportionate impact of suffering of women and girls. Besides bombings, famines, epidemics, mass executions, torture, arbitrary imprisonments, forced migration, ethnic cleansing, threats and intimidation, women and girls also suffer from sexual and gender based violence and different kind of exploitation. (UN, 2002)

Violence against women occurs globally and in all parts of society. In many countries, it is the norm; even worse, it is a part of widely tolerated and supported cultural practices. We see violence everywhere, not only in armed conflicts, where it is used as a weapon, but also during peacetime. Daily, there are news reports about emergencies, natural disasters, terrorist attacks and mass violence. The rise in mental and psychosocial problems is therefore not surprising. Unfortunately, scientific evidence regarding mental health and psychosocial support during such events remains scanty (Inter-Agency Standing Committee, 2007).

Gender

The WHO estimated that in 2007 there were 3.3 billion women globally. Only 15 per cent of them were living in high-income countries, and almost half were in southeast Asia and western Pacific regions (WHO, 2009). Nearly 50 per cent of children under nine years of age live in low-income countries, whereas one in three women over 60 years of age live in high-income countries. (Table 12.1)

Table 12.1 Distribution of women and girls around the world by age and country-income in 2007

	Low-income countries		*Middle-income countries*		*High-income countries*		*Total*	
	n	%	*n*	%	*n*	%	*n*	%
Age group								
0–9	300,768	50	241,317	40	57,456	10	599,541	18
10–19	267,935	45	263,464	44	61,577	10	592,975	18
20–59	580,014	34	875,052	51	276,140	16	1,731,206	52
60+	86,171	22	183,099	48	115,681	30	384,952	12
Total	1,234,888	37	1,562,932	47	510,854	15	3,308,673	100

Source: United Nations Population Division, as cited in WHO (2009)

Most armed conflict occurs in low-income countries, and conflicts are common; 190 armed conflicts have taken place since World War II (WHO, 2002). About a quarter were between states; the rest were within states. Most conflicts lasted under six months. Some went on for many years, or are still active (for example, Viet Nam, Angola, Colombia and Afghanistan). The total number of armed conflicts was under 20 in the 1950s, over 30 in the 1960s and 1970s, and over 50 during the late 1980s. After the 1980s, there was a sharp increase in conflicts in Europe because of the collapse of the communist regimes in eastern Europe and the former Soviet Union. In general, the size and area of the conflict has changed radically in the past two centuries (WHO, 2002).

Today, the lives of women are still affected by health, environmental, economic, demographic, cultural and social factors. However, during armed conflicts, emergencies, and disasters, besides the common problems that such events present, women face specific gender-related problems (WHO, 2009).

Pincha states: 'women typically suffer the burden of gender more than men do. Gender refers to socially constructed stereotypes, roles, opportunities and relationships associated with being male or female' (Pincha, 2008). In her book *Gender Sensitive Disaster Management: A Toolkit for Practitioners*, she describes the common, and often compulsory, roles of women worldwide. Pincha's words are still valid: there is a 'sharp division between reproductive and productive spheres, despite the fact that they form an inter-related whole and feed into each other' (Pincha, 2008).

It is obvious that:

- women do most of the reproductive work, which is completely unpaid;
- women's work is still less valued;
- although women contribute significantly to the household economy, they are still not recognized as breadwinners;
- the unwillingness and/or reluctance of men on acquiring such skills as cooking, taking care of children, and household chores, due to gender role stereotypes has an adverse impact on women;
- women are often excluded from decision-making roles at various levels, though decisions taken usually concern women; and
- socially constructed gender boundaries are fluid and dynamic (Pincha, 2008).

In addition, many stereotypes and myths exist about women globally. Thus, women should be humble, have long hair, have children, take care of their husbands and the elderly, do all domestic work, be shy and not to be heard, and be sacrificing. In contrast, men should not show emotions, should be the only breadwinners, should act rough and tough, should fulfil their sexual urges, drink in order to cope, and show power over women. These stereotypes and myths are systematically described in Table 12.2.

Table 12.2 Myth versus reality

Myths	*Facts*
Women are vulnerable	Women are rendered vulnerable by social, economic and political arrangements of society
Gender equals women and their problems	Gender unpacks and questions the power relationship between women and men, as well as the invisibility of transgender persons
Addressing practical gender needs is enough to empower women	Interventions to be sensitive need to address both practical gender needs of women and men as well as strategic gender needs of women
Only men do 'productive' work	Women's household work sustains the productive work of men and typically consumes more time than men's work
'Access' is enough to empower women	Access is different from having control over what one has access to
Domestic violence is a private affair	Domestic violence impacts societal gender relations
Domestic violence affects only the spouse (typically women)	Domestic violence against women affects the entire household, including children and the elderly; it is a far-reaching problem, affecting all sectors of society and warrants being in the forefront of political discourse
Income-generating activities address the livelihood concerns of women	For women, livelihoods encompass the patterns of expenditure as much as the sources of income generation

Source: Pincha (2008)

The changes in traditional roles of women

With so many conflicts around the world, the traditional role of women is changing everywhere; in families, in communities, and in the public domain. Armed conflicts have led to many female-headed households because men are killed, kidnapped, imprisoned or disappear. Women must take over household responsibilities, care for children, the elderly, farms and animals, earn money, trade, and become active outside their homes. These changes have forced women to develop new survival skills. This is good for them, their confidence, their family and the whole country. Charlotte Lindsey says:

> Some of these 'empowerment' changes may be seen as positive developments for women. However, they must be viewed through the lens of the loss, poverty and deprivation endemic to war, and the fact that in many societies women still only gain status (economic and social) through marriage. (Lindsey, 2001)

This brings us to another problem: widowhood and disappearances. Owing to armed conflicts and the resulting casualties, there are many widows in war-torn countries. But it often happens that 'women who had lost both their husbands and their assets may not receive compensation for their losses' (Pincha, 2008).

The impact of widowhood differs between cultures and religions (Lindsey, 2001). It affects a woman's physical safety, identity and mobility, her access to basic goods and services, and her right to inheritance, land and property, in addition to the wider impact on the community. Besides this, they often face many other problems because they cannot divorce and start a new life.

Research

Few studies focus on political and armed conflict as a determinant of women's health. The research described here brings new knowledge about the suffering of women and the determinants of their health in eight countries. It is a cross-sectional pilot study, performed to demonstrate the feasibility of, and validate methods for a larger study. A multilingual approach was used (Lyamzina, 2011).

Study aim

The study aimed to:

- identify, systematically, countries where women are affected by armed conflict and/or the permanent state of conflict or violence;

- estimate the occurrence of psychiatric morbidity and to identify specific vulnerable groups among women living in the study areas;
- highlight the state of health of women and their access to healthcare;
- highlight the status of mental health of women (stress, depression, anxiety);
- measure levels of anxiety, depression and post-traumatic stress disorder (PTSD);
- reflect on the social coherence of women (e.g. accessibility of education); and
- formulate recommendations related to prevention based on the results.

Study hypotheses

The hypotheses tested were:

1 Depression, anxiety and PTSD are occurring among female civilians who are not 'direct victims' of violence.
2 Women in selected countries are exposed to similar traumatic events and will have similar distributions of PTSD (regardless of nationality, origin, background, religion).
3 Civilian women suffer from social trauma because of the violent environment and permanent fear in which they are forced to live.
4 PTSD correlates with age, education, social, marital status and living conditions.

Methods

Criteria for study countries were gathered from the literature. The following criteria were used:

- presence of armed conflict lasting more than 10 years; and
- feasibility of doing the study within the country (e.g. access, obtaining study permission, technical assistance, cooperation with local NGOs, governments, communication, language skills).

The eight countries meeting the study criteria were Azerbaijan, Chechnya, Colombia, Dagestan, Ethiopia, Palestine, Sudan and Turkmenistan. Sudan and Ethiopia are treated as a single region in the tables below, because the questionnaires came from the border between the two countries.

Participants

Females were selected for each country separately, following two basic criteria: an age between 18 and 71 years, and living within a settled community or refugee camp in the chosen area. Women excluded were:

- members of the army, military, police;
- female prisoners;
- patients confined to institutions (e.g., psychiatric hospitals).

Questionnaires were distributed to 30 women in each country. A stratified random sampling method was used to select participants. The women were invited to volunteer based on their willingness to fill in four questionnaires, respond to questions related to their past traumatic experience, the duration of the study, and our ability to access the completed questionnaires.

Women could refuse to participate, but the survey met almost no resistance, though the degree of distrust was high. The response rate was about 70 per cent.

Measures

No validated diagnostic questionnaires or culturally appropriate tools were available for the chosen countries. Different cultural aspects were accommodated during the research, and all necessary permissions were obtained. Each woman obtained the following material: letter of introduction (in the appropriate language), questionnaire 1, Hopkins Symptom Checklist-25 (HSCL-25), Beck Depression Inventory (BDI) and Post-traumatic Stress Diagnostic Scale (PDS).

QUESTIONNAIRE 1

For this pilot study a special questionnaire was designed in cooperation with several psychotherapists. Its purpose was to collect basic information regarding demographics, living circumstances, psychosocial status, physical health, and coping and support needs. It avoids leading questions, and includes cross-checking questions, and quantitative and qualitative aspects (Lyamzina, 2011).

Simple, mostly yes/no questions were chosen. The questionnaire was created and distributed in Russian, Spanish, English and Arabic. All versions were created and proofread by native speakers from related countries. The questionnaire was pre-tested on approximately 20 women having different education levels in three languages (Russian, Spanish and Arabic) in order to test its simplicity and clarity.

HOPKINS SYMPTOM CHECKLIST-25

The HSCL-25 was used to measure mental health status. It consists of 25 self-administered items. The first 10 symptoms measure levels of anxiety, the following 15 symptoms measure levels of depression and, in total, the 25 symptoms measure level of emotional distress. Item response values ranged from 1 to 4. Response 1 means 'not at all', response 2 'a little', response 3 'quite a bit' and response 4 'extremely'. Results are obtained by summing up the responses and then dividing by the number of answered items. An anxiety score, a depression score and a total score from 1 to 4 were calculated (Garieballa, 2004).

BECK DEPRESSION INVENTORY

The BDI is a free, widely used psychological tool that estimates the severity of depression. It consists of 21 questions, rated from 0–3, with a maximum possible score of 63. Scores of less than 9 reflect an absence of depression symptoms. Those from 10 to 18 suggest mild to moderate levels of depression; scores from 19 to 29 suggest moderate to severe levels of depression. Scores over 30 suggest extreme to severe depression (Malkina-Pych, 2009).

POST-TRAUMATIC STRESS DIAGNOSTIC SCALE

The presence of PTSD disorder was measured by PDS, obtained from Pearson Education. This is a self-administered test of 49 items that can be completed in 10–15 minutes if the person has at least an eight-grade level of education (Foa, 1995). Because the PDS is recommended to estimate and compare rates of PTSD in particular populations, it was a perfect tool to confirm or refute the results of previous questionnaires and to help compare rates of PTSD estimated by previous tools.

Statistical analysis of data

The collected data were analysed using the SPSS version 18 software. Descriptive statistics were determined for Questionnaire 1, HSCL-25 and BDI. Fisher's exact two-tailed test was used to determine the statistical differences of samples in selected countries. Non-parametric tests were used to assess differences between means. A p-value < 0.05 was used to assess statistical significance.

Results

Data were obtained from populations in Azerbaijan (settled community), Dagestan (settled community), Chechnya (settled community), Colombia (settled community and temporary shelters of internally displaced persons, IDPs), Palestine (settled community) and south Sudan–Ethiopia (refugee camp). Tables 12.3 to 12.7 show the results in the order in which they were obtained (Lyamzina, 2011).

Table 12.3 presents data about the questionnaires. About 70 per cent of those surveyed responded to Questionnaire 1, HSCL-25 and BDI, and almost 64 per cent for PTSD. Those declining to participate were similar to participants in terms of traumatic experience, but they either did not want to remember the trauma, or may have been doubtful that another research project would benefit them.

Table 12.3 Questionnaires used versus response frequency

	Dagestan		*Turkmenistan*		*Azerbaijan*		*Palestine*		*Colombia*		*South Sudan–Ethiopia*		*Chechnya*			
	n	%	*n*	%	*n*	%	*n*	%	*n*	%	*n*	%	*n*	%	*Total*	%
Questionnaire 1, HSCL-25, BDI																
Women admitted	30	100.0	30	100.0	30	100.0	30	100.0	30	100.0	30	100.0	30	100.0	210	100.0
Q given	30	100.0	30	100.0	30	100.0	30	100.0	30	100.0	30	100.0	30	100.0	210	100.0
Q rejected	6	20.0	8	26.6	4	13.3	10	33.3	0	0.0	4	13.3	12	40.0	44	21.0
Q not returned or lost	2	6.7	2	6.7	6	20.0	2	6.7	0	0.0	3	10.0	5	16.7	20	9.5
Q returned completed	22	73.3	20	66.7	20	66.7	18	60.0	30	100.0	23	76.7	13	43.3	146	69.5
PTSD																
Women admitted	30	100.0	30	100.0	30	100.0	30	100.0	30	100.0	30	100.0	30	100.0	210	100.0
Q given	30	100.0	30	100.0	30	100.0	30	100.0	30	100.0	30	100.0	30	100.0	210	100.0
Q rejected	6	20.0	10	33.3	4	13.3	20	66.7	0	0.0	4	13.3	12	40.0	56	26.7
Q not returned or lost	2	6.7	2	6.7	6	20.0	2	6.7	0	0.0	3	10.0	5	16.7	20	9.5
Q returned completed	22	73.3	18	60.0	20	66.7	8	26.6	30	100.0	23	76.7	13	43.3	134	63.8

Note Q = questionnaire.

Table 12.4 Socio-demographic characteristics

	Dagestan		*Turkmenistan*		*Azerbaijan*		*Palestine*		*Colombia*		*South Sudan–Ethiopia*		*Chechnya*			
	n	*%*	*n*	*%*	*n*	*%*	*n*	*%*	*n*	*%*	*n*	*%*	*n*	*%*	*Total*	*%*
Number of participants	22	100.0	20	100.0	20	100.0	18	100.0	30	100.0	23	100.0	13	100.0	146	100.0
Place of birth																
This town (village)	10	45.5	1	5.0	1	5.0	7	38.9	5	16.7	0	0.0	11	84.6	35	24.0
Another town (village)	6	27.3	0	0.0	0	0.0	7	38.9	1	3.3	21	91.3	0	0.0	35	24.0
Other region	3	13.6	0	0.0	0	0.0	2	11.1	24	80.0	0	0.0	0	0.0	29	19.8
Other country	3	13.6	19	95.0	19	95.0	2	11.1	0	0.0	2	8.7	2	15.4	47	32.2
Marital status																
Single	6	27.3	3	15.0	4	20.0	6	33.2	16	53.4	16	69.6	4	30.7	55	37.7
Married	13	59.2	16	80.0	12	60.0	10	55.6	10	33.3	0	0.0	7	53.9	68	46.6
Divorced	0	0.0	0	0.0	0	0.0	1	5.6	1	3.3	3	13.0	1	7.7	6	4.1
Widowed	3	13.5	1	5.0	4	20.0	1	5.6	3	10.0	4	17.4	1	7.7	17	11.6
Living																
Alone	5	22.7	2	10.0	3	15.0	0	0.0	5	16.7	18	78.3	2	15.4	35	24.0
With husband	2	9.1	3	15.0	2	10.0	3	16.7	2	6.7	0	0.0	3	23.0	15	10.3
With husband and children	11	50.0	9	45.0	9	45.0	7	38.9	15	50.0	0	0.0	4	30.8	55	37.7
With children	3	13.6	6	30.0	6	30.0	1	5.6	6	20.0	2	8.7	4	30.8	28	19.2
With partner	1	4.6	0	0.0	0	0.0	0	0.0	2	6.6	3	4.3	0	0.0	6	4.1

	Dagestan		*Turkmenistan*		*Azerbaijan*		*Palestine*		*Colombia*		*South Sudan–Ethiopia*		*Chechnya*			
	n	*%*	*n*	*%*	*n*	*%*	*n*	*%*	*n*	*%*	*n*	*%*	*n*	*%*	*Total*	*%*
Number of children																
0	5	22.7	3	15.0	0	0.0	1	5.6	5	16.7	18	78.3	2	15.4	34	23.3
1	3	13.6	4	20.0	6	30.0	1	5.6	4	13.3	2	8.7	2	15.4	23	15.8
2	6	27.3	4	20.0	8	40.0	1	5.6	8	26.7	2	8.7	3	23.1	34	23.3
3	6	27.3	6	30.0	4	20.0	4	22.2	8	26.7	1	4.3	5	38.5	30	20.6
4	2	9.1	3	15.0	2	10.0	1	5.6	3	10.0			1	7.7	11	7.5
5							2	11.1	1	3.3					3	2.1
6							2	11.1	0	0.0					2	1.4
10									1	3.3					1	0.7
Educational level																
No school attendance	0	0.0	0	0.0	0	0.0	0	0.0	3	10.0	10	43.50	0	0.0	13	8.9
Elementary school	0	0.0	0	0.0	0	0.0	0	0.0	12	40.0	5	21.70	0	0.0	17	11.6
Intermediate school	3	13.6	4	20.0	1	5.0	1	5.6	1	3.3	0	0.00	0	0.0	10	6.9
Secondary school	3	13.6	1	5.0	4	20.0	1	5.6	12	40.0	8	34.80	2	15.4	31	21.2
Special school	14	63.7	10	50.0	7	35.0	0	0.0	1	3.3	0	0.00	2	15.4	34	23.3
University	2	9.1	4	20.0	7	35.0	16	88.8	1	3.4	0	0.00	9	69.2	39	26.7
PhD	0	0.0	1	5.0	1	5.0	0	0.0	0	0.0	0	0.00	0	0.0	2	1.4
Occupation																
Employment	13	59.10	14	70.0	11	55.0	15	83.3	11	36.7	0	0.0	7	53.8	71	48.6
Self-employment	7	31.90	1	5.0	1	5.0	0	0.0	1	3.3	0	0.0	2	15.4	12	8.2
Housewife	1	4.50	3	15.0	7	35.0	1	5.6	16	53.3	0	0.0	4	30.8	32	2
Maternity leave	1	4.50	2	10.0	1	5.0	1	5.6	2	6.7	0	0.0	0	0.0	7	4.8

Questionnaire Number 1 demonstrated that there was a high rate of exposure to different traumatic events. The probability of active PTSD is very high in all groups. In most cases there was inadequate evaluation of the psychological condition, and women often don't know that they suffer from psychological consequences from their traumatic experiences. Most women do not have access to or were not provided with any psychological help, and were unwilling to ask for it. Despite high exposure to different traumatic events, many women were willing to release the pain, forgive and continue their lives, mostly for the sake of their children.

The *Post-Traumatic Stress Disorder Scale* showed that civilian women are exposed to a high level of terrible traumatic events as a result of violence; for example (74%, $n = 99$) of women from the total sample were exposed to military combat or a war zone. The lowest score of PTSD was 54.5 per cent in Dagestan and highest (100%) in south Sudan–Ethiopia. We explored the relationship of demographics to the occurrence of PTSD, and found no correlation of PTSD between participants with and without PTSD by age, education level, living conditions or marital status in contradiction with hypothesis number four. The Fisher's exact test confirmed the hypothesis number two about equal presence and distribution of PTSD in five of eight countries.

The *Beck Depression Inventory* was used to measure severity of depression level. In Palestine 88 per cent ($n = 16$) and in Dagestan 64 per cent ($n = 14$) of women had no symptoms of depression. In Colombia 53 per cent ($n = 16$), Chechnya 46 per cent ($n = 6$), and Azerbaijan 45 per cent ($n = 9$) of women showed mild–moderate levels of depression. In all countries, moderate–severe levels were present only in a few women. Extreme–severe depression was mainly present among women from south Sudan–Ethiopia (74 per cent; $n = 17$), but women in Turkmenistan (22 per cent; $n = 4$), Colombia (13 per cent; $n = 4$) and Chechnya (8 per cent; $n = 1$) were also affected.

The results of *Hopkins Symptom Checklist-25* were assessed using values recommended by Mollica *et al.* (1987), with the cut-point for HSCL-10 and HSCL-15 a mean of 1.75, and a mean of 2.25 set up as cut-point for the HSCL-25 emotional distress scale.

The mean scores of depression and anxiety among women with current PTSD were not significantly higher than women without PTSD. Nevertheless in Dagestan, Turkmenistan, Colombia, south Sudan–Ethiopia and Chechnya, the mean HSCL-10 and HSCL-15 scores for women with current PTSD were 1.75 or higher. Among women in Turkmenistan, south Sudan–Ethiopia and Chechnya with PTSD, and women in Colombia and Chechnya without PTSD, mean values for HSCL-25 were higher than 2.25 (Table 12.7).

Table 12.5 PTSD versus non-PTSD participants

	Dagestan		*Turkmenistan*		*Azerbaijan*		*Palestine*		*Colombia*		*South Sudan–Ethiopia*		*Chechnya*			
	n	%	*n*	%	*n*	%	*n*	%	*n*	%	*n*	%	*n*	%	*Total*	%
Number of participants	22	100	18	100	20	100	8	100	30	100	23	100	13	100	134	100
PTSD	12	54.5	17	94.4	16	80	8	100	23	76.7	23	100	9	69.2	108	80.6
Non-PTSD	10	45.5	1	5.6	4	20	0	0	7	23.3	0	0	4	30.8	26	19.4

Table 12.6 Beck Depression Inventory scores

	Dagestan		*Turkmenistan*		*Azerbaijan*		*Palestine*		*Colombia*		*South Sudan–Ethiopia*		*Chechnya*			
	n	%	*n*	%	*n*	%	*n*	%	*n*	%	*n*	%	*n*	%	*Total*	%
Number of participants	22	100.0	18	100.0	20	100.0	18	100.0	30	100.0	23	100.0	13	100.0	144	100.0
Score																
≤ 9	14	64.0	4	22.0	7	35.0	16	88.0	2	7.0	3	13.0	3	23.0	49	34.0
10–18	6	27.0	4	22.0	9	45.0	1	6.0	16	53.0	1	4.0	6	46.0	43	30.0
19–29	2	9.0	6	34.0	4	20.0	1	6.0	8	27.0	2	9.0	3	23.0	26	18.0
30–63	0	0.0	4	22.0	0	0.0	0	0.0	4	13.0	17	74.0	1	8.0	26	18.0

Table 12.7 Comparison of participants with and without PTSD in relation to HSCL-25

	Dagestan		*Turkmenistan*		*Azerbaijan*		*Palestine*		*Colombia*		*South Sudan-Ethiopia*		*Chechnya*	
	Mean	*SD*	*Mean*	*SD*	*Mean*	*SD*	*Mean*	*SD*	*Mean*	*SD*	*Mean*	*SD*	*Mean*	*SD*
HSCL-25 emotional distress														
PTSD	2.1	0.7	2.4	0.8	1.8	0.6	1.5	0.5	2.2	0.7	3.5	0.5	2.3	0.7
Non-PTSD	2	0.6	1.9	0.3	2.2	0.6	1.6	0.4	2.6	0.3	0	0	2.5	0.2

Note: SD = standard deviation.

Discussion

This study demonstrates that women in the study countries were exposed to high levels of violence, largely secondary to war, and significant emotional consequences are associated with these exposures. The severity of emotional distress varies across countries, but in all countries the prevalence of emotional disorder was significant. This knowledge will help in further studies of PTSD symptoms and other serious problems for both the social sciences and for healthcare.

This research has furthered our knowledge in that it:

- has highlighted the mental health status of civilian women in countries affected by war, terrorism and/or political violence;
- brings data from countries with limited accessibility and sheds light on situation inside such countries as Turkmenistan, Chechnya and Sudan;
- has confirmed the usefulness of, and partially validated, the questionnaires used to determine the state of mental, physical and psychosomatic health, and especially the consistency of the relationship between depression, anxiety and PTDS; and
- has demonstrated the relatively low effectiveness of international activities and agencies and has shown that necessary activities and assistance reach a very limited number of people.

The social and economic impact of mental health disorders

Mollica *et al.* (2004) describe links between mass violence, mental health impairment and inadequate services, and the existing damage to economic development, social capital, and human rights. Although these forces create mental health impairments and barriers to mental health service delivery, and even healthcare delivery, they also can foster resilience and mental health recovery (Mollica *et al.*, 2004).

Economic costs of violence

The human costs in grief and pain cannot be calculated. However, there is no doubt that violence and mental health disorders have profound impact on the human and economic toll of nations, and 'cost economies all over the world billions of United States dollars each year in healthcare, legal costs, absenteeism from work and lost productivity' (WHO, 2002). For example, Clayton and Barcel (1999) calculated that total direct and indirect costs, including costs for healthcare services, autopsies, police investigations and lost productivity resulting from premature death, amounted to nearly US$80 billion in 1999.

Gender and sustainable development

Sustainable development can be achieved only through long-term investment in economic, human and environmental capital. At present, women of the world are undervalued and underutilized, and, as a group, women – and their contributions to economic advances, social progress and environmental protection – have been marginalized. These contributions could improve economic activity, reduce poverty, enhance societal well-being and help ensure sustainable development in all countries.

While the importance of investing in economic assets to assure progress is obvious, sustainable development brings attention to the ecological and human dimensions that are also key to economic development. But women must be included! In failing to make the best use of their female populations, most countries are under-investing in the human capital needed to assure sustainability. Although women account for over half of the potential talent base throughout the world, as a group they are marginalized and their economic, social and environmental contributions are largely unrealized. Women represent more than 70 per cent of the world's poor in both developed and developing countries, largely due to unequal access to economic opportunities. There is a link between poverty alleviation in countries and the development of their female human capital. A country cannot advance if its women are left behind.

Conclusion

Despite all knowledge, ten years after the first WHO report on the global burden of disease, mental health remains a low priority, especially in most low- and middle-income countries. Even in the United States, while more than $70 billion is invested annually in global public health research, not even 10 per cent goes to research into the health problems that account for 90 per cent of the global disease burden (Scott, 2008). Mental illness may soon exhibit an even greater disparity.

Mental disorders are an important cause of long-term disability and dependency. Five of the 10 leading disabilities worldwide are psychiatric conditions (Mollica *et al.*, 2004). While depression predicts the onset and progression of both physical and social disability (Bruce *et al.*, 1994; Penninx *et al.*, 1998), depression was the fourth leading disease burden in 1990, but is predicted to move to second place by 2020.

Despite all our knowledge, mental health is missing from the policy framework for health improvement and poverty reduction. Moreover, it has not even been acknowledged as an obstacle in the attainment of the Millennium Development Goals (i.e. promotion of gender equality and empowerment of women, reduction of child mortality, improvement of maternal health, and the reversal and spread of HIV/AIDS, malaria and other diseases; WHO, 2002).

The Universal Declaration of Human Rights, which enshrines the equal value of human life, and the Geneva Convention, which protects civilians and medical personal during conflict, are good starting points to improve the medical and humanitarian response during conflict (Lancet, 2009).

Furthermore, awareness about mental health must become an integral component of primary and secondary healthcare practice. It must be integrated into social and health policies, health systems planning, and healthcare delivery. Healthcare workers need to be trained to recognize and provide appropriate treatment of mental disorders and be supported in these endeavours. Primary and secondary care providers should overcome their reluctance to treat patients with severe mental illnesses, and should learn effective ways to interact and communicate with these patients (Prince *et al.*, 2007).

References

Bruce, M. L., Seeman, T. E., Merrill, S. S. and Blazer, D. G. (1994) 'The impact of depressive symptomatology on physical disability: MacArthur Studies of Successful Aging', *American Journal of Public Health*, vol 84, pp1796–1799

Clayton, D. and Barcel, A. (1999) 'The cost of suicide mortality in New Brunswick, 1996', *Chronic Diseases in Canada*, vol 20, pp89–95

Farmer, R. D. T., Lawrenson, R., Miller, D. (2008) *Lecture Notes on Epidemiology and Public Health Medicine*, fifth edition, Blackwell Publishing, Oxford, UK

Foa, E. B. (1995) *Posttraumatic Stress Diagnostic Scale Manual*, National Computer Systems Inc., New York, NY

Garieballa, S. S. (2004) 'Trauma, post-traumatic stress disorder and psychiatric comorbidity in forensic patients', dissertation, Universität Konstanz, Germany

Inter-Agency Standing Committee (2007) *Guidelines on Mental Heath and Psychosocial Support in Emergency Settings*, Inter-Agency Standing Committee, Geneva, Switzerland.

Lancet (2009) 'Violent conflict: protecting the health of civilians', editorial, *The Lancet*, vol 370, pp859–877

Lindsey, C. (2001) *Women Facing War: ICRC Study on the Impact of Armed Conflict on Women*, International Committee of the Red Cross, Geneva, Switzerland, available at http://www.icrc.org/eng/assets/files/other/icrc_002_0798_women_facing_war.pdf

Lyamzina, Y. (2011) *Political Violence and its Impact on Female Civil Population: Prevention of Health Damage as a Result of Terrorism, Political Violence and its Impact on Civil Population, with Special Focus on Women*, Lambert Academic Publishing, Saarbrücken, Germany

Malkina-Pych, I. G. (2009) *Psychological Help in Crisis Situations*, Eksmo, Moscow, Russia

Mollica, R. F., Cardozo, B. L., Osofsky, H. J., Raphael, B., Ager, A. and Salama, P. (2004) 'Mental health in complex emergencies', *The Lancet*, vol 364, pp2058–2067

Mollica, R. F., Wyshak, G., de Marneffe, D., Khuon, F. and Lavelle, J. (1987) 'Indochinese versions of the Hopkins Symptom Checklist-25: a screening instrument for the psychiatric care of refugees', *American Journal of Psychiatry*, vol 144, pp497–500

Penninx, B. W. J. H., Guralnik, J. M., Ferrucci, L., Simonsick, E. M., Deeg, D. J. H. and Wallace, R. B. (1998) 'Depressive symptoms and physical decline in community dwelling older persons', *Journal of the American Medical Association*, vol 279, pp1720–1726

Pincha, C. (2008) *Gender Sensitive Disaster Management: A Toolkit for Practitioners*, Oxfam America and NANBAN Trust, available at www.eldis.org/vfile/upload/1/document/0812/Gnder%20sensitive%20disaster%20management%20Toolkit.pdf

Prince, M., Patel, V., Saxena, S., Maj, M., Maselko, J., Phillips, M. R. and Rahman, A. (2007) 'No health without mental health', *The Lancet*, 8 September, vol 370, no 9590, pp859–877

Scott, K. A. (2008) *Violence Prevention in Low- and Middle-Income Countries: Finding a Place on the Global Agenda, Workshop Summary*, National Academies Press, Washington, DC

UN (2002) *Women, Peace and Security*, study submitted by the Secretary- General pursuant to Security Council resolution 1325, United Nations, New York, NY

WHA (1996) *Prevention of Violence: A Public Health Priority*. World Health Assembly, Geneva, Switzerland, available at www.who.int/violence_injury_prevention/resources/publications/en/WHA4925_eng.pdf

WHO (2002) *The World Report on Violence and Health*, World Health Organization, Geneva, Switzerland, available at www.who.int/violence_injury_prevention/violence/world_report/en/

WHO (2009) *Women and Health: Today's Evidence Tomorrow's Agenda*, World Health Organization, Geneva, Switzerland

13 The efficiency of cost-control policies in healthcare

Does economic efficiency imply sustainability?

Tomáš Zelený

Introduction

This chapter explores the efficiency of cost-control policies in healthcare systems through an analysis of healthcare systems in three selected countries: the United States, France and Japan. These were chosen because their healthcare systems are well documented, have complete statistics and are quite different from each other, thus covering a wide range of cost-control policies. First, I describe the current state of the three selected healthcare systems and try to evaluate their sustainability. I then investigate the detail of the institutional setup of the given systems, and analyse the actual efficiency of named control policies through a cross-country comparison. Finally, I link the results of the analysis of the cost-control policies to the sustainability of each of the three healthcare systems, thus attempting to explain how sustainable each of the systems is.

The current state of the three healthcare systems

This analysis consists of two parts. In the first part, I provide a concise review of the current literature about the topic to provide a broad base for my research and a scale on which to address it. My own research comprises part two of this section, in which I compare my findings with those of other authors and attempt to explain any differences. Finally, I draw a conclusion about the sustainability of the current state of the three healthcare systems.

The literature review determined that all authors had similar conclusions regarding the present state in each country's system: in each, healthcare costs have been rising at rates much above inflation and show no sign of stopping. The most common example used to demonstrate this phenomenon is the United States, where, for the past 30 years, healthcare expenditures have significantly exceeded inflation rates (Mattoon, 1992; Buchmueller and Valletta, 2006). The identical phenomenon has been shown in Denmark (Bibbee and Padrini, 2006), and in the G7 as a whole (Hitiris, 1999). The reasons are, however, quite different in the named cases.

Mattoon (1992) provides an exhaustive list of reasons for the rise in healthcare expenditures. He divides them into two categories: demand factors and supply factors. The main demand factor is that the price elasticity of demand for medical services may be as low as 0.2, meaning that the consumption of medicine is barely affected by its price. He claims that this insensitivity is caused by health insurance; it makes the consumption of healthcare cost less and therefore is overused. This type of behaviour is pertinent and I later refer to it as 'the effect of insurance'. He supports his argument with data from 1970 to 1988, showing that expenditures on hospital services increased by over 800 per cent; on not fully insured services, such as drugs and eyeglasses, it increased by only about 350 per cent. Lastly, he mentions that ageing populations have a very negative impact on healthcare costs as old people require much higher expenditures, especially towards the very end of life.

On the supply side, Mattoon suggests that the productivity gains from increased expenditures are low. Both insurance and public health usually reimburse medical providers' costs and add profit to that. The providers can be sure that their costs will be covered and therefore they face no incentive to care about productivity or costs. A similar situation applies when considering the use of best practice techniques; there is no reason to use anything but the best and most expensive techniques available even though second-best techniques often have almost identical success rates and at significantly lower cost. Another factor is the limited supply of physicians; medical schools have limited capacities and the limited number of physicians helps keep the costs of their services high. The increased number of highly specialized medical professions has also not helped as their services become less substitutable and so the specialists can charge higher fees despite general practitioners often being capable of doing the same thing for less. Asymmetric information is another important factor. Since medical knowledge is highly specific, patients have no idea about what treatment they actually need. Lastly, the emphasis on medical technology has a significant impact on costs. This is especially true for the United States, or generally for any country where hospitals compete among themselves to gain patients. Because patients do not pay for services being insured, they prefer go to hospitals with the most modern equipment; and, since hospitals will have their costs paid anyway, they have little reason to not buy the equipment. The listed problems could also be classified into the supply side and the demand-side. However, data describing supply-side factors are difficult to obtain, so the significance of these factors remains an enigma.

The demand-side

The demand-side is widely considered the main problem in healthcare expenditures (Hitiris, 1999; Buchmueller and Valletta, 2006; Bibbee and Padrini, 2006). While we want to assume it to be solely dependent on the individual's health status, medical costs and income, this is usually not the case. Both public and private insurance create significant distortions; the patient directly receives full benefits of healthcare, but does not pay the full costs as these are shifted to others. Therefore, a person's demand for healthcare is limited only by their perception of their own health and not by any financial motives.

Other important factors on the demand-side are population ageing and increasing income (Buchmueller and Valletta, 2006; Bibbee and Padrini, 2006). These two factors are closely related. As income increases, a person can spend more on health. This leads to the extension of life expectancy which is the basis for an ageing population. For both practical reasons and political expediency, the age of retirement cannot be adjusted according to life expectancy, at least not as frequently as what full cost efficiency would necessitate. Such an adjustment would inevitably lead to societal resistance, and, since political representatives who would make this decision rely on public opinion, it is hard to imagine that democratic countries could annually readjust the retirement age to adapt to increasing life expectancies. Ultimately, this leads to a decrease in the ratio of productive people versus retired people, which adversely affects healthcare financing. This ratio is further worsened in most western countries because the population pyramid is no longer a pyramid; young people no longer form the largest sector. In fact, the 'pyramid' is slowly becoming an inverted vase. While changing birth rates can be blamed for the altered shape of the age pyramid, it is a function of the population policy of a given country and its culture, and thus is not deemed a part of healthcare.

Healthcare expenditures have become a vicious cycle. People are healthier due to better health services; this leads to people being more productive for longer, which leads to higher incomes, which leads to higher spending on healthcare, which leads to people living longer, which leads to the rise of the healthcare expenditures as people age.

Recent data

The authors reviewed above agree that the status quo is unworkable and action is necessary. However, they differ as to what the main problem is and, more importantly, their data are outdated. Still, the list of possible reasons, and therefore testable hypotheses, they provide is quite exhaustive and it was for this reason that they were selected for review.

Starting with my own analysis, my first goal was to validate the classical theories against actual data, primarily by focussing on two main factors: the absolute ceiling on healthcare expenditures per capita, and the year-by-year trends in these expenditures. Both values will be considered using 2009 US$ purchasing power parity (PPP) to minimize the effect of inflation and exchange rate fluctuations. The analysis takes the past 20 years into account, and is summarized pictorially in Figures 13.1 and 13.2.

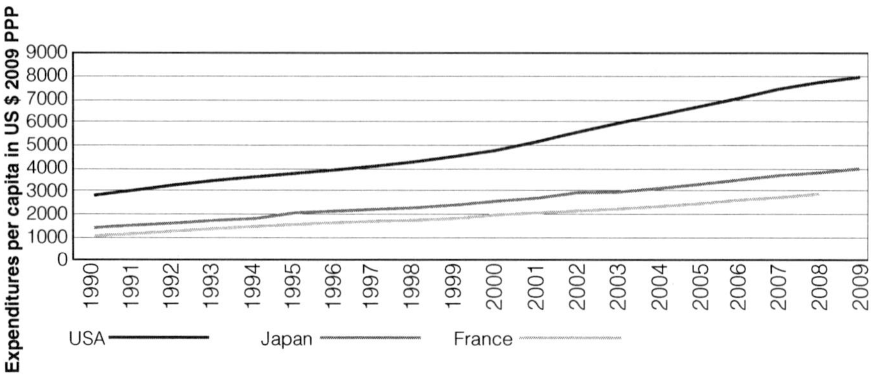

Figure 13.1 Healthcare expenditures per capita (2009 US$ PPP)

Source: own calculations over OECD health data 2011, http://stats.oecd.org/index.aspx?DataSetCode=HEALTH_STAT

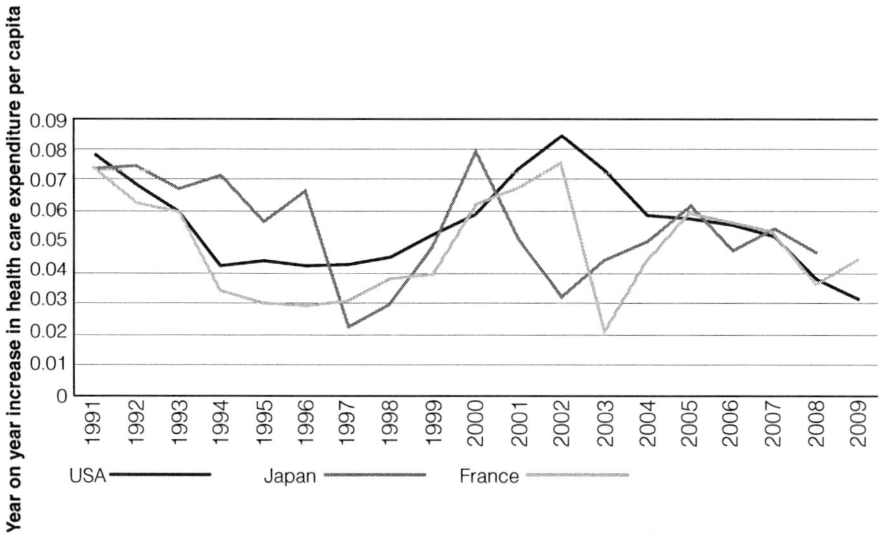

Figure 13.2 Year-by-year trends in healthcare expenditures per capita (2009 US$ PPP)

Source: own calculations over OECD health data 2011, http://stats.oecd.org/index.aspx?DataSetCode=HEALTH_STAT

The trends are quite striking. Healthcare expenditures per capita have been steadily increasing over the past 20 years in each of the three countries examined. Since the expenditures are in constant dollars, this is a net value, and thus even more striking. The trends are particularly interesting and important. In France and Japan, the trends are oscillating and show no sign of stabilising. In the United States, there seems to be a recent convergence to lower expenditure growth values, but there is no way to estimate the limit. There are several reasons which can explain this trend; for example, a general 'running out of money in the economy' (increasing government debt together with increasing households debt), a 'healthcare market responded to the economic recession' explanation, and a 'the system was beginning to stabilise' explanation. Given the new healthcare reform in the United States, we will likely never find out the 'real' reason, and further speculation is beyond the scope of this chapter.

While this piece of evidence seems suggestive, it is not enough to draw any conclusions; the question is: what causes the increase in expenditure? If it reflects an extra expenditure because of a proportional increase in wages, it would be nothing more than people having higher disposable income to spend on the part of healthcare, which could be viewed as a luxury good. This argument makes average net wages a key variable to compare to the change in healthcare expenditures. Other key variables are GDP, ageing and population structure. Checking exact ageing parameters is unnecessary because it changes very slowly. The rate of change in the age of the population is usually quite close to the change in life expectancy at birth. Year-by-year changes in life expectancy at birth are under one per cent, so when talking about a relatively small time-frame of 20 years the absolute effect of ageing is virtually negligible. Population structure is more important, but this is confounded in that the proportion of people at any given age who work, changes over time. Therefore, certain age groups who, in 1990, were effectively not working, now are largely engaged in working. With the age-related changes of roles in society, one cannot compare the age structure of a population across extensive time periods. That leaves us with two variables: average annual income and GDP. Their progress over the past 20 years is shown in Figures 13.3 and 13.4.

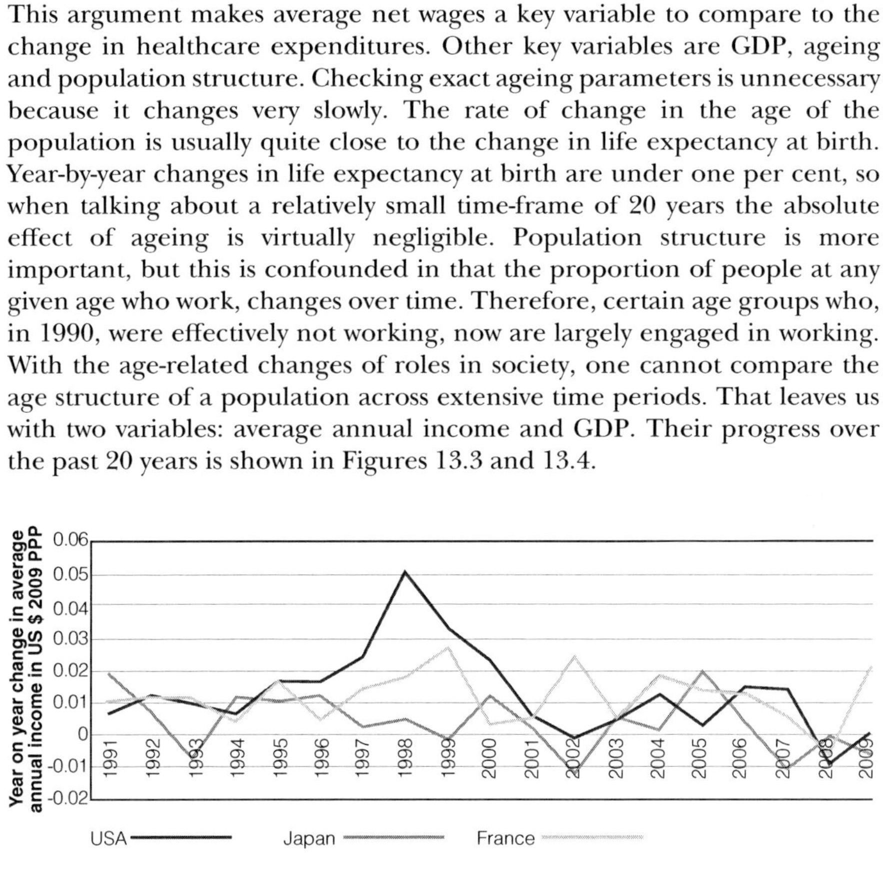

Figure 13.3 Year on year GDP growth at constant prices and constant US$ PPP

Source: own calculations over OECD health data 2011, http://stats.oecd.org/index.aspx?DataSetCode=HEALTH_STAT

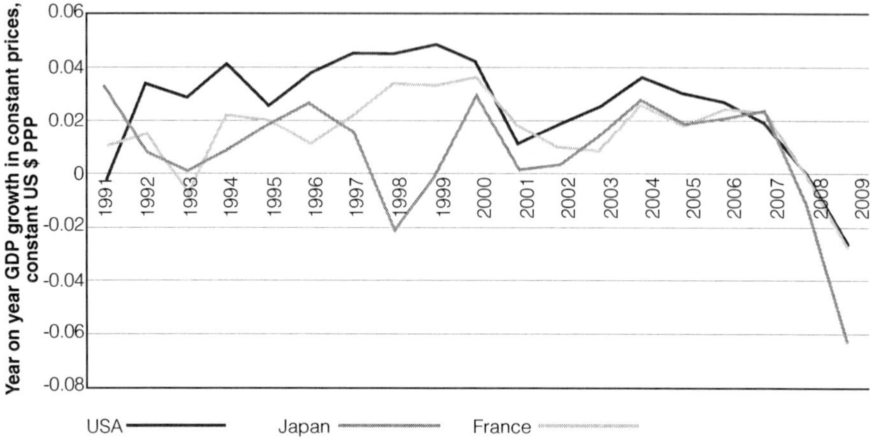

Figure 13.4 Year on year changes in average annual income (2009 US$ PPP)

Source: own calculations over OECD health data 2011, http://stats.oecd.org/index.aspx?DataSetCode=HEALTH_STAT

The *y* axes in both graphs (change in average annual income) are under 5 per cent each year, with 4 per cent and 5 per cent being extremely rare values. Similarly, the year-by-year changes in GDP are a lot lower than the changes in healthcare expenditures. To be more precise, the averages for all variables is listed in Table 13.1.

Table 13.1 Comparison of average values of year-by-year changes in expenditures, income, life expectancy and GDP

Country	*Healthcare expenditures per capita*	*Average annual income*	*GDP*	*Life expectancy at birth*
United States	5.6%	1.3%	2.6%	0.13%
Japan	5.4%	0.4%	0.8%	0.12%
France	4.8%	1.2%	1.6%	0.12%

Source: own calculations over OECD health data 2011, http://stats.oecd.org/index.aspx?DataSetCode=HEALTH_STAT

Table 13.1 reveals that changes in GDP, annual income and ageing (for which life expectancy at birth is a good instrumental variable) are not even close to covering the changes in healthcare expenditures. Thus, factors other than ageing, rising population, income and GDP must be found to account for this gap. There are two reasonable explanations: either the fundamental health status of the population is declining each year, or the institutional setup of the healthcare system is somehow flawed. For the fundamental health status of the population, a statistic that would express it does not exist because it is too crude a measure. Adding up multiple statistics would still miss most of the information, and life expectancy has too many other factors to account for. Thus, we lack a good measure for the health status of the population (see later). Regarding institutional setup and healthcare system efficiency, we are more fortunate because we can compare the systems based on their productivity parameters. The idea is simple: if one system can produce results at least as good as another system without higher cost, it is more efficient. The whole healthcare system comparison is unfortunately the most accurate measure available when comparing the cost-control policies because we cannot effectively pit the policies against each other. The numbers therefore provide basic guidance for the reasoning, rather than an exact proof.

System comparison

As stated earlier, a policy-by-policy comparison is impossible because healthcare policies are combined into whole inter-dependent systems, which make any *ceteris paribus*-based analysis pointless. Therefore, I compare the healthcare systems as a whole. The three countries selected for this chapter all have a combined healthcare financing model, which means that there is both a private and public sector presence in the system. Where they differ is in the allowed amount of involvement of the private sector. I start by a rough characterisation of the given systems and their connection to the cost-controlling policies mentioned earlier. I start with the country with the largest share of the private sector in the healthcare system, namely the United States.

United States

I ignore the recent healthcare reform in the United States owing to the lack of data (given the recency of the legislation). Therefore, everything said relates to the previous healthcare system and may be only somewhat applicable to the new system. The principle of the so-called 'free market' forms the foundation of the United States healthcare system. Citizens have private insurance or they pay out of their pockets (this is the case for about 15.4 per cent of the working population (Blanchflower, 2009). Those who cannot receive treatment because of having no insurance or being unable to pay may be eligible to use the public systems of Medicaid and Medicare. In theory, Medicaid covers the healthcare costs of low-income people, and Medicare covers pensioners. But in practice it is not so clean a division because Medicaid covers only about 40 per cent of the low-income population and, for various reasons, the 60 per cent remaining are left uninsured (Buchmueller and Valletta, 2006). This leads to the core of the problem: because the United States healthcare system is based on 'free market' principles, it is inevitably subject to the market mechanisms of concurrence and profitability requirements. An insurance company needs to attract low-risk insurers (the ones most likely to generate greatest profit for insurers) and weed out the high risk ones having the potential to cause insurers a loss; in the case of healthcare, these are patients with pre-existing disease, more susceptible to illness, or generally those of lower income. If the insurance company does not do so, it would inevitably go bankrupt as the concurrence would take away the profitable patients and leave only the low-profit ones. For private insurance companies to generate profits (which is their purpose), it is necessary to eliminate the high-risk patients from the applicant pool and not insure them, at least not at a standard rate. And there is no way to avoid these extra costs in the private insurance companies because cost-minimization is necessary to generate profits; hence the need to weed out risky patients in the interests of cost minimization. This is something that concurrence generates: if an insurance company were to accept less profitable patients, its costs would rise and it would therefore have to increase the price of insurance, or run at a lower profit margin. An increase in prices would cause the high-profit patients to prefer an alternative company to obtain a better deal, the original insurance company would encounter further problems. The factor that is crucial to this effect is the unique property of healthcare, namely that every insurer should insure an entity of a very similar 'value'. For example, with car insurance it is common that lower income people have cheaper cars, which makes it easier for them to secure insurance. That is clearly not the case with healthcare because the treatment does not become any cheaper with lower patient income.

From the perspective of the earlier policy analysis (above), a key cost-control measure lies in the private payment for healthcare. Ideally, this would make people apply pressure to practitioners to be cost-effective and also make people care more about their own health so as to avoid incurring future health costs. Unfortunately, empirical evidence does not support either of these hypotheses. The reasons for this are discussed in the final part of this chapter.

Japan

In Japan, health insurance companies are paid from the taxes of employees and employers. The structure of the Japanese healthcare system is complex. With respect to administration, most healthcare plans in Japan come from the private sector. However, in practice, they are quasi-public, all offering about the same benefits and covering all variants. The money collected by the state from different insurance plans goes to the national fund, which pays for everything. Individual participation is therefore given from the top, and the only aspect not covered is the traditional healer. About 81 per cent of the hospitals and other healthcare related facilities are privately owned, but their profits are regulated at 0 per cent. Thus, profit is effectively prohibited. Insurance companies also cannot generate a profit; they are paid by the state. The profit motive is therefore excluded from the healthcare system, which is, by law, a non-profit enterprise.

With respect to the previous discussion of cost-control policies in healthcare, none are present in the Japanese system.

France

France presents a unique mixture of public and private sector healthcare. The public sector is composed of compulsory state insurance and state-owned hospitals, which make up about 65 per cent of the total number of hospitals. The roles between public and private hospitals are split: the public hospitals usually provide long-term treatments, education and research, while the private and non-profit sector hospitals focus on individual operations (tertiary care).

There is no significant difference in the quality of care between the differently owned hospitals. This is because they have the same financing scheme; insurance works equally for all types of hospitals and individually operating practitioners. The principle of state insurance is that it covers a given percentage of the costs of treatment, and this percentage rises with the seriousness of the illness. For example, all costs are paid in the case of cancer. Usually, it is in the 75–80 per cent range of the total cost. The remainder is paid by the patient, but for this part, private insurance exists and is used by over 90 per cent of the population. If a patient is not privately insured, he/she pays out of pocket.

From the policy point of view, the demand-side control mechanism is the fact that the patient pays a significant part of the expense of treatment. It is similar to the United States, but here, the system is much more user-friendly because the payments are made regardless.

The costs and results

So far, I have briefly discussed the structure of the systems and their basic cost-control mechanisms. Now, it is necessary to introduce the data in order to compare each system's end results in conjunction with their costs. Three factors are relevant: financing, both in structure and amount; the utilization of the system; and the quality factors. These factors are summarized in Tables 13.2–13.4. The year 2007 was used for the financial data because some data were unavailable for later years; also, in order to have data as comparable as possible, an earlier year was picked (Zelený and Bencko, 2011).

It is obvious that large differences exist between countries with respect to quality/cost ratios. The United States is notable in that the system is used less than in the other countries, while the expenditures per capita are significantly higher and the quality indicators are quite unimpressive. The infant mortality rate is the highest among selected countries, and life expectancy is also lower. The number of preventable deaths is no less than a public health disaster. Japan performs very well and has one very

Table 13.2 Financial indicators

Financial indicators as of 2007	*France*	*Japan*	*United States*
Public financing (%)	78.3	55.2	45.5
Per capita expenditure 2007 US$ PPP	3593	2729	7285
Expenditures (% GDP)	11	8.1	15.7

Source: OECD health data 2011, http://stats.oecd.org/index.aspx?DataSetCode=HEALTH_STAT

Table 13.3 Utilization

Utilization	*France*	*Japan*	*United States*
Active practitioners per 1000 people	3.4	2.2	2.6
Hospital beds per 1000 people	8	13.9	3.1
Average Consultations per person per year	7	13.4	4

Source: OECD health data 2011, http://stats.oecd.org/index.aspx?DataSetCode=HEALTH_STAT

Table 13.4 Quality factors

Quality factors	*France*	*Japan*	*United States*
Life expectancy at birth	80.9	82.6	77.9
Infant mortality rate	3.8	2.6	6.7
Preventable deaths per 100,000 people in years 2002–2003	65	71	110

Source: OECD health data 2011, http://stats.oecd.org/index.aspx?DataSetCode=HEALTH_STAT

interesting feature: the system is heavily used, much more so than in the other two countries. That brings up an interesting hypothesis: from an economic perspective, is it more efficient to let anyone see the doctor for any reason, because the costs of unnecessary consultations are more than compensated for by identifying serious disease early? France performs somewhere in the middle. While it has excellent quality indicators, it pays with higher expenditures. The impressive fact is that France is the best in the world in terms of preventable deaths (Nolte and Marti, 2008).

Why is it all happening?

So far, I have explored the financial sustainability of the healthcare systems and their cost-control policies, their quality indicators, and their architecture. I determined that all three systems are financially exploding despite their completely different architecture, different levels of utilization, and different quality factors. The fact that all indicators are different while the explosive trend remains the same suggests one thing: the examined indicators only partially capture the problem. The question of why the healthcare systems are unsustainable remains unanswered by the hard data; therefore, we need to move to a higher level of analysis. Luckily, there are two fundamental properties that the healthcare systems have in common: they are reactive, and they are democratically selected.

Reactive architecture

By 'reactive', I mean that they are almost entirely focused on healing the patient after the illness starts. If this is so, it is therefore possible and completely consistent that the overall health status of the population of the given country is deteriorating from year-to-year. This hypothesis cannot be tested because no complex data are gathered to provide information about the overall health status of the population (life expectancy has too many other determinants than simply healthcare-related factors). That leaves us with too few hard data for analysis. But this does not negate the hypothesis.

It is entirely possible that the expenditure differences among the three healthcare systems is caused by differences in the overall health status of the population of the respective countries, while the worsening trend is caused by its deterioration. The cause behind the overall healthcare status could, for example, be the country-specific diet and tradition of a healthy lifestyle.

The reactive architecture itself is a closely connected issue and is much easier to grasp. The basic problem flowing from it is that it makes the healthcare system entirely dependent on the health status of the population without affecting it in any way. Economically speaking, it is more efficient to have people who do not become ill. To achieve this, a radical change in our view of the healthcare system would need to happen. The system would need to prevent illness rather than react to it. The main part of such a change would be the rise of all types of preventive measures, especially primary prevention (Bencko, 2011). Such a change cannot happen overnight, but it is a valuable idea to keep in mind. Should healthcare system expenditures continue to explode, perhaps the correct path would be not to keep treating the symptoms, but to start dealing with the fundamental flaws and actually prevent illnesses instead of simply treating them. The exact form of a preventive healthcare system would be country-specific. Its design is beyond the scope of this chapter.

Voluntary choice of future self-destruction

The question that remains to be answered is 'Why are the healthcare systems the way they are?' The answer lies in how they were set up and are kept running, democratically. 'Democratically' means that the healthcare system represents the preferences of the people of the given country. This is a critical point, because system expenditure trends have not changed for decades in most cases. It seems improbable that people would want their system to change and have been unable to make changes over so much time. That brings us to a disturbing hypothesis; the systems are unsustainable because people of the respective countries are, perhaps through sheer inertia, unable to influence and change that which has become systemic.

Why would people want to live with an unsustainable healthcare system? There are two possible answers to this question. The first one is that people make an error while estimating future utility. The idea is quite simple: an individual's perception of his/her current happiness tends to be stable over time. Looking into one`s own distant future, it is very difficult to imagine future preferences, and thus the future utility one might have. In practice, this difficulty results in a bias to expect more than a realistic amount of happiness from good events and a less than realistic amount of happiness from bad events. This has been especially well-documented in the cases involving one's own health (Sackett *et al.*, 1978; Gilbert *et al.*, 1998; Lowernstein *et al.*, 2003). Following this logic, people might simply be aiming too high in anticipating their level of future health. The second possible answer is quite different in style and yet gives the same result: people choose to self-destruct in the end. Such behaviour is easy to observe in an individual life. Almost every natural death could have been delayed should the patient have lived healthier and/or had spent more money on his health (Becker, 1976). To put it more simply, it might simply be that people do not care that the system is going to go bankrupt in the distant future for as long as they currently enjoy an easy ride into the foreseeable future.

Conclusion

I have examined three healthcare system expenditures, trends, individual cost-control policies, system utilization patterns, and their quality indicators. Through this comparison, I determined that, if trends continue, the systems are financially unsustainable and likely to go bankrupt sooner rather than later. Among other variables and individual cost-control policies themselves, I found nothing that could even partially explain the complete lack of sustainability of these systems. Therefore, I looked for more fundamental issues that were large enough to result in unsustainability. At this level, I identified two likely reasons.

The first reason relates to the reactive architecture of each of the three systems investigated. The systems are designed to cure sick people and leave them well after they recover. Such a system does not address the overall health status of the population, which may be the source of its unsustainability. A change to a preventive system, based on prevention, would be necessary in order to remedy the situation. Indeed, the investment in public health (i.e. prevention) is a mere fraction of that invested in healthcare (perhaps about 5% of total health service expenditures).

The second issue lies in the policy choice of each of the healthcare systems. Given that the three systems studied exist in so-called democratic countries, it is very likely that they are unsustainable because people want them to be as they are, perhaps due to unrealistic estimates of their own future utility, or due to a strong preference for immediate gain even at the cost of future self-destruction. To confirm or refute these hypotheses is beyond the scope of this chapter, and thus is left as a subject for further research.

References

Becker, G. S. (1976) *The Economic Approach to Human Behavior*, University of Chicago Press, Chicago, IL

Bencko, V. (2011) 'Primary prevention of diseases: current challenges and opportunities' (in Czech), *Praktický lékař*, vol 91, no 3, pp127–130

Bibbee, A. and Padrini, A. (2006) *Balancing Health Care Quality and Cost Containment: The Case of Norway*, OECD Economics Department Working Paper no 481, OECD Publishing, Paris, France

Blanchflower, G. (2009) *Happiness and Health Care Coverage*, Discussion Paper No. 4450, Dartmouth College, University of Stirling, Stirling, UK

Buchmueller, T. and Valletta, R. (2006) 'Health insurance costs and declining coverage', *FRBSF Economic Letter*, 29 September, available at http://ideas.repec.org/a/fip/fedfel/y2006isep29n2006-25.html

Gilbert, D. T., Pinel, E. C., Wilson, T. D., Blumberg, S. J. and Wheatley, T. P. (1998) 'Immune neglect: A source of durability bias in affective forecasting', *Journal of Personality and Social Psychology*, vol 75, no 3, pp617–638

Hitiris, T. (1999) *Health Care Expenditure and Cost Containment in the G7 Countries*, Discussion paper in economics 99/15, Department of Economics, University of York, York, UK

Lowernstein, G., O'Donoghue, T. and Rabin, M. (2003) 'Projection bias in predicting future utility', *The Quarterly Journal of Economics*, 2003, pp1209–1248

Mattoon, H. R. (1992) 'Can the states solve the health care crisis?' *Economic Perspectives*, November, pp15–27

Nolte, E. and Marti, C. (2008) 'Measuring the health of nations: updating an earlier analysis', *Health Affairs*, January/February, vol 27, no 1, pp58–71

Sackett, D. L. and Torrance, G. W. (1978) 'The utility of different health states as perceived by the general public', *Journal of Chronic Diseases*, vol 31, pp697–704

Zelený, T. and Bencko, V. (2011) 'The splendours and miseries of combined health care financing' (in Czech), *Praktický lékař*, vol 91, no 4, pp206–209

Part IV

Climate Change, Water and Public Health

Introduction

Laura Westra, Colin L. Soskolne and Donald W. Spady

Climate change is considered one of the most severe threats to human security, to human rights in general and to human health specifically. The increasingly frequent and extreme water and weather events associated with a warming planet will negatively affect all aspects of human society. In this part of the book, both climate and water issues are discussed as components of the same problem, starting with the moral obligations we all share.

In Chapter 14, Brown argues that the current emphasis on state responsibility for climate change obscures the equally strong necessity for lifestyle changes by individuals. He argues that individuals should adopt 'climate ethics' and modify their practices accordingly. Not only is this obligation urgent for those living in the affluent 'North', but it applies to all those living an affluent, consumerist lifestyle anywhere. Indeed, all consumers should accept their responsibility for the present impasse.

Ott and Baatz explore further the question of moral responsibility in Chapter 15. After acknowledging the emergence of a sub-field of climate change ethics (beyond the analysis of scientific, economic and political material on this topic), the chapter presents an 'ethical profile of climate change', considered as a 'paradigm case for intergenerational responsibility', as well as a case of 'unfair victimization'. The chapter also discusses such issues as mitigation, adaptation and climate engineering, as well as the likelihood of civil society's ability to accept and implement the steps required to achieve climate change justice.

The next three chapters move us from moral and scientific considerations to the legal aspects of the problem. D'Aloia, in Chapter 16, discusses the role of state constitutions in that regard. He acknowledges that climate change is a 'technological disaster', which places the responsibility for its effects squarely on the shoulders of the inventors and users of technology. These effects are, at least in part, a 'deferred phenomenon', particularly for those who enjoy most of the power to make significant changes. In addition, the effects of climate change are already affecting, and will continue to affect, those people who played no part in producing climate change. Thus far, international law has produced only symbolic documents, which are neither binding nor justiciable. Thus, D'Aloia appeals to constitutions as being effective over longer time periods rather than being subject to short-term political change.

The last two chapters consider water issues, not only as connected to climate change, but specifically relevant to public health. In Chapter 17, Dellapenna starts by discussing customary international law and the importance of its connection to human rights law as expressed in the Berlin Rules. Groundwater, despite its importance, is addressed by very few international legal instruments; but, with the presence of climate change, 'rapidly falling water tables might not appear until some years after a serious overdraft begins'. This would make it too late to devise remedies, as would be suggested by the precautionary principle. The Draft Article on the Law of Transboundary Aquifers and their Report to the United Nations General Assembly would represent a step forward, especially if it became part of a progressive treaty on water.

In Chapter 18, McIntyre discusses international water law from the standpoint of ecological integrity and human rights, starting from General Comment no. 15 (The Right to Water). This document includes both paragraphs that are purely anthropocentric and business oriented, but it also expresses many ecological concerns. Paragraph 11 is particularly important as it asks that water should be treated as a 'social and cultural good' rather than a commercial one. A similar emphasis on the interface between human health and human rights, and the protection of watersheds and aquatic ecosystems, is present in the 2005 Report of the United Nations Sub-Commission on the Promotion and Protection of Human Rights. Many states are now enacting special policies for the future of water and 'eco-system needs', such as South Africa, for instance, as discussed in the next part of this book (see Chapter 22).

The particular orientation of this volume on public health emphasizes the interface between ecological degradation and public health, as discussed in Part I. In fact, Westra (Chapter 1) argues that the denied connection between health and environment is a major component of the multiple failures of today's international instruments regarding the environment and its connection to human rights. The ongoing laissez-faire attitude of major powers regarding climate change is an obvious case in point.

14 Ethical obligations of individuals to reduce greenhouse gas emissions

Donald A. Brown

Introduction

Although the scientific community has understood since the early 1800s how greenhouse gases that naturally appear in the Earth's atmosphere affect global temperatures, the international debate about what should be done to reduce the threat of human-induced warming caused by increasing levels of atmospheric concentrations of greenhouse gases began in earnest in the early 1980s. For most of the time since then, the focus of this debate has been on the obligations of nations to reduce emissions to prevent dangerous climate change. This chapter examines the obligations of individuals for climate change.

As we shall see, the focus on the obligations of nations in the climate change debate is partly responsible for the global community's failure to achieve significant greenhouse gas emissions reductions world-wide. In addition, as we shall see, since all people have duties to reduce greenhouse gas emissions to their fair share of safe global emissions, greater worldwide attention to the duties of individuals to reduce their greenhouse gas emissions is urgently needed given the huge need to dramatically reduce worldwide greenhouse gas emissions to prevent catastrophic harm to tens of millions of people around the world.

The thirty-year climate debate visible to the public has largely focused on two types of issues. First, whether human-induced warming has been sufficiently scientifically proven. Second, whether any proposed national responses to climate change will create unacceptable economic costs to national economies.

In the United States and several other countries there has been a well-financed campaign, often funded by fossil fuel interests, that has fought proposed national responses to climate change on the grounds of lack of scientific certainty and unacceptable economic harms to the nation. And so, despite a highly contested, very publicly visible debate on what to do about climate change, this debate has been almost exclusively focused on the degree of scientific certainty about whether humans are changing the climate and the economic consequences of adopting national policy responses.

Harris has argued that this almost exclusive focus on nations in the public debate about climate change has taken attention off the obligations of individuals who are also responsible for climate change (Harris, 2009, p92). Harris also has claimed that most of the ethics literature on climate change is flawed because it completely overlooks the responsibility of high-emitting individuals in developing countries (Harris, 2009, p122).

Without doubt, most of the international debate about climate change has been about national duties. Yet the largest source of climate change are billions of people who are consuming more than their fair share of fossil fuel energy, and thereby elevating atmospheric concentrations of greenhouse gases to unsafe levels.

Given the magnitude of the emissions reductions needed worldwide to prevent potentially catastrophic climate change, the world is very unlikely to make the huge reductions necessary to prevent dangerous warming unless all individuals accept their moral responsibility to reduce emissions to their fair share of safe global emissions.

Following Harris, this chapter will argue that the responsibility of individuals to reduce their greenhouse gas emission exists both in developed and developing countries. Yet for the most part there has been little discussion in most high-emitting countries, including the United States, about the obligations of entities other than national governments to reduce the threat of climate change, and even less attention to the obligations of individuals in developing countries. However, if the world is going to reduce the enormous threat of climate change, the international community needs to recognize that hundreds of millions of affluent (that is middle- and upper-class) people now live in developing countries and that they have the power to consume as much as people in developed countries (Harris, 2009, p126). There are now hundreds of millions of individuals in developing countries that are buying higher consuming automobiles, houses, and appliances that use energy at levels much greater than necessary to meet basic needs. In fact, individuals are purchasing large mansions and limousines in some of the poorest countries and in so doing exceeding their fair share of safe global emissions. Yet, for the most part, rich people, both in developed and developing states, have thus far escaped moral scrutiny (Harris, 2009, p7).

The debate about climate change at the international level often is framed as a conflict between the rich Northern countries versus the poor Southern countries. Yet these categories are very misleading. As Sachs says:

> [T]he conventional North–South distinction obscures the fact that the dividing line in today's world, if there is any, is not primarily running between Northern and Southern societies, but right across all of these societies. The major rift appears to be between the globalized rich and the localized poor. The North–South divide, instead of separating nations, cuts through each society, albeit in different configurations. It

separates the global consumer class on the one side, from the social majority outside the global circuits, on the other. (Sachs, 2002, p20)

In international negotiations, developing country governments rightfully focus on unjust luxury emissions of rich countries versus survival emissions of poor people in poor countries (Harris, 2009:151). Yet ethical obligations of individuals and organizations exist regardless of country. Consequently, fat cats in Shanghai have just as much ethical obligation to reduce their unfair emissions as do fat cats in London (Harris, 2009:151).

The lack of more widespread discussion of obligations of individuals for climate change is not only to be expected given the strong focus on national obligations in the last several decades. In addition, there have been considerable efforts by organizations and individuals often funded by fossil fuel interests to undermine the notion that anyone has obligations to reduce climate change's threat. Cost arguments against climate change policies are frequently being made in the United States and some other countries that give the impression that there is no obligation of anyone to reduce their carbon footprint if it costs too much to reduce greenhouse gas emissions. In fact, it would appear that at least some people in developed nations believe that decisions to reduce greenhouse gas emissions should be made on the basis of cost alone, without regard to whether people or governments have duties, responsibilities and obligations to others to reduce their emissions.

Given that many people in some developed countries are not convinced that climate change is a real problem, and that there has been a well-financed, well-organized disinformation campaign to convince people that climate change is not a threat, it is not surprising that no visible organized campaign has emerged to encourage individuals to lower their carbon footprint in many developed countries. And so the failure of most individuals to understand their obligations to reduce their carbon footprint is a by-product of the thirty-year debate on climate change which has for the most part ignored the responsibility of individuals around the world to reduce their carbon footprints.

This chapter now examines more rigorously the ethical responsibilities of individuals.

Responsibilities of individuals

All major ethical systems hold that people have obligations not to harm others, regardless of where they are located around the world. That is utilitarian, rights based theories, and justice based ethical theories hold that humans have duties to not harm others. Different ethical theories, as we shall see, might reach different conclusions about how duties should be allocated among people who are causing harm to others but none would deny the responsibility of all people to refrain from harming others no matter where they are located.

Some have argued that individuals are not responsible for climate change because their actions by themselves don't cause climate change; it is only their actions in combination with others that cause harm (see, for example, Sinnott-Armstrong, 2005). Yet since every molecule of greenhouse gases in the atmosphere make the problem worse, it is not true that any individual's greenhouse gas emissions in excess of their fair share of safe global emissions do not contribute to the harm others experience by climate change.

Others have argued that individuals have no responsibility for climate change because individuals contribute such infinitesimal contributions to the global problem that climate change should be understood as a collective problem, not an individual problem (Sinnott-Armstrong, 2005). Yet, because each individual is contributing to the global problem and individuals have a duty to not harm others, individuals have obligations to not exceed their fair share of safe global emissions. As we shall see, determining what is each individual's fair share is a matter of considerable controversy, yet no individual can deny the responsibility to limit their emissions to their fair share of safe global emissions.

Therefore, high-emitting nations and people make ethically flawed claims if they argue that they have no responsibilities, obligations and duties to reduce their greenhouse gas emissions to their fair share of safe global emissions. Such claims are ethically unsupportable because no person or nation has a right either to harm others as a means to achieve their economic health or to endanger others' life, health, or security for self-interested reasons.

Yet the strong ethical conclusion that individuals have duties to not harm others by their release of greenhouse gases into the atmosphere does not lead to precise guidance on what any person's quantitative obligation is. As we shall see, quantifying any individual's obligation for reducing greenhouse gas emissions is a matter of considerable ethical complexity and therefore an issue about which reasonable people that acknowledge their general ethical responsibility may disagree on. Yet, as we shall see, concluding that it is challenging to determine precisely what ethics requires quantitatively of any individual in terms of ethically supportable greenhouse gas emissions is not to conclude that a strong ethical case can't be made that individuals emitting high levels of greenhouse gas are emitting in excess of what justice requires of them even though it might be difficult to define precisely what justice requires quantitatively. In other words, strong ethical condemnation can be made of those individuals who are emitting high levels of greenhouse gases even though it may be difficult to determine what justice requires of them precisely. That is, it is quite easy to spot ethically troublesome individual behaviour on greenhouse gas emissions despite controversies in specifying precise ethically determined greenhouse gas emissions limits for individuals.

Furthermore, although some philosophers have made arguments that individuals only have moral responsibilities to members of their communities and therefore not people outside of their community, this 'communitarian' understanding of ethical obligations is very difficult to justify particularly in cases like climate change where one can demonstrate that individuals are responsible causally for catastrophic harm to others outside their community.

As Harris has argued, climate change is a problem about which only a 'communitarian' ethic makes sense (Harris, 2009). A 'communitarian' ethics holds that all people responsible to all people to prevent harm regardless of where they live. Our moral duty to help protect people from harm in whose production we are implicated is more stringent than our moral duty to help protect people from harm in whose production we are not materially involved (Pogge, 2005). This is not to say that people have no duty to help people who are suffering from causes not attributable to them. Peter Singer has argued that if it is in our power to prevent something very bad from happening without sacrificing something that is morally significant, we have a duty to do it (Singer, 1972, p40). That is, for example, because we are able to do so, we ought to prevent the starvation of thousands of people outside our country according to Singer. And so, a case can be made that even if there were no causally based responsibility for people to reduce their greenhouse gas emissions, they should as matter of ethics do so if they can do so. Nevertheless, in the case of climate change the causal connection between high emitters' behaviour and the suffering of others make duties, obligations, and responsibilities unequivocal.

For this reason, individuals have strong duties to reduce greenhouse gas emissions from activities that are wasteful or are that derive from their use of luxury items that consume large amounts of fossil fuel in their production. And so a case can be made, for instance, that individuals who are exceeding their fair share of safe global emissions should not purchase large automobiles or trucks for which they have no need that consume high amounts of fossil fuel. Similarly, individuals should not purchase large homes that consume large amounts of fossil fuel energy without a compelling need for a large house.

All individuals are responsible for greenhouse gas emissions that have caused and will continue to cause harm to others, and as a result all have responsibilities to limit their harmful emissions to their fair share of safe global emissions without regard to whether their nation has acted. Yet, as we shall see, different theories of justice would reach different conclusions about each individual's fair share of safe global emissions.

Distributive justice requires that burdens of preventing harm among many individuals should be allocated equally unless there are morally relevant criteria for treating some individuals differently. For this reason, high-emitting individuals that are emitting greenhouse gas emissions above per capita emissions limits needed to prevent harm from climate change that cannot make the case that their emissions levels are justified by morally relevant criteria are clearly exceeding their fair share of safe global emissions.

Given differences in distributive justice theories, one might ask: who are the high-emitting individuals exceeding their fair share of safe global emissions? Although different theories of distributive justice would lead to different allocations of responsibility, a matter discussed below, it is safe to say that most individuals in developed nations far exceed any conceivably just global allocation of safe greenhouse gas emissions. This is so because of the huge differences in per capita emissions between developed and developing countries coupled with the need to reduce total global greenhouse gas emissions by 60 to 80 per cent to prevent dangerous climate change. For instance, United States citizens in 2006 were emitting 19 tonnes CO_2 equivalent per capita, compared with 1.9 tonnes for Brazil, 0.8 tonnes for the Philippines and 0.3 tonnes for Kenya. Given that these levels of global emissions must be reduced by as much as 60 to 80 per cent, the vast majority of individuals in countries like the United States are emitting at levels far in excess of their fair share of safe global emissions.

In addition, given that responsibility for past emissions is arguably a factor that should be considered in determining fair allocations and given that people in most developed countries have historically emitted much higher levels than people in developing countries, it is quite clear that the vast majority of individuals cannot reasonably argue that they are not exceeding their fair share of safe global emissions. For instance, if responsibility for reducing greenhouse gas emissions is allocated in part on historic emissions, the largest portion of historic responsibility has to be attributed to the United States, with 25.6 per cent of historic emissions, followed by the 15 European Union countries at 15.9 per cent, OPEC countries at 7.4 per cent, Russia at 7.3 per cent, China at 6.4 per cent, Brazil at 5.2 per cent, the 76 countries of AOSIS (Association of Small Island States) and the LDCs (least-developed countries) at 4.1 per cent, Japan at 2.8 per cent, and finally India with next to no responsibility at 0.3 per cent (Müller *et al.*, 2009). Although there are interesting philosophical questions about when a nation or individual should be presumed to have had enough knowledge about likely climate change harm to make them responsible for past emissions, most citizens in high-emitting nations like the United States also have at least some responsibility for historical emissions.

Given the comparatively large per capita and historical emissions in developed countries and the need to make hard-to-imagine large reductions from existing global greenhouse gas emissions levels to prevent catastrophic climate change, it is extremely unlikely that most individuals in developed countries can make any serious argument that they are not currently emitting far in excess of their fair share of safe global emissions.

However, there may be some in developed countries that are emitting very small amounts of greenhouse gases who can make a credible argument that they are already emitting at levels below their fair share of safe global emissions. Yet, since the world averages 4.5 CO_2 tonnes of per capita emissions while countries like the United States are emitting 19 tonnes per capita, and the world must reduce per capita emissions to perhaps less than 2.0 tonnes per capita to prevent dangerous climate change, it is very unlikely that many people in developed countries can make a respectable argument that they are already below their fair share of safe global emissions. If individuals believe that they are already below their fair share of safe global emissions, they have a duty to articulate the theories of distributive justice they are relying on to justify that belief once they understand that climate change is threatening others.

There are also likely to be many individuals in developing countries that are exceeding their fair share of safe global emissions because wealth differences in many developing countries are great and there are wealthy and middle classes in most countries even in countries where the vast majority of the people are very poor. Those groups and individuals in developing countries who are exceeding their fair share of safe global emissions have a duty to reduce their emissions to levels required by retributive and distributive justice notwithstanding that they are in developing countries.

Quantifying individual responsibility

To precisely ascertain the obligation of groups or individuals below the national level, one must consider theories of distributive and retributive justice and, as we shall see, a variety of factual matters that need to considered before theories of justice can be a guide to calculating individual greenhouse gas emissions obligations.

Distributive justice is concerned with how benefits and burdens of social policies should be distributed throughout society, and so distributive justice is usually concerned with forward-looking responsibilities. Retributive justice is concerned with how responsibility for harms should be allocated among those who have already caused harm. Therefore, retributive justice is usually concerned with backward-looking responsibilities.

Because both questions of distributive and distributive justice are relevant to any quantitative level of individual responsibility determine each person's fair share of safe global emissions one must consider not only what the person's fair share of safe global emissions are in the future but also how the individual may have contributed historically to current elevated levels of global atmospheric concentrations of greenhouse gases. That is there are forward-looking issues as well as backward-looking issues that ideally should be considered in determining any person's responsibility.

Climate change raises questions of both distributive and retributive justice because:

- climate change is a problem caused by some people that inflict harm on others;
- some of the poorest people in the world are extremely vulnerable to its impacts and can do little to protect themselves from those impacts;

- the adverse impacts to some of the world's poorest people are likely to be catastrophic;
- huge reductions from status quo emissions are necessary to prevent catastrophic warming; and
- some people have been much more responsible than others for raising atmospheric greenhouse gas concentrations to dangerous levels that are already causing harm for millions.

Because some people more than others have caused the problem, questions of retributive justice arise about how to allocate responsibility for past behaviour and the harm that it has already been caused. Because the world needs to allocate acceptable levels of future greenhouse gas emissions among all peoples, climate change is a problem of distributive justice.

Retributive justice would require all people who cause harm to others to take responsibility to right the wrong they are responsible for usually in proportion to their contribution to the harm. Yet, most ethical theories will only assign blame if those causing harm did so voluntarily with knowledge that their behaviour was causing harm. Because many people in the world have had no understanding of how their activities were contributing to the harm of others, the forward-looking responsibility for individual climate change harms among individuals that are aware of the threat of climate change is much clearer then backward-looking obligations.

Most ethicists assert that any individual's responsibility for harms that they contribute to turns on whether they have knowledge or should have known that their actions were causing harm and whether they had voluntary options to select behaviours that could have avoided the harm. Some people could choose to buy a low consuming vehicle, others could not. Some could afford solar energy, others could not. Some could bicycle to work, others could not. Therefore, assigning greenhouse gas emissions reductions on the basis of past greenhouse gas-emitting behaviour is ethically complicated because, among other things, the presence of real options is a consideration in determining whether an action is blameworthy.

In fact, determining any person's fair share of greenhouse gas emissions runs into a number of complicated factual; questions when attempts are made to determine climate change responsibility for prior actions. This is so because not all people who have emitted greenhouse gases had knowledge that their behaviour was harmful, nor have all people had equal ability to choose energy options that would reduce the threat of climate change. Most ethicists believe that persons are morally responsible for actions that are made voluntarily that the person knew or should have known were potentially harmful (Sinnott-Armstrong, 2005). For this reason, determining the backward-looking obligations of individuals for greenhouse gas emissions is difficult because of the complexity of the factual context that should be considered before assigning blame. However, once a person is on notice that their behaviour could be contributing to great harm to others, they have a duty to determine what they can do to prevent or minimize that harm.

Not all people have been equally free to choose behaviours that are climate-friendly, and so not all people's activities that have contributed to climate change been completely voluntary. Some people have access to bicycle lanes to commute to work, others don't. Some can use public transportation, and others have no public transportation options. Some individuals can afford to buy low emitting automobiles, others cannot. Some few people can afford to put solar energy on their houses, most others cannot. Because only those bad actions that are voluntary are blameworthy according to dominant ethical theories, assigning responsibility for prior actions that have caused climate change must consider whether people engaged in greenhouse generating activities had options to choose climate change friendly options.

Most theories of ethics also are reluctant to assign blame if the person had no knowledge that their behaviour was causing harm or was threatening harm. Since many people in the world still don't understand that a gas-guzzling car is contributing to famine in Africa, most ethicists would be reluctant to call driving a huge automobile for sheer fun unethical until the driver was warned that driving a large car could be contributing to harm experienced by others. For this reason, ethical duties to desist from behaviour that is increasing atmospheric concentrations would begin once a person knew or should have known that they are contributing to the harm of others. Yet even in this case, an argument can be made that there can be no ethical blame if the person has no options to select climate friendly behaviours. And so determining individual quantitative responsibility for past behaviour is a complex endeavour both factually and theoretically.

Most ethicists would also be reluctant to assign blame for past greenhouse gas emissions if those who emitted emissions above their fairs share of safe global emissions in the past had no options to choose climate benign behaviours. Yet because government institutions can provide the changes in energy consumption options needed to give people a greater ability to choose climate friendly behaviours by such things as building public transportation, bicycle lanes, or by subsidization of renewable energy and individuals can pressure government to make energy options more climate friendly, an ethical case can be made that individuals have a duty to encourage government institutions to make changes in infrastructure or climate friendly energy availability so that individuals can more easily satisfy their obligations to reduce the threat of climate change.

Stating precisely what is required of individuals in regard to future emissions also runs into some ethical disagreement. This is so because there are several different respectable ethical theories about what distributive justice requires concerning how duties and burdens should be distributed. Respectable theories for allocating future responsibility include distributions on the basis of equality, need or Rawlsian allocations that would benefit poor people first, just to name a few. These different theories of distributive justice would reach different quantitative conclusions about what is each person's fair share of future greenhouse gas emissions levels. However, since, as we have seen, most high-emitting individuals can not satisfy any theory of just allocations very few high-emitting individuals can come close to justifying current emissions levels on any respectable theory of just distributions. Therefore it is possible to conclude that those high-emitting individuals that deny responsibility for future greenhouse gas emissions are acting unjustly even in cases where it is difficult to determine unambiguously what distributive justice requires. For this reason, an examination of the ethical obligations of individuals may not lead to a clear consensus of what ethics requires of them in regard to acceptable maximum levels of emissions, yet ethical reflection can achieve universal ethical condemnation of status quo emissions levels for most individuals in developed countries and high-emitting individuals in developing nations. And so we do not need to know what justice requires precisely to spot the injustice of high-emitting individuals.

In addition to the ethical need to comply with some quantitatively determined fair share of safe global emissions where justice is determined by respectable theories of distributive justice, there are several ethical arguments that can be made that those who have the ability to reduce the great suffering of others, have an obligation to do so even if they are complying with a quantitative specification of an individual's fair share of safe global emissions. One such argument for this conclusion is that individuals have obligations to restore the basic conditions necessary for the enjoyment of rights to those whose human rights are being violated.

Without doubt, the kinds of harms that are expected from human-induced climate change will interfere with basic human rights. In fact climate change will put into jeopardy the very lives, health, and indispensible natural resources upon which lives of hundreds of millions of people around the world depend, threatening the poorest and most vulnerable people in particular. In fact, climate change is a threat to things that are the material conditions for human life and it is interference with the dignity of human life that is usually the predicate for recognizing that specifiable human rights have been violated. In fact, climate change is currently threatening the very existence of nations like the Maldives and Kiribati. Since we have no problem acknowledging an ethical obligation to avoid trampling the specifiable rights of others, we may easily extend this principle to climate change and conclude that anyone who can do so should reduce greenhouse gas emissions to levels necessary to restore basic rights even if one is not emitting at levels above some quantitatively level prescribed by distributive justice. In other words, as long as some peoples' human rights are being infringed by climate change all people have a duty to reduce their emissions to zero if they can do so without great harm to themselves.

One might ask how an individual's obligations can be quantified. As we have seen, distributive justice would require that burdens to reduce harms should be divided equally unless another allocation can be justified on morally relevant grounds. And so, equal per capita emissions for all humans need not be the only ethically defensible allocation formula, but it is certainly a helpful way of thinking about individual responsibility initially. The following is not meant to be a final definition of what is each individual's fair share of safe global emissions but only a heuristic device to encourage the refinement of the thinking needed to determine any individual's fair share of safe global emissions. That is, the following is meant as generating a rule of thumb to trigger deeper consideration of any individual's responsibility.

The following are per capita CO_2 emissions for different countries from burning fossil fuels (Guardian, 2011, quoting United States Energy Information Agency):

1 Australia: 19.6 tonnes
2 United States: 17.7 tonnes
3 Russia: 11.2 tonnes
4 Germany: 9.3 tonnes
5 UK: 8.4 tonnes
6 China: 5.8 tonnes
7 World average: 4.5 tonnes
8 India: 1.4 tonnes
9 Africa average: 1.1 tonnes
10 Chad: 0.03 tonnes

And so if the world per capita emissions average is 4.5 tonnes, and if the world must reduce current emissions by 80 per cent by 2050 to prevent dangerous climate change, a case can be made that the global per capita goal should be 0.9 tonnes per person (or 4.5 tonnes minus 80%) by 2050. This would make the average United States reduction a 95 per cent reduction from current per capita levels by 2050. Because mainstream scientists believe that to achieve safe global emissions levels, the world must reduce total existing global emissions by 25 per cent to 40 per cent by 2020, a case can be made that global per capita goal for 2020 should be 3.38 tonnes per person (4.5 tonnes minus 25%) Yet, these calculations would only equalize on a per capita emissions in the future. It does not take into consideration any reductions based upon obligations for historical emissions. Here is some comparative data for historical emissions from 1850 until 2007:

1 United States: 339,174 tonnes or 28.8 per cent
2 China: 105,915 tonnes or 9.0 per cent
3 Russia: 94,679 tonnes or 8.0 per cent
4 Germany: 81,194.5 tonnes or 6.9 per cent
5 UK: 68,763 tonnes or 5.8 per cent
6 Japan: 45,629 tonnes or 3.87 per cent

7 France: 32,667 tonnes or 2.77 per cent
8 India: 28,824 tonnes or 2.44 per cent
9 Canada: 25,716 tonnes or 2.2 per cent
10 Ukraine: 25,431 tonnes or 2.2 per cent

(Guardian, 2011, quoting The World Resources Institute)

If these figures are translated to historical emissions per person, the following amounts could be attributed to different countries (Guardian, 2011, quoting Norwegian University of Industry and Technology):

1 Luxembourg: 1,429 tonnes
2 UK: 1,127 tonnes
3 United States: 1,126 tonnes
4 Belgium: 1,026 tonnes
5 Czech Republic: 1,006 tonnes
6 Germany: 987 tonnes
7 Estonia: 877 tonnes
8 Canada: 780 tonnes
9 Kazakhstan: 682 tonnes
10 Russia: 666 tonnes

And so a case can be made that the 0.9 tonnes per person goal should be reduced further for those individuals that have been historically high-emitters of greenhouse gases. Exactly how these per capita historical emissions should be allocated quantitatively raises the questions about when the historical emission trigger responsibility should start, a matter beyond the scope of this chapter.

And so a strong ethical case can be made that any individual's responsibility should be, at the very minimum:

- 0.9 tonnes per person (4.5 tonnes per capita, reduced by 80%) by 2050
- 3.38 tonnes per person (4.5 tonnes per capita, reduced by 35%) by 2020
- Minus some percentage of the historical emissions per capita of the nation (this would vary depending on the country and the starting point in time that arguably triggered the individual responsibility)

Although determining precisely what any individual's ethically based greenhouse gas emissions target should be is complex due to the complicating factor of responsibility for historical emissions, for purposes of giving individuals a sense of the magnitude of the emissions reduction challenge we can say without fear of contradiction that an individual goal of 3.38 tonnes per person per year by 2020 is the highest defensible goal that can be justified, yet this number could be strongly challenged as still being greatly unfair to poor people who are vulnerable to climate change on a variety of grounds.

Furthermore, as we have seen above, a strong ethical case can be made that any individual's obligation to reduce greenhouse gas should be understood to be zero, if carbon neutrality can be achieved by the individual without great harm to the individual.

References

Guardian (2011) 'Which nations are most responsible for climate change?', *The Guardian,* 21 April, available at www.guardian.co.uk/environment/2011/apr/21/countries-responsible-climate-change? (accessed 24 January 2012)

Harris, P. (2009) *World Ethics and Climate Change: From International to Global Justice,* Edinburgh Studies in World Ethics, Edinburgh, UK

Müller, B., Höhne, N. and Ellermann, C. (2007) *Differentiating (Historic) Responsibilities for Climate Change Summary Report,* Oxford Climate Policy, Oxford, UK, available at www.oxfordclimatepolicy.org/publications/documents/DifferentiatingResponsibility.pdf

Pogge, T. (2005) 'Real world justice', *The Journal of Ethics,* vol 9, no 1–2, pp29–53

Sachs. W. (2002) *The Jo'Berg Memo: Fairness in a Fragile World,* Heinrich Böll Foundation, Berlin, Berlin, Germany, available at www.boell-afghanistan.org/downloads/Joburg_Memo_engl..pdf (accessed 24 January 2012)

Singer, P. (1972) 'Famine, affluence, and morality', *Philosophy and Public Affairs,* vol 1, no 3, pp229–243

Sinnott-Armstrong, W. (2005) *It's Not* My *Fault: Global Warming and Individual Moral Obligations,* Advances in the Economics of Environmental Research, AECE-V005, available at http://sites.duke.edu/wsa/papers/files/2011/05/wsa-itsnotmyfault2005.pdf

15 Domains of climate ethics

Konrad Ott and Christian Baatz

Introduction

Literature on climate change is abundant. Beside the scientific, economic, technological and political literature, there is also a substantial body of ethical analysis of the many moral problems embedded in climate change. The term 'climate ethics' (CE) is used for such analyses.

Our aim in this chapter is to present a systematic overview of CE. We distinguish between different domains (topics) of CE.[1] A comprehensive CE will be established if well-substantiated positions in each domain can be coherently conjoined. We provide an outline of the main components of such theory.

At its core, CE refers to a triangular structure of how to reduce the negative impacts of climate change by:

- *mitigation* (reduction of greenhouse gas emissions),
- *adaptation*, and
- *climate engineering*.

Some sections below refer to this structure, but, prior to that, we refer to the ethical profile of climate change, followed by a reflection on climate economics. In addition, we discuss distribution schemes for remaining emissions entitlements. We assume some familiarity with the basics of climate science and with mainstream economics.

The ethical profile of climate change

The basic physical mechanism of a greenhouse effect is beyond doubt. There are many remaining uncertainties in the details of climate change, but the 'big picture' of a warming world, at least partly due to anthropogenic emissions, has been scientifically established.[2] Recent scientific attention focuses on 'tipping points' and feedback mechanisms in the global climate system. All in all, scientific understanding of the global climate system has increased and the models are more trustworthy than 20 years ago.[3]

Anthropogenic climate change is not repugnant in itself. Imagine a world with low CO_2 concentrations that would allow for only an Inuit-like human life in a species-poor borealis-type world. If human cultures and biodiversity could flourish, and if this 'cold' world could be warmed by releasing some GHGs, most people would not oppose such a scenario.

Climate change is a moral problem because of its negative impacts on human systems (and on biodiversity) in the short, medium and long run. Not all impacts need, however, to be seen as negative. Negative impacts are those that count as evils (i.e. harms/perils) according to our axiological common sense. In human life, we are facing evils that either are naturally induced (e.g. natural disasters) or that result from the behaviour of other persons. Climate change manifests itself in events that look like natural disasters, but may be anthropogenic. However, hardly any single event, except for sea-level rise contributed to by glacial melt, can be attributed to human emissions with certainty.

Although only weather events are directly observable, the increase in risks associated with climate change can be measured and liability for such increases can be assessed (Allen, 2003). What can be predicted with some confidence is a modification in probability, frequency and intensity of events that cause evils for humans. Such disasters are, for instance, floods, droughts, heat waves, forest fires, landslides, spread of diseases, hurricanes, heavy rainfall and inundations, declines in local harvests, desertification, increased water stress in (semi-)arid regions, conflicts over scarce resources, political instability and the like.

The negative (and positive) impacts of climate change will fall upon specific people by chance, but there are some 'patterns of likeliness'. If a person lives on the coast of Bangladesh or in Mali, it is more likely that he/she will be affected by flood or drought than a person in the hills of, say, France or Germany. All models indicate that poor people in the global South will have to face most perils. Risks are imposed upon them. Those people might be unaware or ignorant of the problem that is affecting them. Since these people do not contribute much to climate change, they are, intuitively, victimized by the polluters.

Climate change is a paradigm case for intergenerational responsibility since, once induced, it will continue for centuries (e.g. with the melting of ice shields in Greenland and Antarctica). The ethical literature on responsibility towards posterity can be applied to the case of climate change. Parfit's 'future individual paradox' does not refute the widespread conviction that there is some moral responsibility vis-à-vis future generations (Ott, 2004).[4] Such responsibility implies, minimally, that it is mandatory to bequeath overall environmental conditions that are not inimical to a decent life for all humans. Such decency can be conceived according to the capability-approach of Nussbaum and Sen. This implies the prima facie obligation not to change the global climate by GHG emissions in a way that dignity, decency and the safety of human life is impaired or threatened. This highly unspecific formulation must be specified as CE proceeds through its different domains. The moral profile of climate change can be conceived as:

- Negative external effects in conjunction with market failure (economics).
- Increase in pain, suffering, sorrow which affects the overall welfare function for worse (welfare-based ethics).
- Imposing risks on other people without informed prior consent given by them (ethics of risk).
- Impairing rights of contemporary and future persons (right-based morality).
- Unfair victimization of other people (ethics of justice).

Rights-based morality, ethics of risk, and ethics of justice are close allies. Under these approaches, it seems plausible to conceive of climate change as a case of *victimization*. Victimization is one type of injury against other people. The facets of such victimization are as manifold as the types of evils that are associated with climate change. If one adopts the principle that it is more important to avoid harms than to bring about benefits, the attitude against victimization can be taken by utilitarianism, especially negative utilitarianism. For both Kantian and utilitarian ethicists, it seems hard to accept increases in the standard of living of wealthy persons that impose severe risks on poor people (Shue, 1992). Utilitarian ethicists such as Broome (1992) and welfare ethicists such as Lumer (2002) come to results on mitigation policies that differ significantly from those of economists who calculate the economic optimal (efficient) climate policy (see below). This indicates that neoclassical economics is not simply applied utilitarian welfare ethics, but is, in fact, a very different approach.

Ethical suppositions in climate economics

Neo-classical economists are not willing to avoid climate change 'at any cost'. If energy input by fossil fuels increases production of commodities, but has GHG emissions as unwelcome side-effects, and if the consumption of commodities fulfils preferences while the side-effects create negative external effects, the GHG emissions should be curbed to the extent only to which these external effects outweigh the utilities being created by consumption (Cf. Schröder, 2002). Indeed, standard economic approaches rely on the idea of maximizing net present value. The paradigmatic calculation is Nordhaus's 'classical' DICE model (Nordhaus, 1994). Tol continues this efficiency approach (EA), in which he downplays the moral problems of climate change (Tol, 2008). However, the application of EA to global, unique and long-term problems such as climate change has raised skepticism even among economists.

Meanwhile, it is widely accepted that EA is not neutral with respect to ethics. First of all, it must be clearly understood that in all models, costs are opportunity costs, not payments.[5] Furthermore, there are many ethical assumptions in EA models. Such assumptions are:

- the rate of discount;
- the curving of the damage function;
- aggregation of impacts in a single welfare function;
- the marginal value of future consumption units;
- the assumed value of a statistical life;
- technological innovation as either exogenous or endogenous to climate change;
- monetary value of environmental change and loss of biodiversity; and
- shift in transaction costs, control costs and search costs.

Economic calculations are highly sensitive to these assumptions. It makes a difference whether the damage function is shaped in a linear fashion or whether it allows for non-linearity. A linear damage function models climate change as rather smooth and without unpleasant surprises. Modelling the monetary value of a statistical life may downplay the death of poor humans. The many cultural amenities of a stable natural environment are also downplayed in most economic models. The costs of strong mitigation will increase if technological innovation in carbon-free energy supply systems is modelled as exogenous. Costs will decrease if innovations are modelled as endogenous (which is more likely).

Another important variable is the discount rate. Stern, choosing a far lower rate than Nordhaus, argues for immediate and strong mitigation measures (Stern, 2007). However, both approaches rely on debateable assumptions (Hampicke, 2011; see also the contributions in Hampicke and Ott, 2003).

The debate on the ethical assumptions within EA motivates many (prudent) economists to adopt an alternative approach, called the *standard price approach* (SPA). This approach starts from a standard set by some legitimate authority (democratic politics, fair negotiation, discourse-based). The primary task of economics is to calculate how this standard can be reached by minimizing costs. In SPA, the role of economics is less a master of rational choice than a servant to political objectives.[6] SPA, however, does not answer the question of how to determine such a standard with respect to atmospheric greenhouse gas concentrations. We turn to this question now.

Stabilization level of atmospheric greenhouse gas concentration

Article 2 of the United Nations Framework Convention on Climate Change (UNFCCC) defines the ultimate objective of this convention, and of all related protocols, to stabilize atmospheric greenhouse gas concentration at a level that prevents dangerous anthropogenic interference with the climate system. Very often, a 'tolerable window' approach has been specified with reference to a modest increase in global mean temperature (GMT). Very popular is the so-called '2°C target' proposed by the Wissenschaftlicher Beirat der Bundesregierung Globale Umweltveränderungen (WBGU, 2009). This target claims that GMT should not increase more than 2°C compared to pre-industrial GMT. It has been argued that the sum of evils associated with a higher increase in GMT might become too high. Some scientists, such as James Hansen, argue that a 2°C increase in GMT is still too risky since the ice shields of Greenland and Antarctica might melt down slowly but steadily (over centuries) at such a GMT. Thus, the 2°C target is ambitious from a political perspective, but from a strictly risk-averse position, it might still be too risky.

Some years ago, a study on behalf of the German Environmental Protection Agency (Ott *et al.*, 2004) outlined an ethical argument in favour of very low GHG stabilization levels. The study compared CE approaches that argue from within different ethical theories. Almost all approaches, except ethical contractarianism, came to the conclusion that there is a moral commitment to curb global GHG emissions in order to reach the lowest possible GHG stabilization levels. This agreement encompassed variants of utilitarianism, welfare-based consequentialism, deontological approaches, Rawlsian approaches, Aristotelian prudential approaches, physiocentric approaches and, of course, Jonas's ethics of responsibility. Thus, one can argue with some confidence that, despite all controversies, most current ethical theories demand the stabilization of GHG at the lowest feasible level. This is, indeed, a remarkable convergence of different theories that should not be ignored by politicians. Clearly, the clause 'as low as possible' requires interpretation and specification.

In any case, taking the 2°C target seriously requires that GHG concentrations remain far below 560 parts per million by volume (ppmv) of CO_2 equivalent (CO_2-eq). Given all the carbon on planet Earth, especially coal resources, given economic growth, and given roughly 9.2 billion humans in 2050, it will be very difficult to reduce GHG emissions to the extent needed. All in all, we propose to adopt a prudent and cautious, but not completely unrealistic stabilization level of 450ppmv CO_2-eq. Given current GHG concentrations (430ppmv CO_2-eq) and an increase of 1.5–1.9ppmv $CO_{2\text{-eq}}$ each year, this target would mean that the net intake of GHG into the atmosphere must be stopped within two decades. Global emissions must peak in 2025, and then continuously decline as steeply as possible. This target requires deep cuts in emissions in the North but, meanwhile, it requires cuts in countries like China, too.[7] There might be some overshot above this limit, but it is better to face overshot *as such* than to adapt objectives to emission realities step by step.

Distribution schemes for remaining emission entitlements

Any stabilization target raises the problem of how to distribute the remaining sink capacities (or carbon budget) fairly. There are many schemes of how the carbon should be distributed under the given target structure.[8] Since emission entitlements are only one good among many, it might be tempting to embed the problem at stake into a more comprehensive theory of distributive justice. But, because such a theory will be essentially contested, it seems more viable to isolate emission entitlements as one specific good, the distribution of which is to be determined irrespective of how other goods are distributed in a globalized world. Thus, we set aside all problems of background distribution.

If one assumes, first, that the atmosphere has the status of a *global common good*, and if one, second, adopts the Rawlsian intuition on justice that all goods should be distributed equally unless an unequal distribution benefits all, egalitarian schemes deserve special attention. Recently, we have argued in favour of an egalitarian *per-capita* approach in more detail (Ott, 2010a). The argument claims that it is fair to shift the burden of proof to those who favour unequal distribution schemes for global common pool goods. Reasons in favour of an unequal distribution might be that some people deserve more entitlements from a moral point of view, or that unequal schemes are beneficial to all consumers in the global village. There are only a few articles that defend this position.[9] Another reason is special needs.

The most plausible claim with respect to special needs might be the claim for heating in winter in the North which might be seen as more basic than the 'luxury need' for cooling in the tropical zones. As a matter of fact, income levels can explain the differences in emission profiles better than natural factors (Neumayer, 2002). If so, heating needs can be addressed by technological innovations and social policies in rich Northern countries and should not open Pandora's box of a global debate on special needs. In such a debate, there will be claims for special needs in many countries, such as special needs to visit friends and relatives in large countries with a high mobility (as in the United States). An egalitarian scheme is well advised not to address special needs.

An egalitarian scheme under the target-structure given in the previous section would mean that each person is given a carbon budget of roughly 1.8–2.0 tonnes of CO_2 a year.[10] If the global carbon budget is allocated to national states according to their populations, this implies emission reductions of 80 per cent (Germany) or even 90 per cent (United States). There are different proposals of how to deal with such budgets .The budget might be auctioned or distributed directly to individuals. In most proposals, the budgets can be traded freely on carbon markets. If properly implemented, such an egalitarian scheme has the welcome effect that persons with low emissions (India, Africa) will benefit because they can sell their entitlements.

In any case, the political integrity of such schemes must be secured against misuse.[11]

Adaptation opportunities

Humans are practical beings with large capacities for problem-solving. They are settlers on a global scale who can cope with a great variety of environmental conditions. These capacities can be used for adaptation. Adaptation strategies may include building structures such as dykes, behavioural patterns such as siesta, protective strategies against forest fires, improved water supply systems in arid regions, different crops in agriculture, and so on.[12] Adaptation has a broad spectrum across different dimensions of societal life.

Rich countries can utilize scientific knowledge, financial capital, political administration, and infrastructure in order to implement adaptation strategies on their own. Given only modest climate change and proper adaptation strategies, the prospects for the temperate zones are not completely bleak. The situation is different in Southern countries were many institutional preconditions for effective adaptation are lacking.

The emergent adaptation discourse suggests that there can be no such thing as a global master plan on how to adapt. Adaptation is literally 'concrete' because internal and external resources, cultural lifestyles, and patterns of environmental practices must be rearranged within adaptation strategies. Details are beyond the competencies of ethicists.

It is very likely that there will be adaptation funding for Southern countries under the UNFCCC regime. The extent of payments coming from Northern countries will need to be negotiated. Some calculations indicate that even US$100 billion per year would not be sufficient. This cost does not include costs for the provision and resettlement of climate refugees.[13] It is very likely that there will never be enough money in the fund. Since adaptation funding is done under the condition of scarcity of resources, applications for such funding must be governed and controlled by fixed criteria. In order not to fall prey to strategic behaviour, the financing of adaptation has to be done with sobriety and prudence.

By intuition, the most vulnerable and marginalized groups should be the first beneficiaries of adaptation funding. Grasso proposes the following vulnerability-based decision rule for spending: the lower the overall level of human security, the more adaptation funds are due (Grasso, 2007). It can not be denied that vulnerability and human security are important criteria for funding priorities. But if these criteria remain out of balance with other criteria, there is an incentive to present oneself as poor, helpless, ignorant, devoid of capabilities and initiative, and so on. If such an outcome is to be avoided, the criterion of vulnerability should not be the only one.

Many poor people do not live in misery, but use their indigenous knowledge to reproduce a decent livelihood. Why not allocate a substantial portion of adaptation funding to communities that have sustained a non-miserable livelihood for generations and might continue to do so even under climate change impacts? Most experts would agree that adaptation must be something other than an intensification of emergency aid. Adaptation funding should reward and stimulate activities by which adaptation is linked to other objectives of sustainable development. It should pay special attention to the conservation and restoration of natural capital (cf. Ott and Döring, 2008). Activities that combine local adaptation, biodiversity conservation, ecosystem restoration, and carbon storage should be most encouraged. Adaptation funding should give priority to 'eco-carbon' activities.

Climate engineering

In his most recent publications, Teller proposes solar radiation management as a technical measure against climate change (Teller *et al.*, 2002). According to Teller, a doubling of CO_2 concentrations could be compensated by a decrease of roughly 2–3 per cent of solar radiation reaching the surface of planet Earth. Solar radiation management (SRM) is one type of climate engineering, defined as deliberate human interference with the global carbon cycle or composition of the atmosphere. Carbon dioxide removal (CDR) is another type of climate engineering. CDR has much overlap with 'eco-carbon' adaptation strategies and is often close to nature conservation and restoration. The effects of CDR are promising, but rather slow to materialize.

The profile of SRM is different. Ignoring the SRM-option of placing some thousand reflexive discs in outer space on economic grounds (costs of some trillion United States dollars), attention falls upon one specific SRM option: *continuous release of large amounts of sulphate aerosols into the stratosphere.* This option seems attractive to many scientifically credible scholars, especially those in the United States (Blackstone and Long, 2009; Keith *et al.*, 2010).[14] SRM has already become a tempting 'superpower' option. The more popular message is often quite simple: If there is a quick, cost-efficient, effective technological solution (like SRM) to the problem of climate change by which a decline in economic growth and a change in consumerist lifestyle can be avoided, the United States should not hesitate to embrace such a solution.[15] In case of emergency, even unilateral action by technological advanced national states might be the *ultima ratio.*

Together with Betz, we have mapped arguments both for and against SRM (Ott, 2010b; Betz and Cacean, 2011). The contra-side of this map of arguments is quite crowded. There are arguments using the concept of hubris used by Jonas: engineering planet Earth might be an instance of such hubris. Since injecting sulphate aerosols into the stratosphere will affect weather patterns all around the world, it can be questioned on the grounds of distributive justice, among others (cf. Svoboda *et al.*, 2011).

With respect to the political economy of SRM, it might be argued that SRM should be seen as a protective measure in favour of outdated United States industries with their high-emission profiles against the global diffusion of smart 'green' industries with comparatively low GHG emissions. SRM fits frightening well within the profile of the most questionable variant of capitalism and its military-industrial complex. Launching SRM as an economic-political project will discourage investments in carbon-poor economics. Moreover, there are risk-based ethical concerns against sulphate-based SRM.

Once fully deployed, SRM could not be easily stopped if it is not combined with stringent mitigation. SRM, however, once tested in large field tests and fully deployed, may realize itself as a *replacement* of mitigation efforts. In this case, there would be a future world with unmitigated high GHG concentrations in the lower atmosphere and a sulphate-based shield against solar radiation in the upper atmosphere. Both kinds of human interferences with the atmosphere must be kept in some balance over a long period of time (Matthews and Caldeira, 2007). If it turns out that SRM has substantial negative side-effects and, thus, should be stopped, future generations may be trapped in a dilemma. One course of action would be stopping SRM. If so, there would be sudden and rapid climate change (some °C in few decades). The second course would be to continue SRM. It seems highly repugnant to impose such a risk upon future generations without adequate justification (cf. Gardiner, 2010). One should consider in advance how such a dilemmatic situation might be avoided. The old criterion of reversibility (Birnbacher, 1988) requires a robust and viable exit-strategy for SRM. Without such a strategy, SRM should be rejected. It has often been said that SRM should be *supplementary* to mitigation, adaptation and CDR. In reality, however, SRM, once tested in large field tests and fully deployed may come to *replace* mitigation efforts.

All arguments considered, CDR should be researched and tested in the field, while SRM might be researched theoretically by experiments and modelling. There should be a ban on large field test for, at least, the next 20 or, better, 30 years. Meanwhile, the risks and threats of SRM can become a useful 'stick behind the door' that might motivate national states to co-operate on a proper global mitigation and adaptation regime. SRM will again become prominent on the agenda if the prediction that all global climate policies are bound to fail should materialize.

Conclusions

It is mandatory that CE should provide some reasonable ethical orientation. Without a common moral grounding, climate negotiations will fall prey to the predicament of becoming a mere 'muddling through', governed by strategic and tactical cleverness of the thousands of stakeholders and negotiators gathering each year at conferences. Thus, let us summarize some preliminary results of our 'topical' reasoning:

- Ethical profiling: impacts seen as evils, objections against imposing risks and victimization, intergenerational responsibility.
- Standard price approach in climate economics, discarding 'efficiency' approaches.
- Ultimate stabilization objective at '2°C ↔ 450ppmv CO_2-eq'.
- Long-term egalitarian distribution at 1.8–2 tonnes per person per year in conjunction with emissions trading.
- Mandatory attitude for Northern countries to assist adaptation strategies in the global South in conjunction with sustainability 'eco-carbon' criteria for funding.
- Research on CDR options, ban (or moratorium) on SRM.

The triangular tensions among mitigation, adaptation and climate-engineering strategies should not be seen as a portfolio. Within this triangular affair, mitigation deserves priority because mitigation is a precondition for adaptation, and for CDR being successfully performed.

Mitigation on a global scale is not utopian any longer. Despite the continuing rise of GHG emissions (they added 1.9ppmv CO_2-eq to the atmosphere in the year 2010), substantial change is in the making. Public awareness has increased worldwide. Renewable energies already are going to be established globally. The diffusion of existing carbon-poor technologies can be accelerated by political strategies and economic incentives. GHG emissions have been decoupled from GDP growth in advanced industrial societies.[16] There is scientific knowledge, plenty of capital for carbon-low investments, established technologies waiting to be mainstreamed, and global civil society is becoming more aware. Interestingly enough, the major achievements of modern societies (science, technology, capital, public reasoning) are available for problem-solving. If the course of action proposed here could be agreed upon and become a safely paved and reliable pathway, the speed of taking steps may be increased substantially.

Notes

1 The idea to distinguish different domains is taken from Grasso (2007).

2 Minor mistakes of IPPC which have attracted the media are painful according to IPCC's review standards but do not shatter this overall picture.

3 So-called 'climate skepticism' still presumes to adopt the scientific virtue of being skeptical but, as climate science proceeds, this presumption has become misleading.

4 The famous future-individual paradox was outlined in Parfit (1983).

5 Most costs are decreases or delays in growth rates of GDP. Given the magnitude of global GDP, even small declines in growth rates amount to huge monetary costs.

6 At least with respect to environmental problems SPA has several advantages over EA since it is hard to see how the 'efficient' pollution of air, rivers, and marine systems or the 'efficient' number of species on planet Earth might be calculated.
7 For a discussion of the duties of individual persons to reduce GHG emissions see Baatz (2012a).
8 Grandfathering, basic needs, Rawlsian difference principles, proportionality, per-capita schemes.
9 The most inspiring criticism of egalitarianism is to be found in Caney (2009). Caney's idea is to embed GHG emissions in a holistic scheme of goods, capacities, and sources of anthropogenic forcing. This holistic approach adds complexity to an already complex matter.
10 This approach should be based on a benchmark to avoid incentives for pronatalistic population policies.
11 Our proposal would result in something akin to contraction and convergence (Meyer, 1999). Due to the space available we omitted a critical discussion of a rivaling concept, the Greenhouse Development Rights Framework (Baer *et al.*, 2008; but see Kraus and Ott, 2009). However, contraction and convergence is plausible only when combined with a robust scheme of financing adaptation in developing countries. In this way it is also possible to account for the historical dimension of climate change (for detailed analysis see Baatz, 2012b).
12 A conceptual framework on adaptation strategies is given by Smit *et al.* (2000).
13 See overview in Biermann and Boas (2008).
14 Many think tanks that supported climate skepticism some years ago quickly shifted towards SRM enthusiasm.
15 Sometimes it is added that the problem of global cooperation in mitigation GHG can be easily turned into a technological joint effort problem.
16 The German Environmental Advisory Board has outlined scenarios under which Germany could, with modest costs, reach a safe supply system for electricity that runs without nuclear power plants and without conventional coal in the 2030s (cf. Sachverständigenrat für Umweltfragen, 2011).

References

Allen, M. (2003) 'Liability for climate change', *Nature*, vol 421, pp891–892

Baatz, C. (2012a) 'Climate change and individual responsibility to reduce GHG-emissions', forthcoming in *Ethics, Policy and Environment*

Baatz, C. (2012b) 'Compensating those vulnerable to climate change – who should pay and how to raise the funds?', forthcoming in *Ethics, Policy and Environment*

Baer, P., Athanasiou, T., Kartha, S., Kemp-Benedict, E. (2008) *The Greenhouse Development Rights Framework*, Heinrich Böll Foundation, Christian Aid, EcoEquity and the Stockholm Environment Institute, Berlin, Germany

Betz, G. and Cacean, S. (2011) *Sondierungsstudie Ethische Aspekte des Climate Engineering*, Karlsruhe Institute of Technology, Bonn, Germany

Biermann, F. and Boas, I. (2008) 'Protecting climate refugees: the case for a global protocol', *Environment*, vol 50, no 6, pp10–16

Birnbacher, D. (1988) *Verantwortung für Zukünftige Generationen*, Reclam, Stuttgart, Germany

Blackstone, J. J. and Long, J. C. S. (2009) 'The politics of geoengineering', *Science*, vol 327, p527

Broome, J. (1992) *Counting the Cost of Global Warming*, The White Horse Press, Oxford

Caney, S. (2009) 'Justice and the distribution of greenhouse gas emissions', *Journal of Global Ethics*, vol 5, no 2, pp125–145

Gardiner, S. M. (2010) 'Is "arming the future" with geoengineering really the lesser evil? Some doubts about the ethics of intentionally manipulating the climate system', in S. M. Gardiner, S. Caney, D. Jamieson and H. Shue (eds) *Climate Ethics. Essential Readings*, Oxford University Press, New York

Grasso, M. (2007) 'A normative ethical framework in climate change', *Climatic Change*, vol 81, pp223–246

Hampicke, U. (2011) 'Climate change economics and discounted utilitarianism', *Ecological Economics*, vol 72, pp45–52, available at www.sciencedirect.com/science/article/pii/S0921800911003612

Hampicke, U. and Ott, K. (eds) (2003) *Reflections on Discounting*, special issue of *International Journal of Sustainable Development*, vol 6, no 1

Keith, D., Parson, E. and Morgan, M. G. (2010) 'Research on global sun block needed now', *Nature*, vol 463, pp426–427

Kraus, K. and Ott, K. (2009) 'How fair is fair enough? Two climate concepts compared', in T. Böll (ed.) *Climate Change and Justice: On the Road to Copenhagen*, Heinrich Böll Foundation, Berlin, Germany, pp33–36

Lumer, C. (2002) *The Greenhouse: A Welfare Assessment and Some Morals*, University Press Of America, Lanham, MD

Matthews, D. and Caldeira, K. (2007) 'Transient climate-carbon simulations of planetary geoengineering', *PNAS*, vol 104, no 24, p9,952

Meyer, A. (1999) 'The Kyoto Protocol and the emergence of "contraction and convergence"', in O. Hohmeyer and K. Rennings (eds) *Man-made Climate Change*, ZEW Economic Studies, Springer, Heidelberg, Germany, pp291–345

Neumayer, E. (2002) 'Can natural factors explain any cross-country differences in carbon dioxide emissions?', *Energy Policy*, vol 30, pp7–12

Nordhaus, W. (1994) *Managing the Global Commons: The Economics of Climate Change*, MIT Press, Cambridge, MA

Ott, K. (2004), Essential components of future ethics', in R. Döring and M., Rühs (eds) *Ökonomische Rationalität und Praktische Vernunft*, Königshausen & Neumann, Würzburg, Germany, pp83–110

Ott, K. (2010a) 'Ethical foundation of climate change policies', in S. Bergmann and D. Gerten (eds) *Religion and Dangerous Environmental Change*, Lit, Münster, Germany, pp195–203

Ott, K. (2010b) 'Kartierung der Argumente zum Geoengineering', in *Jahrbuch Ökologie 2011*, Hirzel, Stuttgart, Germany, pp20–32

Ott, K. and Döring, R. (2008) *Theorie und Praxis starker Nachhaltigkeit*, second edition, Metropolis, Marburg, Germany

Ott, K., Klepper, G., Lingner, S., Schäfer, A., Scheffran, J. and Sprinz, D. (2004) *Reasoning Goals of Climate Protection. Specification of Article 2 UNFCCC*, report on behalf of the Federal Environmental Protection Agency of Germany (UBA), Berlin, Germany

Parfit, D. (1983) 'Energy policy and the further future', in D. MacLean and P. Brown (eds) *Energy and the Future*, Rowman & Littlefield, Totowa, NJ, pp166–179

Sachverständigenrat für Umweltfragen (SRU) (2011) *Wege zur 100% erneuerbaren Stromversorgung*, Sachverständigenrat für Umweltfragen (SRU), Berlin, Germany

Schröder, M. (2002) *Klimavorhersage und Klimavorsorge*, Springer, Berlin, Heidelberg, Germany

Shue, H. (1992) 'The unavoidability of justice', in A. Hurrel and B. Kingsbury (eds) *The International Politics of the Environment*, Oxford University Press, Oxford

Smit, B., Burton, J., Klein, R. and Wandel, J. (2000) 'An anatomy of adaptation to climatic change and variability', *Climatic Change*, vol 45, pp223–251

Stern, N. (2007) *The Economics of Climate Change: The Stern Review*, Cambridge University Press, Cambridge, UK

Svoboda, T., Keller, K., Goes, M. and Tuana, N. (2011) 'Sulfate aerosol geoengineering: the question of justice', *Public Affairs Quarterly*, vol 25, no 3, pp157–179

Teller, E., Hyde, R. and Wood, L. (2002) *Active Climate Stabilization: Practical Physics-Based Approaches to Prevention of Climate Change*, United States Department of Energy, Washington, DC

Tol, R. (2008) 'Why worry about climate change? A research agenda', *Environmental Values*, vol 17, no 4, pp437–470

WBGU (2009) *Kassensturz für den Weltklimavertrag – Der Budgetansatz*, Wissenschaftlicher Beirat der Bundesregierung Globale Umweltveränderungen, Sondergutachten, Berlin, Germany

16 Climate change and law

A constitutional perspective

Antonio D'Aloia

Introduction

Today climate change is one of the most serious and controversial problems in human experience, and this situation seems likely to intensify (Emanuel, 2007, p84).

In 2010, greenhouse gas (GHG) emissions rose by 5 per cent over 2009, when they had fallen because of the world economic crisis and recession. This crisis temporarily resulted in reduced GHG emissions; however, it also changed governmental priorities and brought forward recession-linked financial and social issues. As a consequence, governments found it hard to implement an eco-oriented agenda. This is an irrational consequence because issues arise from environment crises that are as urgent and dramatic as economic ones.

Climate change still faces various relevant scientific uncertainties as to its cause, its seriousness and how to face it. Somehow these uncertainties still influence opinion as to how to approach these uncertainties and derive solutions. Even so, all these things cannot blur the fact that this is an epochal time for our world, and we cannot yet identify all of its implications.

In the same way, even if climate change is produced in part by natural causes, nobody seriously doubts that human activity has influenced and continues to influence the causative factors and climate change itself. Climate change is not only a 'natural' disaster: it is also, and probably primarily, a 'technological' disaster (Nespor, 2011, p6).

Moreover although many of the risks and challenges of climate change will occur in the future; climate change is not a problem for the future, it is here now. The world is already living this situation, feeling its weight and its power to modify behaviours, lifestyles, expectations and choices.

The interaction between the present and the future works in various ways. The problem is already in progress and doing something (or even many things) is not enough to produce readily visible positive effects. The consequences of climate change will last for decades, even if stringent GHG reductions were immediately and universally applied. Gardiner (2006, p151) stated it in a very effective way: 'climate change is a substantially deferred phenomenon. These facts suggests that intra-generational motivation for acting on climate change may be low.'

Thus, we must not only aim to reduce or control the emission of GHGs, we must be ready to live with the inevitable effects of existing conditions. We also learn to face situations that will exist regardless of what is done now and to manage emergencies that we cannot avoid; their countdown has already started.

In addition, climate change effects are not placed only in time, but also in space. Its effects can show years later and in distant places, affecting countries and people who played no or little part in producing climate change (Pellegrino, 2010, p13).

Climate change and law

Considering this complex and novel scenario, it is easy to understand why the response of law to climate change is difficult to visualize. Law is brought back to its elementary and primary aim: to guarantee man's survival and coexistence, and to preserve environmental and physical conditions in which this survival is possible. It tries to answer a profound question: 'what is the future for our planet and mankind?' (see D'Aloia, 2003; Bifulco, 2008, p61).

Legal responses are beginning, with some initiatives but few results. As Posner and Weisbach (2010, p59) wrote, 'most of legislation and other forms of government action that have taken place have been largely symbolic'. What climate change law exists has been primarily international law, but it faces limits and difficulties, especially regarding the primacy and binding force of a country's internal law and policy. This is particularly the case in those fields (of which climate change is the most pervasive and disastrous) where the fundamental economic interests of states and their internal subjects are involved.

It could not be different. Climate change is a global problem and national law is the wrong agent to develop the regulatory foundations to address it. Nevertheless, national law could have the force that international law cannot have, and its execution can be guaranteed in every state.

We know the first substantive steps that international law took to fight climate change. The heart of this political–juridical strategy was the United Nations Framework Convention on Climate Change (UNFCCC), approved at the 1992 Rio de Janeiro conference. It was non-binding, only containing directives, principles and commitments, but with no compulsory and specific aims.

But the UNFCCC formed the base of the 1997 Kyoto Protocol, which did have concrete commitments and targets for GHG emissions reduction, quantified in a percentage and linked to a date of expiry. However, the Kyoto Protocol took effect only in 2005 and some states (e.g. United States) did not sign it, thus compromising its effectiveness.

Some problems were not solved by Kyoto; for example, how emissions reductions should be distributed amongst industrialized and developing states. These were shifted to later conferences, such as the Copenhagen conference in 2009.

It is simplistic to put the obligation to reduce emissions only on those states considered as primarily responsible for the production and emission of GHGs. Climate change is expected to affect poorer nations more than richer ones. 'Poorer nations are in warmer areas, are more dependent on agriculture, and cannot afford seawalls and other countermeasures' (Posner and Weisbach, 2010, p79). While industrialized states were the major contributors to climate change, today the emerging countries are the big contributors ('rich enough to make use of raw materials but too poor to do without an environmentally hazardous exploitation'; Birnbacher, 2006, p27). Thus it is absurd and contradictory not to bind these states to emissions reductions. While not forcing emerging countries to reduce emissions may be corrective justice, if we do not we worsen the climate situation.

Government response to climate change

Climate change is not manifested identically across the globe, and its consequences also are not uniform. This variation in effect and consequence clearly affects how different governments (even neighbouring governments) may adapt to and plan for climate change. This can result in (hopefully non-militaristic) conflict between national and territorial agents and institutions. Such conflict could occur when some territories are more exposed than others to climate change associated risks (Farber, 2008, p1). Moreover, the responsibility for many of the issues that revolve around the causes and effects of climate change, such as transportation, urban mobility, agriculture, industry, town planning, bio-housing and renewable energy resources, falls to local states and governments, and not the federal government.

In principle, climate change is a global issue, and thus it seems illogical to have sub-national governments carry the load. Their role should be relegated largely to implementing national climate change policies and plans and also to help in developing and promoting local action plans and providing social support as needed.

With respect to this, an interesting case study is that of the United States. Against a traditionally hostile position to the international emissions agreements, some state governments adopted 'aggressive' initiatives. A good example is California's Global Warming Solutions Act of 2006, in which the state assumed emissions reduction objectives similar to Kyoto, in terms of both the time frame and amount of reduction. Unlike the Italian Constitution, the American Constitution has no 'environmental' clause. However, every regulation or administrative intervention that affects the economy or industrial activity (and the Global Warming Solutions Act certainly would have this effect) must comply with the Interstate Commerce Clause, a cornerstone of the American federal system, a clause which has been used several times by the Supreme Court to restrict the actions of individual states.

With respect to climate change, the scope of the state intervention was not intended to give a competitive advantage to in-state businesses, but was to help mitigate a serious global problem, one which is ultimately a problem for the whole country.

In a recent 5/4 decision (*Massachusetts v. EPA*), even though this was not a 'climate change' issue per se, the Supreme Court gave important indications as to how it might interpret the questions just highlighted. The majority opinion emphasized that when considering global issues, the role of the national government has some limits. The four dissenting Justices argued that the state challengers did not have standing to sue over harm caused by climate change and they would have allowed the Environmental Protection Agency to reject GHGs as pollutants under the Clean Air Act. The Supreme Court should emphasize that the threat to the state's citizens and even its territory (e.g. as a result of sea level rise) due to climate change raises particular problems in regard to some parts of the country. This legitimates the interest by a semi-sovereign state in responding to the problems and challenges of climate change: these rising seas have already begun to swallow Massachusetts's coastal land. Because the Commonwealth owns a substantial portion of the state's coastal property, it has alleged a particularized injury in its capacity as a landowner. The severity of that injury will only increase over the course of the next century: if sea levels continue to rise as predicted, one Massachusetts official believes that a significant fraction of coastal property will be 'either permanently lost through inundation or temporarily lost through periodic storm surge and flooding events'.

We can conclude the discussion on this aspect of the problem, by entering evidence that the unique problems raised by climate change are also reflected in the governance system. The policies of mitigation of and adaptation to climate change no longer fit within the traditional competences between federal and state authorities. The traditional patterns evolved in response to problems totally different from climate change. New problems need new measures and new organizing schemes, and familiar doctrines should be remoulded (see Farber, 2008, p43). The models must be adapted to the reality, not the opposite.

The relationship between two 'words'

The impact of climate change on the distribution of power in a federal system is a constitutional subject, a way to look at the relationship between these two conceptual giants (Chemerinsky *et al.*, 2007, p51). The relationship between the two 'words' (constitution and climate change) and the 'worlds' that they represent is complex, and requires several levels of analysis.

Both constitution and climate change reflect global reality. A constitution is a global vision of a society, it expresses its identity, or at least what it aspires to being. Similarly, the causes and effects of climate change are the consequence of what the human experience has been and of what it could become. Behind the challenges of climate change, we can find a deep rethinking of our lifestyle and of a way to mould the development of the world and of social communities. Climate change is a global experience that invests the topics of distributive equality, our duty to future generations, ecosystem protection and the ultimate survival of humanity.

The two perspectives are conditioned and are mutually integrated. The constitutional state of the twenty-first century is destined to be an environmental state, as that of the twentieth century was largely a 'welfare state'.

We need to clarify what we mean by constitution, and constitutional law. At least in Europe, we allude to a reality in which there are many levels of legal speech. It is not only the constitution as a document, or how it is interpreted; it is a combination, like a form and a living experience. More clearly, EU law is part of the constitutional law of the states; and now, under certain conditions, international law also acts to define constitutional parameters operating inside a state.

The constitutions of the twentieth century, especially in Europe, have been considered as instruments designed to transfer ideas and concepts and circulate within national, supranational and international law. In doing so, the sovereignty of the states is extended to a new level: that of a dialogue with other states and other systems constituted within them. This has eroded the exclusive feature of state law and sovereignty, but it has also made the constitutional systems open to external contributions, which rightfully ultimately become part of constitutional law.

EU law and the decisions of the European Court of Justice prevail on the national law, even at the constitutional level. The only limits are the supreme principles and the inviolable rights: limits which are more symbolic than concrete.

The EU law has now assumed a fundamental role regarding the general principles and priority objectives of its member states. After the Lisbon Treaty, the European Charter of Fundamental Rights (ECFR) was included in the EU Law Treaty, and is thus directly binding in national law. Regarding environmental themes (among which climate change is key) the ECFR contains important assertions. The preamble affirms the principles of sustainable development and our responsibility to future generations. As well, Article 37 establishes the protection of the atmospheric and improving its quality. The base of common constitutional traditions that recognize the centrality of sustainable development and intergenerational responsibilities is becoming increasingly visible. In this process, the development of the two perspectives, one from the EU, the other from individual nation, benefits from mutual influence.

The pressure exercised by EU law in this field has been positive, because it has forced the states to take the climate change problem seriously. There is no doubt, however, that the EU, through the implementation of the Kyoto Protocol and through developing mechanisms and policies for emissions reduction, has become a leader. It can play a significant role regarding implementing international decisions, as well as in further climate change negotiations.

We can generally be satisfied with the results. Emission levels in recent years have been steadily dropping, and the more industrialized countries have adopted appropriate and effective political strategies, especially through strong incentives for renewable energy (Fracchia and Marcovecchio, 2010, p13).

The European Court of Justice has significant influence through EU law to bind states institutions. It has also begun to develop useful guidelines with respect to climate law. For example, a recent decision, 'Lesoochranárske zoskupenie' of March 2011, concerned the role of the Convention of Aarhus on access to information, public participation in decision-making and on access to justice in environmental matters.

The European Court recognizes that the dispositions of the convention of Aarhus, as undersigned by the Community and then approved through the decision 2005/370, are integrating part of the legal system of the European Union. Moreover, in principle, since is a matter concerning an agreement concluded by the union and its Member States with other states, this convention must be considered able to make direct effects when it establishes a clear and precise obligation that is not subordinated, in its implementation or its effects, to some further action. As stated, Article 9, no 3 of the Convention of Aarhus does not contain the mechanisms to directly regulate citizens; and thus its implementation is subordinate to an ulterior action, and it does not carry judicial force regarding the law of the union. Nevertheless, national judicial interpretations should be in conformity both with the scope of Article 9, no 3 of this convention and with the legal protection of the rights recognized by the EU. This will allow an organization or agency, directed to protecting the atmosphere, such as the *Lesoochranárske zoskupenie*, to counter legal decisions that do not conform to EU environmental law.

This was an important advance, because legal issues regarding effective protection of the atmosphere also consider appropriate case law, and it allows participation in situations where the protection of the ecological balance is involved or, as in this case, of mitigation and adaptation to climate change. Ensuring active intervention by interested governmental or non-governmental organizations is consistent with interests involved in climate change legislation (Tulumello, 2010, pp134–137) is important because of the enormous political and social importance that responding to climate change involves. This is especially important given that the cause–effect relationships of climate change can be broken up in space and time.

Responding to climate change is not just a scientific or technical exercise. It requires democratic action remoulded to accommodate the challenges of climate change. Increasing the numbers and effectiveness of individuals that can defend environmental interests permits advocacy for those who may play no role in making decisions, such as future generations, and also the members of the natural world (animals, plants, lakes, rivers and oceans) that will face the very serious effects of climate change.

Finally, when the Court of Justice states that the agreements reached by the EU and its Member States can produce directed effects, at least when clear and precise obligations are defined, then it is not subordinated in implementation or effects to some ulterior action. An important consequence of these agreements is that they acknowledge the full acceptance of binding agreements regarding climate change, such as when creating emissions targets and detailed time frames.

In many states (e.g. Italy), this result can be considered as being acquired in a way that differs from community law. The Constitutional Court has recognized that international treaties concerning the protection of fundamental rights (the reference is to the European Court of Human Rights) are more effective than state law, and they prevail in the state system. Through the constitutions and their acceptance of international law on human rights as guiding internal legislation, international agreements on climate change, on environmental protection and concerning key problems for human life and rights could consolidate the necessary legal force that until now they have not fully reached.

Time: the element that binds constitutional language and climate change

Time (or, more importantly, the needs of future generations) is an element that joins constitutional language and climate change. With their complex structures, principles and rationales for permitting and limiting power, through the creation of traditions of rights and responsibilities and civil duties and respect for law, constitutions provide transgenerational stability to a country. Their contents and effects flow from regime to regime. This is exemplified in an early document of modern constitutionalism, the Virginia Declaration of Rights of 1776, where the preamble states that 'these rights belong to it [i.e. the people of Virginia] and their posterity, as the basis and foundation of government'.

The relationship between constitutional language and future generations is demonstrated in the rigidity of constitutional rules, which cannot be changed except by special proceedings, and in some cases are radically removed from the possibility of review. In other words, the constitutional 'constraint' requires passage from one generation to another; there are no 'exclusive' governments. But there are moments when this stability and promise of continuing principles and values are compromised, along with the resources that enable continuance of these principles and values. There is normally an expectation of 'intergenerational solidarity' – the concept that future generations will maintain the above-stated principles, especially about inviolable rights, is predicated on a commitment by past and present generations to maintain the conditions that enable their maintenance. By compromising these principles today, this expectation is in danger of being lost. All principal categories of constitutional law contain this projection to the future. The state is not a provisional, temporary figure; it is a fundamentally permanent figure and by its action it must maintain community living conditions and work for the present and future public interest of the community (see Romano, 1969 [1909]).

This may be true in theory, but the reality is different. The experience of constitutional democracies and modern representative states move in completely different directions. State-based decisions are usually short-term and reflect current consensus, even at the expense of long-term objective interest. The need to respect the wishes of those who vote and those who make law produces an unavoidable bias for the interests of the present. This obsession by modern democracy for the 'present' is called 'presentism' by Thompson (2007), and is characterized by a difficult to find adequate space for the interests and expectations of future generations. Democracy and constitutionalism both face the serious problems of climate change, and its present and future consequences; the challenge is imagine institutions, procedures, tools and rules that solidify the principle of intergenerational solidarity.

Climate change is a typical intergenerational problem. As Gardiner says, 'climate change is a ... deferred phenomenon. These facts suggests that intra-generational motivation for acting on climate change may be low' (Gardiner, 2006, p151). In fact, the link between climate change and the protection of future generations is the premise of the 1992 Rio Convention on Climate Change.

The causes and results of climate change are temporally widely separated. Future generations will pay for the consequences of GHG emissions that started many decades previously; with luck, they will also enjoy the benefits of emission reductions (Posner and Weisbach, 2010, p144).

Today, causes and consequences are mixed, because we are still releasing GHGs and we are already experiencing climate change disasters. This fact can help raise the awareness in the present generation of the serious consequences of climate change and perhaps make today's generation aware of what future generations will face. This intragenerational motivation can give visibility and strength to an intergenerational perspective, thus strengthening the political weakness of future generations, generations who otherwise have no vote and no voice (Farber, 2008, p38).

The most effective way to consolidate the moral legitimation and juridical strength of commitments and solutions is to regard the problem of climate change through this perspective of intergenerational responsibility, this perspective of protecting the rights of future generations and the perspective of (inherently intergenerational) sustainable development. Both the perspectives of intergenerational justice and sustainable development have to gain a place in human discourse that is not just theoretical or moral, but real, and able to produce politically effective and legally enforceable results.

On the political and juridical side, the concept of sustainable development dates back to the Brundtland Report of 1987, meaningfully entitled *Our Common Future*. Since then, dozens of laws, court decisions and international rules make reference to the concept of sustainable development. We are accumulating laws, still imperfect in their content and capacity to enforce, but increasingly tending to become a general principle of international law, and this is having an evident impact on the evolution and conformation of national juridical systems. This principle, it has been suggested, should be holistic; it should cross the principal areas of environment, economic development, social cohesion, peace and security, and proceed even to the weighty issue of disparity between areas of the world.

A similar, but less intense, process of juridical consolidation is emerging regarding the concept of intergenerational responsibility or justice. This is closely related to the concept of sustainable development, which reflects the principle that the use of a good or resource is sustainable only when its object is not irreversibly consumed, when its capacity for reproduction or repair is respected, and when its transmission to future generations is permitted.

Clauses and formulas oriented to intergenerational justice are emerging in the constitutional language of states and also in international normative documents. These formulas are general but are characterized by an awareness of ecological and financial intergenerational problems. For example, for the first group, consider Article 20a of the German Constitution, which states: 'Mindful also of its responsibility toward future generations, the State shall protect the natural bases of life by legislation and, in accordance with law and justice, by executive and judicial action, all within the framework of the constitutional order.' Similar statements can be found in the preambles of the Constitution of Estonia, the Constitution and Charter of Fundamental Rights and Freedoms in the Czech Republic, and in Poland, Ukraine and Switzerland.

For the second group, which is more relevant to the present topic, reference must be made to various articles in which the protection of the environment (as well as of natural resources and of the landscape) becomes a chance to indicate the protection of future generations and their interests as targets of public policies to implement constitutional mandates. These include: Article 41 of the Constitution of Argentina, Article 225 of the Constitution Brazil, the French Charter for Environment, Article 59 of the Constitution of Albania, Article 110 of the Constitution of Norway, Article 74 of the Constitution of Poland, Article 66 of the Constitution of Portugal (which refers to 'sustainable development'), Articles 5 and 73 of the

Constitution of Slovenia and Article 9, 44, 117/2s of the Constitution of Italy (see Tremmel, 2006, p191.)

Even in a scenario that considers a 'broken world' (see Mulgan, 2010, p59), the constitution seems maintained, so the capacity to be a point of reference for political and institutional choices, and individual and collective human behaviour, still exists. In specific cases, they can function to legitimate and strengthen measures to prevent, adapt and mitigate the consequences of climate change, and to safeguard the interest of future generations, using institutions or written law (Tremmel 2006, 89).

From this perspective, it does not matter if we ask ourselves if future generations have rights, or if present generations even have duties towards future generations. The difference among these two perspectives is not as clearly defined as it may seem. At any rate, to talk about rights through the lens of the present day, and forget the dramatic changes that can arise because of climate change, seems abstract and illusory (Mulgan, 2010, p59).

If the constitutionalism perspective of an environmental state can only be 'responsibility (or solidarity) of all and each towards all things and peoples' (Sirimarco, 2000, p117), it means that rights and duties have many points of connection and reciprocal influence. Of course, rights contain the perspective of responsibility towards others (both today and in the future), but also the awareness that any right can be used in a way that is unreasonable and unsustainable so as to preserve its object of interest.

From another point of view, rights exist not only as individual claims, but also as an expression of fundamental principles, collective action, the evolution of society and public opinion, and a way to perceive the problems occurring to contemporary man.

The problem, therefore, is not just to define the interests of future generations, but how to protect and safeguard them, and with which (necessarily renewed and remoulded) normative tools, institutional machineries, administrative procedures and trial mechanisms. The progressive achievement of constitutional importance for intergenerational issues and the principle of sustainable development can therefore be a very precious resource.

Conclusion

I am from Italy, and Italy is a country of cathedrals, of great and beautiful churches, built over decades by thousands of people, all of whom knew well that they would not see the results of their work (Letta, 2009, p.3). In spite of this, they continued to build because they knew that was the inheritance that they could give to future generations. They had the awareness that they were building something great for the future.

The challenges of climate change present the same problem: to know that the future reflects what we do now; that the world will be, and will have, that which we define through our choices. When building the cathedral there was often anxiety about the future. The same perspective exists today with respect to our response to climate change. But we must replace today's common obsessions, the ones that have dominated (and continue to do so) the political and cultural scene, with the obsession of responding effectively to climate change.

In this sense, climate change is not only a challenge, but an opportunity to improve our ethical and political system: as stated by D. Jamieson (2010, p43), 'an effective answer to it will make us better people, and will help us to take back our democracy'.

References

Bifulco, R. (2008) *Diritto e generazioni future*, Franco Angeli, Milan, Italy

Birnbacher, D. (2006) 'Responsibility for future generations – scope and limits', in J. C. Tremmel (ed.) *Handbook of Intergenerational Justice*, Edward Elgar Publishing, Northampton, UK

Chemerinsky, E., Daniels, B., Hardy, B., Profeta, T., Schroeder, C. H. and Siegel, N. S. (2007) 'California, climate change and constitution', *Environmental Law Forum*, vol 25, no 4, July/August, available at nicholasinstitute.duke.edu/climate/policydesign/california-climate-change-and-the-constitution

D'Aloia, A. (2003) *Diritti e Costituzione. Profili evolutivi e dimensioni inedite*, Giuffré, Milan, Italy

Emanuel, K. (2007) *What We Know About the Climate Change*, MIT Press/Boston Review Books, Cambridge, MA

Farber, D. (2008) 'Climate change, federalism, and the constitution', UC Berkeley Public Law Research Paper no. 1081664, available at http://ssrn.com/papers

Fracchia, F. and Marcovecchio, A. (2010) 'Il cambiamento climatico: problema e opportunità per il diritto', in F. Fracchia and M. Occhiena (ed.) *Climate Change: la risposta del diritto*, Editoriale Scientifica, Naples, Italy

Gardiner, Stephen M. (2006) 'Protecting future generations: intergenerational buck-passing, theoretical ineptitude and a brief for a global core precautionary principle', in J. C. Tremmel (ed.) *Handbook of Intergenerational Justice*, Edward Elgar Publishing, Northampton, UK

Jamieson, D. (2010) 'Le sfide morali e politiche del cambiamento climatico', in *La società degli individui*, vol 39, pp35–43

Letta, E. (2009) *Costruire una cattedrale*, Il Mulino, Bologna, Italy

Mulgan, T. (2010) 'Teoria etica e intuizioni in un mondo in frantumi', *in La società degli individui*, vol 39, no 3, pp44–60

Nespor, S. (2011) 'Catastrofi naturali e catastrofi tecnologiche. Riflessioni sul caso giapponese', 23 March, available at www.federalismi.it/document/editoriale/EDITORIALE_23032011125751.pdf

Pellegrino, G. (2010) 'Cambiamento climatico e generazioni future', in *La società degli individui*, vol 39, no 3, pp7–17

Posner, E. A. and Weisbach, D. (2010) *Climate Change Justice*, Princeton University Press, Princeton, NJ

Romano, S. (1969) [1909] *Lo Stato moderno e la sua crisi*, Giuffré, Milan, Italy

Sirimarco, M. (2000) 'Il dubbio della sopravvivenza', in E. Baglioni (ed.), *Ospiti del futuro*, Giappichelli, Turin, Italy

Thompson, D. (2007) 'In rappresentanza delle generazioni future. Presentismo politico e amministrazione fiduciaria democratica', *Filosofia e Questioni pubbliche*, no 1, pp13–29

Tremmel, Joerg C. (2006) 'Establishing intergenerational justice in national constitutions', in J. C. Tremmel (ed.) *Handbook of Intergenerational Justice*, Edward Elgar Publishing, Northampton, UK

Tulumello, G. (2010) 'Sviluppo sostenibile, discrezionalità amministrativa e sindacato giurisdizionale', in F. Fracchia, M. Occhiena (ed.) *Climate Change: la risposta del diritto*, Editoriale Scientifica, Naples, Italy

17 International groundwater law

Joseph W. Dellapenna

Introduction

Human health is impossible without an adequate supply of safe drinking water. Increasingly, this requires recourse to groundwater because groundwater makes up 97 per cent of the world's unfrozen fresh water (Puri and Aureli, 2009, p16). That, in turn, requires an adequate legal regime for groundwater both as a national and an international resource. Yet, until recently, nations have made few international agreements regarding groundwater – in sharp contrast to the numerous international agreements regarding surface waters. This is not surprising.

Before the spread of advanced pumps after World War II, groundwater was strictly a local resource, the use of which could not affect users at any considerable distance from the water withdrawal (Ashley and Smith, 1999, pp6–7). Newer technologies and exponential growth in demand for water combined to make groundwater a critically important resource, the focus of disputes between nations, and the focus of a small, but growing number of agreements between nations for cooperative management and protection (Burchi and Mechlem, 2005).

Still, there are no generally applicable agreements for internationally shared groundwater. The UN Convention on the Law of Non-Navigational Uses of International Watercourses, which would apply to groundwater to some extent, has not yet entered into effect (UN, 1997). Customary international law therefore is of even greater significance than it is for surface waters. This customary law derives from the limited relevant practice of states and from international environmental law and international human rights law (Berlin Rules 2004, introductory note); it also applies both to internationally shared groundwater and to groundwater generally. This chapter, after introducing the extent of existing international agreements that appear to regulate internationally shared groundwater, discusses the nature of customary international law, the patterns of state behaviour that validate the customary law applicable to groundwater, and the recent attempts to summarize this law in an authoritative statement.

International agreements

Only rarely do international agreements on water expressly mention groundwater. Initially, if groundwater was mentioned at all, it was through a definition of the waters within the scope of a general water treaty without any provisions specific to groundwater issues (Burchi and Mechlem, 2005). Groundwater was an afterthought even in an occasional treaty that mentions groundwater in its specific operative provisions. Some agreements are even vaguer regarding groundwater. Thus, the Mekong agreement addresses, in certain respects, the 'environment', defining that term as including '[t]he condition of water and land resources, air, flora, and fauna that exists in a particular region' (Mekong Agreement, 1995, article 2). Whether such vague agreements actually apply to groundwater as well as surface waters is at least unclear. Yet the gradual spread of such agreements did serve to establish that the same general legal principles apply to groundwater as apply to surface water (Berlin Rules, 2004, article 36; Eckstein and Eckstein, 2003). One could hardly reach a different conclusion given that groundwater and surface water are the same water moving through a single hydrologic cycle.

At the end of the twentieth century, growing pressure on water resources often did not lead to international agreements specifically focused on groundwater. Only slowly did treaties begin to address groundwater more specifically (Burchi and Mechlem, 2005). Agreements referring to groundwater may be grouped into three types (Caponera and Alheritiere, 1978). In some agreements, groundwater is seen as a problem impeding the development of other resources, producing agreements focusing on the dewatering of aquifers. In other agreements, groundwater is seen as a resource to be developed or exploited, producing agreements focusing on the allocation of groundwater withdrawals among the concerned states. Yet other agreements approach groundwater as a resource to be managed and protected, producing agreements focusing on the prevention of harm to aquifers or their users, or on the management of aquifers and related resources. The different sorts of agreement did not follow any set sequence for a particular groundwater basin; nor does each groundwater basin feature all three types of agreements. Instead, states sharing a groundwater basin enter into an agreement that they see as necessary for a particular situation, and a particular agreement sometimes includes elements of each type of agreement.

Groundwater treaties usually were made without full knowledge of the relevant facts: the actual condition of the resource, the effect of water withdrawals from the aquifer, or the sustainability of such withdrawals (Dellapenna, 2010b, §49.06). States dealt with this problem either by providing that uses shall continue in their established or historic pattern, or by providing for the use of specific – often, but not always equal – quantities of groundwater by the several states without any real attempt to manage or even to assess the groundwater resource (Burchi and Mechlem, 2005).

Some agreements provide that a state has the exclusive use of certain springs, without limits on the quantities to be taken. Several recent treaties simply provide for the equitable utilization of groundwater, requiring a balancing process involving the sort of factors listed in the UN Convention and the Berlin Rules – without any specific allocation and dependant on further negotiations to determine the amounts (Burleson, 2006, pp388–409). This is more of an invitation to negotiate than an allocation of the groundwater.

Customary international law generally

Customary international law consists of the practices of states undertaken out of a sense that the practice is required by law (*opinio juris sive necessitatus*, or simply *opinio juris*) (Lepard, 2010; Wolfke, 1993). When these two elements combine, law results regardless of how long or briefly the practice has continued. Customary law is binding because the participating states have expressly or implicitly consented to the rule (Lepard, 2010, pp97–121; Wolfke, 1993, pp160–167). References to law tie a customary practice to a sense of legitimacy and constitute the practice as law in a highly decentralized and institutionally undeveloped system like international law (or among subsistence farmers or nomadic tribesmen).

Customary international law emerges through a process of claim and counterclaim between states. When a state undertakes an action that affects other states, the other states either acquiesce in the action or oppose it, usually at first through rhetorical strategies; if the matter is important enough, an objecting state will escalate its opposition through various sanctions up to the possibility of military operations. Eventually the states involved reach a consensus, expressed through an exchange of notes or otherwise, about what each state is entitled to do under the circumstances. Over time, a practice emerges that allows one to predict how states will behave. If nothing more were involved, one might question whether this could properly be termed law, yet beginning with the simplest rhetorical strategies and continuing through to outright war, the states refer to international law as a justification of their claims and their practices (Byers, 2000). Diplomats know very well the difference between appeals to law, appeals to morality, and appeals to expedience; they often express these different propositions at appropriate points in a single communication.

Customary international law has been remarkably successful. Focusing exclusively on the relatively few, but highly dramatic, failures of international law can create an impression that the system is ineffective, yet no form of international life could exist without a shared set of norms that are largely self-effectuating in the conduct of that life (Rittberger and Mayer, 1993). Customary international law often works satisfactorily, either because there is a broad consensus on what is proper, or because other states are unwilling to challenge the states with a strong interest in the matter (Koh, 1997).

It serves to empower international actors by legitimating their claims, but it also constrains them by limiting the claims they can make (Norman and Trachtman, 2005). Yet the uncertainties about customary international law plus the lack of a neutral enforcement mechanism makes exclusive reliance on customary international law both undesirable and impossible.

Custom frequently is ill-defined and uncertain, and often leaves gaps and ambiguities in the law. The process of determining whether customary international law exists and its content is 'inelegant' (Kolb, 2003). These determinations require diplomats, international tribunals, lawyers and scholars to examine widely varied evidence of state practice through research into often obscure sources; finding evidence of the reasons for that practice is even more challenging. Turning as it does on a question of motive, examination of the primary evidence for a customary rule is often inconclusive. A widespread pattern of international agreements may demonstrate that the treaty obligations have become customary requirements binding even on states not party to the treaties (Lepard, 2010, pp191–207; Wolfke, 1993, pp68–72). Even an unratified treaty might indicate customary law. Resolutions of international organizations also may be evidence that states consider a particular rule to be a legal obligation, although legal experts sometimes overlook whether state practice is actually consistent with such resolutions (Lepard, 2010, pp208–228; Wolfke, 1993, pp79–84, 100–104).

Successful areas of customary law often are codified under UN or other auspices precisely because the rules are so seldom questioned and so generally followed. The UN usually begins such a codification through the International Law Commission, a body of 34 jurists and diplomats representing a broad range of legal cultures and political ideologies. It was created by the General Assembly in 1947 to help codify and 'progressively develop' customary international law. Consensus often comes after years of discussion, lending a high degree of credibility to the results. The Commission reports its findings to the General Assembly, which might take steps to turn the Commission's 'draft articles' into a legally binding instrument. The rules prepared by the Commission often are accorded 'quasi-legal effect' as rules of customary international law even without taking becoming a binding legal instrument. Even when a body of customary law has been codified, however, parts or even a great deal of it survive as customary law. Private groups also codify customary international law. One such group is the International Law Association, founded in 1873 by lawyers, jurists, and scholars of international law. Its efforts often are accepted as accurate summaries of customary international law, including the Helsinki Rules on the Uses of Waters of International Rivers (ILA, 1966). This effort was so successful that the General Assembly instructed the International Law Commission to draft a set of articles to be based on the Helsinki Rules in 1970 (UN, 1970).

Customary international law and groundwater

The application of the well-established rules of customary international law to groundwater is more problematic than the application of those rules to surface waters because of the uncertainty about groundwater's hydrogeologic characteristics. We often have accurate and ongoing measurements of surface waters for a century or more. Groundwater, however, was long seen as a mysterious substance the sources or behaviour of which were unknown; even now we often do not know a great deal about particular aquifers (Dellapenna, 2010a). Acquiring knowledge is possible, but it is expensive and time consuming. Because of such problems, we often can only make tentative decisions regarding groundwater – decisions that the informal processes of customary regimes are ill adapted to revise or supplement. Proper management of groundwater requires more than bare promises to cooperate or to take specific steps to protect and enhance the waters in question. Participating states need to agree to collect and share data, to formulate joint plans and programs for groundwater, to implement common groundwater management policies, and to undertake the joint training of technical personnel and of environmental studies (Burleson, 2006, pp418–23). Participating states could agree to coordinate their separate management regimes or to partial or complete joint management, or they could establish a new, at least quasi-independent agency to manage the groundwater of behalf of all the participating states (Burchi and Spreij, 2003). Such fully developed regimes remain rare.

The usual codification processes have been applied to water resources. The International Law Commission drafted a set of articles that the General Assembly approved as the UN Convention on the Law of Non-Navigable Uses of International Watercourses (UN, 1997). This convention, which has not yet entered into force, would apply only to some internationally shared groundwater, leaving out groundwater that, while internationally shared, is not hydraulically connected to an international watercourse. The UN Convention also ignores the extent to which customary international law, primarily international environmental law, applies to groundwater within a single state. The UN Convention will only apply, if at all, as evidence of customary international law for some time to come. In the face of these deficiencies in the UN Convention, both the International Law Association and the International Law Commission undertook to codify the customary international law applicable to groundwater.

The International Law Association completed its project first, approving the Berlin Rules on Water Resources in 2004 after eight years of work. The Berlin Rules are an ambitious reconsideration of the international law applicable to water, including the extent to which international law applies to water entirely within a single state. Chapter VIII of the Berlin Rules is the first attempt at a detailed summary of the emerging customary international law applicable to groundwater. The Association had addressed groundwater in the Seoul Rules on International Groundwater in 1986, but those rules only said that the governing principles of the Helsinki Rules also apply to groundwater (ILA, 1986).

Chapter VIII of the Berlin Rules focuses mostly on groundwater as such, although some rules in Chapter VIII address aquifers as the primary object of management for groundwater (ILA, 2004, articles 36–42). While the Berlin Rules apply to all groundwater, and not just to groundwater connected to international drainage basins, the rules also indicate that the application of the general rules require attention to the special characteristics of groundwater (ILA, 2004, article 36). The rules also recognize that aquifers, like other water sources, should be managed conjunctively and in an integrated fashion (ILA, 2004, articles 5, 6, 36; Kallis and Butler, 2001). The difficulty and expense of determining just what is happening with groundwater along with the difficulty of remediating any damage that might result from poor management make application of the precautionary principle particularly compelling (ILA, 2004, articles 23, 38), applying this obligation to groundwater entirely within a single state because the obligation derives from international environmental law rather than from instruments directed specifically at transboundary waters. To achieve these goals, the responsible states must acquire the necessary information (ILA, 2004, article 39; UN, 1997, articles 9, 11–19, 24(1), 28(2), 31), including by:

1 monitoring groundwater levels, pressures, and quality;
2 developing aquifer vulnerability maps;
3 assessing the impacts on groundwater of industrial, agricultural, and other activities; and
4 any other measures appropriate to the circumstances.

This obligation to acquire the necessary information derives from, but is more specific than, the generalized obligation to gather and exchange data on transboundary waters expressed in other articles of the Berlin Rules and in the UN Convention (ILA, 2004, articles 56–60; UN, 1997, articles 9, 11–19, 24(1), 28(2), 31). Even if the obligation to gather information is limited to transboundary contexts, often a state cannot know whether an aquifer is transboundary, and thus a state cannot fulfil its duties unless it develops comprehensive information for all aquifers within its jurisdiction without waiting for proof of international connections.

In addition to the specific requirements of the Berlin Rules on groundwater, states must fulfil their general obligations to protect the aquatic environment and to respond to extreme situations (ILA, 2004, articles 22–35), including the obligation to undertake the impact assessments (ILA, 2004, articles 29–31). Three articles of the Berlin Rules set out the specific substantive obligations of states relative for groundwater. The first of these articles addresses the application of the principle of sustainability to aquifers (ILA, 2004, articles 7, 40). Fewer issues are more controversial than 'groundwater mining' – abstracting groundwater as an exhaustible rather than renewable resource (Albiac *et al.*, 2006; Chavez, 2000). Sustainability cannot altogether preclude the abstraction of water from a non-renewable aquifer because if use is limited to the recharge rate, such waters cannot be used at all (ILA, 2004, article 40(2)). If groundwater is mined, the water table will decline, pumping will become more expensive, and eventually pumping will have to stop from total depletion or impaction, or because pumping becomes too expensive. In order to ensure sustainability, states should establish a maximum allowable drawdown for each aquifer, with the maximum reflecting somewhat the natural and artificial recharge (ILA, 2004, article 40(1)). Treaties and other international instruments relating to surface waters and connected groundwater after 1990 stressed the concept of sustainability in just this fashion (e.g. EU, 2000, article 4(1)(b)(ii)). Ultimately, whether to extract groundwater faster than the rate of recharge is left to the judgement of the particular states concerned (e.g. EU, 2000, article 4(7); Fuentes, 2002; Gupta, 2002).

Groundwater managers must be particularly sensitive to the reality that rapidly falling water tables might not appear until some years after a serious overdraft begins, by which time it might be too late. The precautionary principle, as well as the sustainability principle, thus requires special care in setting allowable drawdowns and in assessing other risks to the aquifer or of the aquatic environment related to the aquifer (ILA, 2004, articles 23, 38). Biodiversity can become an issue in setting the maximum allowable drawdown; the precautionary principle again cautions against over optimistic exploitation of the resource (ILA, 2004, articles 22, 25, 38). Because groundwater moves slowly and unpredictably, it is particularly vulnerable to environmental damage and thus requires special steps to ensure the protection of aquifers (ILA, 2004, article 41). These provisions add to the general obligations to protect the aquatic environment and to respond to extreme situations (ILA, 2004, articles 22–28, 32–35). Because the obligation to protect aquifers derives from international environmental law, it applies even to an aquifer entirely within a single state.

States cannot exploit more than their appropriate share of groundwater, whether from a renewable or a non-renewable aquifer, under the principle of equitable utilization (ILA, 2004, article 42). Several international agreements now limit the drawdowns of groundwater in order to ensure that states limit their use to an equitable and reasonable share. In setting drawdown rates, basin states are to have due regard for the obligation not to cause significant harm to another state (ILA, 2004, article 16) and to the obligation to protect aquifers (ILA, 2004, article 41). Under Article 41(5), states are to cooperate in protecting the recharge of groundwater. Similarly, under article 41(6), the obligation to prevent significant harm applies to transboundary groundwater, having due regard to the rule of equitable utilization. States sharing groundwater must resolve all questions regarding its proper management jointly if they are to ensure that the resource or its beneficial uses are shared equitably (ILA, 2004, article 42). Other legal principles that arguably apply to groundwater management – particularly relating to public participation and related rights (ILA, 2004, articles 17–21) – find only limited support thus far in actual groundwater treaties.

The International Law Commission's Draft Articles on the Law of Transboundary Aquifers

Shortly after the General Assembly approved the UN Convention on the Law of Non-Navigable Uses of International Watercourses (UN, 1997), the International Law Commission undertook to craft a set of Draft Articles on the Law of Transboundary Aquifers, completing its first reading in 2006 and its second reading in 2008 (ILC, 2006, 2008; Eckstein, 2007). The Commission drew upon the Berlin Rules and the comments of an International Law Association working group that reviewed the first reading (ILC, 2008, preamble), but the Draft Articles are closer to the UN Convention's provisions on surface waters than to the Berlin Rules chapter on groundwater. The Draft Articles focus on the transboundary dimensions of 'aquifers' and related 'aquifer systems.' They define an 'aquifer' as 'a permeable water-bearing underground geological formation underlain by a less permeable layer and the water contained in the saturated zone of the formation' (ILC, 2008, article 2(a)) and an 'aquifer system' as 'a series of two or more aquifers that are hydraulically connected' (ILC, 2008, article 2(b)). The articles focus on the rights and duties of 'Aquifer States,' states 'in whose territory any part of a transboundary aquifer or aquifer system is situated' (ILC, 2008, article 2(d)).

One of the more controversial and perplexing articles in the Draft Articles reaffirms the sovereignty of Aquifer States over the portions of transboundary aquifers within their borders, while also declaring that 'a State is to exercise its sovereignty in accordance with international law and the [Draft Articles]' (ILC, 2008, article 3). Given that both international law and the Draft Articles limit state sovereignty, this article upholds and denies sovereignty at the same time. What, if anything, this article actually means, is unclear. Some see it as a fundamental error, a focusing on sovereignty over and management of the rock in which groundwater is found rather than, as in the UN Convention or the Berlin Rules, on rights in and management of the groundwater itself (McCaffrey, 2009).

Otherwise, the Draft Articles present 19 articles that largely track the UN Convention, particularly the principles of equitable utilization and avoidance of harm (ILC, 2008, articles 4(a), 5, 6). Other provisions track the UN Convention's duty to cooperate (ILC, 2008, article 7), the regular exchange of data and information (ILC, 2008, articles 8, 19), the protection and preservation of the environment (ILC, 2008, article 10), the prevention, reduction and control of pollution (ILC, 2008, article 12), the obligation to consult on the management of internationally shared groundwater and on planned activities likely to affect such groundwater (ILC, 2008, articles 14 and 15), the obligation to cooperate regarding emergency situations (ILC, 2008, article 17), and the protection of internationally shared groundwater in time of armed conflict (ILC, 2008, article 18). Aquifer States are also required to monitor their transboundary aquifers and aquifer systems and to exchange the resulting data (ILC, 2008, article 13). This is necessary if the other obligations are to have real meaning.

The articles do not fully embrace the principle of sustainability, requiring only that Aquifer States shall 'aim at maximizing the long-term benefits' derived from the use of groundwater (ILC, 2008, article 4(b)), that they shall 'establish ... an overall utilization plan, taking into account present and future needs of, and alternative water sources for, the Aquifer States' (ILC, 2008, article 4(c)), and that they 'shall not utilize a recharging transboundary aquifer or aquifer system at a level that would prevent continuance of its effective functioning' (ILC, 2008, article 4(d)). Several important aspects of sustainability are omitted from these specific obligations, including the obligation of protect aquifers from pollution. The Draft Articles do not discuss non-recharging aquifers, failing to take a position on groundwater mining. Nor do the Draft Articles define what an aquifer's *function* is. Would exhaustion in 20 years be its function? Without some indication of what that word means, there is no effective limitation on exploitation and thus no real commitment to sustainability.

The Draft Articles do recognize the hydro-geologic realities of groundwater somewhat. They require Aquifer States to identify recharge and discharge zones of their transboundary aquifers and aquifer systems and to take 'special measures' to minimize detrimental impacts on recharge and discharge (ILC, 2008, article 11(1)). The Draft Articles would also extend this duty to non-aquifer States in which a recharge or discharge zone is located (ILC, 2008, article 11(2)). Why non-Aquifer States would do so without sharing the benefits of such actions is not explained. The Draft Articles also would impose an obligation for advanced states to promote capacity building in developing nations (ILC, 2008, article 16). This, like the obligations ostensibly imposed on non-Aquifer States regarding recharge and discharge, is easier to articulate than to enforce.

The Commission recommended in its report that the General Assembly 'take note' of the Draft Articles, recommend that states make 'appropriate arrangements' for their shared aquifers on the basis of the principles in the Draft Articles, and consider the possibility of convening a negotiating conference to draft a convention on the topic (Yamada, 2008). This approach avoids either suggesting amendments to the UN Convention on the Law of Non-Navigable Uses of International Watercourses or proposing a protocol to that convention. Either approach would be troubling given the difficulties the UN Convention has experienced in obtaining the ratifications necessary to enter into force (Salman, 2007), although the pace of ratification has picked up recently. On 11 December 2008, the

General Assembly adopted a resolution incorporating the suggestions made by the Commission (UN, 2008). Whether the Draft Articles will ever become a treaty, either through incorporation in a larger treaty on transboundary waters or as a stand-alone instrument, is entirely uncertain at this point.

Conclusion

The International Law Commission's Draft Articles on the Law of Transboundary Aquifers, having received the imprimatur of the UN General Assembly (UN, 2008), stands as a significant step in the regularization and codification of the customary international law applicable to internationally shared groundwater. Like so much of the Commission's work, however, it is extremely cautious, neglecting the Commission's charge to undertake the progressive development of customary international law. States and water users alike will find a useful starting point for working out arrangements for managing internationally shared groundwater (or aquifers, if you prefer), but they will quickly discover that satisfactory management will require them to go beyond the articles. One of the most obvious points where this will be true is if a recharge zone (or part of a recharge zone) is located outside of an Aquifer State. Satisfactory arrangements will be possible only if the non-Aquifer State is accorded a role in managing the aquifer or aquifer system as a whole, including sharing in the benefits derived from that management, if the non-Aquifer State is to be held to the duty as set forth in the Draft Articles. In this regard, and perhaps in other ways, the Berlin Rules on Water Resources provide a more progressive blueprint for the management of internationally shared groundwater.

References

Albiac, J., Hanemann, M., Calatrava, J., Uche, J. and Tapia, J. (2006) 'The rise and fall of the River Ebro transfer', *Natural Resources Journal*, vol 46, pp727–757

Ashley, J. S. and Smith, Z. A. (1999) *Groundwater Management in the West*, University of Nebraska Press, Lincoln, NE

Burchi, S. and Mechlim, K. (eds.) (2005) *Groundwater in International Law: Compilation of Treaties and Other International Instruments*, Legis. Study no. 86, FAO, Rome, Italy

Burchi, S. and Spreij, M. (2003) *Institutions for International Freshwater Management*, UNESC0 SC-2003/WS/41, UNESCO, Paris, France

Burleson, E. (2006) 'Middle Eastern and North African hydropolitics: From eddies of indecision to emerging international law,' *Georgetown International Environmental Law Review*, vol 18, pp385–424

Byers, M. (ed.) (2000) *The Role of Law in International Politics: Essay in International Relations and International Law*, Oxford University Press, Oxford, UK

Caponera, D. A. and Alheritiere, D. (1978) 'Principles of international groundwater law', *Natural Resources Journal*, vol 18, pp589–619

Chavez, O. E. (2000) 'Mining of internationally shared aquifers: The El Paso-Juarez case', *Natural Resources Journal*, vol 40, pp237–251

Dellapenna, J. W. (2010a) 'The physical and social bases of quantitative groundwater law', in A. Kelly (ed.) *Waters and Water Rights*, LexisNexis, Newark, NJ, ch. 18

Dellapenna, J. W. (2010b) 'The international law applicable to water resources generally', in A. Kelly (ed.) *Waters and Water Rights*, LexisNexis, Newark, NJ, ch. 49

Eckstein, G. E. (2007) 'Commentary on the UN International Law Commission's draft articles on the law of transboundary aquifers', *Colorado Journal of International Environmental Law and Policy*, vol 18, pp537–610

Eckstein, G. and Eckstein, Y. (2003) 'A hydrogeological approach to transboundary ground water resources and international law,' *American University International Law Review*, vol 19, pp201–258

EU (2000) 'Water framework directive', EU Dir. 2000/60/EC, 43 OJ (L 327) European Union

Fuentes, X. (2002) 'International law-making in the field of sustainable development: the unequal competition between development and the environment', *International Environmental Agreements: Policy, Law and Economics*, vol 2, pp109–133

Gupta, J. (2002) 'Global sustainable development governance: institutional challenges from a theoretical perspective', *International Environmental Agreements: Policy, Law and Economics*, vol 2, pp361–388

ILA (1966) 'The Helsinki rules on the uses of the waters of international rivers', in *Report of the Fifty-second Conference* 447–533 (Helsinki), International Law Association, London, UK

ILA (1986) 'The Seoul rules on international groundwaters', in *Report of the Sixty-second Conference*, 251–276 (Seoul), International Law Association, London, UK

ILA (2004) 'Berlin Rules on Water Resources', in *Report of the Seventy-First Conference* 334–421 (Berlin), International Law Association, London, UK

ILC (2006) 'The Law of Transboundary Aquifers', UN Doc. A/CN.4/L.688 (first reading), International Law Commission, New York, NY

ILC (2008) 'The Law of Transboundary Aquifers', UN Doc. A/CN.4/L.724 (2008) (second reading), International Law Commission, New York, NY

Kallis, G. and Butler, D. (2001) 'The EU water framework directive: measures and implications', *Water Policy*, vol 3, pp125–142

Koh, H. H. (1997) 'Why do nations obey international law?', *Yale Law Journal*, vol 106, pp2,599–2,659

Kolb, R. (2003) 'Selected problems in the theory of customary international law', *Netherlands International Law Review*, vol 50, pp119–150

Lepard, B. D. (2010) *Customary International Law: A New Theory with Practical Applications*, Cambridge University Press, Cambridge, UK

McCaffrey, S. C. (2009) 'The International Law Commission adopts Draft Articles on transboundary aquifers', *American Journal of International Law*, vol 103, pp272–293

Mekong Agreement (1995) 'Agreement on cooperation for the sustainable development of the Mekong River Basin', signed 5 April 1995, Cambodia–Laos–Thailand–Vietnam, reprinted in *International Legal Materials*, vol 34, pp864–880

Norman, G. and Trachtman, J. P. (2005) 'The customary international law game', *American Journal of International Law*, vol 99, pp541–580

Puri, S. and Aureli, A. (2009) *A Global Atlas of Transboundary Aquifers of the World*, UNESCO IHP, Paris, France

Rittberger, V. and Mayer, P. (eds.) (1993) *Regime Theory and International Relations*, Clarendon Press, Oxford, UK

Salman, S. M. A. (2007) 'The United Nations watercourses convention ten years later: why has its entry into force proven difficult?', *Water International*, vol 32, pp1–15

UN (1970) 'Progressive development and codification of the rules of international law relating to international watercourses', GA Res. 2669 (XXV), 8 December 1970, UN Doc. A/8028, United Nations, New York, NY

UN (1997) 'Convention on the law of non-navigable uses of international watercourses', GA Res. 51/229, 21 May 1997, UN Doc. A/51/49, United Nations, New York, NY

UN (2008) 'The law of transboundary aquifers', GA Res. A/Res/63/124, 11 December 2008, United Nations, New York, NY

Wolfke, K. (1993) *Custom in Present International Law*, second edition, M. Nijhoff, Dordrecht, The Netherlands

Yamada, C. (2008) *Fifth Report on Shared Natural Resources: Transboundary Aquifers*, UN Doc. A/CN.4/591, United Nations, New York, NY

18 Environmental protection and the human right to water

Complementarity and tension

Owen McIntyre

Introduction

Though it is patently obvious that, in certain situations, measures intended to realize aspects of the emerging human right to water and sanitation (hereafter human right to water) might come into conflict with objectives of environmental protection, and thus with measures intended to pursue such objectives, neither the various declaratory instruments nor the vast majority of the academic literature driving the discourse on the human right to water appear ready to address this issue.[1] Taking General Comment No. 15, adopted by the UN Committee on Economic, Social and Cultural Rights (CESCR) in November 2002,[2] as the most authoritative analysis of the normative content of the emerging human right to water, one can clearly see that, while environmental protection is inherent to ensuring the availability of sufficient and adequate water for human needs, the approach taken is by definition anthropocentric rather than ecocentric, and the extent of the entitlements advocated therein may compete with ecological requirements for water resources. This potential tension is most apparent in respect of the purported obligation to provide water for livelihoods and where a narrow understanding of the right to sanitation might be adopted. This chapter sets out to examine the nature of the environmental protection elements included within the elaboration on the human right to water under General Comment No. 15 and explore the potential for both complementarity and tension as between social and environmental objectives. In addition, it seeks to examine the possibilities for reconciling the requirements of the human right to water and of environmental protection both under international and national law, as well as to explore the need for better integration of the potentially competing social and environmental values inherent to water resources law.

Environmental protection under General Comment No. 15

A cursory survey of General Comment No. 15 reveals a surprising number of references to the need to utilize water resources sustainably and to protect waters from pollution. However, more careful scrutiny of the relevant provisions further reveals that they are heavily biased towards an anthropocentric view of environmental problems, involving an approach to addressing such problems which clearly emphasizes human needs over ecological requirements. While one should not be surprised that a human rights instrument would prioritize human needs – particularly one which is itself an interpretation of Articles 11 and 12 of the 1966 Covenant on Economic, Social and Cultural Rights (ESCR Covenant) conferring, respectively, the right to an adequate standard of living and the right to the highest attainable standard of health - this approach is to ignore somewhat the potential for conflict with quite highly developed normative regimes requiring the strict protection of aquatic ecosystems.

Anthropocentric versus ecocentric approach

Examples abound of environmental concerns set out under General Comment No. 15 which are viewed through an anthropocentric lens. Paragraph 7, for instance, notes 'the importance of ensuring sustainable access to water resources for agriculture to realize the right to food', while also noting the duty in Article 1(2) of the ESCR Covenant, which provides that a people may not 'be deprived of its means of subsistence'. Similarly, paragraph 8 deals with the obligation of states parties 'to prevent threats to health from unsafe and toxic water conditions' and to 'monitor and combat situations where aquatic ecosystems serve as a habitat for vectors of diseases wherever they pose a risk to human living environments'. Quite clearly, the health or integrity of the aquatic ecosystems themselves was not a key concern for the Committee. In the same vein, the Committee's concerns about the quality of water to which people are entitled focus on the safety of such water for personal or domestic uses, which must be, according to paragraph 12(b), 'therefore free from micro-organisms, chemical substances and radiological hazards, that constitute a threat to a person's health', as well as 'of an acceptable colour, odour and taste for each personal or domestic use'. Paragraph 16, which identifies those groups and individuals to whom states parties should give special attention, only refers to the protection from pollution of traditional water sources in rural areas and the water resources of indigenous peoples on their ancestral lands. More generally, paragraph 11 advises that '[w]ater should be treated as a social and cultural good, and not primarily as an economic good', thus ignoring the immense ecological significance of water except to the extent that '[t]he manner of the realization of the right to water must also be sustainable, ensuring that the right can be realized for present and future generations'. This in turn appears to betray a narrow conception of sustainability which focuses very much on *human needs*, present and future.

As regards the specific obligations of states set out under General Comment No. 15, paragraph 21 refers to the duty to 'refrain from interfering directly or indirectly with the enjoyment of the right to water' by, inter alia, 'unlawfully diminishing or polluting water', while paragraph 23 sets out states' duty to prevent third parties from interfering with the right by 'polluting and inequitably extracting from water resources, *including natural sources*, wells and other distribution systems'. Thus, the pollution of natural water bodies *per se* is not a central concern, which suggests that the Committee understands environment-related human rights obligations inherent to the human right to water to be completely disconnected from the wider and longer established body of norms on the environmental protection of water resources. This is unfortunate on a number of levels, not least of which is the failure of the Committee to rely upon virtually universal legal restrictions on the pollution of water resources to support the legal status of key elements of the still contested human right to water concept.[3] This approach is mirrored in paragraph 44, which sets out a list of specific violations of the human right to water, but only includes those situations where a state causes 'pollution and diminution of water resources affecting human health' and a state's 'failure to enact or enforce laws to prevent the contamination and inequitable extraction of water' and thereby permitting 'infringements of the right to water by third parties'.

In relation to the participative and informational obligations imposed upon State parties to the ESCR Covenant, which are arguably among the most significant and effective elements of the human right to water,[4] paragraph 48 of General Comment No. 15 provides that '[i]ndividuals and groups should be given full and equal access to information concerning water, water services and the environment, held by public authorities or third parties'. Similarly, the indicators and benchmarks identified in order to assist in monitoring states' compliance with their obligations under the human right to water exhibit little evidence of any wider environmental focus. Paragraph 53 suggests, for example, that '[i]ndicators should address the different components of adequate water (such as sufficiency, safety and acceptability, affordability and physical accessibility)'. However, paragraph 53 does include the United Nations Environment Programme (UNEP) among the list of international agencies from whom states may obtain guidance on appropriate indicators.

It would be a mistake, however, to suggest that General Comment No. 15 completely ignores the need for a broader ecological approach to the protection of water resources and, at least implicitly, the potential of measures intended to implement the human right to water to impact upon aquatic ecosystems. Most significantly, paragraph 28, which provides that 'States parties should adopt comprehensive and integrated strategies and programmes to ensure that there is sufficient and safe water for present and future generations', further advises that:

> Such strategies and programmes may include: (a) reducing depletion of water resources through unsustainable extraction, diversion and

> damming; (b) reducing and eliminating contamination of watersheds and water-related eco-systems by substances such as radiation, harmful chemicals and human excreta; ... (e) assessing the impacts of actions that may impinge upon water availability and natural-ecosystems watersheds, such as climate changes, desertification and increased soil salinity, deforestation and loss of biodiversity; ...

Of course, the inclusion in paragraph 53 of UNEP among the international agencies from whom states may obtain guidance on the development of appropriate indicators for monitoring implementation of the human right to water suggests that broader ecological values might in many cases characterize the concept's practical implementation.

The potential problem with such a clear focus on anthropocentric 'environmental' protection over ecological protection is that it fails to emphasize the need to protect water resources more generally, stressing instead the need to protect water bodies exploited as sources of water used for human purposes or to protect water distribution systems. This approach might suggest to states the adoption of short-term options, such as the intensive treatment of water intended for human consumption and use which is abstracted from polluted natural water sources, rather than the maintenance of aquatic ecosystems and the development of the ecosystems services which they might provide. In addition, though legal regimes for the ecological protection of water resources are generally quite highly developed at the national, regional and international levels, if not always very effectively implemented or enforced, a greater emphasis on the environmental and ecological protection of water bodies and of wider aquatic ecosystems within this definitive elaboration of the human right to water concept would have allowed the concept to derive further support from this additional source of legal authority and legitimacy. Many influential commentators[5] and initiatives for legal codification[6] have sought to link the human right to water to the pre-existing obligations of states to protect water resources and aquatic ecosystems, but the CESCR would appear almost to eschew this assistance through the isolated approach to the concept's normative implications adopted under General Comment No. 15.

Complementarity and tension

Of course, in the vast majority of instances, measures designed to implement the human right to water and measures intended to ensure the environmental protection of water resources, and even of broader aquatic ecosystems, will be mutually supportive and complementary. Often the availability of sufficient and adequate water for a variety of human needs will be dependent upon the effective function of aquatic and other ecosystems and on the ecosystems services they provide. At a more specific level, aspects of the entitlements envisaged under the human right to water, and the corresponding obligations imposed upon states parties to the ESCR Covenant, contribute directly to environmental protection. In addition to the environmentally relevant provisions of General Comment No. 15 cited above, other elements of the right to water, such as the inherent informational and participative rights, would normally be expected to have a direct and positive impact on environmental status and ecological integrity.

It is also clear, for example, that the issue of access to adequate sanitation may play a key role and paragraph 29 of General Comment No. 15 acknowledges that '[e]nsuring that everyone has access to adequate sanitation is not only fundamental for human dignity and privacy, but is one of the principal mechanisms for protecting the quality of drinking water supplies and resources'. However, much may depend on how 'sanitation' is defined. For the specific purpose of articulating a human right to sanitation, the CESCR has more recently adopted the definition of the UN Independent Expert on Water and Sanitation, which describes 'sanitation' quite generally as 'a system for the collection, transport, treatment and disposal or reuse of human excreta and associated hygiene ... which is safe, hygienic, secure, socially and culturally acceptable, provides privacy and ensures dignity'.[7] It might be considered somewhat disappointing that neither the Independent Expert nor the Committee saw fit to include any reference to environmental factors along the lines adopted by the Sub-Commission on the Promotion and Protection of Human Rights, which advised in its 2006 guidelines on the realization of the human right to water and sanitation that 'everyone has the right to have access to adequate and safe sanitation *that is conducive to the protection of public health and the environment*'.[8]

Indeed, it is quite clear from a close examination of the text that General Comment No. 15 is primarily concerned with access to safe drinking water and that the CESCR regards the human right to sanitation as ancillary to that primary concern, rather than as an autonomous human right. Indeed, the opening paragraph of General Comment No.15 makes clear the significance of sanitation for realization of the human right to water, and thus the ancillary nature of any right to sanitation, by noting that '[o]ver one billion persons lack access to a basic water supply, while several billion do not have access to adequate sanitation, *which is the primary cause of water contamination and diseases linked to water*'. Paragraph 29, cited above, also describes the right of access to adequate sanitation as 'one of the principal mechanisms for protecting the quality of drinking water supplies and resources'. Thus, the focus of General Comment No. 15 is clearly much more on the continued availability on safe and adequate water than the provision of adequate sanitation for the purposes of preserving human dignity, which suggests that the CESCR employs quite a narrow conception of the right to sanitation, requiring only such steps as are necessary to prevent unacceptable risks to human health, and certainly not one encompassing broad environmental objectives.[9] While this is, perhaps, to be expected given the focus of General Comment No. 15, it is regrettable that the Committee did not aim to articulate the human right to water and sanitation in a manner that was more in keeping with the well-established tenets of international environmental law and international water resources law. In relation to the latter field, Article 6(1) of the 1999 Protocol on Water and Health[10] to the 1992 UNECE Helsinki Convention on the Protection and Use of Transboundary Watercourses[11] notably requires that the parties shall pursue the aims of access to drinking water and sanitation for everyone 'within a framework of integrated water resources management systems aimed at sustainable use of water resources, ambient water quality which does not endanger human health, *and protection of water ecosystems*'. Similarly, A World Health Organization report from 2003[12] argues that the human right to water should be balanced in an integrated catchment policy with all other water needs, such as irrigation, power generation and *nature conservation*. The 2005 report by the UN Sub-Commission on the Promotion and Protection of Human Rights, prepared by the Special Rapporteur, Judge El Hadji Guissé, specified in respect of the water quality obligations of states arising under the human right to water that 'States should prevent and progressively *reduce contamination of watersheds and aquatic ecosystems* by substances such as bacterial pathogens and chemical pollutants'.[13]

It would appear to be a missed opportunity on the part of the Committee, and other proponents of the human right to water concept, to have declined to link the concept more closely to general environmental requirements and thereby avail of the normative legitimacy of water and environmental law and of its substantive, procedural and technical sophistication. Including the human right to water within the general rubric of 'water law', one leading commentator observes that '[w]ater law is noticeable at the national and international levels for often dissociating the recognition of the human right to water from actual water laws and regulations', and argues that '[s]ince water law is in some respects less developed than environmental law, it must start by borrowing elements from the existing regime'.[14]

However, the greatest potential for conflict between the social objectives of the human right to water and the increasingly prominent ecological objectives of international water resources law, and international environmental law more generally, arises from the potentially extensive scope of the entitlements specified under General Comment No. 15, at least in respect of agricultural and livelihood uses. In paragraph 7 of General Comment No. 15, the Committee stresses 'the importance of ensuring sustainable access to water resources for agriculture to realize the right to adequate food' and notes, in connection with this duty to provide water for agricultural purposes, 'the duty in article 1, paragraph 2, of the Covenant, which provides that a people may not 'be deprived of its means of subsistence'. Though this provision would appear to be intended to limit agricultural entitlements strictly to the needs of subsistence farmers, by proceeding to outline the duty of states parties to 'ensure that there is adequate access to water for subsistence farming and for securing the livelihoods of indigenous peoples', there is a very real danger that it might be interpreted expansively so as to favour agricultural purposes over ecological integrity. For example, in his highly influential report prepared for and adopted by the Sub-Commission on the Promotion and Protection of Human Rights, Special Rapporteur, Judge El Hadji Guissé, stated that 'in order to realize the right to adequate nutrition and the right to earn a living through work, marginalized or disadvantaged farmers and other vulnerable groups should be given priority in access to water resources for their basic needs.' Indeed, in paragraph 6 of General Comment No.15, the Committee recognizes that '[w]ater is essential for securing livelihoods (right to gain a living by work)', before adding that, in addition to personal and domestic uses, '[p]riority should also be given to the water resources required to prevent starvation and disease, *as well as water required to meet the core obligations of each of the Covenant rights*'. It is worth remembering that under Article 6 of the Covenant the states parties recognize the 'right to work, which includes the right of everyone to the opportunity to gain his living by work'. Having regard to the statement in the preamble to the ESCR Covenant that the rights contained therein 'derive from the inherent dignity of the human person', Ziganshina suggests that 'the human right to water should be the basis for states' obligations to supply water not only for drinking and sanitation, but also for the water-dependent livelihoods of their residents'.[15]

Any extension of the scope of the human right to water to meet, even fairly basic, livelihood needs, understood in terms of water-dependent activities, no matter how inefficient, has the potential to bring the social objectives of the concept into direct conflict with environmental objectives. In cases where ecologically important wetlands, including some protected under international environmental regimes such as the Ramsar Convention,[16] would have to compete for water with programmes intended to reduce unemployment and poverty, the human right to water concept as currently articulated under general Comment No. 15 would appear to prioritize and favour the latter. Short-term benefits gained through such an approach might come at a significant longer-term cost. Indeed, the potential for such conflict in certain basins is increasing all the time in the light of relentless population growth and climate change. For example, some assessments concerning the potential impacts of climate change included in a recent UNDP report forecast that the Syrdarya and Amudarya river basins may see a reduction in water volume of thirty and forty per cent respectively.[17]

Reconciling the human right to water with environmental protection

Notwithstanding the dissociation of the human right to water concept from broader environmental objectives, there nevertheless exist numerous frameworks and models for reconciling these fields, both in international law and national legal regimes. At the international level, the principle of equitable and reasonable utilization, the pre-eminent rule of general international law relating to the inter-State allocation of shared international water resources, provides a sophisticated mechanism for balancing social, economic and environmental requirements, which has been informed and nuanced by decades of State practice. Taking the 1997 UN Watercourses Convention[18] as the most authoritative articulation of general international law in this area, it is instructive that it provides in Article 6 a comprehensive yet non-exhaustive list of the social, economic and environmental factors to be taken into account in determining an 'equitable' water allocation regime, while also setting out detailed environmental and ecosystems requirements under Articles 20-23 and singling out 'the requirements of vital human needs' for special consideration under Article 10. While the 'social and economic needs of the watercourse States concerned' are clearly and prominently listed under Article 6, the concept of 'vital human needs' corresponds very closely to and is likely to be informed by the ongoing discourse on the human right to water. Similarly, the requirement for States 'to protect and preserve the ecosystems of international watercourses' set out under Article 20 is likely to be largely informed by key instruments of international environmental law, such as the Ramsar Convention or the Convention on Biological Diversity.[19] Though the UN Watercourses Convention is primarily concerned with water allocation among co-riparian States and the cooperative management of shared water resources, it clearly aims to take on board the broader but related requirements of environmental protection as well as the emerging requirements of the human right to water paradigm. A corresponding effort at integration would have been helpful in General Comment No. 15, which could have aimed towards achieving a convergence of social, economic and environmental objectives.

An integrative approach is also evident in the regime created under the UNECE 1992 Helsinki Convention on the Protection and Use of Transboundary Watercourses which, though principally concerned with environmental protection through the adoption of a highly developed ecosystems approach, has given rise to a 1999 Protocol on Water and Health which, though not a human rights instrument, is entirely supportive of the human rights-based approach to water entitlements. The most integrative instrument of all, however, is the International Law Association's 2004 Berlin Rules on Water Resources Law which attempts both vertical integration, between international and national water law regimes, and horizontal integration, between social and economic needs for water, an ecosystems approach to the environmental protection of all water resources, and a human rights-based approach to individual water entitlements.

There are numerous examples at the national level of legal mechanisms designed to implement the human right to water which also have due regard to the need for ecological protection. For example, in the Flanders

Region of Belgium the relevant water services law guarantees each individual free access to 15 cubic metres of water per year, or 40 litres per person per day, whereas the average daily consumption per person amounts to 100 litres. In order to incentivize water conservation, a progressive tariff for water provided above 40 litres per person per day is prescribed under a legal regime that is intended to function as a combined social and ecological measure. Similarly, the Free Basic Water Policy adopted by South Africa in 2001 creates an entitlement to water free of cost up to a limit of 6,000 litres of water per household per month or 25 litres per person per day (based on each household notionally containing 8 persons), after which progressive charges are applicable. However, this policy is based on the stipulation in the 1996 South African Constitution that '[e]veryone has the right to have access to … sufficient food and water' and the 1998 National Water Act, which provides that 'reserves' of water must be identified and maintained in order to meet both the basic human needs and ecological sustainability needs before allocating water for other uses.[20] In Uruguay, Article 47 of the Constitution, which is primarily concerned with environmental protection, also asserts that water is an essential national resource and a human right and provides that the first principle guiding the development of water policy is the protection of the environment.[21] Therefore, it is quite clear that the imperative social demands of a human rights-based approach to water entitlements can easily be balanced with broader ecological demands and can benefit from the legal and political legitimacy of environmental protection requirements, as well as from the relative substantive and procedural sophistication of the wider corpus of environmental laws.

Conclusion

It would be mutually beneficial to both areas of law and practice if international declarations and guidance documents on the emerging human right to water concept could articulate environmental and ecological values more trenchantly. While such an approach would lend ever-welcome support to environmental protection efforts, it would also allow human rights-based approaches to borrow from the established legitimacy and substantive and procedural sophistication of environmental law and water law. In addition, a clear elaboration of the place of ecological values within the concept of a human right to water would assist in resolving conflicts between its social and environmental objectives whenever they might arise, an issue which Salman M. A. Salman has described as remaining 'unresolved'. Further, such an approach would facilitate integration of the human right to water concept with that of a human right to a clean environment, while also lending much needed support to the latter, hotly debated and somewhat embattled project.[22] One key element in integrating ecological values into the human right to water concept would involve the elaboration of a broader understanding of the associated human right to sanitation, so that states would be unambiguously required to provide sanitation systems which function to protect aquatic ecosystems as well as human health. The comprehensive and systematic integration of ecological values into the international discourse on the human right to water would encourage and guide national policy-makers in developing integrated legal regimes for water resources management, where the human right to water would not be considered in isolation from other uses and values associated with water. As things currently stand, leading commentators appear able to agree that 'human rights documents pay little attention to the necessity to integrate water supply for basic human needs into a wider water policy, taking into account 'ecosystem needs' as well'.[23]

Notes

1 One notable exception is Verschuuren, J. (2010) 'The right to water as a human right or a bird's right? Does co-operative governance offer a way out of a conflict of interests and legal complexity?', in P. Cullet, A. Gowlland-Gualtieri, R. Madhav and U. Ramanathan (eds) *Water Law at the Crossroads in India: National and International Perspectives*, Cambridge University Press, New Delhi, India.

2 Committee on Economic, Social and Cultural Rights, *General Comment No. 15, The Right to Water (Articles 11 and 12 of the International Covenant on Economic, Social and Cultural Rights)*, UN Doc. E/C.12/2002/11, 26 November 2002. Available at www.unchr.ch/html/menu2/6/gc15.doc.

3 See, for example, McCaffrey, S. (2005) 'The human right to water', in E. Brown Weiss, L. Boisson de Chazournes and N. Bernasconi-Osterwalder (eds) *Fresh Water and International Economic Law*, Oxford University Press, Oxford, UK.

4 See further, McIntyre, O. (2011) 'The human right to water and global administrative law: mutually supporting concepts', in L. Westra, K. Bosselmann and C. Soskolne (eds) *Globalisation and Ecological Integrity in Science and International Law*, Cambridge Scholars Press, Newcastle upon Tyne, UK.

5 Cullet, C. (2011) 'Water law in a globalised world: the need for a new conceptual framework', *Journal of Environmental Law*, vol 23, no 2, pp233–254.

6 International Law Association, *Berlin Rules on Water Resources*, Report of the Seventy-first Conference of the International Law Association (Berlin, 2004), available at www.internationalwaterlaw.org/documents/intldocs/ILA_Berlin_Rules-2004.pdf.

7 UN Committee on Economic, Social and Cultural Rights, Statement on the Right to Sanitation, UN Doc. E/C.12/2010/1, 19 November 2010, referring to C. de Albuquerque, 'Report of the Independent Expert on the issue of human rights obligations related to access to safe drinking water and sanitation', UN Doc. A/HRC/12/24, 1 July 2009, para. 63, at 20–21, available at www2.ohchr.org/english/bodies/hrcouncil/docs/12session/A-HRC-12-24_E.pdf.

8 Commission on Human Rights, Sub-Commission on the Promotion and Protection of Human Rights, 'Realization of the right to drinking water and sanitation: Report of the Special Rapporteur, El Hadji Guissé', UN Doc. E/CN.4/Sub.2/2005/25, 11 July 2005, para. 4.3, available at www.ohchr.org/Documents/Issues/Water/SUb_Com_Guisse_guidelines.pdf.

9 See further, Smets, H. (2010) 'The right to sanitation: a new human right in developed countries', *Environmental Policy and Law*, vol 40, no 2/3, pp112–114.

10 London, 17 June 1999, UN Doc. MP.WAT/AC.1/2000/1.
11 (1992) 31 *ILM* 1312.
12 World Health Organization (2003) *The Right to Water*, World Health Organization, Geneva, Switzerland, pp18–21.
13 Commission on Human Rights, Sub-Commission on the Promotion and Protection of Human Rights, 'Realization of the right to drinking water and sanitation: Report of the Special Rapporteur, El Hadji Guissé', UN Doc. E/CN.4/Sub.2/2005/25, 11 July 2005, para. 4.3, available at www.ohchr.org/Documents/Issues/Water/SUb_Com_Guisse_guidelines.pdf.
14 Cullet, C. (2011) 'Water law in a globalised world: the need for a new conceptual framework', *Journal of Environmental Law*, vol 23, no 2, pp233–254.
15 Ziganshina, D. (2008) 'Rethinking the concept of the human right to water', *Santa Clara Journal of International Law*, vol 6, no 1, pp113–128, at p117.
16 1971 Convention on Wetlands of International Importance Especially as Waterfowl Habitats (Ramsar, 2 February 1971), 11 *ILM* 969.
17 UNDP, *Water – Critical Resource for Uzbekistan's Future* (2007), at 15, cited by Ziganshina, D. (2008) 'Rethinking the concept of the human right to water', *Santa Clara Journal of International Law*, vol 6, no 1, pp113–128, at p121.
18 1997 United Nations Convention on the Law of the Non-Navigational Uses of International Watercourses (New York, 21 May 1997), 36 *ILM* 700.
19 1992 United Nations Convention on Biological Diversity, (1992) 31 *ILM* 818.
20 Ziganshina, D. (2008) 'Rethinking the concept of the human right to water', *Santa Clara Journal of International Law*, vol 6, no 1, pp113–128.
21 Cullet, C. (2011) 'Water law in a globalised world: the need for a new conceptual framework', *Journal of Environmental Law*, vol 23, no 2, pp233–254.
22 For a comprehensive overview of this concept, see Boyle, A. E. and Anderson, M. R. (eds) (1996) *Human Rights Approaches to Environmental Protection*, Oxford University Press, Oxford, UK.
23 Verschuuren, J. (2010) 'The right to water as a human right or a bird's right? Does co-operative governance offer a way out of a conflict of interests and legal complexity?', in P. Cullet, A. Gowlland-Gualtieri, R. Madhav and U. Ramanathan (eds) *Water Law at the Crossroads in India: National and International Perspectives*, Cambridge University Press, New Delhi, India.

Part V

New Approaches

Introduction

Laura Westra

This whole volume supports our indictment of the international instruments and other legal regimes as they persistently fail to protect the health of individuals and populations. Although often their language is strong and just, such documents are not consistently applied or appropriately used in jurisprudence. However, as is demonstrated by the World Health Organization's recent work on the Social Determinants of Health, and the Commission on Human Rights Resolution of 2002, on the Right of Everyone to the Enjoyment of the Highest Attainable Standards of Physical and Mental Health, those who bear most of the burden for global ill health are the most vulnerable: Indigenous peoples, the poor in developing countries and local communities.

The chapters in this part of the book consider the plight of Indigenous peoples from three different perspectives. In Chapter 19, Kathleen Mahoney argues that the basic cause of the worsening public health considerations affecting racial and other minorities is the 'globalized hate discrimination' that prevails in our interconnected world. Hate discrimination used to be localized to a place, or a nation; at most, a region. Today it manifests itself as a grave human rights violation and a form of 'incipient violence' everywhere.

In Canada, the first steps in that direction were the systematic denial of the identity of First Nations, Métis and Inuit peoples, as their children were placed in residential school, in order 'to kill the Indian in the child'. A similar attitude prevails still today, not only in the approach towards Indigenous peoples, but also to migrants and asylum seekers in all countries and minorities everywhere.

Valentina Vadi, in Chapter 20, emphasizes the importance of Indigenous peoples' cultural and traditional heritage, as their territorial entitlements are (or should be) protected, in many treaties intended to defend their ancestral lands from encroachment. Many of these territories are inscribed in the World Heritage List. As their traditional territories are under threat, not only their culture and their lifestyle are at risk, but also their health, as their natural resources are exploited and the 'clash between economic development and indigenous peoples' rights' remains an ongoing problem.

Particularly relevant is the regulatory regime dealing with investment in extractive industries, the impact of which is devastating for the traditional lifestyles of Indigenous peoples – and such trade-oriented organizations as NAFTA come in conflict with the mandates of the World Heritage Convention. Thus, as the 'effective protection of indigenous cultural heritage benefits all humanity', it is necessary to introduce specific clauses in investment treaties to ensure a protective shield for Indigenous culture.

The final chapter in this part, Chapter 21 is particularly relevant to South Africa, as Louis Kotzé addresses the plight of its native peoples and of the 'poor nations of the former Third World'. The environmental and public health inequalities that have emerged are clear examples of environmental injustice. Because of climate change and other issues, the question of access to water is particularly acute in that region.

The dire situation affecting the native people of South Africa shows that they bear a double burden of poverty and lack of good health; thus the effort to reach 'sustainable equity' is a pressing imperative in that region, as 'between 12 and 14 million people in South Africa have inadequate access to water, while approximately 20 million have inadequate access to sanitation'. The right to water in South Africa has been litigated in the courts, and the issue is further complicated by the conflict between the immediate needs of local indigent people, and the need for the High Court of South Africa to conserve water resources for future generations in those drought-affected regions.

19 State sponsored hate discrimination

The challenge to human rights at home and abroad

Kathleen Mahoney

Introduction

Globalised hate discrimination is a new phenomenon in our increasingly interconnected world. It used to be said in Canada (in the pre-Internet age) that it was a mistake to be concerned about hatemongers because all of them could be accommodated in a telephone booth.[1] Even if this characterization resonated at one time, it cannot be said to do so today. Economic, political and technological change has altered the social context so significantly that hate discrimination, with its profoundly harmful effects, is now widely disseminated through a broad variety of media capable of reaching millions of people all over the world instantly, at no cost, and with very little effort.[2]

In the past, purveyors of hate victimized people in their own communities or countries. Now they target victims everywhere.[3] An example is the increasing, generalized stereotyping and scapegoating of perceived 'non-citizens' in all countries – expressed through sexist, racist, homophobic, or xenophobic forms of hatred.

The altered social context of globalization enables hate discriminators to not only cause harm by undermining the security, equality, religious, expression and other rights of many millions of individual citizens and groups, they can now undermine the peace and security of entire nations.[4]

This chapter argues that because of the way it operates and the harms it creates,[5] hate discrimination must be understood as a human rights violation[6] rather than as simply a form of expression. It is a form of expressive conduct that goes beyond relaying messages because its utterances alone can perform harmful actions. The chapter concludes that the legal challenges of managing hate discrimination require an approach which carefully weighs all the conflicting and intersecting rights engaged by its proliferation. Hate discrimination engages international and domestic legal and constitutional norms of equality, nondiscrimination, freedom of religion, freedom of expression, security of the person, indigenous rights and multiculturalism that must all be weighed in the rights calculus in order to develop a principled approach that will maximize freedoms and equality for all, while at the same time enhancing and protecting national security.

Although currently under attack, Canada's dual approach, both civil and criminal, is highlighted because it provides some guidance and doctrinal space within which to take on the challenges of establishing a constitutional relationship between rights, as opposed to arrangements that rank some rights as more important than others.

What is hate discrimination?

Hate discrimination is a process. It involves at least three steps: first, singling out a targeted group on the basis of their immutable characteristics; second, targeting them for differential and discriminatory treatment; and third, furthering their social definition in society as inferior, unequal, and rightly disadvantaged, not deserving equal treatment or legal protection because of their group identification.[7] Further steps to enforce its messages usually follow, from the denial of employment, services or accommodation to terrorizing, bullying, beatings and murder.[8] In its most virulent forms, hate discrimination singles out certain groups for existential or genocidal assault.[9]

Like forms of racial and sexual harassment, hate discrimination most often takes the form of words and symbols, leading some to argue that it must be tolerated because it is a form of free expression. But just as the regulation of racial or sexual harassment is not considered a regulation of free speech, the regulation of hate discrimination, properly understood must be treated similarly.[10] Like sexual and racial harassment, some hate speech can facilitate or enact overt violence and other discriminatory acts. International terrorism activity such as providing instruction manuals for making bombs and detonators with which their hated targets can be attacked, recruiting converts to carry out violent hate crimes, and silencing criticism by targeting human rights defenders with violence, threats, and harassment have all been used for the furtherance of hate discrimination.[11]

The expression of hatred is thus incorrectly categorized as political or religious speech or a form of legitimate debate. It is an act, an injury, and a consequence in itself.[12] The 'acts–words' or 'content–form' dichotomies used in the jurisprudence to differentiate between protected and unprotected expression cannot capture the harms perpetrated through hate discrimination in the form of words.[13] Hate speech combines content and form. Color, race, religion, nationality, sexual orientation, or other identity provides the content. Promoting hatred on those grounds is its form. Furthermore, hate discrimination is not merely speech indicating an intention to act in the future. Its harms are immediate. The Supreme Court of Canada in the leading case on hate discrimination opined that: 'the Holocaust did not begin in the gas chambers. It began with words. These are the chilling facts of history – the catastrophic effects of racism.'[14] This passage makes it clear that the Supreme Court of Canada did recognize that hate discrimination is more than just words or expression.[15] By upholding the legislation that forbids the public, wilful promotion of hatred, the Court opined that hate expression can amount to a practice of racism that should not be allowed to hide behind the principle of freedom of expression.[16]

The proliferation of state-sponsored hate discrimination

The globalization of racism, religious hatred, homophobia, sexism and ethnic hatred is a new phenomenon exacerbating the harms to groups and even nations. It is made possible through the use of mass communication systems and the Internet. Hatemongers, including terrorists, religious extremists and rogue politicians, use freedom of expression or religion to transmit their hate messages. Recent instances of crimes against humanity and genocide facilitated by the use of easily accessed sources of mass communication demonstrate how ludicrous such "democratic" claims are. Even as the genocidal slaughter of Tutsi and moderate Hutu citizens began in Rwanda in 2008, free speech was raised in the international community as a reason for not blocking airwaves that would have prevented the killers from getting their deadly genocidal instructions from radio.

State-sanctioned hate discrimination is a particularly serious matter because it can legitimize and normalize hatred of citizens through the use of the prevailing power structure through politics, religion, and culture.[17] Like a virus, it spreads through the media, schools, courts, legislatures, and other national and international institutions such as religious organizations and international political bodies like the United Nations.[18] When state apparatuses of government generate hatred, the perpetrators act on behalf of the law and the state rather than outside of it and are able to make sincere claims to be representative of the values at large in the society.[19]

In furthering state sponsored hate discrimination, politicians often denounce the targeted group's right to their identity and self-determination through denying their history. This is especially damaging when that history includes the systematic destruction or refusal by the state to recognize their rights to exist as a people. Not only does this make it much more difficult for the target group to establish their core identity, it creates an impression that they are seeking something they do not deserve or warrant and they can be rightfully denied. In Canada, examples of state-sponsored vilification of a target group were the systematic attempts to officially deny First Nations, Métis and Inuit peoples their identity by taking their children from their parents, communities and cultures and placing them in residential schools often hundreds of miles from home to 'kill the Indian in the child',[20] legislating who could qualify to be an 'Indian',[21] expropriating treaty lands without compensation,[22] or withholding benefits of citizenship unless they renounced their Indian identity.[23]

When Iranian President Mahmoud Ahmadinejad denies the Holocaust,[24] Dutch party leader Geert Wilders' persistently vilifies Muslims,[25] or

Parliamentarians in Uganda campaign to criminalize and imprison homosexuals,[26] they legitimize and encourage non-governmental groups, businesses and individuals and others in the private domain to participate in the hate discrimination as well.[27]

In addition to politically generated hatred, state-sponsored religious hatred is a powerful mechanism of discrimination.[28] It usually takes the form of characterizing one or more religions as the treacherous enemies of the officially favored religion and promotes their destruction on the theory of 'it's either us or them'.[29] This often leads to assaults upon, and desecration of, the minorities' religious places of worship, cemeteries, and violent repudiation of identifiable members of the targeted religions.[30] In Canada, the project to supplant Aboriginal Spirituality with Christianity held no room for compromise. The basic premise of resocialization from 'savage' to 'civilized' was violent. Aboriginal cultures were to be brought to civilization through discipline and punishment and nowhere was this more obvious than in the treatment of Aboriginal children in residential schools, and in laws prohibiting, through criminal sanctions, the native spiritual and ceremonial practices.[31] The treatment of Coptic Christians by Egyptian officials,[32] and China's persecution of the Falun Gong are further examples of this form of state sponsored hate discrimination.[33]

The third type of state-sanctioned or state-sponsored hate propaganda – cultural vilification of particular groups – can be much more subtle than other forms of hate discrimination. It includes the promotion of negative stereotypes in the media and forms of entertainment and in otherwise legitimate and enjoyable art forms of music, poetry and literature. As Eli Wiesel has famously said in reference to the Holocaust, 'Cold blooded murder and culture did not exclude each other. If the Holocaust proved anything it is that a person can both love poems and kill children.'[34]

The portrayal of indigenous peoples in popular culture and sports as wild, sadistic brutes or inferior, lustful, promiscuous women fits the category.[35] Television shows, movies, comics and novels have dehumanized, obliterated or appropriated the identity of indigenous groups and subordinated them, leading the public to the conclusion that the group is inferior and less worthy of respect and regard.[36] The portrayal of Aboriginal women as 'squaws' is particularly damaging.[37] A Manitoba Justice Inquiry investigating the rape and brutal murder of a young First Nations woman, Helen Betty Osborne[38] concluded that the men who abducted and killed her were driven by vicious stereotypes borne of ignorance and aggression. They 'believed that young Aboriginal women were objects with no human value beyond sexual gratification.' The Inquiry relied on evidence that '[t]he portrayal of the squaw is one of the most degraded, most despised, and most dehumanized anywhere in the world … she has no human face, she is lustful, immoral, unfeeling and dirty. Such a grotesque dehumanization has rendered all Native women and girls vulnerable to physical, psychological and sexual violence.'[39]

Economic forms of hate discrimination single out particular groups and encourage discrimination through expression against its members with respect to housing, jobs and services. Other forms go much farther, advocating that extraterritorial restrictive covenants be placed against corporations that do business in countries where the dominant group is the target of their hatred, or even conditioning trade on the basis of the religion, ethnicity or race of the employees of the trading partner. All of these forms of transmitting hatred to achieve a negative economic effect are currently thriving,[40] many of them state-sponsored.[41] The controversy over fishing rights for First Nations in British Columbia is another Canadian example. Members of Parliament and even the Prime Minister, Stephen Harper, argued that aboriginal rights to fish were race-based and should be ignored.[42] As a result, racial tensions were exacerbated, including the threat of violence between First Nation and non-First Nation fishers.[43]

Legal responses to hate discrimination in Canada

Hate discrimination through various forms of expression creates tensions between the targeted groups or individuals and those who wish to promote hatred against them. Deciding where the line should be drawn between free speech rights and the equality rights of the targeted groups falls to the legislatures and the courts.

At one extreme, the free speech advocates argue for the freedom to say, print or videotape anything they want without restriction. On the other extreme, there are those who would use non-discrimination principles to prevent anyone from saying anything that criticizes or insults their fundamental beliefs. Striking a balance between these two points of view is difficult when both sides see the problem as standing at the peak of two slippery slopes. On one side, any restriction of speech is seen as removing safeguards that keep us from sliding towards group think, tyranny and despotism. On the other, unrestricted speech promoting hatred is seen as sliding toward a place where cruelty, violence and even genocide could be inflicted on the disadvantaged, marginalized or despised.

The Canadian approach has been to create both civil and criminal laws to prohibit hate speech when the speech crosses the line of causing harm to others. Civil laws in the form of human rights legislation are designed to educate wrongdoers and acknowledge the equality rights of the targeted groups or individuals. Criminal laws are designed to punish the hate propagandist.

At the present time, the human rights provisions regarding hate speech are under attack,[44] mainly in the media and by some government authorities. Some politicians also think the human rights provisions protecting minorities from hate speech go too far.[45] To resolve this matter, the Canadian Charter of Rights and Freedoms must be brought into the debate to ensure the fundamental values of the state are the lens through which the laws and fundamental freedoms are evaluated, rather than the rough and tumble of the media and popular opinion that serves the interest of politicians.

Hate propaganda laws in Canada, both Criminal and civil, derive support from section 15 equality rights in the Charter. As the hate speech laws impact on the right to expression, also a Charter right, a way must be found to ensure that the two fundamental rights can co-exist. Neither freedom of expression nor equality claims should ever be invisible, relegated to the background or allocated a lower place. There is no hierarchy of rights in the Charter. It must be remembered when seeking this balance between the two sets of rights, hate discrimination through words is a practice of inequality. The law's response to it must be tested against a standard of equality found in the Charter. The resulting limitations are the vehicle through which coexistence can be achieved.

In the Canadian context, especially with our history of state sponsored discrimination against the indigenous population, it is essential to find a non-discriminatory understanding of the limits on expression which avoids privileging certain cultural and racial perspectives in setting the objective tests. Otherwise, it is likely that the result will be a hierarchy of rights with those that benefit the majority rising to the top. Giving meaning to co-existing rights in a non-discriminatory fashion is an important challenge that, if met, will go a long way to resolving the hate speech controversy. The Charter provides some doctrinal space to resolve it.

Conclusion

It could be argued that a coexistence of expressive rights with equality rights could help to create a culture of respect where the opportunity for freedom of expression is equally enjoyed by both minorities and majorities. When seen from this perspective, restrictions on hate speech actually facilitate free speech by protecting voices and by decontaminating social discourse infused with blatant and harmful hatred.

Justice Dickson in the *Keegstra* case recognized that not only can expression be used to the detriment of our search for the truth, it can undermine rationality in an unregulated marketplace of ideas and promote forms of intolerance and prejudice.[46] This destroys the marketplace of ideas founded on equality values. Thus, legal restrictions of hate speech are not and should not be understood as limitations on freedom. They represent a refined understanding of what freedom is. The marketplace of ideas is a limited response to the search for truth. The challenge is to find the best way of responding.

Justice Dickson believed that fostering of tolerant attitudes among Canadians is best achieved through a combination of diverse measures. He said that dealing with the harm done through hate propaganda may require that especially stringent responses be taken to suppress and prohibit a modicum of expressive activity where deterrence and condemnation is necessary. But he also said having both the criminal and civil means of redress (through human rights legislation) is justified in a free and democratic society because it gives the state some leeway in use of the law depending on the circumstances which may require a less severe response. Furthermore, Justice Dickson's analysis is consistent with Canada's international obligations with respect to hate speech and racial, ethnic and religious equality although the international human rights regime has yet to recognize the equality rights of sexual minorities. The challenge is to find adequate legal protection that will work, pass constitutional muster and also provide a framework for a broader commitment to respect.

Irwin Cotler argues that a culture of respect is needed and that it must be anchored in a set of foundational principles found in international human rights jurisprudence and domesticated in Canadian law.[47] He claims that over the past 25 years the Canadian Supreme Court in passing judgment on many hate speech cases has provided a workable set of legal principles and precedents within a comprehensive appreciation of international human rights law and constitutional law. Cotler sees these principles as at least a starting point for a discussion about the creation of a culture of respect.[48]

It is logically irrational to assert that there should be unlimited liberty of either action or speech. Justice should prevent harm, not require it. The need for courts to apply hate laws with firmness, consistency and wisdom is essential if the norms of behaviour we wish to promote in society are to be encouraged.

Notes

1 This was a favourite expression of Alan Borovoy who was the long-time Director of the Canadian Civil Liberties Association, which opposed any regulation of hate discrimination on the grounds that it violated free speech principles. See A. Borovoy, *When Freedoms Collide: The Case for Our Civil Liberties* (Toronto: Lester and Orpen Dennys, 1988). See also Kathleen Mahoney's book review of the same publication at [1990] *Alberta L. R.* p. 715.

2 J. Bailey, 'Twenty years later Taylor still has it right: how the Canadian Human Rights Act's hate speech provision continued to contribute to equality', in S. Rodgers and S. McIntyre, eds. *The Supreme Court of Canada and Social Justice: Commitment, Retrenchment or Retreat* (Markham: LexisNexis, 2010, 349 at 350–351); R. Klein and A. Bromberg, '2010 audit of antisemetic incidents: patterns of prejudice in Canada' (Toronto: B'nai Brith Canada, 2010), at 2, 9–10, http://jewishtribune.ca /tribune/PDF/audit2010/ENAudit2010.pdf; Statistics Canada, 'Police-reported hate crime in Canada 2009' (Ottawa: StatsCan, 2011), http://www.statcan.gc.ca/pub/85-002-x/2011001/article/11469-eng.pdf.

3 D. K. Citron, 'Cyber civil rights' (2009) *Boston Univ L R* 89:61 at 64-66, 68-84; 'Law's expressive value in combating cyber gender harassment' (2009) *Michigan L Rev* 108:373 at 374–375; Egale Canada Human Rights Trust, 'Every class in every school: final report on the first national climate survey on homophobia, biphobia, and transphobia, in Canadian Schools, executive summary,' May 2011, http://www.egale.ca/extra%5C1489.pdf.

4 See Robert M. O'Neil, 'Hate propaganda and national security' in Moore and Turner, *Legal Issues in the Struggle Against Terror*, Carolina Academic Press, 2010; Rudiger Wolfrum, 'Genocide and crimes against humanity, prevention', www.enotes.com/genocide-encyclopedia/prevention; Department of Justice 'Backgrounder: parliamentary review of the Anti-Terrorism Act', http://www.justice.gc.ca/eng/news-nouv/nr-cp/2004/doc_31338.html.

5 Ibid.

6 A term borrowed from Canada, Minister of Justice, *Report to the Minister of Justice of the Special Committee on Hate Propaganda in Canada*, (Cohen Committee) Queen's Printer, Ottawa, 1966.

7 The author discusses many strategies of hatemongers, noting in particular the activities of a group called Anonymous which has devoted itself to systematically attacking minorities and feminists sites with a common approach of dehumanizing the targets followed by intimidation through threats of rape and violence.

8 The Supreme Court of Canada described the harmful effects of hate speech in the two of the leading Canadian cases *Canada (Human Rights Commission) v. Taylor*, [1990] 2 SCR 892, at 918–919 and *R. v. Keegstra*, [1990] 3 SCR 697, at 746–747, 812. Subsequent jurisprudence and literature further document the nature and extent of the harm. For example, see R. Delgado and J. Stefanic, *Understanding Words That Wound* (Boulder: Westview, 2004), at 16–18; M. J. Matsuda, 'Public response to racist speech: considering the victim's story,' in M. J. Matsuda *et al.*, *Words That Wound: Critical Race Theory, Assaultive Speech and the First Ammendment* (Boulder: Westview Press, 1993) 17 at 24; *Bou Malhab v. Diffusion Metromedia CMR inc.*, 2011 SCC 9 at paras 68 107; *Mugusera v. Canada (Minister of Citizenship and Immigration)* 2005 SCC 40 at paras 102, 147; A. Tsesis, *Destructive Messages: How Hate Speech Paves the Way for Harmful Social Movements* (New York: New York University Press, 2002) at 94–98; G. M. Herek, 'Hate crimes and stigma-related experiences among sexual minority adults in the United States' (2009) *J Interpers Violence* 24:55 at 57.

9 Samantha Power discusses contemporary genocides where hate speech was a critical factor in motivating the mass murders in *A Problem From Hell America and the Age of Genocide* (Perennial, 2002). See also hallmarks of hate discussion, infra, note 87 and following.

10 The Supreme Court of Canada recognized that discrimination may be carried out through expression, as in the poisoning of work environments through sexual harassment in *Janzen v. Platy Enterprises Ltd.*, [1989] 1 SCR 1252 and in *Keegstra*, n 10 at 746.

11 The use of the Internet to promote terrorism and provide instruction on how to make bombs to kill large numbers of civilians in a terrorist attack was part of the evidence read into court proceedings in the sentencing hearing of a Canadian terrorist. See 'He pumped gas and plotted destruction, now jihadist faces life in jail' *The Globe and Mail*, 9 October 2009, page 1. For an example of the use of the Internet to target human rights defenders, Canadian lawyer Richard Warman was targeted by neo-Nazi and other hate groups in the United States for his campaign against hate speech on the Internet. He has taken numerous cases before the Canadian Human Rights Commission against various hate groups (see a list of the cases in *Richard Warman v. Canadian Heritage Alliance and Melissa Guille* 2008 CHRT 40), and succeeded in many. An American neo-Nazi was recently indicted over death threats made to Mr Warman (Stewart Bell, *National Post*, 11 December 2008.)

12 This is why the regulation of hate speech is central to human rights law both in Canadian domestic law as well as in international human rights instruments. Hate speech fits logically within the range of anti-discrimination measures

human rights statutes are designed for when it is recognized as a practice of discrimination in the form of words and a integral link in systemic discrimination, keeping target groups in subordinated positions through fear, intolerance, segregation, exclusion, disparagement, vilification, and degradation.

13 United States First Amendment Jurisprudence, while making the distinction between content and form, saying all content-based utterances are protected speech, nevertheless accepts that some content-based expression such as libel, threats and false advertising is not protected. Mari Matsuda argues there is mush speech that is close to action. Conspiratorial speech, defamatory speech, obscene phone calls, and fraudulent speech (Mari Matsuda *et al.*, *Words That Wound: Critical Theory*, Madison: Univ. of Wisconsin Press, 1993, 32.)

14 *R v Keegstra* [1990] 3SCR 697.

15 Ibid at 746.

16 Ibid, at 746–747, 812.

17 Robert Kelly and Jess Maghan, 'Introduction', pp9–22 in *Hate Crime: The Global Politics of Polarization*, Robert Kelly and Jess Maghan, Southern Illinois University Press (1998).

18 Ibid.

19 Anthony E. Simpson, 'Spectacular punishment and the orchestration of hate: the pillory and popular morality in eighteenth century England', in *Hate Crime*, op. cit. note 21.

20 See Milloy, John Sheridan (1999) *A National Crime : The Canadian Government and the Residential School System, 1879 to 1986*, University of Manitoba Press; Ward Churchill, *Kill the Indian, Save the Man: The Genocidal Impact of American Indian Residential Schools*, City Lights Books, San Francisco, 2004; Assembly of First Nations, *Residential Schools: A Chronology* (2009).

21 *The Indian Act* R.S., 1951, c 1–5.

22 See *Oliver (Town) v. Osoyoos Indian Band*, [2001] EXLAW 342. See also http://www.expropriationlaw.ca/news/news.asp?id=48.

23 See *The Act to Encourage the Gradual Civilization of Indian Tribes in this Province, and to Amend the Laws Relating to Indians* 3rd session 5th Parliament, 1857, see at http://en.wikipedia.org/wiki/Gradual_Civilization_Act.

24 President Mahmoud Ahmadinejad recently used the podium of the General Assembly of the United Nations to make a speech broadcast internationally, denying the Holocaust. See Michael B. Oren, 'Deep denial,' *National Post*, 14 October 2009, pA15.

25 Mr Wilders, a popular Dutch politician, was recently acquitted of hate speech charges in The Netherlands. He is well known for promoting a video equating the Qur'an with Mein Kampf and Muslims with Nazis. An appeal to the UN Human Rights Commission is anticipated.

26 Bill No. 18 Anti Homosexuality Bill 2009, Uganda Gazette No. 47 Vol CII, 25 September 2009, which can be found at https://docs.google.com/leaf?id=0B7pFotabJnTmYzFiMWJmY2UtYWYxMi00MDY2LWI4NWYtYTVlOWU1OTEzMzk0&hl=en.

27 See Michelle Goldberg, *The Uganda Anti-Gay Bill's U.S. Roots*, www.thedailybeast.com/articles/2011/05/11uganda-anti-homosexual-bill-inspired-by-american evangelicals.htlm; Jeffery Gettlemen, 'American's role in Uganda anti-gay push', *New York Times*, 11 May 2011; Adrian Phoon, 'The role of United States evangelists in Uganda's kill the gays bill', *The Age*, 12 January 2010.

28 Charles Kimball, in his book *When Religion becomes Evil* (HarperOne, 2002), addresses non-official religious discrimination but maintains that it too is a danger to democracy and to the general welfare of the society. He says there are five warning signs to define such corruption: claims of absolute truth, demands of blind obedience, establishment of the 'ideal' time, justification of means by

the end and declaration of holy war. He cites examples, from the Branch Davidians of David Koresh, to Heaven's Gate and Jim Jones, on through to Osama bin Laden. They all led to death and destruction for their followers and often innocent bystanders. He argues that others, while not so extreme, are dangerous enough to warrant observation. These include several organizations of the so-called religious right who often advocate violence indirectly by condemning certain groups that are deemed unworthy or under the control of Satan.

29 Danchin, Peter G., 'Defaming Muhammad: dignity, harm, and incitement to religious hatred', *Duke Forum for Law and Social Change*, vol 2, pp5–38, 18 August 2010; University of Maryland Legal Studies Research Paper No. 2010-34, available at SSRN: http://ssrn.com/abstract=1661764.

30 Ibid, *Duke Forum*, pp34–36.

31 Wendy Chan and Kiran Mirchanani (eds) *Crimes of Color: Racialization and the Criminal Justice System in Canada*, Peterborough, Ontario: Broadview Press, 2002; Report of the Royal Commission on Aboriginal Peoples, vol 1, *Looking Forward, Looking Back*, pp137–191.

32 David G. Littman, 'Teaching religious hatred', and Magdi Khalil 'The Ordeal of Arab Christians', both in Martyn Thomas, Adly A. Yousef, Heinz Gstrein, Meinrad Strassle (eds) ,*Copts in Egypt: A Christian Minority Under Siege*, Vandenhoeck & Ruprecht GmbH & Co KG, 2006.

33 According to Amnesty International, the persecution of the Falun Gong by the Chinese state includes a multi-faceted propaganda campaign, a program of enforced ideological conversion and re-education, as well as a variety of extralegal coercive measures, such as arbitrary arrests, forced labour, and physical torture, sometimes resulting in death. See 'China: The crackdown on Falun Gong and other so-called "heretical organizations"', Amnesty International, 23 March 2000. See also Mickey Spiegel, 'Dangerous meditation: China's campaign against Falungong', Human Rights Watch, 2002.

34 Cited by Irwin Cotler in 'Hate speech, equality, and harm under the charter: towards a jurisprudence of human dignity for a "free and democratic society"' in G. Beaudoin and E. Mendes (eds) *The Canadian Charter of Rights and Freedoms*, 3rd ed. (Scarborough: Carswell, 1996).

35 Media Awareness Network, *Common Portrayals of Aboriginal People*, http://www.media-awareness.ca/english/issues/stereotyping/aboriginal_people/aboriginal_portrayals.cfm.

36 Ibid.

37 Aboriginal Justice Inquiry of Manitoba, *The Changing Image of Aboriginal Women*, ch13, vol 1 (Manitoba Aboriginal Justice Implementation Commission, 1999), http://www.ajic.mb.ca/volume1/chapter13.html#5.

38 Helen Betty Osborne was a nineteen-year-old Cree student who was abducted, sexually assaulted and brutally murdered by four white men. Fifteen years passed before the first charges were laid against any of the perpetrators.

39 Emma LaRoque, Department of Native Studies, University of Manitoba quoted in Amnesty International, *No More Stolen Sisters* (London, UK.,2009) at 5. http://www.amnesty.ca/amnestynews/upload/AMR200122009.pdf at 5 and in the Manitoba Aboriginal Justice implementation Commission, ibid.

40 One of the most clear examples of this form of hate discrimination is the boycott by the Arab League Against Israel. See Nancy Turck, 'The Arab boycott of Israel'. *Foreign Affairs* (Council on Foreign Relations), vol 55, no 3, pp472–493 (April 1977).

41 Feiler, Gil. 'Arab boycott', *The Continuum Political Encyclopedia of the Middle East*, ed. Avraham Sela, New York: Continuum, 2002, pp54–57. The author states the Arab League officially boycotts products and services that originate in Israel,

businesses in non-Arab countries that do business with Israel, and businesses that ship or flow to Israeli ports. Companies that violated the instructions of the boycott offices were blacklisted. The products of foreign artists, filmmakers, and musicians are also boycotted if they are considered to be too close to Israel. In addition to goods and businesses, many Arab states refuse to allow entrance to anyone who uses an Israeli passport or who has any Israeli stamp in their passport. At one point the boycott was observed by the entire Arab League. Today, only Lebanon and Syria adhere to it stringently.

42 John Cummins MP, 'Supreme court erred on race-based fishery', *Times Colonist* (Victoria), 17 July 2008, pA13.

43 Poneil, 'Harper vows to end race-based fisheries', *Canwest News Service,* 12 July 2006.

44 Alan Shanoff, 'Fatal flaws in hate speech law', *Toronto Sun,* 3 December 2011. Canadian Human Rights Commission Free Speech Controversy, http://en.wikipedia.org/wiki/Canadian_Human_Rights_Commission_free_speech_controversy.

45 Hansard (Canada), 39th Parliament, 2nd Session, Notice Paper, No. 41 Thursday, 31 January 2008, 10:00 a.m.

46 Jane Bailey in her article compares the dangers of the unregulated free market system with the danger of the unregulated marketplace of ideas, arguing for the reasonable regulation of both. 'Twenty years later Taylor still has it right: how the Canadian Human Rights Act's hate speech provision continued to contribute to equality', in S. Rodgers and S. McIntyre, eds. *The Supreme Court of Canada and Social Justice: Commitment, Retrenchment or Retreat* (Markham: LexisNexis, 2010, 350–351).

47 Irwin Cotler, Stockholm International Forum, Key-note Speech at www.manskligarattigheter.gov.se/stockholmforum/2001/page 1219.html.

48 Ibid.

20 The protection of cultural landscapes and indigenous heritage in international investment law

Valentina S. Vadi[1]

Introduction

Indigenous cultural heritage plays an essential role in the building of the identity of indigenous peoples. Its protection thus has profound significance for their dignity and the realization of their human rights. Although the recognition of indigenous peoples' rights and cultural heritage has gained some momentum at the international law level since the adoption of the 2007 United Nations Declaration on the Rights of Indigenous Peoples (UNDRIP)[2] and a number of indigenous cultural landscapes are now inscribed in the World Heritage List, the management of natural resources in traditional lands remains a contentious issue. Law and policy tend to favour macroeconomic notions of growth regardless of actual or potential infringement of indigenous entitlements (Barrera-Hernández, 2005, p1). Many of the estimated 370 million indigenous peoples around the world have lost, or are under imminent threat of losing, their ancestral lands, because of the exploitation of natural resources (Pillay, 2011).

While the clash between economic development and indigenous peoples' rights is by no means new, this chapter approaches this well known theme from a new perspective by focusing on international investment law and arbitration. In recent years, there has been a boom in investment treaties, which protect foreign investments and provide foreign investors direct access to an international arbitral tribunal. Thus, a potential tension exists when a state adopts regulation interfering with foreign investments as this may be deemed to amount to indirect expropriation, or to a violation of other investment treaty provisions. The key question is whether international investment law has embraced a pure *international economic culture* or if, on the other hand, it is open to encapsulating cultural concerns in its modus operandi.

Until recently, international investment law had developed only limited tools for the protection of cultural heritage through investment dispute settlement (Vadi, 2011). However, recent arbitral awards have shown an increasing awareness of the need to protect indigenous cultural heritage and cultural landscapes within investment disputes. Increasingly, arbitrators have balanced the different values at stake (Vadi, 2011).

This chapter will proceed as follows. First, the international norms protecting cultural landscapes and indigenous cultural heritage will be scrutinized. Second, the investment law framework shall be sketched out. Third, a relevant case study will be analysed and critically assessed. Fourth, this contribution offers some legal options to better reconcile the different interests at stake. Fifth, some conclusions shall be drawn.

The international protection of cultural landscapes and indigenous heritage

Cultural landscape is a geographic area which represents the combined work of man and nature.[3] According to Sauer's classic definition: 'The cultural landscape is fashioned from a natural landscape by a cultural group. Culture is the agent, nature is the medium, cultural landscape is the result' (Sauer, 1925). Virtually all landscapes have cultural associations, because all landscapes have been affected in some way by human action. Thus, according to some authors, cultural landscape would represent 'a way of seeing landscapes that emphasizes the interaction between human beings and nature over time' (Ingerson, 2000, p1).

Landscapes have traditionally fallen within the sphere of sovereignty and 'domestic jurisdiction' of the territorial state, with little influence by international law and international institutions. Only in recent decades has landscape increasingly become the focus of a wide range of international legal regimes that directly regulate it and emphasize its cultural, economic and social importance.[4] These developments have been furthered by two different regulatory streams. First, since the adoption of the 1972 Stockholm Declaration,[5] international environmental law has gradually eroded the domain of 'domestic jurisdiction', as environmental governance is increasingly seen as a matter of international concern.

Second, the very notion of 'cultural heritage' has gradually comprised the link between peoples and their land. In international law, the World Heritage Committee first introduced the concept of 'cultural landscapes' in 1992 as an autonomous category to justify the inscription of properties on the World Heritage List.[6] By adopting this new category, the Committee aimed to overcome the traditional dichotomy between nature and culture and to promote an integrated approach to the safeguard of the world heritage (Whitby-Last, 2008, pp51–62). The Committee also aimed to achieve a greater balance in the World Heritage List by including cultural expressions of underrepresented regions of the world. In a sense, the concept of cultural landscape favours a less Western approach, as it goes beyond the appreciation of mere natural or monumental beauty to include intangible cultural heritage values. The form of legal protection of landscape which placed emphasis on humanity being *within* the environment, rather than being disconnected from it, is particularly appropriate in protecting indigenous cultural heritage.

As a result, a number of indigenous cultural landscapes have been inscribed in the World Heritage List. Landscape is central to indigenous peoples' cultures. For indigenous peoples, land is the basis not only of economic livelihood, but also the source of spiritual and cultural identity (Gilbert, 2010, p31). Geographic features often have important spiritual significance for indigenous peoples[7] who 'see the land and the sea, all of the sites they contain, and the knowledge and the laws associated with those sites, as a single entity that must be protected as a whole' (O'Faircheallaigh, 2003, p27). Because of this holistic approach by indigenous peoples, a UN study insists that 'all elements of heritage should be managed and protected as a single, interrelated and integrated whole' (Daes, 1993). The UNDRIP recognizes the dignity and diversity of indigenous peoples' culture and their right to maintain their distinctive spiritual and material relationship with the land which they have traditionally owned, occupied or otherwise used.[8]

Among the different theoretical models that have been proposed to deal with indigenous peoples' rights (Westra, 2008, p10), the cultural integrity approach 'emphasizes the value of traditional cultures in and of themselves as well as for the rest of society' and links environmental concerns to cultural entitlements which are firmly rooted in the human rights catalogue. In sum, the cultural integrity model includes both environmental and cultural considerations to protect indigenous peoples' identity and acknowledges the dynamic nexus between indigenous peoples and their lands. While landscape protection has only a very recent pedigree in international law and no enforcement mechanism (Mashood, 2000, p360), cultural rights may be claimed before national courts and regional human rights courts, as well as through particular complaint mechanisms at the UN level.

Some scholars have criticized this approach contending that emphasizing the cultural entitlements of indigenous peoples de facto reduces their political rights and limits their claims to self-determination (Cutler, 2010). According to these authors, over-emphasizing culture can undermine self-determination. Nonetheless, if one deems the cultural integrity approach as complementary to other approaches, such an approach is of fundamental importance to understand and better protect the culture and human rights of indigenous peoples.

International investment law

The law of foreign investment is one of the oldest and most complex areas of international law. As there is no single comprehensive global treaty, investors' rights are defined by a plethora of bilateral and regional investment treaties and by customary international law. International investment law provides extensive protection to investors' rights in order to encourage foreign direct investment (FDI) and to foster economic development. At the substantive level, investment treaties provide inter alia for: adequate compensation for expropriated property; protection against discrimination; fair and equitable treatment; full protection and security; and assurances that the host country will honour its commitments regarding the investment.

Treaty provisions lack precise definition of these standards and their language encompasses a potentially wide variety of state regulation that may interfere with investors' property rights. Therefore, a potential tension exists when a state adopts regulatory measures interfering with foreign investments, as regulation may be considered as violating substantive standards of treatment under investment treaties and the foreign investor may require compensation before arbitral tribunals.

At the procedural level, investment treaties provide investors direct access to an international arbitral tribunal, creating a set of procedural rights to their direct benefit (Paulson, 1995). This is a major novelty in international law, as customary international law does not provide such a mechanism. The use of the arbitration model is aimed at depoliticizing disputes, avoiding potential national court bias, and ensuring the advantages of confidentiality and effectiveness (Shihata, 1986, p4).

However, given the architecture of the arbitral process, significant concerns arise in the context of disputes involving cultural landscapes and indigenous heritage. While arbitration structurally constitutes a private model of adjudication, investment treaty arbitration can be viewed as public law adjudication (Van Harten, 2007a, p372). Arbitral awards ultimately shape the relationship between state, on the one hand, and private individuals on the other (Van Harten, 2007b, p70). Arbitrators determine matters such as the legality of governmental activity, the degree to which individuals should be protected from regulation, and the appropriate role of the state (Sornarajah, 2002, p17).

Investor-state arbitration, however, distinguishes between two types of non-state actors:

- the investor engaged in foreign direct investment; and
- the FDI impacted non-state actors (Gal-Or, 2008–2009).

While indigenous peoples do have access to local courts, and eventually, regional human rights courts, the resolution of disputes arising from the investment within the territory of the host state is delegated to an international dispute settlement mechanism, thus undercutting the authority of national courts to deal with investment disputes (Francioni, 2009, p. 72). Furthermore, court decisions in the host state upholding complaints brought by private parties against a foreign investor may be challenged by the investor before an arbitral tribunal on the grounds that they constitute wrongful interference with the investment (Francioni, 2009, p72).

The increasing impact of FDI on the social sphere of the host state has raised the question of whether the principle of access to justice, as successfully developed to the benefit of investors through the provision of binding arbitration, ought to be matched by a corresponding right to a remedial process for individuals and groups adversely affected by the investment in the host state (Francioni, 2009, p71). While the recognition of multinational corporations as 'international corporate citizens' has progressed (Muchlinski, 1997, p79), by comparison, the procedural rights of indigenous peoples have remained unchanged. The paradox is that the foreign company and indigenous peoples lie at the opposite ends of the same spectrum: the company is characterized by its foreignness; indigenous peoples are characterized by their indigeneity (Langfield, 2010, pp135–152), descending from those who inhabited the area before colonization. At the same time, however, indigenous peoples have clearly defined rights under international law (Vadi, 2011). The following section addresses the question as to whether indigenous peoples' rights play any role in the context of investor-state arbitration.

Indigenous cultural heritage and the promotion of foreign investments

The development of natural resources is increasingly taking place in, or very close to, traditional indigenous areas (Barrera-Hernández, 2005). While development analysts point to extractive projects as anti-poverty measures and advocate for FDI as a major catalyst for development (OECD, 2002, p3), as one author puts it, 'for the most part, the peoples in the areas where the resources are located tend to bear a disproportionate share of the negative impacts of development through reduced access to resources and direct exposure to pollution and environmental degradation' (Barrera-Hernández, 2005, p6). Rising investment in the extractive industries can have a devastating impact on the livelihood of indigenous peoples and their culture (Tienhaara, 2006, pp73–100).

The linkage between economic globalization and indigenous peoples' rights has been discussed by administrative and constitutional courts at the national level (Chapman, 2008), and by human rights bodies at the regional and international levels (Westra, 2008). This case law and the relevant literature are extensive; what is less known is the emerging case law of arbitral tribunals dealing with elements of indigenous cultural heritage. Given the impact that arbitral awards can have on indigenous peoples' life and culture, scrutiny and critical assessment of this case law is of the utmost relevance. In general terms, investment disputes with indigenous cultural elements are characterized by the need to balance the protection of indigenous cultural heritage by the host state and the property rights of foreign investors.

Case study

To date, several investment disputes have involved indigenous cultural heritage elements (Vadi, 2011). For reasons of space, it is not possible to examine all of these awards in the context of this chapter; I will thus examine and critically assess the *Glamis Gold* case.[9] The case is significant because it involved a mining project within the California Desert Conservation Area, which includes a number of cultural and religious sites of the Native American Quechan Tribe. The area was heavily used by pre-contact Native Americans as a travel route, and more recently the Quechan used to walk the Trail of Dreams[10] while performing ceremonial practices. Although the area is not listed in the World Heritage List, its cultural importance for the tribe is similar to the importance of Mecca or Jerusalem for other believers.[11] When Glamis Gold, a Canadian mining company, planned the Imperial Project to mine gold on this federal land, the Department of the Interior withdrew the Project from further mineral entry for 20 years to protect historic properties.[12] In 2002, however, permission for the project was granted and regulations required the backfilling of all open-pit mines to re-create the approximate contours of the land prior to mining.[13]

In response to the federal and state actions, the claimant filed its Notice of Arbitration, arguing that state and federal measures constituted an indirect expropriation in violation of Article 1110 of the North American Free Trade Agreement (NAFTA).[14] According to the claimant, the expropriation began with the federal government's unlawful refusal to approve the Claimant's plan of operations[15] and continued with the backfilling requirement. In particular, backfilling would be uneconomical and arbitrary since it would not be rationally related to its stated purpose of protecting cultural resources.[16] The claimant pointed out that 'once you take the material out [of] the ground and if there are cultural resources on the surface, they are destroyed. Putting the dirt back in the pit actually does not protect those resources, but may lead to the burial of more artefacts and cause greater environmental degradation.[17] In addition, the claimant contended that the review process of its project violated the fair and equitable standard.[18]

The arbitral tribunal found the claimant's arguments to be without merit.[19] The tribunal found that the California backfilling measures 'did not cause a sufficient economic impact on the project to effect an expropriation of the claimant's investment'.[20] With regard to the purpose of the legislative measures, the tribunal deemed the measures to be rationally related to their stated purpose.[21] The tribunal admitted that 'some cultural artefacts will indeed be disturbed, if not buried, in the process of excavating and backfilling',[22] but concluded that, without such legislative measures, the landscape would be harmed by significant pits and waste piles in the near vicinity.[23] The arbitral tribunal also expressly referred to Article 12 of the World Heritage Convention (WHC),[24] which requires states to protect their cultural heritage even if not included in the World Heritage List. This is rather extraordinary as cultural heritage experts have repeatedly stressed that Article 12 of the WHC is an often-neglected provision (Lenzerini, 2008).

With regard to the alleged breach of the fair and equitable treatment standard, the Tribunal concluded that the acts of the federal government and the State of California did not violate the fair and equitable treatment standard.[25] The tribunal noted that the cultural review of the claimant's plan of operations was undertaken by qualified professionals who provided reasoned and substantiated opinions and was not biased: 'It is not the role of this Tribunal or any international tribunal, to supplant its own judgment of underlying factual material and support for that of qualified domestic agency'.[26] In addition, the contested California legislation was deemed to be of general application and did not target the claimant's investment.[27] The tribunal also stressed that investor expectations were not created by specific assurances.[28]

Critical assessment

In the *Glamis Gold* case, the arbitrators had to decide which of the rights in question carried more weight. The rights of the foreign company and the protection of indigenous cultural heritage were jointly considered, and the arbitral tribunal ascertained to what degree the limitation of the rights of the foreign company was justified by the importance of providing for the protection of indigenous cultural heritage. Implicitly, the arbitral tribunal deemed that protection of indigenous cultural heritage did not affect the core of investors' rights, but legitimately restricted the periphery of such rights. From an international investment law perspective, the award has to be welcomed as the arbitral tribunal 'took an especially sensitive approach in reviewing a State's decision to restrict property rights as a means of protecting non-investment interests' (Schill, 2010, p257).

From a cultural heritage perspective, however, one may wonder whether the result is fully satisfying. While such an assessment was outside the arbitral tribunal mandate, as arbitral tribunals are of limited jurisdiction and can adjudicate on investment claims only, one may question whether the state and federal measures were fully adequate to ensure the protection of indigenous heritage. As the respondent correctly pointed out, digging and backfilling may destroy indigenous cultural artefacts. Furthermore, one may wonder whether backfilling can ensure that the cultural rights of indigenous peoples are fully respected. To clarify, I have some doubt that backfilling can preserve the sacred value of certain landscapes. If digging is obviously not possible under Mecca and Jerusalem, which are both pilgrimage destinations for other believers – Jerusalem is also a world heritage site – one may wonder why the Trail of Dreams, which is sacred for indigenous peoples, should receive a different treatment. In conclusion, the case ultimately points out that international investment arbitration is not the most suitable forum for adjudicating cultural heritage related disputes.

Cultural exceptions in investment treaties

While *ex post* approaches to the protection of indigenous cultural heritage in the context of arbitral proceedings include interpretation, negotiation and balancing (Vadi, 2011), this section explores the *ex ante* or legislative approach to cultural heritage. Cultural exceptions might provide a useful tool in balancing the different interests at stake.

For instance, the Trans-Pacific Strategic Economic Partnership Agreement establishing a free trade area between Brunei Darussalam, Chile, Singapore and New Zealand (hereafter Trans-Pacific SEP),[29] sets out an exception to its obligations for the trade in goods and services to protect historical or archaeological heritage. More importantly, the Trans-Pacific SEP expressly states that New Zealand can provide more favourable treatment to Maori in respect of matters covered by this Agreement including in fulfilment of its obligations under the Treaty of Waitangi.[30] Derogations including preferential treatment for aboriginals are included in an annex to Canada's model foreign investment protection agreement (Peterson, 2004). Malaysia has similarly excluded measures designed to promote economic empowerment of the Bumiputras ethnic group from the scope of BITs (Sornarajah, 2004, pp120–121).

The merit of introducing a cultural clause in investment agreements is proven also by the recent *UPS* case,[31] which involved debate over the applicability of the cultural industries clause in a North American Free Trade Agreement (NAFTA) claim. The United States claimed that Canada's Publications Assistance Program (PAP) – a policy designed to promote the wider distribution of Canadian periodicals – was discriminatory to foreign investors. The tribunal upheld Canada's argument that the PAP was exempted from review under NAFTA by virtue of the cultural industries exception.[32]

The lack of careful drafting in investment treaties can affect the police power of the host state to adopt and implement social programmes, as affirmative actions aimed at encouraging the economic, cultural and social opportunities of disadvantaged aboriginal groups may conflict with investment treaty provisions. For instance, in the immediate post-Apartheid period, South Africa adopted an ambitious social and economic programme to advance the standing of historically disadvantaged persons. In particular, the Minerals and Petroleum Resources Development Act (MPRDA)[33] terminated the common law concept of ownership of mineral rights and provided that the mineral and petroleum resources of South Africa are the common heritage of its people and that the State is the custodian of those resources. Businesses have had to pay royalties on mineral rights since 2009.[34]

The MPRDA has generated much controversy among foreign and domestic investors and recently has been challenged before local courts[35] and in an investor state arbitration.[36] A number of Italian investors complained inter alia that the MPRDA amounted to an indirect expropriation of their rights without providing compensation. Because the case was settled, what is publicly available does not provide a clear picture of how the case would have been adjudicated by the arbitral tribunal.

Nonetheless, this case demonstrates the merit of introducing a specific clause or exception in the context of investment treaties in order to create a shield for policies of particular cultural or social relevance. As a matter of dispute avoidance, the inclusion of an *ad hoc* clause can prevent possible conflicts. In this sense, recent South African BITs expressly shelter those government measures which are designed to advance the interests of the previously disadvantaged (Peterson, 2006, p11).[37]

Conclusions

The effective protection of indigenous cultural heritage benefits all humanity by better ensuring diversity. In particular, cultural landscapes are a legacy for everyone as they reveal aspects of a country's history and yield a sense of identity for present and future generations. The interplay between investors' rights and indigenous cultural heritage in international investment law and arbitration is an almost unexplored field. Thus, further study is needed to shed light on this complex interplay.

At a procedural level, disputes between states and foreign investors often present a constitutional dimension because they involve the conflict between fundamental rights, such as the right to property, and cultural rights. Investor-state arbitration is not the most suitable forum to settle this kind of dispute. Nonetheless, as some arbitrations have dealt with indigenous heritage, their scrutiny is of topical importance. In a previous study, I focused on the procedural aspects of the arbitral process and on the need of its limited 'judicialization' to integrate indigenous participation to the same (Vadi, 2011). This chapter has focused on substantive issues and argues for a constitutional balancing between foreign investors' rights and legitimate State concerns flowing from international human rights treaties and the WHC.

As arbitral tribunals may face difficulties in finding an appropriate balance between the different interests concerned, improved legal drafting is very much needed. In this regard, cultural exceptions should be introduced in the text of investment agreements. On the one hand, this would provide certainty and black letter rules to foreign investors. On the other hand, it would adequately protect indigenous cultural heritage. In conclusion, this chapter acknowledges that FDI can represent a potentially positive force for development. Yet state policy and practice concerning resource exploitation must be mindful of its implications for the culture of indigenous peoples.

Notes

1 The author wishes to thank Laura Westra, Francesco Francioni, Claire Cutler, Colin Soskolne, Donald W. Spady and Judy Carter for their comments. The usual disclaimer applies.

2 United Nations Declaration on the Rights of Indigenous Peoples, A/RES/61/295 (2007).

3 The word landscape probably comes from the Dutch word *landschap*, which was used by Dutch painters in the sixteenth century to indicate paintings representing natural inland sceneries. The word originates from the German: 'Land shaffen' means to work or to shape the land. Literally, landscape means 'cultivated land' and, thus, 'shaped land'.

4 European Landscape Convention, adopted on 20 October 2000, entered into force on 1 March 2004, CETS No 176.

5 United Nations Conference on the Human Environment, Stockholm Declaration on the Human Environment, 16 June 1972, 11 ILM 1416 (1972).

6 1992 Operational Guidelines to the 1975 UNESCO Convention on the Protection of World Natural and Cultural Heritage.

7 For instance, the Maori personify the sacred places and venerate them as visible traces of their ancestors. See Smith (2001, p3).

8 See Declaration on the Rights of Indigenous Peoples, preamble, Articles 8, 11, 12.1 and 13.1.

9 *Glamis Gold Ltd v. United States* Award (*Glamis Gold* Award), 8 June 2009, available at www.state.gov/s/l/c10986.htm, accessed 16 September 2011, §§100–101.

10 *Glamis Gold* Award, §107.

11 *Glamis Gold* Award, §§103–108.

12 *Glamis Gold* Award, §152.

13 *Glamis Gold* Award, §183.

14 North American Free Trade Agreement, 32 ILM 1480 (1993).

15 *Glamis Gold* Award, §321.

16 *Glamis Gold* Award, §321.

17 *Glamis Gold* Award, §687

18 *Glamis Gold* Award, §639.

19 *Glamis Gold* Award, §360.

20 *Glamis Gold* Award, §536.

21 *Glamis Gold* Award, §803.

22 *Glamis Gold* Award, §805.

23 *Glamis Gold* Award, §805.

24 Article 12 of the WHC reads as follows: 'The fact that a property belonging to the cultural or natural heritage has not been included in either of the two lists mentioned in paragraphs 2 and 4 of Article 11 shall in no way be construed to mean that it does not have an outstanding universal value for purposes other than those resulting from inclusion in these lists.'

25 *Glamis Gold* Award, §824.

26 *Glamis Gold* Award, §779.

27 *Glamis Gold* Award, §765.

28 *Glamis Gold* Award, §799.

29 Trans-Pacific Strategic Economic Partnership Agreement signed on 18 July 2005 and entered into force on 1 May 2006, www.mfat.govt.nz/downloads/trade-agreement/transpacific/main-agreement.pdf, accessed 22 September 2011.

30 Treaty of Waitangi (Māori Te Tiriti o Waitangi) 1840. www.nzhistory.net.nz/politics/treaty/read-the-treaty/english-text, accessed 22 September 2011.

31 *United Parcel Service of America v. Government of Canada*, Award on the Merits, May 24, 2007, §156ff.

32 NAFTA, Annex 2106.

33 *Minerals and Petroleum Resources Development Act* (MPRDA), Act No. 28 of 2002. *Republic of South Africa Government Gazette*, vol 448, issue 10, October 2002, no. 23922.

34 MPRDA, Section 3(1).

35 *Agri South Africa v. Minister, Minerals & Energy*; *Van Rooyen v. Minister, Minerals & Energy* (55896/2007; 10235/2008) [2009] ZAGPPHC 2 (6 March 2009).

36 *Pietro Foresti, Laura De Carli and Others v. Republic of South Africa*, ICSID Case No. ARB(AF)/07/1, Award, 4 August 2010, http://icsid.worldbank.org/ICSID/FrontServlet?requestType=CasesRH&actionVal=showDoc&docId=DC1651_En&caseId=C90 , accessed 22 September 2011.

37 See, for instance, Article 3(3) (c) of the 1998 Treaty between the Czech Republic and South Africa.

References

Barrera-Hernández, L. (2005) 'Indigenous peoples, human rights and natural resource development: Chile's Mapuche peoples and the right to water', *Annual Survey of International and Comparative Law*, vol 11, no 1, article 2, available at http://digitalcommons.law.ggu.edu/annlsurvey/vol11/iss1/2

Chapman, T. (2008) 'Corroboree shield: a comparative historical analysis of (the lack of) international, national and state level indigenous cultural heritage protection', *Macquarie Journal of International and Comparative Environmental Law*, vol 5, pp81–96

Cutler, C. (2010) 'The globalization of international law, indigenous identity, and the 'new constitutionalism', in W. Coleman (ed.) *Property, Territory, Globalization: Struggles over Autonomy*, University of British Columbia Press, Vancouver, Canada

Daes, E. I. (1993) *Study on the Protection of the Cultural and Intellectual Property of Indigenous Peoples*, Sub-Commission on Prevention of Discrimination and Protection of Minorities, UN Doc. E/CN.4/Sub 2/1993/28, UN, New York, NY

Francioni, F. (2009) 'Access to justice, denial of justice, and international investment law' in P.-M. Dupuy, F. Francioni and E.-U. Petersmann (eds) *Human Rights in International Investment Law and Arbitration*, Oxford University Press, Oxford, UK

Gal-Or, N. (2008–2009) 'The investor and civil society as twin global citizens: proposing a new interpretation in the legitimacy debate', *Suffolk Transnational Law Review*, vol 32, pp271–301

Gilbert, J. (2010) 'Custodians of the land: indigenous peoples, human rights and cultural integrity' in M. Langfield, W. Logan and M. Craith (eds) *Cultural Diversity, Heritage and Human Rights*, Routledge, Abingdon, UK, pp31–44

Ingerson, A. (2000) 'What are cultural landscapes?', available at http://home.comcast.net/~jay.paul/landscapes.doc, (accessed 26 January 2012)

Langfield, M. (2010) 'Indigenous peoples are not multicultural minorities: cultural diversity, heritage and indigenous human rights in Australia' in M. Langfield, W. Logan and M. Craith (eds) *Cultural Diversity, Heritage and Human Rights*, Routledge, Abingdon, UK

Lenzerini, F. (2008) 'Article 12', in F. Francioni (ed.), *The 1972 World Heritage Convention- A Commentary*, Oxford University Press, Oxford, UK

Mashood, S. J. (2000) 'Kakadu and the politics of world heritage listing', *Australian Journal of International Affairs*, vol 54, no 3, pp357–372

Muchlinski, P. (1997) 'Global Bukovina examined: viewing the multinational enterprise as a transnational law making community', in G. Teubner (ed.) *Global Law Without a State*, Dartmouth, London

OECD (2002) *Foreign Direct Investment for Development*, Organisation for Economic Co-operation and Development, Paris

O'Faircheallaigh, C. (2003) 'Negotiating cultural heritage? Aboriginal mining company agreements in Australia' *Development and Change*, vol 39, no 1, pp25–51

Paulson, J. (1995) 'Arbitration without privity', *ICSID Review–Foreign Investment Law Journal*, vol 10, p2ff

Peterson, L.-E. (2004) 'Clarification on Aboriginals and Canada's investment treaties', *Investment Law and Policy Weekly News Bulletin*, 11 June, available at http://www.iisd.org/pdf/2004/investment_investsd_june11_2004.pdf (accessed 8 September 2011)

Peterson, L.-E. (2006) *South Africa's Bilateral Investment Treaties, Implications for Development and Human Rights*, Friedrich Ebert Stiftung, Geneva, Switzerland

Pillay, N. (2011) 'Statement by the United Nations High Commissioner for Human Rights', United Nations, New York, NY, available at www.un.org/en/events/indigenousday/message_unhchr.shtml (accessed 16 September 2011)

Sauer, C. O. (1925) 'The morphology of landscape', *University of California Publications in Geography*, vol 2, pp19–54

Schill, S. (2010) 'Glamis Gold v. United States', *American Journal of International Law*, vol 104, pp253–259

Shihata, I. F. I. (1986) 'Towards a greater depoliticization of investment disputes: the role of ICSID and MIGA', *ICSID Review–Foreign Investment Law Journal*, vol 1, no 1, pp1–25

Smith, R. K. M. (2001) 'Traditional lands and cultural rights: the Australian experience', *International Journal of Human Rights*, vol 5, no 3, pp1–18

Sornarajah, M. (2002) 'The clash of globalizations and the international law on foreign investment', *The Simon Reisman Lecture in International Trade Policy*, availableatwww.ctpl.ca/publications/speeches-presentations/clash-globalizations-and-international-law-foreign-investment (accessed 18 September 2011)

Sornarajah, M. (2004) *The International Law on Foreign Investment*, Cambridge University Press, Cambridge, UK

Tienhaara, K. (2006) 'What you don't know can hurt you: investor-state disputes and the protection of the environment in developing countries', *Global Environmental Politics*, vol 6 no 4, pp73–100

Vadi, V. (2011) 'When cultures collide: foreign direct investment, natural resources and indigenous heritage in international investment law', *Columbia Human Rights Law Review*, vol 42, no 3, pp797–889

Van Harten, G. (2007a) 'The public–private distinction in the international arbitration of individual claims against the state', *International and Comparative Law Quarterly*, vol 56, no 2, pp371–393

Van Harten, G. (2007b) *Investment Treaty Arbitration and Public Law*, Oxford University Press, Oxford, UK

Westra, L. (2008) *Environmental Justice and the Rights of Indigenous Peoples*, Earthscan, London

Whitby-Last, K. (2008) 'Article 1 cultural landscapes' in F. Francioni (ed.) *The 1972 World Heritage Convention*, Oxford University Press, Oxford, UK, pp51–62

21 'Some for all, forever'

A Southern perspective on poverty, access to water, environmental health and the North–South divide

Louis J. Kotzé

> People are not equal in their struggle for access to resources. Some are rich, and live in green and pleasant suburbs or modern cities; others are trapped halfway along the path to material wealth, in polluted villages and towns; while many scratch a meagre living on tiny farms threatened by drought and soil erosion. (Rodney R. White, *North, South, and the Environmental Crisis,* University of Toronto Press, 1993, p3)

Introduction

The North–South dimension of global developmental politics has featured strongly in literature since it was first coined and popularized in the mid-twentieth century.[1] It is commonly associated with terminology such as: 'development', 'globalization', 'Third World', 'First World', 'industrialized and non-industrialized nations', 'emerging and developed economies', 'polarization', 'distribution of global wealth', 'hierarchy of wealth', 'income disparities', 'injustice' and 'inequality', among others. While its manifestation and severity are constantly changing, it continues to dominate the development discourse: 'the divide between the rich nations of the former First World and poor nations of the former Third World ... remains a fundamental dimension of contemporary global dynamics'.[2] Even though international cooperation and concerted, collective and mutually supportive action increasingly occur in an effort to address many global development challenges, the world remains polarized along distinct political, social, cultural, religious and economic lines – a consideration that inhibits a comprehensive cooperative approach to global developmental issues.[3]

The North–South divide manifests particularly starkly in global environmental and public health contexts as the unequal distribution of environmental burdens and benefits between countries of the North and the South, specifically with respect to the effect this has on the environment and the health and well-being of people.[4] In the health context, the divide is exemplified by the so-called '10/90 gap', which posits that 90 per cent of research funding addresses diseases affecting only 10 per cent of the world's population.[5] This is a clear example of extreme inequality, disproportionally allocated resources and irrational priorities with respect to social justice, fairness and equity. In the environmental context, this inequality is often termed 'environmental injustice', a theme that is growing in importance worldwide and which has been extensively canvassed by various GEIG scholars, among others.[6] There is no need to repeat their views here. Instead, in this chapter I will reflect on the North–South divide and its related issues as they occur *within* a country as opposed to *between* Northern and Southern countries.

Within many countries, deep socio-economic rifts exist; between the empowered elite and marginalized groups, among others. South Africa is an example in this respect. Even after 15 years of democracy and constitutional governance, severe inequalities remain, which are also evident in the environment and health context. This divide finds clear expression in the issue of access to water. While a small privileged minority has sufficient access to water, most of the population – including the poor, unemployed and generally marginalized sectors – have no or insufficient access.[7] South Africa's Gini cofficient is one of the worst in the world, a fact that will necessitate 'government interventions through demand or supply side management ... to address the gaps in service delivery and access to water ... while at the same time being mindful of the increasing poverty gap'.[8] While I have written elsewhere on various legal aspects related to access to water in South Africa,[9] I will focus here on the North–South divide in the country in the context of access to water. I attempt to indicate the implications of the divide for environmental health in light of the rights-based approach to environmental governance as measured against the – famously controversial – Constitutional Court decision in *Mazibuko v. City of Johannesburg* (Mazibuko).[10]

The North–South divide

The North–South divide collectively refers to the common experiences of inequality of people in African, Asian and South American (third or developing world) countries as opposed to the rest of the developed world.[11] It is less a geographical division,[12] a 'qualitative dividing line' between countries of the South from the North', than a line cutting across political, cultural, economic, social and environmental aspects.[13] The divide is often used as a paradigm to understand the divisions or inequalities between the developed and developing world, especially insofar as this manifests in terms of trade, the environment, global diplomacy, economic development, resource exploitation, human rights protection, and transfer of technology, to name a few.[14] While these areas are varied, they do share a common denominator: they are all concerned with issues of *development* which, in turn, is related to basic needs, poverty, health and well-being. No doubt, in modern society:

> What we want for everybody is that they have food for every day, sufficient clothing, shelter, drinkable water, basic health care, fundamental education, etc; in short, that what we often think of as basic needs and rights are satisfied. This reminds us of the fundamental concern of development; that is, human beings and their needs.[15]

Despite this truism being justifiably subject to criticism, development is therefore concerned with the satisfaction of basic needs of humans who require environmental resources to do so. Where demand for environmental resources exceeds supply, as it currently does, it becomes unsustainable; that is to say, there will not be 'some for all forever'.[16] A profound challenge of our time will be to ensure that everyone on Earth has their basic needs and rights satisfied within the limits of available renewable and non-renewable resources. *Equitable* access and use of environmental resources of a sufficient quantity and quality will be paramount; as would an *equal* distribution of environmental externalities and benefits be important to achieve sustainable equality. It is *unsustainable equality* – persistent inequality – that drives and deepens the North–South divide, and also in the environmental health context where poverty plays a decidedly important role.[17]

Aspects of the North–South divide

Equality, poverty, health and sustainability concerns are reciprocal, consequential and interwoven, or, put differently, '[p]opulation health and equity are central to "sustainability" and vice versa'.[18] Poverty is likely *the* major consideration in the North–South divide and in the health context because it is a cause, consequence and exacerbating factor in this respect:

> Most of the disease burden in low-income countries finds its roots in the consequences of poverty, such as poor nutrition, indoor air pollution and lack of access to proper sanitation and health education. The WHO estimates that diseases associated with poverty account for 45 per cent of the disease burden in the poorest countries.[19]

While environmental resources such as water of an acceptable quantity and quality are necessary to sustain life and livelihood, many people lack access to these resources because of societal North–South divisions manifesting primarily as inequality. Bridging the North–South divide, in part by promoting equality in access to and sustainable use of water, would be critical for ensuring and sustaining good health.

The Millennium Development Goals (MDGs), despite their soothing and often disingenuous political rhetoric, illustrate the inextricable link between development, poverty, North–South inequalities, and health.[20] The MDG's primary objective is to enhance and secure development, especially for people in the South. They identify eight objectives directly related to North–South inequalities, environmental health and sustainability, including: eradication of extreme poverty and hunger (Goal 1); reduction of child mortality (Goal 4); improvement of maternal health (Goal 5); combating HIV/AIDS, malaria and other diseases (Goal 6); and ensuring environmental sustainability (Goal 7).[21] Access to water bears on all of these goals: '[t]he availability of safe water has a direct effect on the likelihood of success for each of the other MDGs, most notably the three health-related targets'.[22] To the extent that unequal access and use of water resources of an acceptable quantity and quality would lead to deteriorating public health, one could argue that there is a clear link between the North–South divide and environmental health issues in the water context. No doubt, '[w]here water supply and water treatment are deficient, human health status is low, life expectancy is low, and infant mortality is very high ... As human beings cannot live without water its supply must be viewed as the single most critical variable in the current global crisis.'[23]

In real terms, the link between the North–South divide, poverty, health and access to water is evident from the fact that water is fundamental to the lives and ways of life of all people. Poor people, however, have few means and opportunities to gain access to water; they are stuck in a vicious cycle and separated from their empowered 'Northern' fellow citizens by a continuously deepening divide. In fact, globally, most people that are deprived of access to water live in the South, and within Southern countries there are further divisions that separate those that have access to water and those who have not.[24]

It is in this context that one must consider the suggestion of Soskolne *et al.*:

> ... sustainable global health is fostered by minimizing the exclusion of vulnerable groups. This calls for a truly large-scale effort to reduce poverty and ignorance, including more effective provision to poor populations of tools needed to advance their own health.[25]

In other words, vulnerable, excluded, and marginalized groups that are discriminated against in terms of the distribution of life-sustaining environmental resources such as water, must be afforded the opportunity and means (or tools) to take corrective and redistributive action. These opportunities and means could come from various places and could take many different forms including, for example, better laws and policies, better governance, and improved education. The remaining sections of this chapter explore the extent to which the Constitution of the Republic of South Africa, 1996 (Constitution), as the 'supreme law of the Republic'[26] serves the purpose of being such a tool to advance the health of the poor, vulnerable and marginalized groups in South Africa in the context of access to water in an attempt to bridge the divide.

South Africa, the North–South divide and access to water

Providing people with access to water in South Africa is a daunting challenge for various reasons. During most of its apartheid past, South Africa's water governance regime had exclusively favoured a small, yet politically powerful, white minority which benefited from virtually unrestricted use of water resources and water services.[27] Water is an extremely scarce resource in South Africa which is classified as a 'water-stressed' country.[28] In addition to resource scarcity, further factors, such as poverty, HIV/AIDS and other diseases,[29] unemployment, general social decay and socio-economic inequalities, add to the complexities and difficulties of water service provision. In its policy on water services that forms the foundation of the current statutory water regime, the government estimated that between 12 and 14 million people in South Africa have inadequate access to water, while approximately 20 million have inadequate access to sanitation.[30] With few gains in poverty alleviation and improvement of the living standard of most South Africans, and coupled with a marked recent increase in the influx of destitute foreigners from neighbouring countries seeking better fortunes in South Africa, this estimation could very well be too optimistic.

A constitutional approach

In South Africa, correcting inequalities and ensuring better health and well-being for all with a view to bridging the North–South divide in relation to access to water, presents a mammoth challenge. As with all other governance, legal and societal matters in South Africa, the Constitution, as the supreme law of the country, is crucial in that it can provide some of the opportunities and 'tools' permitting corrective and redistributive action. The Bill of Rights provides three basic types of rights which are potentially applicable, namely, political rights (first generation), socio-economic rights (second generation) and, so-called group rights (third generation). I refer to these collectively as the 'three-pronged' rights-based approach to environmental governance and argue that when applied collectively to issues such as environmental deterioration, health and environmental justice, may provide a holistic, comprehensive and sustainable foundation for the protection and promotion of health and well-being that is cast in powerful constitutionalist language.[31]

The first collection of political rights provides that:

- everyone 'is equal before the law and has the right to equal protection and benefit of the law';
- everyone 'has inherent dignity and the right to have their dignity respected and protected'; and
- everyone 'has the right to life.'[32]

The second collection of socio-economic rights guarantees that '[e]veryone has the right to have access to adequate housing' and, more importantly for present purposes, section 27 states that '*[e]veryone has the right to have access to* health care services, including reproductive health care [and] sufficient food and *water*', among others.[33] The third collection consists primarily of the environmental right which provides that '[e]veryone has the right to an environment that is not harmful to their health or well-being'.[34] Clearly, the nature, scope, purpose, and formulation of all of these rights directly relate to issues such as poverty alleviation, redistributive and corrective justice, protection of environmental health and well-being, and satisfying basic needs. Consequently, these rights could be ideally suited to bridge the North–South divide in the South African water provision context. To what extent have they been used in the water context to bridge the divide?

Some for all forever?

In 2009, the Constitutional Court had the opportunity to address the North–South divide in water by means of the rights-based approach explained above in the case of *Mazibuko v. City of Johannesburg* (Mazibuko). The central issue was the interpretation of section 27 of the Constitution: the right of access to water. The case was instituted by Lindiwe Mazibuko and other poor, destitute residents (the applicants) living in Phiri, a township near Johannesburg,[35] after their water services provider (the City of Johannesburg and the respondent *in casu*) decided to install prepayment water meters to recover costs for any water that consumers used in excess of the City's free basic water supply of 25 litres per person per day, or of 6,000 litres per household per month.[36] The applicants claimed, inter alia, that the prepayment meters violated their constitutional right of access to water (section 27), and that the city's free basic water supply was, quantitatively speaking, insufficient. The case commenced in the High Court,[37] was appealed to the Supreme Court of Appeal,[38] and ended up in the Constitutional Court in 2009. The High Court declared that the prepayment water system was unconstitutional and unlawful and consequently ordered the City to provide the residents of Phiri with a free basic water supply of 50 litres per person per day, and the *option* of a metered supply installed at the cost of the City. The City appealed this decision to the Supreme Court of Appeal which replaced the order of the High Court with one declaring that 42 litres of water per person per day would constitute sufficient water in terms of section 27(1) of the Constitution. This decision was finally appealed to the Constitutional Court where the applicants argued, inter alia, that the Supreme Court of Appeal erred in determining that the sufficient amount of water required by section 27 was 42 litres instead of 50 litres. They essentially sought a reinstatement of the High Court Order. The Constitutional Court unanimously dismissed the applicants' appeal and held that a court cannot prescribe to government how much water it must supply to people; a court can only decide on whether the government's water provision policies and laws are reasonable or not. It determined that the City's free water policies and laws were reasonable and that the installation of the prepayment water meters was neither unfair nor discriminatory. The result was that, after several years of litigation, the applicants were back to square one in all respects.

The Constitutional Court's decision admittedly contains several elements for critique and, as I have noted elsewhere,[39] could not have been easy to make. The result in the Mazibuko decision is a consequence of steadfast adherence to judicial precedent which the Constitutional Court itself created in the earlier judgments of the *Government of the Republic of South Africa and others v. Grootboom and others* (Grootboom),[40] and *Minister of Health and others v. Treatment Action Campaign (TAC) and others*,[41] where it considered the rights of access to adequate housing and access to health care services, respectively. In line with these precedents, the Court was forced not to focus on the right per se, but rather on the obligation on government to progressively realize the right in question. In other words, any constitutional challenge must test whether the state's actions have met the constitutional standard of reasonableness in the state's efforts to realize the right.

A court will typically intervene only where this standard has not been met; it will not intervene in those instances where the state has failed to provide a specific quantity of a socio-economic entitlement such as water. This test is known as 'reasonableness review', and entails that, in the absence of minimum core obligations (a notion which the Constitutional Court has consistently rejected), it would only be required of a court to determine whether the legislative and other measures taken by government to realize a positive obligation in terms of socio-economic rights are reasonable or not.[42] The decision is a further result of respect for the separation of powers doctrine that prevails in the South African constitutional state (*Rechtsstaat*), which posits that the judiciary cannot intervene in the executive functions of governments. The court evidently did not see its way open to prescribe to government how much water it must supply to people:

> ... it is institutionally inappropriate for a court to determine precisely what the achievement of any particular social and economic right entails and what steps government should take to ensure the progressive realisation of the right. This is a matter, in the first place, for the legislature and executive, the institutions of government best placed to investigate social conditions in the light of available budgets and to determine what targets are achievable in relation to social and economic rights. Indeed, it is desirable as a matter of democratic accountability that they should do so for it is their programmes and promises that are subjected to democratic popular choice.[43]

While the decision may be debatable, it is more useful here to reflect on its consequences in the context of the North–South divide. First, Mazibuko made it clear that considerations of environmental justice and equality are manifestly intertwined with the availability, distribution, and use of environmental resources. Nowhere else is this perhaps more evident than in the water context:

> Although rain falls everywhere, access to water has long been grossly unequal. This inequality is evident in South Africa. While piped water is plentifully available to mines, industries, some large farms and wealthy families, millions of people, especially women, spend hours laboriously collecting their daily supply of water from streams, pools and distant taps.[44]

There are no winning formulas for addressing environmental and social injustice, otherwise there would not be poor, deprived and destitute people in the world. The problem of achieving environmental justice and equality in resource availability, distribution, and use is compounded by the deeply difficult conundrum of inter-generationality. It is doubtful whether we will be able to ensure equity for future generations if we cannot even achieve more equitable access to water for the present generation. While there are no evident solutions, governments, water users, and all other interested and affected parties would be well-advised to carefully reconsider the design, objectives, content, and implementation of current and future laws, policies and other means of governance if they are to achieve inter- and intragenerational equity.

Second, as Mazibuko has illustrated, not even one of the most progressive constitutions and constitutional courts in the world with the strongest rights to access to water can remedy the situation; it was beyond the scope of the Court's power to order government to provide more access to free water. Moreover, even if it had made such an order, it probably would have taken years for the government to implement it and provide poor people access to more free water. In 2000, the Constitutional Court ordered in the *Grootboom* case that the applicant, Mrs Irene Grootboom and others in her position could demand that the state act reasonably to provide access to housing for people by devising and implementing a housing policy that did not neglect the most poor and vulnerable members of society.[45] Yet, eight years later, in 2008, she died, without a house of her own. While this may point to a lethargic government, admittedly constrained by the lack of resources, it also demonstrates the need to refocus on fundamental empowerment aspects such as education, poverty alleviation and inventing and providing 'poor populations [with] tools needed to advance their own health'[46] in addition to those legal mechanisms that already exist in legislation, namely, Bills of Rights and constitutions. While I agree with Westra[47] that ' public health requires regulations and legal instruments to implement the collective rights it supports', laws and rights, even those backed by a constitutional court, have their limits and alone cannot achieve any significant advance in bridging the North–South divide. What is required instead is a collective multi- and cross-disciplinary effort to reconsider, resituate and possibly redesign governance priorities and the entire governance effort which relates to the environment, to health, poverty and access to basic resources. This effort must aim to bridge the North–South divide by focusing on redistributive and corrective justice (for past injustices), justice for the present generation, and justice for future generations; it must be sustainable.

Third, in light of the previous consideration, the road to bridging the North–South divide in this context will no doubt be a long and difficult one littered with many obstacles. Providing people who have had no access to water or who have insufficient access will take time, and not even a powerful constitutional text or court can achieve immediate tangible results. While this must never become an excuse for inaction or neglect, it is important to face reality:

> At the time the Constitution was adopted, millions of South Africans did not have access to the basic necessities of life, including water. The purpose of the constitutional entrenchment of social and economic rights was thus to ensure that the State continue to take reasonable legislative and other measures progressively to achieve the realisation of the rights to the basic necessities of life. It was not expected, nor could it have been, that the State would be able to furnish citizens immediately with all the basic necessities of life.[48]

Fourth, courts can only adjudicate issues that are presented to and argued before them. In Mazibuko, the constitutional challenge was brought in light of the right of access to water and consequently this right was the primary focus of the Constitutional Court. None of the rights listed in the previous section were extensively invoked, argued, or adjudicated by either of the parties or the Court.[49] This is surprising if one considers that, in fact, most of the aspects that the three-pronged rights based approach to environmental governance seeks to address were present in Mazibuko. While mere speculation, it could be that the Court might have come to an entirely different decision if the applicants had argued more of these rights, thereby forcing the Court to also consider environmental, health, well-being and human dignity aspects, among others.

Conclusions

The rights-based approach to environmental governance is a powerful tool for bridging the North–South divide. When properly applied to its full extent in relevant cases, it could provide the ideal platform for a representative and balanced sustainability evaluation by a court to the extent that the court will have to engage with environmental, social-cultural and economic issues simultaneously. In this way, the need to provide all people with equal access to a life-sustaining resource assumes new dimensions which raise critical ecological, ethical, social and economic issues. The result is that the singular issue of providing access to water becomes a broader one of providing equal access for present *and* future generations in a manner which respects the limits of the resource by balancing ecological and biological integrity with growing demand and myriad exacerbating resource pressures.

Acknowledgement

Funding from the Alexander von Humboldt Stiftung is acknowledged with thanks.

Notes

1 The North–South divide was popularised in the 1980s by the work of the Brandt Commission. See André Gunder Frank, 'North–South and East–West paradoxes in the Brandt Report', 1980, *Third World* Quarterly, 2(4), 669–680.

2 Giovanni Arrighi, Beverly J. Silver, and Benjamin D. Brewer, 'Industrial convergence, globalization, and the persistence of the North–South divide', 2003, *Studies in Comparative International* Development, 38(1), 3–31 at 4.

3 Ulrich Beyerlin 'Bridging the North–South divide in international environmental law', 2006, *Zeitschrift für ausländisches öffentliches Recht und Volkerrecht*, 66, 259–296 at 260.

4 Selected reading: Ruchi Anand, *International Environmental Justice: a North–South Dimension* (Ashgate, Hampshire 2004), 1–139; Mickelson Karin, 'South, North, international environmental law, and international environmental lawyers', 2000, *Yearbook of International Environmental Law*, 52–81; Henry Shue, 'Global environment and international inequity', 1999, *International Affairs*, 75(3), 531–545.

5 Colin L. Soskolne *et al.*, 'Toward a global agenda for research in environmental epidemiology', 2007 *Epidemiology*, 18(1), 162–166 at 163. See also Global Forum for Health Research available at www.globalforumhealth.org/about/1090-gap/ [accessed September 2011].

6 See, for example, Laura Westra, *Environmental Justice and the Rights of Unborn and Future Generations: Law, Environmental Harm and the Right to Health* (Earthscan, London, 2006).

7 H. Thompson, *Water Law: A Practical Approach to Resource Management and the Provision of Services* (Juta, Cape Town, 2005), 9.

8 N. A. King, G. Maree and A. Muir, 'Freshwater systems', in H. A. Strydom and N. D. King (eds), *Fuggle and Rabie's Environmental Management in South Africa*, 2nd edn (Juta, 2009), 439.

9 Louis J. Kotzé, 'Access to water in South Africa: constitutional perspectives from a developing country', 2009, *Finnish Environmental Law Review*, 1, 70–106; Louis J. Kotzé 'Phiri, the plight of the poor and the perils of climate change: time to rethink environmental and socio-economic rights in South Africa?', 2010, *Journal on Human Rights and the* Environment, 2(1), 135–160.

10 *Mazibuko and Others v. City of Johannesburg* 2010 (3) BCLR 239 (CC).
11 Ruchi Anand, *International Environmental Justice: a North–South Dimension* (Ashgate, Hampshire 2004), 1.
12 Even though most developed countries are in fact geographically situated in the Northern Hemisphere and most developing countries in the Southern Hemisphere.
13 Ruchi Anand *International Environmental Justice: a North–South Dimension* (Ashgate, Hampshire 2004) 1.
14 See David M. Malone and Lotta Hagman, 'The North–South divide at the United Nations: fading at last?', 2002, *Security Dialogue,* 33(4), 399–414; David Gillies, *Between Principle and Practice: Human Rights in North–South Relations* (McGill-Queen's University Press, Montreal, 1996).
15 Gro Harlem Brundtland, 'The Scandinavian perspective on the North–South dialogue', in Kofi Buenor Hadjor (ed) *New Perspectives in North–South Dialogue: Essays in Honour of Olof Palme* (IB Tauris & Co, London, 1988), 20.
16 'Some for all forever' is the notion that informed the formulation of South Africa's water law and policy framework.
17 The link between poverty and the divide is even more pronounced when the divide is considered against the many dimensions/parameters in terms of which poverty is measured. Arie M. Kacowicz, 'Globalization, poverty and the North–South divide', 2007, *International Studies Review,* 9, 565–580 at 569–570.
18 Colin L. Soskolne *et al.*, 'Toward a global agenda for research in environmental epidemiology', 2007 *Epidemiology,* 18(1), 162–166 at 163.
19 Philip Stevens, *Diseases of Poverty and the 10/90 Gap* (International Policy Network, London, 2004) available at www.who.int/intellectualproperty/submissions/InternationalPolicyNetwork.pdf [accessed 27 September 2011] at 4.
20 Phyllida Travis *et al.*, 'Overcoming health system constraints to achieve the Millennium Development Goals', September 2004, *Lancet,* 364(9437), 900–906 at 900.
21 United Nations Development Programme (UNDP) available at www.beta.undp.org/undp/en/home/mdgoverview.html [accessed 27 September 2011].
22 Editorial, 'Clean water alone cannot prevent disease', September 2004, *Lancet,* 364(9437), 816 at 816.
23 Rodney R. White, *North, South, and the Environmental Crisis* (University of Toronto Press, Toronto, 1993), 122.
24 Rodney R. White, *North, South, and the Environmental Crisis* (University of Toronto Press, Toronto, 1993), 123.
25 Colin L. Soskolne *et al.*, 'Toward a global agenda for research in environmental epidemiology', 2007 *Epidemiology,* 18(1), 162–166 at 163.
26 Section 2 of the Constitution.
27 Department of Water Affairs and Forestry *White Paper on Sanitation and Water Supply* (1994) 4–5. Available at www.dwaf.gov.za/Documents/Policies/WSSP.pdf [Accessed 6 June 2011].
28 H. Thompson, *Water Law: A Practical Approach to Resource Management and the Provision of Services* (Juta, Cape Town, 2005), p7.
29 Limited access to water is a strong determinant of disease. Access to adequate and safe water is essential for an acceptable standard of health and well-being and to avoid diseases like cholera, hepatitis and typhoid.
30 Department of Water Affairs and Forestry *White Paper on a National Water Policy for South Africa* (1994) 15. Available at www.dwaf.gov.za/documents/policies/nwpwp.pdf (accessed 2 June 2011); Department of Water Affairs and Forestry *White Paper on Sanitation and Water Supply* (1994) 1. Available at www.dwaf.gov.za/Documents/Policies/WSSP.pdf (accessed 2 June 2011).

31 These three generations are all substantive rights. Procedural rights also play an important role in environmental governance especially insofar as they guarantee and enforce rights of access to information; administrative justice; broad access to courts; and transparent, participative and accountable governance. See Louis J. Kotzé and Anel Du Plessis, 'Some brief observations on fifteen years of environmental rights jurisprudence in South Africa', 2011, *Pace Journal of Court Innovation*, 3(1), 101–120.

32 Sections 9–11.

33 Sections 26 and 27.

34 Section 24.

35 Phiri is part of Soweto, created under the previous apartheid regime as an exclusive 'black residential area'.

36 Access to water is regulated in terms of the *Water Services Act* 108 of 1997.

37 *Mazibuko and others v. City of Johannesburg and others (Centre on Housing Rights & Evictions as amicus curiae)* [2008] JOL 21829 (W).

38 *City of Johannesburg v. L Mazibuko* (hereafter *City of Johannesburg v. Mazibuko*) (489/08) [2009] ZASCA 20.

39 Louis J. Kotzé, 'Phiri, the plight of the poor and the perils of climate change: time to rethink environmental and socio-economic rights in South Africa?', 2010, *Journal on Human Rights and the Environment*, 2(1), 135–160.

40 2001 1 SA 46 (CC). See, among others, Pierre De Vos 'The right to housing' in D. Brand and C. Heyns (eds) *Socio-economic Rights in South Africa* (Pretoria University Law Press, 2005), 85–106.

41 2002 5 SA 721 (CC). See, among others, C. Ngwena and R. Cook, 'Rights concerning health' in D. Brand and C. Heyns (eds) *Socio-economic Rights in South Africa* (Pretoria University Law Press, 2005), 107–151.

42 'Reasonableness review' does not stand isolated from criticism. See S. Liebenberg 'Chapter 33: the interpretation of socio-economic rights' in M. Chaskalson *et al.* (eds) *Constitutional Law of South Africa*, 2nd edn (Juta Original Service, 2003), 33–41.

43 *Mazibuko and Others v. City of Johannesburg* 2010 (3) BCLR 239 (CC) at paras 61, 65.

44 *Mazibuko and Others v. City of Johannesburg* 2010 (3) BCLR 239 (CC) at Par 2.

45 Pierre De Vos, 'Constitutionally speaking: Irene Grootboom died, homeless, forgotten, no C-class Mercedes in sight', 11 August 2008, available at http://constitutionallyspeaking.co.za/irene-grootboom-died-homeless-forgotten-no-c-class-mercedes-in-sight/ (accessed 29 September 2011).

46 Colin L. Soskolne *et al.*, 'Toward a global agenda for research in environmental epidemiology', 2007 *Epidemiology*, 18(1), 162–166 at 163.

47 Laura Westra, 'Collective human rights: public health v. structural and ecological violence (the example of Ecuador v. Colombia)', 2010, *ILSA Journal of International and Comparative Law*, 16(2), 557–572 at 559.

48 *Mazibuko and Others v. City of Johannesburg* 2010 (3) BCLR 239 (CC) at Par 59.

49 With the exception of the right to equality (section 9 of the Constitution) which was briefly referred to by the Court in the context of the applicants' contention that the prepayment water meters resulted in unfair discrimination. *Mazibuko and Others v. City of Johannesburg* 2010 (3) BCLR 239 (CC) at Paras 105; 148–158.

Part VI

Environmental Laws and Human Health

Introduction

Colin L. Soskolne and Donald W. Spady

In this, this final part of the book, the five chapters bring together the most pressing issues of our time. These include global warming, agriculture, food security, the role of financial regimes in precipitating and fomenting ongoing declines, some of the public health ramifications and regulatory approaches to their mitigation, and also the role of international law as a mechanism for bolstering global governance to more ensure a sustainable future for generations to come. The notion of ecological law is introduced as a potential enabler of a change in course from one of decline to one of sustainability.

In Chapter 22, Gottwald addresses the very serious issues of global warming, greenhouse gases and food security from the perspective of the beef cattle industry. Beef consumption is often criticized because cattle production contributes to global warming through the production of methane and through water use. However, Gottwald argues that 'it is not the cow that is detrimental to the climate; it is the way it is raised', and the true climate culprits are 'agribusiness and factory farming'. He advocates a return to small-scale, regional and organically run farming.

Food also plays a role in Chapter 23, where Quinn and Bencko discuss the perplexing problem of food security and its importance in maintaining human health. They describe briefly the market economics of food security and the development of financial tools to help maintain food price stability. However, this chapter is also a description of how, in an unregulated market, money rules, and how the manipulation of these tools, combined with human greed and indifference to (or perhaps ignorance of) the essential human value of what is being sold, created a major crisis of food security for vulnerable populations globally. Given the importance of food security to meet a growing population at a time when food production is threatened by global change, market manipulations are unethical and regulatory reform is essential.

However, if one can transfer expectations from one area of law to another, Onzivu, in Chapter 24, raises only modest hope that such reform is likely. He reviews the current body of international environmental law with respect to public health protection and its domestic implementation. He comes up wanting, but remains somewhat optimistic and offers a possible remedy. Onzivu provides good arguments that there is a need for public health to have its own pillar to be added to the existing three pillars of sustainability. 'Health in All Policies', a recent initiative of the World Health Organization, may help in this regard.

Chiarelli in Chapter 25 takes us on a journey from mankind's origins, five million years ago, in an untouched environment, to today's over-exploited, over-populated, fragile and failing world. It is a history of imagination and brilliance. But it is also a history of unbridled anthropocentrism and hubris, describing a species that must now face and resolve the consequences of its actions, not through technology (although that will help), but through changes in attitude, behaviour and perspective.

Finally, in Chapter 26, Garver eloquently sums it all up and makes a plea for the rule of ecological law, paraphrased by Thomas Berry as '*articulating the conditions for the integral functioning of the Earth process, with special reference to a mutually enhancing Earth–human relationship*'. Garver extends this concept and provides ten features that ecological law would embrace. Adopting ecological law has profound consequences for our current way of life, including the need to live within nature's limits, rather than the limits of our pocketbooks or our social class. Our current commitment to the paradigm of infinite economic growth is mathematically, physically and biologically unsustainable – indeed, impossible – and is resulting in global socio-ecological catastrophe. Yet those who have aspired to affluence are afraid of change, and change is difficult. Thus, the adoption of the rule of ecological law is an opportunity for transformation, an exciting opportunity, a challenging opportunity, a requisite opportunity, and possibly the only opportunity.

Solutions for ensuring a sustainable future have been identified in this part of the book. These solutions require that we confront the collapse of life as we know it. The changes required rest in attitudinal and behavioural shifts among all people who embrace the need for 'contraction and convergence' for greater global equity. Given humankind's historical path and its current predicament, stronger regulations and legal regimes that embrace human rights at the supranational level of governance will represent a practical formula for ensuring a future for our children.

22 Are cows 'climate killers'?

Franz-Theo Gottwald

Global warming: a danger to agriculture?

Global warming has become a reality: between 1906 and 2005, global mean temperatures have risen by 0.7°C, indicating that a further 2°C increase in the temperature of Earth's atmosphere by the middle of the twenty-first century (relative to nineteenth-century figures) is inevitable, no matter what measures might be taken (Schulz, 2008, p14). Any and all political parties and organizations have been discussing a wide variety of approaches aimed at reducing anthropogenic, climate-relevant gases. Even if the impact of global warming has not yet been acutely felt everywhere, in the long run, climate change poses a major challenge for feeding an ever-growing world population.

Prognostications by the Intergovernmental Panel on Climate Change (IPCC) state that the developing countries, most of which are in Africa, will be most harmed. Countries where small-scale agriculture is dependent on rain for watering have observed that precipitation has become more and more sporadic (Bals *et al.*, 2008, p172). Southern Europe also has begun to experience seasonal droughts and water is becoming ever scarcer. Within fifteen years, demand for water will exceed supply by more than 50 per cent (Gottwald and Boergen, 2009, p101). In these regions, rising temperatures will lead to changes; pleasingly, these will not be wholly negative. Changes in yields are dependent on changes in temperature and precipitation, as well as the fertilizing effect of carbon dioxide (CO_2), but also the ability of farmers to adapt their choice of plants and irrigation practices (Rahmsdorf and Schellnhuber, 2007, p19). This will lead to an increase in yields in colder regions (i.e. mainly the richer industrialized countries, which are predominantly responsible for the majority of emissions of harmful gases), while sub-tropical, already arid, water-starved regions will have to deal with additional reductions (Rahmsdorf and Schellnhuber, 2007, p19). Hence, the countries that will suffer the most from climate change are those least responsible for causing it.

For instance, Ethiopian nomads have been adjusting to environmental changes over the centuries. Global warming, however, is pushing their ability to adjust to the limit. The decreasing availability of water forces them to migrate over ever greater distances. More frequent crop failures have caused malnutrition among nomads. In addition, their animals are less fertile and more susceptible to diseases (Riché *et al.*, 2009).

The impacts of global warming are not only on present-day crop yields, but are also likely to cause as yet inestimable harm to (agro)biodiversity, lead to dysfunctional ecosystems and the emergence of new diseases, and also negatively impact available resources, while fostering extreme weather events and weather-related natural disasters.

Global warming and the emission of harmful gases: the role of agriculture

To a great extent, industrialized agriculture is implicated in the emission of greenhouse gases harmful to the climate. Agriculture worldwide is responsible for about 30 per cent of all greenhouse gas emissions. It is the main source of methane (CH_4) and nitrous oxide (N_2O) emissions, which, compared with CO_2, are potentially 300 times more harmful. CO_2 emissions are due to changes in land use, mainly agriculture on previously wooded areas (Schulz, 2008, p12).

Table 22.1 Greenhouse gas emissions by economic sector, 2004

Economic sector	*Share (%)*
Refuse and waste water	3
Buildings	8
Transport	13
Agriculture	14
Shift in land use	17
Industry	19
Energy provision	26

Source: IPCC (2007)

Beef farming, more than any other practice, has been the target of critics. Scientists and authors worldwide seem to have chosen agricultural beef cattle as their number one 'climate killer'. This may be based in part on the role of beef farming in reducing the area of the world's rainforests.

In particular, South America has seen its rainforests clear-cut for pastures and feed cultivation for cattle. The American sociologist and journalist Jeremy Rifkin estimated that, as early as the 1980s, one American hamburger required six square metres of rainforest to be converted to pasture land (Rifkin, 1994). It is true that the clear-cutting of rainforests represents a huge ecological threat. The Amazon forest alone has an enormous impact on world climate. Close to 50 per cent of solar energy that falls on forested areas is absorbed through the transpiration of water through the leaves. Water originating from these forests and draining into the Atlantic makes up 15 to 20 per cent of total world freshwater effluence. Additionally, these rainforests are huge, highly sensitive, carbon sinks. Cutting and burning cause carbon to be released and thus the creation of carbon dioxide which then adds to global warming. If this kind of destructive exploitation continues unabated, within 15 years, more than half of the Amazonian rainforests will have vanished or have become unsustainable. One consequence would be the emission of 26 billion tonnes of carbon into the atmosphere (Nepstad, 2007, pp4–5).

Additionally, beef and dairy products are reputed to carry a substantial carbon footprint (Bals *et al.*, 2008, p297). To be sure, during their digestive processes, ruminants emit methane and, in fact, they are responsible for a major share of total CH_4 emissions:

Table 22.2 Share of various sources of emissions of total methane emissions, 2006

Source of emissions	*Share (%)*
Beef cattle	38
Garbage dumps	23
Pigs	7
Sheep	5
Coal mining	4
Natural gas	7
Others	16

Source: European Environmental Agency (2008)

In comparison with other ruminants, cattle produce the highest amount of methane. However, there are differences within the species. Non-lactating milk cows emit 150 to 300 grams of CH_4 per animal per day, lactating cows up to 600 grams. Feeder cattle emit between 80 and 220 grams (Flachowsky and Brade, 2007, p423).

It is estimated that the total number of cattle worldwide cause methane emissions equal to two billion tonnes of greenhouse gases (Reichholf, 2006a). Recently, the German press made the not overly original demand of 'gas masks for cattle', while other reports claimed that the problem could be solved by using climate-friendly feed mixes ('less grass, less gas'). There are, in fact, scientists who are convinced that a change in diet for cows could reduce methane emissions by up to 30 per cent. A reduction in the share of green fodder, while simultaneously increasing concentrated feed and certain fats, is reputed to reduce methane production in the rumen (Westphal *et al.*, 2010).

Let us examine how detrimental cows really are for the global climate and how decisive factors like feeding and farming practices are. The following will give an exhaustive overview of these and other questions.

'The cow – our climate killer': rehabilitation of a purported climate-damaging perpetrator

Having branded the cow as Enemy Number One of our global climate, more and more critical voices were raised pointing out the enormous significance of foraging animals for the environment, soil fertility and climate. Cows and other ruminants are able to forage on marginal land unsuited for cultivation and turn grass into meat and milk. In this very primordial way, grazers have been using grasslands for thousands of years. Grasslands have always supported high concentrations of mammals. For instance, the 16,000km^2 Serengeti supports more than a million and a half large animals (Reichholf, 2006b). Grazers assure superior soil fertility of grasslands in many parts of the world and hence contribute substantially to climate protection.

It is known that pastures and meadows have particularly high humus content. The process of grazing contributes much more than simply cutting back vegetation. Their hoof prints encourage turf building, their excrement returns energy to the soil and also spread plant seeds widely across the grasslands. The excrement contains microorganisms that interact with soil organisms. Grazers help humus formation and soil health and thus help sequester carbon.

Soil-sequestered carbon is three times that of carbon bound up in vegetation. The soil of grasslands worldwide stores more than a third of global carbon (Idel, 2010, p36). European grasslands and forests sequester an annual amount of up to 100 million tonnes of CO_2 and thus form the most important carbon sinks (Ruppaner, 2010, p27). Here lies the problem: for decades, supposedly useless grasslands are being converted into fields. This simultaneously ends any climate-related function as carbon sinks, while setting free additional CO_2 through this change in land use.

Meadows and pastures in farming have always been a vital part of ecologically sound rural agriculture. However, substituting concentrated feed for green fodder as well as increasing the cultivation of fodder and energy-producing plants has counterbalanced the positive effects of grasslands (Ruppaner, 2010, p27). Concomitant with factory farming, livestock were bred for high performance, and, by being fed agriculturally produced feed, were artificially forced to compete for food with humans. While grasslands lie fallow, animal feed is grown on millions of hectares worldwide. In turn, these areas are no longer available for growing cereals for human consumption. In this way, important CO_2 sinks, grasslands, forests and rains forests are sacrificed for monocultures

This is the core of the problem: cows in their original function as grazers can play an important role in the maintenance of soil fertility, biodiversity and for the climate – if they are allowed to do so. The reason for this ability is their special digestive tract: a cow can eat up to 100kg of green fodder, followed by up to nine hours of ruminating. Their stomachs are made up of several chambers and – with the help of billions of microorganisms – enable cattle to digest grasses, and even straw, and turn them into useful human food. The system is ingenious, considering that these hard-to-digest grasses are useless for most animals and human beings, and cannot serve as food. But agribusiness strives to optimize the meat and milk production of cattle. Before the bovine spongiform encephalopathy (BSE) crisis, plant eaters were fed animal meal; nowadays, feed is predominantly made up of energy- and protein-rich cereals, especially soy. Two-thirds of the protein fed in the EU comes from developing or emerging countries (Idel, 2010, p23). Thus, industry turned the once-ingenious grazer into an animal metabolically unsuited for what it consumes, with the unintended consequence that it is now regarded as a 'climate killer' (Idel, 2010, p24).

This accusation is not only absurd, but downright wrong. It is not the cow that is detrimental to the climate; it is the way it is raised. Science is becoming more aware of this fact. Sustainably used grasslands, their root mass and humus building, can function as CO_2 sinks (Heissenhuber and Zehetmeier, 2010). Sustainable grazing practices furthermore help reduce nitrous oxide (N_2O, laughing gas) emissions into the atmosphere. German scientists (Wolf *et al.*, 2010) spent a year studying the effects of animal husbandry in Inner Mongolia and demonstrated that emissions of N_2O would be significantly reduced by grazers. The study showed that previous studies significantly overestimated the harm to the climate caused by animal husbandry, while underscoring the need for further study concerning animal husbandry's impact on the environment and the climate.

In the past, it was erroneously assumed that an increase in the intensity of cattle breeding would lead to a reduction in the harmful effects of cows on climate. According to these figures, two cows producing 5,000 litres of milk each a year will consume twice as many resources and emit twice as much as one high performance cow producing 10,000 litres per year (Idel, 2010, p65). This ignores the importance of how this milk is produced (i.e. compound feed versus green fodder, pasture versus indoor farming, imported feed stuff versus closed loop recycling management). An additional factor is the life performance of cows: high-performance cows produce more milk, but due to their significantly shorter lives and expected useful life spans, their climate and eco-balances are much worse.

Agribusiness and factory farming: the true climate culprits

Worldwide agribusiness causes approximately 31 per cent of greenhouse gases. This is due to high amounts of chemical fertilizers and pesticides, removal of CO_2 sinks, clear cutting of rainforests, draining of swamps for monocultures and plantations, as well as large-scale use of machines. A further problem with regard to the emission of climate-related gases is the increase in globalization and transportation of farm produce.

People in western industrialized countries live well beyond their means. Agrarian economies with their extreme demand on resources, energy and water, function only because the actual costs are hidden and will be left for future generations and so-called developing countries to pay. Climate gases are produced in agribusiness mainly through the conversion of forests and grasslands into cultivated fields, fuel for machines and transport as well as synthetic nitrogen fertilizers. It is not only the high energy use in the production of these fertilizers that damages the climate, but also its field use: For every 100 tonnes of fertilizer, there are up to three tonnes of nitrous oxide (Galloway *et al.*, 2010). Even though nitrous oxide is the most problematic of agricultural climate gases, in the past it has frequently been ignored. Economic interests and their fatal erroneous assumptions as well as the invention of nitrogen fertilizers have rendered soil fertility less significant (Idel, 2010, 55). Therefore, climate computations have, thus far, not taken into account components like ammonia and nitrous oxide that are set free during the conversion and break-down processes of nitrogen fertilizers (Galloway *et al.*, 2010).

In Germany, soil use is one of the main culprits as far as carbon dioxide and nitrous oxide emissions from agriculture are concerned. Loss of humus, soil calcification, soil erosion, changes in land use, ploughing up of grasslands as well as large amounts of mineral nitrogen fertilizers cause more than 76 per cent of emissions harmful to the climate (Bioland, 2009, p3). Industrial-style agriculture is mainly to blame for these figures. Years of over-exploitation have both reduced soil fertility as well as sequestration capabilities for CO_2.

Factory farming is responsible for the highest concentrations of gaseous emissions in agriculture (Idel, 2010, p57). The reasons are changes in the type of use, large-scale monocultures and high density of livestock, as well as soil compaction. Ever since the decoupling of livestock and animal feed production, feed grain has predominantly been grown in developing or emerging economy countries and exported to the rich industrialized countries. This practice is particularly damaging to the climate especially when grown on land derived from the clear-cutting of tropical forests. During the growing season of 2004–2005 alone, more than a million hectares of Brazilian rainforest were converted into fields for growing soya (Greenpeace, 2006, p8). This loss of biodiversity and of a unique habitat, coupled with the clear-cutting of the Amazon basin, has had an enormous impact on the climate: two-thirds of Brazil's greenhouse gas emissions are due to deforestation and slash-and-burn practices (Greenpeace, 2006, p5). And yet, these soils are not at all suited to cultivation for animal feed. A significant number of these areas are known for their weak ecological viability and high vulnerability to soil degradation (Schlatzer, 2010, p20).

In these cases, producing meat cheaply on land that is ultimately 'thrown away', represents a type of agricultural colonialism. It might prove to have far-reaching and lasting consequences for world food production and global climate.

High concentrations of livestock breeding operations also dramatically increase and concentrate the accumulation of animal excrement which fouls soils, bodies of water and the atmosphere. Thus, factory farming, which is still supported by all European political factions, negatively impacts human health. The development of antibiotic resistance by pathogens has become a major concern. Factory farming continues to use increasing amounts of antibiotics, despite reasoned warnings from consumer advocates and physicians. This trend is particularly dire in poultry farming. For example, in Germany, antibiotics are given up to six times per fattening round (32 days). This process is used as a prophylactic measure for all animals and not applied only to sick birds. This increases the risk of bacteria building up resistance, hence rendering these medications useless in the treatment of human beings.

Every year, more than 66 billion farm animals are slaughtered worldwide (Schlatzer, 2010, p15). An increase in prosperity in emerging countries has led to a trend toward higher meat consumption. For instance, in China annual meat consumption quadrupled to 59.5kg per person between 1980 and 2005 (FAO, 2010). During the same time span, meat consumption more than doubled in developing countries (almost 31kg per person per year). The Food and Agriculture Organization of the United Nations (FAO) expects worldwide meat production to grow to 463 million tonnes by 2050.

Milk and egg consumption has also increased dramatically during the past decades. Worldwide annual milk consumption has risen to 82kg per capita while 9kg per capita of eggs are consumed (Schlatzer, 2010, p34).

It is a fact that far too many animal-derived products are consumed in industrial nations. The unbridled consumption of food from intensive-farming practices not only has direct negative implications for human health, but increasingly it has dire consequences for the environment, resources and the climate. Any additional increase would prove fatal. An increase in the number of farm animals would simultaneously mean higher demand for animal feed. This, in turn, would result in more monocultures, more clear-cutting of the last remaining rainforests, as well as a reduction in available areas for the cultivation of food plants for human consumption.

In addition to cutting down on the consumption of animal-derived foods, meat, sausages and cold cuts, there will have to be a change in the way these products are made. Sustainable, social and ecologically fair as well as species-proper production systems will play a key role.

Will 'bio' alleviate the climate crisis?

There are many indications that organically produced ('bio') foods are more benign to the climate than conventionally produced products. This is due to several factors, including the use of fertilizers and pesticides, type of soil preparation, use of machines and tractors, transport routes, and type of animal husbandry. Organically produced foods average ten to twenty per cent fewer CO_2 emissions than conventional foods (Bals *et al.*, 2008, p299). Table 22.3 illustrates the climate balance of selected products, listed according to production method. The calculations show total greenhouse gases emitted (also CH_4 and N_2O), not only CO_2 as expressed in CO_2 equivalents.

Table 22.3 Climate footprint of organic versus conventional animal-based foods

Food	*CO_2 equivalents*	
	Conventional	*Organic*
Beef	13.311	11.374
Pork	3.252	3.039
Poultry	3.508	3.039
Butter	23.794	22.089
Yoghurt	1.231	1.159
Cheese	8.512	7.951
Milk	940	883
Cream	7.631	7.106
Eggs	1.931	1.542

Note: CO_2 equivalents in grams, calculated per kilogram product, differentiated by production method.

Source: Fritsche and Eberle (2007, p5)

It is noteworthy that there is not a substantial difference between the two methods of production. Other tests yield more significant differences (e.g. Lindenthal *et al.*, 2010). While factors of production are important, the degree of processing and the length of transport routes weigh more heavily. Frozen products require a lot of energy: one kg of fresh boiled potatoes causes the release of 197 grams of CO_2, while the same amount of french fries adds up to 5,714 grams CO_2 (Bals *et al.*, 2008, p298).

Regional products win hands down when considering emissions due to long transport routes. But each case must be treated separately because some vegetables or fruits from overseas actually prove less harmful to the climate if regional cultivation requires a high amount of energy and resources (like heating of greenhouses or non-sustainable irrigation systems).

It is a fact that organic agriculture is more benign for the environment and less harmful to the climate than industrial agriculture. This is due to various factors. First, through planting of perennial legumes and use of high-quality organic fertilizers, organic agriculture enhances the carbon sequestration ability of soils. Mean carbon accumulation in organic farms is 402kg per hectare per year, while conventional operations register carbon reduction in the soil (Hülsbergen and Küstermann, 2007). Organic agriculture also increases humus content in soils. Soils containing humus are more fertile due to an increase in water conductivity and storage capacity. Moreover, humus plays an important part in the storage capacity for carbon (Bioland, 2009, pp6–7).

In organic agriculture, the use of chemical-synthetic fertilizers, pesticides and herbicides is prohibited. This is beneficial for soil health, biodiversity, water protection and human health, and positively impacts resource and climate balances. As well, the production of mineral nitrogen fertilizers uses a very large amount of energy.

In organic agriculture, feed production and animal husbandry are closely linked. The animals are directly integrated into the production cycle and farms are limited to raising only as many animals as their own fields are able to feed. There are strict regulations imposed on what additional animal feed may be purchased. This system-oriented approach reduces the leaching of nitrates and increased nitrous oxide emissions into the atmosphere. Farmers growing their own animal fodder reduce the amount of feed purchases; large-scale feed imports from developing countries as practiced in factory farming is not common in organic agriculture.

Organic husbandry prescribes pasturing of animals (obligatory during the summer, otherwise whenever possible). This leads to appropriate use of grasslands and a reduction in the share of concentrated feed. This gives ruminants the appropriate and proper nutrition they need, and allows them to fulfil the function for which they are eminently suited: utilizing plants that are not appropriate for human consumption (grass, straw). At this time, only a small fraction of organic animal-derived food stuffs are consumed in Germany (Table 22.4). According to current data, 60 per cent of German households are in favour of species-appropriate husbandry, but only 33 per cent would pay a higher price for their food (Nestlé, 2011). This discrepancy between moral claims and actual purchasing behaviour explains why changes in buying patterns are always short-lived, despite various food scandals. Price still remains the principal deciding factor rather than (supposedly) non-monetary values like quality, health, sustainability, and protection of the climate, the environment and the animals.

Table 22.4 Percentage share of organic food in Germany, 2010

Foods	%
Eggs	6.4
Milk	3.8
Cheese	1.8
Beef	1.9
Pork	0.4
Poultry	0.3

Source: AMI Analysis based on GfK Consumer Index (http://marktundpreis.de)

Agrarian policies of the past are mainly responsible for this as long as the immense costs inherent in harm to the climate, the environment and the waste of resources incurred by agribusiness are still externalized.

The destruction of forests, the high levels of fossil energy consumption, the loss of biodiversity, antibiotic residues polluting soils, pesticides and liquid manure as well as the health costs associated with excessive consumption of animal proteins are not included in discounters' rock-bottom prices (Idel, 2010, p53).

The opposite is true: agricultural subsidies are not given in keeping with criteria like sustainability, environmental and soil protection. In fact, they have been handed out to the huge agribusiness and food multinationals, institutions where these environmental values are disparaged. In 2008, Südzucker, a global player, received more than 34.4 million Euros from the EU. Other recipients included the German subsidiary of Doux, the French poultry company, the Nordmilch and Campina dairy companies and the chocolate makers Storck and Ferrero, while direct payments to farmers and small businesses figured only marginally.

A new way of thinking is therefore needed in the future: ecological and social justice will have to become more important. Farms and businesses must be run in a sustainable, more climate-friendly way, thereby contributing to saving resources, improving soil health and biodiversity. The practice of having taxpayers bear the burden of non-sustainable industrialized production methods cannot be continued, while competition is skewed in favour of those who guarantee the lowest prices with the help of state subsidies.

It is not only the International Assessment of Agricultural Knowledge, Science and Technology for Development (IAASTD) report of 2008, studiously ignored by politicians and industrialists, that concludes that 'business as usual' can no longer be tolerated. All 400 contributing agricultural experts from all over the world agree that there is much potential in small-scale, regional and organically run farming (IAASTD, 2008). Following their argument invalidates statements that stigmatize cows as climate killers. After all, the animals are not responsible for ecological problems that are due to animal husbandry; this blame can be laid at the doorstep of non-sustainable farming practices.

References

Bals, C., Hamm, H., Jerger, I. and Milke, K. (2008) *Die Welt am Scheideweg: Wie retten wir das Klima?* Rohwolt, Reinbek b. Hamburg, Germany

Bioland (2009) *Im Blickpunkt: Klimaschutz und Biolandbau in Deutschland*, Hintergrundpapier, Bioland e.V., Mainz, Germany

European Environmental Agency (2008) *Annual European Community Greenhouse Gas Inventory 1990–2006 and Inventory Report 2008*, European Environmental Agency, Copenhagen, Denmark

FAO (2010) *Asia Pacific Food Situation Update*, Food and Agriculture Organization of the United Nations, Bangkok, Thailand

Flachowsky, G. and Brade, W. (2007) 'Potenziale der Reduzierung von Methanemissionen bei Wiederkäuern', *Züchtungskunde*, vol 7, no 6, pp417–465

Fritsche, U. R. and Eberle, U. (2007) *Treibhausgasemissionen durch Erzeugung und Verarbeitung von Lebensmitteln*, Öko-Institut e.V., Darmstadt, Germany

Galloway, J., Dentener, F., Burke, M., Dumont, E., Bouwman, L., Kohn, R., Mooney, H., Seitzinger, S. and Kroeze, C. (2010) 'The impact of animal production systems on the nitrogen cycle', in H. Steinfeld, H. A. Mooney, F. Schneider, L. E. Neville (eds) *Livestock in a Changing Landscape: Vol. 1. Drivers, Consequences, and Responses*, Island Press, Washington, DC, pp83–95

Gottwald, F.-T. and Boergen, I. (2009) 'Wasser als Lebensmittel', in P. C. Mayer-Tasch (ed.) *Welt ohne Wasser. Geschichte und Zukunft eines knappen Gutes*, Campus, Frankfurt a. M., Germany, pp100–120

Greenpeace (2006) *Eating up the Amazon*, Greenpeace, Amsterdam, The Netherlands

Heissenhuber, A. and Zehetmeier, M. (2010) *Ökonomische und ökologische Aspekte der Nutzung von Biomasse durch den Wiederkäuer*, Hülsenberger Gespräche, Hamburg, Germany, pp47–55

Hülsbergen, K.-J. and Küstermann, B. (2007) 'Ökologischer Landbau. Beitrag zum Klimaschutz', in K. Wiesinger (ed.) *Angewandte Forschung und Beratung für den ökologischen Landbau in Bayern*, Bayerische Landesanstalt für Landwirtschaft, Freising-Weihenstephan, Germany

IAASTD (2008) *Agriculture at a Crossroads*, Island Press, Washington, DC

Idel, A. (2010) *Die Kuh ist kein Klima-Killer! Wie die Agrarindustrie die Erde verwüstet und was wir dagegen tun können*, Metropolis Verlag, Marburg, Germany

IPCC (2007) *IPCC Fourth Assessment Report: Climate Change 2007 (AR4)*, Cambridge University Press, Cambridge, UK

Lindenthal, T., Markut, T., Hörtenhuber S., Rudolph, G. and Hanz, K. (2010) 'Klimabilanz biologischer und konventioneller Lebensmittel im Vergleich', *Ökologie und Landbau*, vol 153, no 1, pp51–53

Nepstad, D. C. (2007) *Der Teufelskreis am Amazonas. Bericht für den World Wide Fund for Nature*, WWF International, Gland, Switzerland

Nestlé (2011) 'So is(s)t Deutschland. Zusammenfassung der Studie 2011', available at http://nestle-studie.de/downloads (accessed 27 July 2011)

Rahmsdorf, S. and Schellnhuber, H. J. (2007) 'Die Vorboten ernst nehmen' in *Klimawandel: Gerechtigkeit im Treibhaus*, Politische Ökologie vol 106–107, Oekom verlag, Munich, Germany, pp16–20

Reichholf, J. H. (2006a) *Der Tanz um das Goldene Kalb: der Ökokolonialismus Europas*, Verlag Klaus Wagenbach, Berlin, Germany

Reichholf, J. H. (2006b) 'Gräser, Fleisch und Humus: Tiere in Grasland-Ökosystemen', in Bayerische Akademie der Wissenschaften (ed.) *Gräser und Grasland: Biologie – Nutzung – Entwicklung*, Rundgespräche der Kommission für Ökologie vol 31, Pfeil Verlag, Munich, Germany, pp47–59

Riché, B., Hachileka, E., Awuor, C. B. and Hammill, A. (2009) *Climate-Related Vulnerability and Adaptive Capacity in Ethiopia's Borana and Somali Communities: Final Assessment Report*, International Institute for Sustainable Development, New York, NY

Rifkin, J. (1992) *Beyond Beef: The Rise and Fall of the Cattle Culture*, Dutton Books, New York, NY

Ruppaner, M. (2010) 'Zukunft von Wiesen und Weiden. Plädoyer für eine Umkehr im Umgang mit Grünland', in AgrarBündnis e.V. (ed.) *Der kritische Agrarbericht 2010*, ABL Verlag, Hamm, Germany, pp27–34

Schlatzer, M. (2010) *Tierproduktion und Klimawandel. Ein wissenschaftlicher Diskurs zum Einfluss der Ernährung auf Umwelt und Klima*, LIT Verlag, Berlin, Germany

Schulz, D. (2008) 'Die Rolle der Landwirtschaft beim Klimawandel – Täter, Opfer, Wohltäter', *Local Land and Soil News*, vol 24/25, no 1, pp12–15

Westphal, S., Steingaß, H., Drochner, W. and Rodehutscord, M., (2010) 'Efficiency of several combinations of potential inhibitors of ruminal methane formation in vitro', *Berichte der Gesellschaft für Ernährungsphysiologie*, vol 19, p99

Wolf, B., Zeng, X., Brüggemann, N., Chen, W., Dannenmann, M., Han, X., Sutton, M. A., Wu, H. and Yao, Z. Butterbach-Bahl, K. (2010) 'Grazing-induced reduction of natural nitrous oxide release from continental steppe', *Nature*, vol 464, pp881–884

23 Food security, public health, financial regimes and international law

John Quinn and Vladimír Bencko

Introduction

Humankind has rarely been able to achieve balance among adequate food production, food allocation, food distribution, safe financial mechanisms in agriculture, consumption and economies of scale that provide satisfactory nutrition for all. It has been duly noted that pestilence and drought may be caused by nature, but that famine and starvation are caused by people. Food security is the availability of and adequate access to nutritious food. An adequate food supply is foundational to human security and development. Owing to the complex interplay of economic issues, global change, population development and consequent increased demands, altered social expectations, resource depletion, and geopolitical instability, global food security is now a regional public health crisis.

Public health and food security

Access to adequate food and water are fundamental to population health. Adequate and clean water help stave off infectious diseases and waterborne illnesses. Access to a nutritious and consistent food supply aids normal child growth and development and helps individuals to thrive and provide for others in both family and community. Excess or shortage can lead to either over- or under-nutrition, both of which have significant and possibly permanent negative consequences, even death. Over-consumption in both the developed and developing worlds is a leading factor accounting for the world's growing pandemics of obesity, diabetes and cardiovascular disease. The reality of under-nutrition is increasingly obvious. This arises not only through access issues, but the soil itself must be capable of producing foods that are rich in nutrients. Through over-farming, the depletion of elements essential to nutritious food is becoming evident everywhere. Soils, water supply, inclement weather are only some of nature's services that are under extreme stress.

For the poorest billion people on Earth, poverty is inversely proportional to food security. With the ability of a region or population to grow or purchase its food, food security becomes increasingly tenuous and the risk of food shortages and political instability rises. Despite the fact that more of the developed world has health issues associated with over-consumption, the developing world is quickly catching-up in all of these entirely preventable diseases. However, despite some areas of the developing world experiencing over-nutrition, many still suffer from the effects of micronutrient deficiencies, a completely preventable health problem.

Some highlighted micronutrient deficiencies in the developing world include the following (Heimburger, 2008):

- *vitamin* A (retinol) deficiency, leading to vision and eye disorders;
- *iron* deficiency, leading to muscle weakness and abnormalities, anaemia and mental development disorders;
- *zinc* deficiency, leading to developmental retardation and congenital malformations;
- *fluoride* deficiency, leading to dental carries;
- *iodine* deficiency leading to thyroid enlargement (goiter) and cretinism;
- *copper* deficiency, leading to anaemia and mental retardation;
- *vitamin C* deficiency, leading to scurvy and poor wound healing;
- *vitamin D* deficiency, leading to rickets and osteomalacia;
- *folate* and *vitamin B12* deficiency, leading to megaloblastic anaemia;
- *niacin* deficiency, leading to pellagra, memory loss and disorientation; and
- *thiamine* deficiency, leading to beriberi, muscle weakness and wasting.

All of these are preventable nutrient deficiencies affecting countries with inadequate food security and unbalanced food consumption. Equitable access to food and stable food markets can greatly improve the micronutrient deficiencies facing the developing world today.

But feeding the world's hungry is not an entirely possible or credible and evidenced-based policy that has proven effective and reproducible around the globe (Moyo 2011, pp29–47; Seybolt, 2009; Fleck and Kilby, 2009). Using double-blind field research, it has been demonstrated that poverty leads to a world where those without enough to eat may save up to buy a television instead of adequate food for their family, where more money does not translate into more food, and where making rice cheaper can sometimes even lead people to buy less rice (Banerjee and Duflo 2011a, b; Banerjee and Duflo, 2008, Banerjee and Duflo, 2007). Indeed, when many communities have gained more access to wealth and can afford adequate and balanced food supplies, many opt for the better tasting and less nutritious option purely as a right of becoming 'civilized'. As communities and societies gain more access to wealth, the greatly needed outcome of more balanced consumption is not guaranteed and is sometimes even hindered as more and more market forces encourage the purchase of luxuries instead of adequate nutrition. Education for these at-risk communities is needed in the form of primary prevention to prevent misguided family and household expenditures on poorly nutritious food and other superfluous purchases that are not directly linked to their own food security, public health, and overall well-being.

The public health issues of unbalanced nutrition, inadequate access to food, and misappropriation of resources – at the governmental and household levels – are present globally and affect billions of people. They are compounded by inadequate access to nutritious food, plus large scarcities building up in the world of global agriculture. Among these scarcities are: arable land, freshwater, fossil fuels for energy and for fertilizer production, appropriate farm technology and access to this technology, and fish supplies. In addition, the excessive use of fertilizers, and inappropriate and aggressive farming techniques have led to macro- and micro-nutrient depletion in soils. Other factors include diminishing access to appropriate financial support and an increasingly unstable climate. A final and increasingly important factor is the use of food crops for biofuel production and energy, as opposed for consumption (Reilly and Willenbockel, 2010; Tenenbaum, 2008). All of these factors make increasing global food output extremely difficult (Cribb, 2010; Pimentel, 2006). We will see that the cornerstone to public health action and improvement in the food security crisis is found in climate change reduction. The public health situation in relation to agriculture and food security is worsening, but why?

Economics of food security

Supply and demand are the driving forces in the pricing of commodities. Items that are scarce fetch a higher price, while items in abundance tend to be cheaper. Global economic markets and economies of scale are directly linked to food security. When harvest yields on crops change, even by very small amounts, the effects are long-lasting, and greater than one might anticipate at first glance. These can lead to food insecurity and an associated spike in human suffering.

Owing to unknown future crop yields in most types of agriculture, financial instruments have been developed for investors to wager on the future price of many agricultural commodities; this helps offset the economic effects of potential crop losses. If crop yields for a commodity (e.g. wheat and grain) are greater than expected in a certain market, the market price may drop. Conversely, if there is a poor harvest and less grain is harvested, the market price would rise.

In 1991, in order to limit risk and maximize the potential profit from uncertain commodity prices, the firm of Goldman Sachs developed the Goldman Sachs Commodity Index (GSCI; www2.goldmansachs.com/services/securities/products/sp-gsci-commodity-index/index.html). In 1999, the Commodity Futures Modernization Act of 2000 was promulgated.

This act deregulated over-the-counter financial products or derivatives. This included the commodity market and it let investors engage in commodity trading without limit. An unintended consequence was the development of a food crisis that would leave one billion people hungry. How this arose is described below.

Before the GSCI was constructed, the Commodity Research Bureau (CRB) index functioned to help measure the overall direction of commodity sectors. It was also used by other investors to help assess the risks associated with long- and short-term investments. However, this index was less sophisticated than the GSCI, which let investors focus their investments more tightly, and eventually dictate price changes that resulted in considerable food insecurity and ultimately public health catastrophes in several countries.

For example, the price of grain was traded between buyers and sellers at its future price – before the bushel had been grown, harvested or valued by that market. This may sound like a questionable gamble with large stakes, but this practice helped stabilize the price of grain. It also allows farmers to hedge investment for times of poor crop yield years and to invest within their own farms and business. Furthermore, over time these practices helped decrease the price of grain. This greatly affected public policy and humanitarian aid and promoted food security for many countries and markets; these are defining features of a very connected global grain market. However, many countries still attempt to impose subsidy interventions, including grabs of arable land in poor nations by wealthier nations in order to farm a variety of crops that enhance the investor country's food security. These crops, now grown in a poorer nation by wealthier agricultural firms, will, due to rising prices, make it to market only in wealthier nations. The link between the price variability of grain on local and international markets is complex. However, when grain is traded on one of the three major American primary grain exchanges in Chicago, Kansas City or Minneapolis, the price affects global food pricing. Some factors influencing price are weather and conflict, but market influences, like speculation, also affect price. These factors may be present in one region but can affect other markets and, ultimately, the price of bread in distant countries. Land rights and equity in access to land can lead to food security across communities and populations. There are many aspects that must be in play to enable food security for any individual, family, community, region or country. Yet the need for equity in access to food security is lacking the world over (Deninger and Squire, 1998).

In this context, the advent of the GSCI slowly set the stage for great disruption in the global market through long-term investment in grain but with no commitment to food production. The ability to buy and sell grain commodities, as well as to provide liquidity in the market with actual grain storage and food production, became disconnected. The market could treat grain or other commodity futures on the GSCI just like a stock or other financial product; it did not have to produce, store or actually sell any grain at all. This was a departure from what grain really is, namely a tangible, agricultural product of nature essential for life, and it was quickly transformed into an investment product with limitless paper value (Levin and Coburn, 2009). But what happens to the grain market when investors wish to take their money out of the investment, placing orders to sell in large volumes? Did the commodity index, through such a simple process of speculative selling (or buying), enable skyrocketing grain prices and eventual human suffering?

This new investment tool attracted many investors to consider their investment in grain futures as safe; after all, everyone must eat. Although this investment strategy led to significant investments in grain futures, it also led to extreme market speculation and subsequent wide fluctuations in price (Kaufman, 2011). The GSCI enabled futures to be traded as stocks, with prices linked more to investor interest and greed than to the true value of the commodity. While perhaps 'rational' investor behaviour, these actions are not rational from the perspective of maintaining natural ecosystems, ensuring equitable and adequate food supply or even human life. Investor sentiment of profiting from commodities is not sustainable and there are inherent biophysical limits to global ecosystems (Daly, 2005). The GSCI thus precipitated a crisis of food security experienced by about one billion people.

As these 'commodity-financial' products became increasingly profitable, more and more investment occurred. This led to gross food price inflation, excessive price variability, and consequential food insecurity and, ultimately, famine. The problem was particularly apparent during the financial crises of 2007–2008, when investors sold their stocks and invested in gold and grain, thus driving their prices to new heights. Grain and many other commodities, were seen as safer investments to park capital than other risky products. In market terms, the competition to maximize crop yields, especially in wheat, and to enable basic food security to support public health, faced the unscrupulous investment banker who artificially increased the price of grain to maximize financial yield but, in doing so, orchestrated a manmade food security crisis affecting some one billion people (UN 2011; Koning and Mol 2009). Put simply, if the price of grain was rising considerably, the producer in a poor country would profit more by selling his grain to wealthier nations rather than to local markets for local consumption.

Market manipulation occurs the world over. However, manipulators can be detected and should be held accountable when people starve as a result. Presently, we are at a stage in human economic development where the actions of a very few on one side of the globe can greatly influence millions globally, whether these actions are intentional or not. Sadly, the ones that should be held responsible are often anonymous, and today's economic structure and practices, such as speculation buying and computer assisted trading, makes the risks of manipulation even greater. The consequences of these actions can be disastrous and irreparable on a global social, economic and environmental scale. Investors and speculators must be regulated especially where the right to food is concerned. Non-compliance in a regulated environment would require that culprits be held accountable for their actions on the global market. Corporations are considered people under the law and can be held accountable as such (*Santa Clara v. Southern Pacific Railroad*).

Food pricing and food security

The basic economic principles of supply and demand hold true in agriculture. Recent price fluctuations in the market have been influenced by factors such as grain-fed beef cattle for human consumption and grain crops grown for biofuels instead of for food (Southgate, 2009). These are examples of 'food affluence'; where the price of food is not a key deciding determinant to purchase the food. Most humans do not enjoy this luxury. The consequences and negative impacts of a rise in the price of food are not felt equally across markets (Brown, 2011). People who spend a large proportion of their income on food, such as in Egypt, Jordan or Ukraine, feel the effects of a relatively small rise in the futures price of food far more than those living where food costs are relatively low, such as in Europe or North America.

To gauge food price variability across the globe, the Food and Agriculture Organization of the United Nations (FAO) monitors the monthly change in international prices of a basket of food commodities (FAO, 2011). It is called the 'FAO Food Price Index' (FFPI) and is a weighted average of the commodity group price indices of meat, dairy, cereals, oils and fats, and sugar. The FFPI helps gauge food security across the globe; it results in numerical 'points' based on pricing in each commodity field. In 2000, the FFPI was 90; in 2007 it was 159; in 2008 it reached 200 points, when the most recent food crisis hit. In June 2011, it was reported at 234 (FAO, 2011), a value so high it made front-page news. Before investment products like the GSCI were created, such commentaries would not be top news at Bloomberg or anywhere on Wall Street; however, at 234, many speculators and investors became more interested in using food as an investment product despite drastic consequences to the world's poor (Ruitenberg, 2011).

While the FAO collects and analyses global agricultural data and provides technical assistance, there is no organized effort to ensure the adequacy of world food supplies or food security (Brown, 2011). Indeed, within the last decade, major investment bank interest rates have risen sharply with that of food prices and commodity indices as market volatility, geopolitical and other socio-economic factors make food a speculative investment. However, this 'investment product' and its variation in price can make one billion hungry and lead to a public health crisis that no investor has any obligation or responsibility to consider.

A reduction in crop yields, environmental and political instability, war and conflict, all lead to food insecurity. After World War II, in order to mitigate the problem of food insecurity, the United States Department of Agriculture instituted a programme where the United States government would purchase surplus wheat and grain from United States farmers so as to stabilize United States market prices. In so doing, it found itself in control of a sizable quantity of United States grain that was not available on the open market – a surplus that did not negatively impact market price. In fact, the surplus became so huge that the United States government at times paid farmers to not grow wheat at all, because the potential future price might have been adversely affected. This practice of government wheat subsidies is still carried out today, but to a much smaller extent than it was in the 1950s and 1960s. Nevertheless, it was a major influence on the global wheat market.

The wheat surplus enabled many governmental and humanitarian programs to shift off-market wheat held by the United States government to global areas with greatest need. These programmes employed United States farmers and helped to maintain a stable wheat price via government subsidization. Recently, United States government food surpluses have evaporated because of record high prices and farmers are selling their crops on the open market (Kirchhof, 2008). In light of recent environmental and economic instability, the United States wheat surplus has been eliminated, along with any governmental or humanitarian programmes.

Biofuels and food security

Biofuels are fuels derived from organic matter, namely raising crops, and converting or adding them to burnable material to be used in combustible engines. Biofuels have also contributed to an unprecedented rise in the food market. Precious arable land once used for edible wheat and grain has been supplanted by a more profitable commodity such as oil seed rape, used in the production of biofuels. The rate at which the United States is converting grain into ethanol has grown significantly. For example, in 2000, in the United States, 16 million tonnes of grain was used to make ethanol, whereas 126 million tonnes were used in 2010. As a consequence, the price of grain is now tied to the price of oil (Brown, 2011); this is good for investors, but disastrous for those who need grain for food.

Brazil, which obtains ethanol from sugar cane, is second in production of biofuels after the United States, and the European Union aims to obtain 10 per cent of its transport fuel from biofuels by 2020. All these efforts serve to divert land from growing food to 'growing energy', and they all are leading to food scarcity (Eissentraut, 2010). Indeed, the economics of food and food price play a much larger role than simply to feed the hungry or than the need of food as a human right.

Conflict, war, disaster and food security

Food is as critical to national security as are resources like oil, steel, rubber, water and raw materials, which often pre-empt food security in a country

(Fullbrook, 2010). Access to a consistent food supply provides a minimum level of security. Indeed, food *is* security, and the ability of a state to provide basic infrastructure and free market access to purchase affordable and sustainable food is a key state role; the inability to do this is a mark of a failed state. Failed states do not guarantee human security or food security and they open the door to an increase in human suffering through inadequate public health and security. Thus, ensuring access to reliable and sufficient food during a crisis must be a public health priority. Failure to do so often leads to political instability and endangered public health. These problems will only be compounded by a growing population and by the consequences of climate change.

Access to arable land, rule of law and ownership of the rights to land and agriculture and safe and secure access to food do not exist in many countries even in times of peace, and in even more countries during times of crisis (Westra, 2011). Conflict and food security are multifaceted and inextricably connected. Those countries and communities that experience active conflict are at an increased risk of food insecurity (Messer and Cohen, 2006). The many determining factors of human conflict that affect food security are:

- access to food at the market: price variability and supply;
- rural and agricultural infrastructure destroyed;
- loss of livestock and access to arable land;
- deforestation, desertification and rising water levels;
- no access to water for irrigation;
- no consistent access to seed, farm technology or human capital experience;
- migration and human flow (e.g. a large influx of people into one region, with insufficient quantities in another region);
- the use of landmines and other explosive devices throughout arable land; and
- the use of food as a weapon.[1]

Ecological integrity, the environment and food security

From a natural and environmental perspective, access to arable land, seed, sustainable water supplies and environmental sustainability are the bulwark of food security and sustainability. Geopolitical instability, human conflict, economic and market manipulation and volatile market fluctuations can lead to significant barriers to food security. However, without environmental sustainability, arable land, access to seed and water, communities cannot grow food. With an imbalance in any of the above-listed factors, a food crisis can easily ensue despite best efforts made by aid agencies and governments (Westra, 2006). The prevailing paradigm in food markets and food security holds that the health of the environment drives agriculture, agriculture drives commodity markets and pricing, price and food demand drives food production which in turn drives local and international economies of scale. Ecological integrity reflects the resilience of the relevant environment to respond to natural and man-made influences. Public health and food security for the global population are directly linked to the environmental health and integrity of the planet. Only a healthy and sustainable approach to Earth's ecological integrity will prove successful in providing for healthy populations. Decades of global policies for the pursuit of growth at all costs through energy and ecological exploitation, has resulted in declines in ecological integrity (Yergin, 2011). An exploding global population compounds the already tenuous challenge of ensuring food security while simultaneously maintaining global ecological integrity.

Climate change is linked to security, public health and food security. Adverse effects of climate change will aggravate existing threats to international peace and security and new threats due to the loss of territory in some states due to sea-level rise, desertification and low-lying island states, presents significant regional, food and international security implications (UN Security Council, 2011). Environmental degradation leading to the loss of topsoil, depleted and polluted water supplies, the use of genetically modified or immunologically tainted seed, and drought brought on by a warmer climate all lead to food insecurity. Preventable desertification, poorly planned crop rotation and land abuse, an over-dependence on specific crops and climate change indicate that the seams on any remaining global ecological integrity have been blown open. These factors are leading to a global food crisis and public health disaster.

Conclusions

Most of the famine, starvation, and food insecurity experienced by people around the world are of human origin. Natural events such as drought and flood often exacerbate food insecurity, but underlying man-made problems and events bring it to the fore. Failed states, investment speculators and climate change lead to food insecurity. Policy and human action can mitigate these problems. Adequate food production, balanced consumption and economies of scale that provide satisfactory nutrition for all, define the needed pillars of a global health framework in order to sustain life by ensuring food security. Food security is defined as a person's availability and access to food. With continued market manipulation, conflict, a deteriorating environmental situation with climate change, exponential population growth, food security is not guaranteed for all. Adequate food supply is the foundation of human security and development, and this must be pursued under a global policy framework from both practical and theoretical vantage points in order to bring one billion hungry people into the fold of a civilized world and to provide food security for all.

With the complex interchange of economic markets, market manipulation and economic arbitration, climate change, the lack of water, widespread geopolitical instability, growing food demand and supply issues, food security is a global public health crisis. Market misadventure has led to the current food crisis plus significant food insecurity for nearly one billion people or more. Eliminating unacceptable speculation on future markets is not the only policy option, nor would it stop climate change, water scarcity or population growth. True policy options must include not only market reform, but also by encouraging sustainable agriculture for emerging markets and developing nations. This provision must guarantee equal and fair access of small farmers and agricultural workers to their own local and wider global food markets in the form of fair trade. This global policy shift to sustainability at a small and organic-paced level can engender an environment for increased food security. Presently however, worldwide food security is deteriorating and a global public health crisis is imminent and chronic. The underlying causes are not only speculation and greedy global markets, but rather diminishing crop yields, abuse and depletion of precious water supplies, the destruction and desertification of topsoil, climate change and a booming population in a world of increasing inequality. A stable climate means stability in food price and food security. By tackling market reform, climate change and ecological degradation, food security can follow.

Note

1 Some explanation of what we mean by 'the use of food as a weapon' may be useful. Food security would be possible if countries would be willing to rely on international markets – however, many countries do not 'trust' international markets. One reason for this distrust is the propensity of the United States and other countries to apply economic embargoes against countries for various political reasons. When countries perceive that their food security may be jeopardized by such international economic sanctions (or embargoes resulting from wars), they feel vulnerable; thus, they insist on pursuing 'self-sufficiency' policies even in the face of total lack of comparative advantage. Another aspect of the 'food as a weapon' thesis concerns the manipulation of food supplies by interests within certain countries. Certain privileged and powerful groups may restrict food supplies (directly or indirectly by controlling distribution systems, etc.) to segments of the population that are out of favour (see www.apcss.org/Publications/Report_Food_Security_98.html). More can be found at http://endthelie.com/resources/declassified-government-documents/u-s-government-white-papers/food-as-a-weapon-national-security-study-memorandum-nssm-200/#axzz1lDxAL2Ss.

References

Banerjee, A. and Duflo, E. (2007). 'The economic lives of the poor', *Journal of Economic Perspectives*, vol 21, no 1, pp141–167

Banerjee, A. and Duflo, E. (2008) 'What is middle class about the middle classes around the World?' *Journal of Economic Perspectives*, vol 22, no 2, pp3–28

Banerjee, A. and Duflo, E. (2011a) 'More than 1 billion people are hungry in the world: but what if the experts are wrong?' *Foreign Policy*, May/June, available at http://www.foreignpolicy.com/articles/2011/04/25/more_than_1_billion_people_are_hungry_in_the_world

Banerjee, A. and Duflo, E. (2011b) *Poor Economics: A Radical Rethinking of the Way to Fight Global Poverty*, Public Affairs Press, New York, NY

Brown, L. (2011) 'The new geopolitics of food: from the Middle East to Madagascar, high prices are spawning land grabs and ousting dictators. Welcome to the 21st-century food wars', *Foreign Policy*, May/June, pp53–62

Cribb, J. H. J. (2010). *The Coming Famine: The Global Food Crisis and What We Can Do to Avoid It*, University of California Press, Berkeley, CA

Daly, H. (2005) 'Economics in a full world', *Scientific American*, September, vol 293, no 3, available at www.scientificamerican.com/article.cfm?id=economics-in-a-full-world

Deninger, K. and Squire, L. (1998) 'New ways of looking at old issues: inequality and development', *Journal of Development Economics*, vol 57, pp259–287

Eissentraut, A. (2010) *Sustainable Production of Second-Generation Biofuels: Potential and Perspectives in Major Economies and Developing Countries*, February, Information Paper, International Energy Agency, Paris, France, available at www.iea.org/papers/2010/second_generation_biofuels.pdf

FAO (2011) *FAO Food Price Index*, Food and Agriculture Organization of the United Nations, Rome, Italy, available at www.fao.org/worldfoodsituation/wfs-home/foodpricesindex/en (accessed August 2011)

Fleck, R. and Kilby, C. (2009) 'Changing aid regimes? United States foreign aid from the Cold War to the War on Terror', *Journal of Development Economics*, vol 91, no 2, March, pp185–197

Fullbrook, D. (2010) 'Food as security', *Food Security*, vol 2, pp5–20

Heimburger, D. (2008) 'Malnutrition and nutritional assessment', in D. L. Longo, A. S. Fauci, D. L. Kasper, S. L. Hauser, J. L. Jameson and J. Loscalzo (eds) *Harrison's Principles of Internal Medicine*, 18th edition, McGraw-Hill, New York, NY, pp605–611

Kaufman, F. (2011) 'How Goldman Sachs created the food crisis', *Foreign Policy*, April 27, available at http://www.foreignpolicy.com/articles/2011/04/27/how_goldman_sachs_created_the_food_crisis?page=0,1 (accessed 28 January 2012)

Kirchhof, S. (2008) 'Surplus United States food supplies dry up', *United States Today*, 1 May, available at www.usatoday.com/money/industries/food/2008-05-01-usda-food-supply_N.htm (accessed 28 January 2012)

Koning, N. and Mol, A. (2009) 'Wanted: institutions for balancing global food and energy markets', *Food Security*, vol 1, pp291–303

Levin, C. and Coburn, T. (2009) 'Excessive speculation in the wheat market: majority and minority staff report, permanent subcommittee on investigations', *United States Senate*, June 24, available at http://blog.thederivativeproject.com/files/6/7/3/9/5/268450-259376/PSI_WheatSpeculation_062409.pdf

Messer, E. and Cohen, M. J. (2006) *Conflict, Food Insecurity, and Globalization*, Discussion Paper 206, May, Food Consumption and Nutrition Division, International Food Policy Research Institute (IFPRI), Washington, DC, available at: www.ifpri.org/sites/default/files/publications/fcndp206.pdf

Moyo, D. (2011) *Dead Aid: Why Aid is Not Working and how There is a Better Way for Africa*, Farrar, Straus and Giroux, New York, NY

Pimentel, D. (2006) 'Soil erosion: a food and environmental threat', *Environment, Development and Sustainability*, vol 8, no 1, pp119–137

Reilly, M. and Willenbockel, D. (2010) 'Managing uncertainty: a review of food system scenario analysis and modeling'. *Philosophical Transactions of the Royal Society B*, vol 365, no 1554, pp3,049–3,063

Ruitenberg, R. (2011) 'World food prices climb to record as UN sounds alarm on further shortages', *Bloomberg*, 3 March, available at www.bloomberg.com/news/2011-03-03/world-food-prices-climb-to-record-as-un-sounds-alarm-on-further-shortages.html (accessed 28 January 2012)

Seybolt, T. (2009) 'Harmonizing the humanitarian aid network: adaptive change in a complex system', *International Studied Quarterly*, December, vol 53, no 4, pp1027–1050

Southgate, D. (2009) 'Population growth, increases in agricultural production and trends in food prices', *The Electronic Journal of Sustainable Development*, vol 1, no 3, available at www.ejsd.org

Tenenbaum, D. (2008) 'Food vs. fuel: diversion of crops could cause more hunger'. *Environmental Health Perspectives*, June, vol 116, no 6, ppA254–A257

United Nations (UN), (2010) 'Somalia: famine & drought situation', *Report No. 9*, 17 Office for the Coordination of Humanitarian Affairs (OCHA), Somalia, available at http://reliefweb.int/sites/reliefweb.int/files/resources/OCHA%20Somalia%20Situation%20Report%20No.%209%2017%20August%202011.pdf (accessed 28 January 2012)

UN Security Council (2011) 'Security Council, in statement, says "contextual information" on possible security', Security Council Session SC/10332, 20 July 2011, Department of Public Information, New York, Security Council 6587th Meeting (AM & PM), available at www.un.org/News/Press/docs/2011/sc10332.doc.htm (accessed 28 January 2012)

Westra, L. (2011) *Globalization, Violence and world Governance*, Studies in Critical Social Sciences, Brill, Leiden, The Netherlands

Westra, L. (2006) *Environmental Justice and the Rights of Unborn and Future Generations: Law, Environmental Harm and the Right to Health*, Earthscan, London

Yergin, D. (2011) *The Quest: Energy, Security, and the Remaking of the Modern World*, Penguin Group Press, London

24 Re-examining health protection in international environmental regulation

William Onzivu

Introduction

A vast body of international environmental law and its domestic implementation provide for the protection of human health and the environment, but in this chapter I argue that this has not happened. Using examples from the regulation of water, climate change and environmental health in the European Community, I examine the inherent pitfalls of the legal regimes in maximizing health protection and then explore the health and environmental protection linkages in both law and fact, and argue for more robust environmental legal regimes to protect human health and the environment.

The health deficit in environmental regulation

General

The importance of environmental law for health protection has prompted a re-examination of the role of environmental legal regimes for the protection of health (Von Schirnding *et al.*, 2002). However, there is increasing concern that international and national environmental law have not been optimized to advance the protection of public health (Onzivu, 2006). Six examples demonstrate the ineffectiveness of international and domestic environmental law to buttress health protection:

1 The need to highlight social and health protection in the global environmental agenda, including sustainable development, was stressed in the outcomes of the Report of the World Summit on Sustainable Development in Johannesburg (United Nations, 2002).
2 Global water regulation is focused more on water allocation than on protecting water quality (Biswas *et al.*, 2009), a key determinant of health.
3 The regulation of transboundary waste under the Basel Convention on Transboundary Movement of Hazardous Waste and their Disposal has failed to optimize health protection. For these reasons, the Conference of the Parties to the Convention adopted the Bali Declaration on Waste

Management for Human Health to bolster health protection under the Convention (Secretariat of the Basel Convention, 2008).

4 The global climate legal regimes under the United Nations Framework Convention on Climate Change and the Kyoto Protocol have focused on mitigation and energy issues and constrained human health issues to adaptation (Onzivu, 2010).

5 The importance of strengthening health protection in environmental regulation has led to renewed action by the European Union to integrate health protection measures in European Commission (EC) environmental regulation. For example, the EC has adopted legal and policy instruments to strengthen health protection in European Community environmental law (McEldowney and McEldowney, 2010).

6 Key tools for domestic environmental regulation that serve to implement international treaties have constrained health protection especially in developing countries (Onzivu, 2006).

Obsolete environmental and public health laws, limited impact assessment of health issues, and the fractious collaboration between the health and environmental sectors, is a challenge. This has led to rethinking the need to reinvigorate health in global environmental regulation; this chapter contributes to this discourse.

Environment–health linkages

Health protection is interlinked with environmental regulation. Environmental law is derived from public health law, notably from the public health regulation of environmental ills in Victorian Britain (Bell and McGillivray, 2008). Environmental law in the United States also originated in public health laws, developing largely from the statutory and public policy precedents in public health and worker safety legislation throughout the twentieth century' (Lazarus, 2007).

Environmental challenges such as poor sanitation, lack of access to safe water, air pollution, use of chemicals, and climate change have continued to adversely affect public health (UNDP, 2006; Onzivu, 2009). Furthermore, a plethora of international environmental legal instruments provide for health protection as a core objective (Sand, 1992).

A healthy balance between the managing natural resources for their aesthetic benefits and sustainable development requires a higher level of health protection in environmental protection. Health is human capital, essential for ensuring intergenerational equity (Pearce and Barbier, 2000). Human health is also intimately tied to ecosystem health that sustains human life, as well as to complex interactions between the environmental, socio-cultural and economic factors (Forget and Lebel, 2000).

The social pillar of sustainability is defined to include human and societal capabilities, implying public health protection (Lehtonen, 2004). Natural capital includes humans, flora and fauna, and their complementarities have been expounded by the following questions (Daly, 1995).What good are human lungs without the natural capital of flora that take up carbon dioxide that helps to replenish oxygen essential to human life? What is the use of fossil fuels healthy human capital? To address these questions, health and safety risk assessment has integrated human health, ecosystem integrity and economic concerns (Mehta, 1997). Human capability as social capital highlights health as a bridge between the ecological, economic and social in sustainable development (Chiesura and de Groot, 2003).

Environmental law as global health law

The World Health Organization (WHO) defines health as a 'state of complete physical, mental and social well-being and not merely the absence of disease or infirmity' (World Health Organization, 2006). This definition implicates the importance of protecting health in environmental law, a view echoed by scholars who have linked health to human capability and quality of life (Ruger, 2009; Gostin, 2008).

Global health law includes environmental treaties, rules, regulations, and dispute settlement mechanisms that all promote health (Fidler, 1999). Environmental treaties with a health objective such as the Stockholm Convention on Persistent Organic Pollutants arguably constitute a body of global health law. WHO's influence in environmental health law derives from the vast body of soft law adopted by WHO and the provision of vital scientific evidence for environmental regulation. WHO has provided scientific evidence for global environmental normative instruments in, inter alia, water, climate change, toxic substances, pollution and the urban environment (Burci and Henri-Vignes, 2004; Westra, 2006). WHO hosts UN environmental forums such as the Intergovernmental Forum on Chemical Safety. WHO contributes to the global climate legal regime by providing expert input to the Subsidiary Body of Scientific and Technological Advice and the Nairobi Work Programme (Onzivu, 2010). Additionally, the WHO African Region and UNEP have convened the Interministerial conference on health and environment in Africa to address African environmental health challenges (WHO, 2011). The resulting Libreville, Luanda and Yamoussoukro Declarations highlight the need to reinvigorate health protection in environmental regulation and governance.

On the effectiveness of environmental treaties

Effectiveness is a concept that requires difficult normative, scientific and historical judgements. There are several types of effectiveness: legal, problem-solving, economic, political and normative (Young, 1999). Others view effectiveness in terms of treaty objectives, levels of participation, implementation and information, financial and capacity building support as well as operation, review and treaty adjustment (Sand, 1992). Legal effectiveness offers the best means to assess environmental treaties on health protection because of the challenges of obtaining accurate data for problem solving and political effectiveness.

International environmental treaties require State parties to implement and enforce a treaty. Treaty compliance helps reduce threats to human health (Onzivu, 2006). While good compliance rates have been observed (DiMento, 2003; Bankobeza, 2003), weak implementation also occurs (Barrett, 1999; Emory, 2000). Compliance must achieve the ultimate goals of a treaty to make it successful.

A treaty should be interpreted in good faith including in the light of its object and purpose (United Nations, 1969). A material breach of a treaty includes the violation of a provision essential to the accomplishment of the object or purpose of the treaty (United Nations, 1969). The following three case studies highlight the limits of environmental law in reinforcing health protection.

Case studies of legal regimes

Freshwaters: limits of the legal regime and example of the Senegal River Basin

Diarrhoeal diseases continue to kill and cause disease especially in children in the developing world (UNDP, 2006). Globally, about 2.5 million child deaths from diarrhoea occur annually (Boschi-Pinto *et al.*, 2008). International water law helps in tackling health challenges facing shared freshwaters but this law is largely pre-occupied with allocating water quantity rather than the quality and health challenges of water management (Bruch, 2009).

Four legal principles underpin the management of shared water resources (McCaffrey, 2007):

1. Absolute territorial sovereignty grants the state the unlimited right to exploit its water resources.
2. Absolute territorial integrity provides that no action of one state shall have influence on the territory of another.
3. Limited territorial sovereignty and integrity attempts to reconcile the freedom of use of water resources with the right to freedom from unwanted interferences to the water resource, and establishes equality of rights of each riparian state to an international water course (Caponera, 1992; Brunee and Toope, 2002).
4. The doctrine of community of interests provides that parties of a shared river have a community of interests in the use of a river. (PCIJ, 1929; ICJ, 1997).

Unfortunately, these principles and the integration of sustainable development and human rights into water law have not effectively optimized public health protection in water quality regulation. These shortcomings have led to several legal strategies. First, riparian states have adopted sustainable water management laws such as the Protocol for the Sustainable Management of Lake Victoria (East African Community, 2003). Second, riparian states have adopted legal instruments addressing public health issues regarding the management of shared freshwaters. An example has been the Protocol on Water and Health to the Convention on the Protection and Use of Transboundary Watercourses and International Lakes that aims to protect human health through better governance of water, ecosystems and waterborne diseases (United Nations, 1999). A third example is the integration of human rights principles in basin legal regimes as is seen with Incomati and Senegal. The UN General Assembly Declaration of a human right to water and sanitation has reinforced this trend (United Nations, 2010). Efforts to include health when managing shared fresh waters face further challenges. The regional procedural mechanisms of these shared freshwater regimes are weak as is their domestic governance of health. This undermines health protection.

The legal regime governing the Senegal River Basin demonstrates this situation. The Senegal River Basin is home to millions of people, and many of whom live along the river. The states of the Basin are Guinea, Mali, Mauritania and Senegal. The Convention on the Statute of the River Senegal of 11 March 1972 declared the Senegal River an international river, affirmed cooperation in the development of river resources, freedom of navigation and creation of an Organization for the Development of River Senegal. The convention creating this organization aimed to implement the purposes of the statute, to perform technical and economic studies, and create a legal capacity to carry out these purposes. After the creation of the L'Organization Pour la Mise en Valeur du Fleuve Senegal (OMVS) in 1972, and the later adoption of the 1978 Works Convention, several dams were built. However, the dams increased the waterborne diseases of bilharzia, malaria and cholera. By 1994, 90 per cent of the inhabitants of the river basin were infected; malaria and cholera became endemic and the human health costs far outweighed the economic gains (Sow *et al.*, 2002).

This case shows the limits of one of the most innovative international water instruments of the time to promote health, but an integrated water basin management agreement that included the protection of public health was not envisaged. Even more recently, the innovative 2002 Water Charter provides for sustainable development and a human right to water (De Chazournes *et al.*, 2005), but without comprehensive health-protecting measures.

Health in evolving domestic climate legislation around the world

Climate change poses a grave threat to human health (IPPC, 2001, 2007). However, health protection in the UN Framework Convention on Climate

Change (United Nations, 1992) and Kyoto Protocol (United Nations, 1998) law has not been optimized. This is because the substance of the treaties is biased towards mitigation, but health is largely confined to adaptation measures. With few Conference of the Parties health decisions, limited participation of the health sector, poor reporting and financing of health, health is relegated to the peripheries of both UNFCCC and Kyoto (Onzivu, 2010).

These limitations also exist in climate laws adopted by developed nations. For example, the United Kingdom and New Zealand have adopted comprehensive climate legislation, but the laws have not optimized public health requirements. The UK Climate Act of 2008 focuses on emission and carbon reduction (OPSI, 2008), despite recognizing the need to address the social costs of climate change (Stern, 2006). The act lacks synergy with UK public health law. The act's committee and sub-committee on climate change lack a clear mandate to address climate change and health coordination as well as fragmentation. The New Zealand Climate Change Act faces similar health deficits (Parliamentary Counsel Office, 2002).

These examples demonstrate the failure by the parties to optimize health protection. Several developing countries are streamlining and adopting new climate-specific legislation to implement their obligations under the UNFCCC or Kyoto Protocol, but they do not optimize health protection (Onzivu, 2006).

An LSE study has reviewed climate legislation in Brazil, China, India, Indonesia, Mexico, Philippines and South Africa (Townshend *et al.*, 2011). It found that trends in domestic legislation focus on carbon markets, energy efficiency, renewable energy, forestry and adaptation but health issues have low priority. Weak inter-sectoral coordination undermines health protection and what legislation exists is compromised by poor implementation and enforcement, inconsistent policies and legislative priorities across health and other sectors, poor compliance, and inadequate capacity and resources (Onzivu, 2009). Moreover, framework environmental laws have not effectively addressed public health issues and impact assessments lack a comprehensive health component.

Comprehensive public health laws in developing countries could address the weaknesses of climate law. Unfortunately, public health laws in many developing countries are dangerously obsolete (Onzivu, 2006, 2009). They were largely adopted in the colonial era to deal with localized public health threats without trans-boundary considerations. Therefore, buttressing health protection in the implementation of global climate law is pivotal for the international community.

Health in European Union (EU) environmental law and policy

The EU is a leader in developing and implementing international environmental law (Kramer, 2006). The Treaties of Maastricht, Amsterdam and Lisbon, have progressively expanded the legal basis for environmental protection in the European Union. As a result, the European Community has adopted environmental Regulations, Directives, Decisions, Recommendations and opinions on many environmental issues (Kramer, 2006). The European Court of Justice has also passed important environmental regulatory decisions.

EC environmental law aims to protect both human health and the environment. However, the laws have failed to coherently and progressively optimize health protection in an integrated manner. Several developments highlight this deficiency. First, environmental quality and its link to human health are highlighted in the EU Sixth Environmental Action Plan. Framework EU legislation that regulates environmental health includes: the Water Framework Directive, the Regulation concerning the Registration, Evaluation and Authorisation and Restriction of Chemicals (REACH), the proposal for a directive on ambient air quality and cleaner air for Europe, and the proposal for a framework directive on pesticides.

Second, in 2003, the Commission adopted a Communication on a European Environmental and Health Strategy. The strategy aimed to reduce the disease burden caused by environmental factors in the EU, to identify and prevent health threats caused by environmental factors, and to strengthen EU capacity for policymaking in this area. This Communication was followed up by the European Environment and Health Action Plan (EEHAP) 2004–2010 which proposes an integrated information system on environment and health as well as a coordinated approach to human biomonitoring to assess the environmental impact on human health. The action plan aimed to generate the information to analyse all potential impacts, assess whether current action is sufficient, and identify areas where new action is needed.

In June 2004, a communication on the EEHAP focused on health priorities in health information, human bio-monitoring, research, indoor air pollution, traffic pollution, plus training and education. Despite these corrective measures, a 2007 mid-term review of the action plan highlighted some achievements, but significant failures in implementing the plan.

Third, health is a priority of the 2006 EU Sustainable Development Strategy, which reaffirms the importance of impact assessment, where the social, environmental and economic dimensions of policies are assessed in a balanced way (Council of the European Union, 2006). A Strategy review in 2009 determined that the overall development of health in the EU is inadequate (European Commission, 2009). Despite EC collaboration with WHO on issues such as climate change, indoor air quality, tobacco control and injury prevention, continued exposure to air pollution, the limited integration of public health concerns across EC environmental law has undermined the efficacy of the strategy for health protection.

Implications for policy

Environmental health as a global public good

The UNDP defines a global public good as one with benefits that are strongly universal in terms of countries (covering more than one group of countries), people (accruing to several, preferably all population groups) and generations (extending to both current and future generations, or at least meeting the needs of current generations without foreclosing development options for future generations; Chen *et al.*, 2003). Hence, environmental health is a global public good because it provides a positive externality in reduced health burdens around the world, at the community, national and global levels (Smith *et al.*, 2003). As a global public good, health promotion in international law, including environmental protection, is pertinent (Von Schirnding *et al.*, 2007).

The challenge for the international community lies in the financing of global public goods. For example, poorer countries have contributed least to the climate problem, but they have the fewest resources to mitigate its consequences (Onzivu, 2010). Developed countries must combine the binding legal obligation with ethical responsibilities to finance adaptation programmes promoting human health and the environmental objectives of climate change mitigation (WHO, 2011). A strong argument exists that richer countries must compensate poorer developing countries for their greater contribution to climate change by financing adaptation costs (Farber, 2007). The United Nations Compensation Commission set a precedent in awarding compensation for both environmental and public health claims (United Nations, 1991; Payne, 2005). Therefore, a global public goods perspective provides a critical framework to optimize health protection in international environmental legal regimes on a wide range of issues.

Reinforcing impact assessments for health

A key type of instrument to bolster the protection of human health in environmental regulation is the mandatory impact assessment. These include environmental impact assessment (EIA), strategic impact assessment and sustainability impact assessment (Sand, 2003). However, the requirement to assess the health impact of all environmental actions under environmental laws in many countries has been limited (Morgan, 2003). When health aspects are addressed, EIAs tend to focus on only the negative effects of changes in the (bio)physical environment and ignore the effects of modifications on other health determinants, such as socio-economic and health promoting benefits (Kwiatkowski and Ooi, 2003; Onzivu, 2006). Owing to the limitations of environmental impact assessments for health and other social issues, many developed countries have established legal and institutional frameworks for integrated environmental impact assessment, but most developing countries have not (Onzivu, 2006). Optimizing health protection in environmental regulation requires an evaluation of the scope of health protection in any environmental regime. Evaluation refers to a careful retrospective assessment of the merit, worth and value of administration, output, and outcome of government interventions, which is intended to play a role in future, practical situations (Vedung, 1997). The EU has institutionalized the evaluation of laws and policies under its 'smart regulation' through the policy cycle, from the design of legislation to when it is revised (European Commission, 2010). This has helped to improve the functional quality and effectiveness of new legislation. A key feature of smart regulation is the Impact Assessment Board which provides independent quality control over the Commission's impact assessments. Since its creation in 2006, it has produced over 400 opinions accessible to the public.

Enhance institutional coordination

The constituents of environmental regulation often involve the environmental, health and other sectors that may stem from the objectives of a specific environmental treaty or other law. To optimize health protection in environmental law, collaboration should occur amongst the inhabitants of an environmental regulatory space. Some treaties mandate the creation of multi-sectoral coordination bodies for domestic implementation. Therefore, the membership of such coordinating mechanisms should include both the ecological and health aspects of the legal regime. Significant membership from the health sector can enhance equity, participation and recognition for health issues. Multi-stakeholder governance also requires that not only state interests be considered but also civil society (Karkkainen, 2002). Hence, a treaty regime process becomes an administrative, shared, exercise where multi-stakeholder processes are sites where, to enhance quality and legitimacy, regulatory problems are defined, innovative solutions devised, and institutional relationships enhanced (Freeman, 1997). Additionally, public health laws in developing countries must bolster the political, economic, social, environmental, and institutional contexts of emerging environmental health threats such as climate change. Similarly, domestic environmental laws need to be reformed to promote interventions that maximize health benefits.

Redefining the scope of the social pillar – a health pillar?

The social dimension is commonly considered the weakest 'pillar' of sustainable development, most notably in reference to its analytical and theoretical underpinnings (Lehtonen, 2004). Despite the increasing discourse on social sustainability, the interaction between the 'environmental' and the 'social' is largely uncharted. Until recently, sustainable development was perceived essentially as an environmental issue, concerning the integration of environmental concerns into economic decision-making. The political acceptability of sustainable development depends on its capacity to respond to the persistent social problems that seem to have surpassed environmental issues as matters of public concern (Lehtonen, 2004). The demand for an appropriate analytical framework for the three pillars of sustainability is demonstrated by the Organisation for Economic Co-operation and Development (OECD) Council of Ministers' call for OECD Environmental Performance Reviews (OECD, 2001).

According to the EC, achieving sustainability in practice requires that economic growth supports social progress and respects the environment, that social policy underpins economic performance, and that environmental policy is cost-effective (European Commission, 2001). As the twentieth anniversary of the Rio Declarations approaches, it is timely to adopt a specific legal instrument that clarifies the scope of each pillar of sustainability.

It can also be argued that the health deficit in global environmental regulation can be cured by adopting a public health pillar of sustainable development. This will address the ambiguities of public health being classed in the social pillar, plus applying an effective advocacy tool for environmental health protection under the environmental pillar and avoiding the consideration of public health as utilitarian, reflecting the economic pillar. Therefore, a public health pillar would provide an effective framework to protect the health of the world's poorest, especially those in the developing world.

Conclusions

The linkages between health and the environment and the goal-oriented nature of environmental regulation have demonstrated the need to reinforce public health protection in global environmental law. Support for the recognition of a fourth pillar of sustainable development has a sound justification in both law and fact: the health protection potential of environmental regulation has been underutilized in the progressive development and implementation of international and domestic environmental law.

Acknowledgements

I thank Jenny, Rianna, Genevieve and Alexandra for their patience. Thanks to Colin Soskolne, Laura Westra, Don Spady and Luc Quenneville for their editorial and intellectual support.

References

Bankobeza, G. M. (2005) *Ozone Protection: The International Legal Regime*, Eleven International Publishing, The Hague, The Netherlands, pp307–08

Barrett, S. (1999) 'International Cooperation and the International Commons', *Duke Environmental Law and Policy Forum*, vol 10, pp131–138

Bell, S. and McGillivray, D. (2008) *Environmental Law*, Oxford University Press, Oxford, UK, pp17–23

Biswas, A. K., Tortajada, C. and Izquierdo-Avino, R. (Eds.) (2009) *Water Management in 2020*, Water Management and Development, Springer, Berlin, Germany

De Chazournes, B., Desgagne, R., Mbengue, M. M., Cesare Romano, C. (2005) *Protection international del'environment*, Editions Pedone, Paris, pp297–312

Boschi-Pinto, C., Velebit, L. and Shibuya, K. (2008) 'Estimating child mortality due to diarrhoea in developing countries', *Bulletin of the World Health Organization*, vol 86, no 9, pp710–717

Bruch, C. (2009) 'Adaptive water management: strengthening laws and institutions to cope with uncertainty', Water Resources Development and Management, in A. K. Biswas *et al.* (eds) *Water Management in 2020*, Springer, Berlin, Germany, pp89–113

Brunnee, J. and Toope, J. (2002) 'The changing Nile basin regime: does law matter', *Harvard Intl. Law Journal*, vol 43, p105

Burci, G. L. and Henri-Vignes, C. (2004) *The World Health Organization*, 1st edition, Kluwer Law International, The Hague, p172

Caponera, D. A. (1992) *Principles of Water Law and Administration*, Taylor and Francis, Abingdon, UK, p213

Chen, L. C., Evans, T. G. and Cash, R. A. (1999) 'Health as a global public good', in I. Kaul, I. Grunberg and M. A. Stern (eds) *Global Public Goods: International Cooperation in the 21st Century*, Oxford University Press, New York, NY

Chiesura, A., de Groot, R. (2003) 'Critical natural capital: a sociocultural perspective', *Ecological Economics*, vol 44, no 2–3, pp219– 231

Council of the European Union (2006) Renewed EU Sustainable Development Strategy as adopted by the European Council on 15/16 June 2006, accessible at http://register.consilium.europa.eu/pdf/en/06/st10/st10917.en06.pdf, Annex, paragraph 13

Daly, H. E. (1995) 'On Wilfred Beckerman's critique of sustainable development', *Environmental Values*, vol 4, pp49–52

DiMento, J. (2003) 'International environmental law: a global assessment', *Environmental Law Reporter*, vol 33, pp10, 387–89

East African Community (2003) Protocol on Sustainable Development of Lake Victoria, signed on November 29 2003, and ratified in November, 2004, accessed at www.fao.org/fishery/shared/faolextrans.jsp?xp_ISIS_MFN=035651&xp_faoLexLang=E&xp_lang=en

Emory, R. W. (2000) 'Probing the protections in the rotterdam convention on prior informed consent', *Colorado Journal of International Law and Policy*, yearbook 47, pp67–68

European Commission (2001) *A Sustainable Europe for a Better World: A European Union Strategy for Sustainable Development*, COM (2001)264 final, Brussels, May 15, 2001

European Commission (2009) *Mainstreaming Sustainable Development into EU Policies: 2009 Review of the European Union Strategy for Sustainable Development*, COM(2009) 400 final, Brussels, 24.7.2009, Article 11, accessible at http://eur-lex.europa.eu/LexUriServ/LexUriServ.do?uri=COM:2009:0400:FIN:EN:PDF

European Commission (2010) *Smart Regulation in the European Union*, COM(2010) 543 final, Brussels, 8.10.2010, accessible at http://eur-lex.europa.eu/LexUriServ/LexUriServ.do?uri=COM:2010:0543:FIN:EN:PDF

Farber, D. A. (2007) 'Basic compensation for victims of climate change', *University of Pennsylvania Law Review*, vol 155, p1,605

Fidler, D. (1999) 'International law and global public health', *Kansas Law Review*, vol 48, pp1–26

Forget, G. and Lebel, J. (2001) 'An ecosystem approach to human health', *International Journal of Occupational and Environmental Health*, April–June(Supplement), ppS15–S16

Freeman, J. (1997) 'Collaborative governance in the administrative state', *UCLA Law Review*, vol 45, no 1, pp1–98

Gostin, L. O. (2008) 'Meeting basic survival needs of the world's least healthy people toward a framework convention on global health'. *Georgetown Law Journal 96*: 331–392 ICJ, (1997) Case Concerning Gabcikovo-Nagymaros Project (Hungary v. Slovakia) 1997 ICJ 54 (5 February) 78

ICJ (International Court of Justice) (1997) *Case Concerning Gabcikovo-Nagymaros Project (Hungary v Slovakia)*, 1997 ICJ 54 (5 February), 78

IPCC (2007) *Climate Change : The Physical Science Basis – Summary for Policymakers*, Intergovernmental Panel on Climate Change, Geneva, Switzerland

IPCC (2001) *Climate Change : Impacts, Vulnerably and Adaptation*, Cambridge University Press, Cambridge, UK

Karkkainen, B. C. (2002) 'Collaborative ecosystem governance: scale, complexity, and dynamism', *Virginia Environmental Law Journal*, vol 21, pp189–243

Kramer, L. (2006) *EC Environmental Law*, sixth edition, Sweet & Maxwell, London

Kwiatkowski, R. E. and Ooi, M. (2003) 'Integrated environmental impact assessment: a Canadian example', *Bulletin of the World Health Organization*, vol 81, pp434, 437

Lazarus, R. J. (2004) *The Making of Environmental Law*, University of Chicago Press, Chicago, IL

Lehtonen, M. (2004) 'The environmental–social interface of sustainable development: capabilities, social capital, institutions', *Ecological Economics*, vol 49, pp199–214

McCaffrey, S. C. (2007) *The Law of International Watercourses*, Second Edition, Oxford University Press, Oxford, p113

McEldowney, J. and McEldowney, S. (2010) *Environmental Law*, Pearson, Harlow, UK, pp88–98

Mehta, M. D. (1997) 'Risk assessment and sustainable development: towards a concept of sustainable risk', *Risk: Health, Safety and Environment*, vol 8, p137

Morgan, R. K. (2003) 'Health impact assessment: the wider context', *Bulletin of the World Health Organization*, vol 81, p390

Onzivu, W. (2006) 'International environmental law, the public's health and domestic environmental governance in developing countries', *American University International Law Review*, vol 21, no 4, pp597, 634–638

Onzivu, W. (2009) 'Tackling the public health impact of climate change: the role of domestic environmental health governance mechanisms in developing countries', *The International Lawyer*, p1311

Onzivu, W. (2010) 'Health in global climate change law: the long road to an effective legal regime protecting public health and the climate', *Carbon and Climate Law Review*, vol 4, pp364–382

OPSI (2008) UK Climate Change Act, CAP 27 available at www.legislation.gov.uk/ukpga/2008/27/pdfs/ukpga_20080027_en.pdf

Parliamentary Counsel Office (2002) Climate Change Response Act, 2002, Public Act 2002 No 40(New Zealand)

Payne, C. (2005) 'UN Commission Awards Compensation for Environmental and Public Health Damage from 1990–91 Gulf War', available at www.asil.org/insights/2005/08/insights050810.html

PCIJ (1929) Case Relating to the Territorial Jurisdiction of the International Commission of the River Oder, 1929 PCIJ (Ser. A) No.23, at 27 (10 September)

Pearce, D. and Barbier, E. B. (2000) *Blueprint for a Sustainable Economy*, Earthscan, London, pp23–24

Ruger, J. P. (2009) 'Global health justice', *Public Health Ethics*, vol 2, no 3, pp261–275

Sand, P. H. (1992) *Effectiveness of International Environmental Agreements: A Survey of Existing Legal Instruments*, Cambridge University Press, Cambridge, UK, pp4–15

Sand, P. (2003) *Principles of International Environmental Law*, Cambridge University Press, Cambridge, UK, pp104–106

Secretariat of the Basel Convention (2008) Bali Declaration on Waste Management for Human Health and Livelihood, accessible at www.basel.int/convention/XX%20Anniversary/Press%20kit/Bali%20declaration.pdf

Smith, R., Beaglehole, R., Woodward, D. and Drager, N., (2003) *Global Public Goods for Health: Health, Economic and Public Health Perspectives*, Oxford University Press, Oxford, UK, p7

Sow, S., de Vlas, S. J., Engels, D., Gryseels, B. (2002) 'Water-related disease patterns before and after the construction of the Diama dam in northern Senegal', 96 *Annals of Tropical Medicine and Parasitology*, p575

Townshend, T., Fankhauser, S., Mathews, A., Feger, C., Liu, J. and Narcisu, T. (2011) *Globe Climate Legislation Study*, Global Legislators Organisation for a Balanced Environment (GLOBE) and the Grantham Research Institute on Climate Change and the Environment, London, p16

United Nations Development Programme (2006) *Human Development Report, 2006, Beyond Scarcity: Power, Poverty and the Global Water Crisis*, UNDP, Nairobi, Kenya, p42

United Nations (1969) Vienna Convention on the Law of Treaties, May 23, 1969, 1155 UNTS 331 8 ILM 679 (1969) Article 31, Article 60(3) (b)

United Nations (1991) UN Security Council Resolution 687, Para 16, UN Doc. S/RES/687 (April 8, 1991)

United Nations (1992) United Nations Framework Convention on Climate Change, 31 ILM 849(1992)

United Nations (1998) Kyoto Protocol, 37 ILM 2

United Nations (1999) Protocol on Water and Health to the 1992 Convention on the Protection and Use of Transboundary Watercourses and International Lakes, available at www.unece.org/env/water/text/text_protocol.htm

United Nations (2002) Report of the World Summit on Sustainable Development, Johannesburg, South Africa, 26 August – 4 September 2002, UN Doc. A/CONF.199/20 (UN, New York)

United Nations (2010) United Nations General Assembly Resolution on the human right to water and sanitation (document A/64/L.63/REV.1) Sixty-fourth General Assembly Plenary 108th Meeting, available at www.un.org/News/Press/docs/2010/ga10967.doc.htm

Vedung, E. (1997) *Public Policy and Program Evaluation*, Transaction Publishers, New Brunswick, NJ

Von Schirnding, Y., Onzivu, W. and Adede, A. O. (2002) 'International environmental law and global public health', *Bulletin of the World Health Organization*, vol 80, no 12, pp970–971

Westra, L. (2006) *Environmental Justice and the Rights of Unborn and Future Generations: Law, Environmental Harm and the Right to Health*, Earthscan, London, pp3–4

World Health Organization (2006) 'Preamble', in *Constitution of the World Health Organization*, 45th Edition, World Health Organization, Geneva, Switzerland

World Health Organization (2011) Regional Committee for Africa, Framework for Public Health Adaptation to Climate Change in Africa, Doc. AFR/RC61/10, 22 June, WHO Regional Office for Africa

Young, O. (1999) *The Effectiveness of International Environmental Regimes: Causal Connections and Behavioural Mechanisms*, MIT Press, Cambridge, MA

25 The human impact on the ecosystem

Past, present and future

Brunetto Anton Chiarelli

This chapter provides a brief history of population growth, the factors determining human energy needs and the impact of the interaction between energy use and populations on the health of ecosystems. It explores the need for population control, effective and equitable food production and the stimulus to develop renewable energies. The importance of culture in reasserting ecosystem health and the continuance of the human species is emphasized.

The history of population increase and their needs

Since the origin of humans around 5 million years ago, both sexes, under all living conditions, from birth to death, have required about 2000kcal daily to meet the three basic needs of human populations: food, fuel and fibres. However, this would be insufficient to enable the material and cultural development of human civilizations. This minimum '3F' requirement was established before humankind developed a technological and consumer oriented culture. The 2000kcal reflected human needs when all of humanity consisted of less than five hundred thousand people, living mainly as hunter–gatherers in the savannahs of Africa and south Asia.

In our present culture it is easy to define the nature and quantity of the first F (food) that we use daily, often to excess. It is more difficult to estimate the energy needed for the second F (fuel), which is invested in movements to collect food or to socialize or to perform other tasks of daily life, and which may be equivalent to walking or running in a savannah environment, more recently travelling on horseback and today in cars. We generally do not give much consideration to the third F (fibres, or clothing). In the earliest times these were non-existent, or made of vegetable fibres or animal skins; at present they are sophisticated and expensive when considering the material required and the amount of work needed to prepare garments.

In the Lower Pleistocene (from 2 million years ago to 780,000 years BC), due to the early development of stone tools, the global population increased from about 800,000 to 1.2 million in the Middle Pleistocene, and further still to 9 million in the Upper and Late Pleistocene (about 10,000–8,000 years BC). Some of this population growth was due to better climatic conditions spreading all over the world.

The development of crop-based agriculture and the breeding of animals took place around 8,000–6,000 years BC, and to a large degree met the demand of the first F (food). This led rapidly to the creation of different cultures and an increase in global population to about 50 million people over a period of less than a thousand years.

A great change in the growth of populations was the transition from bronze to iron technologies in the Mediterranean area (A. Vannini, 2011) that coincided with the inception of the Etruscan culture (Chiarelli, 2010). At the time of Christ, the global population approached 250 million people. At this time, many of the basic norms of social life were accurately defined in the large area under the rule of the Roman Empire.

Technologies were poorly developed in the Early Christian Era, and it took 15 centuries for the population to double to 500 million, roughly at the time when Columbus arrived at what is now known as San Salvador. It took only four centuries, until 1835, for the next population doubling to one billion to occur. Population rose more rapidly as fossil fuels were increasingly exploited (a prime example of the second F, fuel) and industrialization took hold. After only 90 more years, in 1925, the human population reached about two billion, and then three billion in 1950, in spite of the disaster of World War II.

The combination of fossil fuels and modern agricultural science enabled a huge increase in global food production and by the beginning of the present century six billion people lived on Earth (Table 25.1).

Global population is expected to reach seven billion by October 2011, after only 16 years. If population growth rates are maintained, we should reach a total of nine billion people by year 2040.

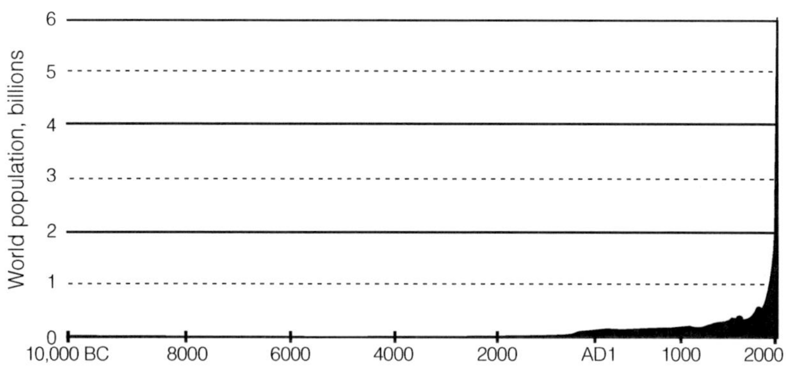

Figure 25.1 World population growth
Source: http://www.census.gov

Table 25.1 World population from the Low Palaeolithic to the present

Chronology	*World population (millions)*	*Population increase index (year %)*
Lower Pleistocene	800,000	0.00007
Middle Pleistocene	1,200,000	0.0054
Upper Pleistocene	6,000,000	0.0100
Late Pleistocene	9,000,000	0.0033
Neolithic	50,000,000	0.085
BC/AD	300,000,000	0.046
1300	400,000,000	0.022
1650	553,000,000	0.37
1750	800,000,000	0.44
1800	1,000,000,000	0.52
1850	1,300,000,000	0.54
1900	1,700,000,000	0.79
1950	2,500,000,000	1.74
1977	4,300,000,000	2.01
2000	6,000,000,000	
2008	6,700,000,000	

Source: Chiarelli (2002)

This rapid increase in population, and in the accompanying industrial development and material consumption, has led to significant effects on the global world ecosystem. This poses a major problem for the survival of our species. Being a naturalist, I share the view of T. Dobzhansky, who often reminded us that in considering the development of life on Earth, there are more extinct species than there are those still in existence, and we might be joining that unfortunate former group.

We expect to reach the 10 billion mark before 2050. But, everything considered, population cannot grow much beyond that figure because of ecological incompatibility with the present demand on resources available on planet Earth.

What to focus on?

Population control

Obviously one way to reduce the human impact on the ecosystem is to impose a strict control on the birth rate. This aim can be achieved by personal choice, such as observing a vow of abstinence, or through various methods of contraception. The imposition of a one child per couple policy was used to control population growth in China, but it had serious negative consequences due to a strong preference for male offspring in the Chinese traditional culture. In 2005, the male-to-female sex ratio at birth in China was 120.5:100 (Li, 2007). This will cause heavy social imbalance problems, particularly from 2030 onwards.

In the Western industrialized countries, knowledge of birth and sex control practices contribute towards keeping human population growth under control. Additional measures contribute to this process. These include increased availability of employment for women, as well as better education (sexual education specifically included), equal opportunity for male/female work, liberal professions and others. Family planning is common, often with not more than two children per family. However, family planning has not been as successful in the so-called developing countries because of a lack of knowledge regarding contraception, and because of a scarcity of employment opportunities for women.

Perspectives for an increase of the '3F', towards survival of humankind after reaching 10 billion in 2050

Food

An increase of food production for a population of ten billion people is theoretically possible using various bio-technologies such as genetically modified (GM) organisms. However, current evidence does not support the claims that GM plants actually produce more than appropriately managed traditional farms. Additionally, some GM products are designed only to be effective for one planting, and new seed must be purchased for every new crop. This poses the real danger that a commercial product, such as GM wheat with a 'killer' gene, could place the livelihood of traditional farmers at great risk and with little benefit to society at large.

Some other examples of GM food include:

- The (theoretically possible) insertion of a lysine (an essential amino acid) producing gene into corn. This would make the amino acid profile of corn more suitable for human consumption and could reduce the demand and consumption of other lysine-rich foods, such as animal meat.
- The use of bacteria growing in petrol to synthesize proteins that may be consumed as food for humans. However, in this example, there are significant problems of scaling that make this approach problematic.

An important approach is to avoid wasting food, either at the time of harvest and storage, or at the time of consumption. A significant proportion of food is lost simply because of poor food management.

Perhaps the most important way to ensure that huge populations can be fed is to develop systems that ensure equitable food distribution within a country or a society and also to ensure that food costs do not become prohibitive or susceptible to market manipulation.

Fuel

There is a growing tendency to invest in so-called renewable resources that can produce energy. These include solar and wind energy, as is being demonstrated in the Atlas Mountain chain and with the Sahara project. Other sources include hydroelectric power, and tidal and geothermal energy. These do not produce CO_2 and thus do not contribute to the greenhouse effect. However, they will not replace the convenience and abundance of energy provided by fossil fuels. A critical problem with fossil fuels is that they are non-renewable and their production over the next few decades will drop significantly, thus there is a strong impetus to explore all available potential sources of renewable energy.

Fibre

Great possibilities are anticipated regarding the development of synthetic fibre, which will cut the use of the currently common fibre production process.

Sociological interaction

The growth of the urban population creates problems of agglomeration and proximity of people. The necessity of changing direction towards a proper social survival must be considered.

Generally speaking, the social organization of any group of mammals follows four stimuli. Two are related to the biology of the species: the mother–child stimulus (A) and the sexual urge (B). The other two are related to the environment in which the population is living: cooperation in the search for food (C) and defence of the group (D). The relation between these stimuli and the environment (*k*) determines the best adaptive choice of a social structure. The variety of intensity of the biological stimuli among the different species determines the minimum number of individuals needed for the survival of the population over time (*deme*), while the productivity of the environment within which the population lives determines the maximum number:

$$(A+B) + k(C+D) = \Delta.$$

However 'culture', which originated in the brain (intelligence), generates the possibility of an increased impact on the ecosystem. therefore the previous equation should be:

$((A+B) + k(C+D))^I = \Delta+$, where I reflects the (negative or positive) impact of culture on the ecosystem, and $\Delta+$ reflects the altered maximum population. Culture allowed a dramatic increase in population speed of transportation and communication. However, the survival of humankind is still related to the maintenance of biodiversity and the heterogeneity of cultures. In some way we can foresee the same condition we had during the Tertiary Age, during which several species of insect developed very complex social structures.

Culture

Compared with animals, present-day humans are born with simpler instinct equipment, but a greater power of learning, and therefore they have a relatively longer period of dependence on their family. Moreover, due to the development of language, humans can communicate and discuss their problems and the relative solutions with one another, passing information down to future generations. Various societies, over long periods, develop a variety of ways of using their powers of learning and instinct, and producing tools, to ease their lives and to satisfying biological drives. These alternative solutions are called 'cultures'.

Culture includes:

- a shared way of perceiving and thinking about the world;
- agreed forms of non-verbal communication;
- agreed rules and conventions about what shall be done under different situations; and
- agreed morals and other values, and a system of religious and allied beliefs.

The future possible survival of our species has to consider these different aspects.

Conclusion

From its origin 5 million years ago, humankind has spread across the globe more effectively than any single species. It has demonstrated an astonishing ability to adapt to its environment. It has also tied its unique gifts of imagination with superior intelligence and creativity to create advanced civilizations and cultures. In doing so, humankind attained an arrogance and attitude of superiority over the natural world and exploited this world to the advantage of humanity. It was too successful. This exploitation pushed the world to its biophysical limits, and now it is failing. Humanity knows the reason why. Whether the various groups of humans who make up the constituencies of the world can come and work together to mitigate and adapt to the consequences of their actions is the great question. It is not just a technical question. To a large extent it is a question of attitude, of behaviour and of culture.

References

Chiarelli, B. (2002) *L'uomo tra passato e future: Dalla natura alla cultura*, vol II, Piccin, Padua, Italy

Chiarelli B. (2010) 'Dal bronzo al ferro: sulla possibile origine anatolica degli etruschi', in *Systema Naturae*, vol 10, Altravista, Padua, Italy

Li, S. (2007) *Imbalanced Sex Ratio at Birth and Comprehensive Intervention in China*, Proceedings from the 4th Asia Pacific Conference on Reproductive and Sexual Health and Rights, Hyderabad, India, October 29–31, UNFPA, New York, NY, available at www.unfpa.org/gender/docs/studies/china.pdf

Vannini A. (2010) 'La bussola dei fenici', in *Systema Naturae*, vol 10, Altravista, Padua, Italy

Further reading

Accademia Pontificia delle Scienze (1993) *Popolazioni e Risorse*, report, Accademia Pontificia delle Scienze, Vatican City

Chiarelli, B. (1992) 'Man, nature and ethics', *Global Bioethics*, vol 5, pp13–20

Chiarelli, B. (2003) 'The evolution of mankind and the origin of global bioethics', *Studia Bobolanum*, vol 4, pp105–110

Chiarelli, B. (2003) *Dalla Natura alla Cultura. Principi di Antropologia Biologica e Culturale*, Piccin, Padua, Italy

Cipolla, C. (1994) *Before the Industrial Revolution: European Society and Economy: 1000–1700*, Norton, New York, NY

Cohen, J. E. (1995) 'Population growth and Earth's human carrying capacity', *Science*, vol 269, pp341–346

Hern, W. M. (1993) 'Is human culture carcinogenic for uncontrolled growth and ecological destruction?', *BioScience*, vol 43, pp768–773

Jonas, I. H. (1990) *Il principio della responsabilità*, Einaudi, Torino, Italy

Lieberman, P. (2007) 'The evolution of human speech: its anatomical and neural bases', *Current Anthropology*, vol 48, no 1, pp39–66

Leopold, A. S. (1949) *A Sand County Almanac, with other Essay on Conservation from Round River*, Oxford University Press, Oxford, UK

Malthus, T. R. (1798) 'An essay on the principle of population,' in G. Himmelfarb (ed.)1970, *On Population*, Modern Library, New York, NY

Marchetti, C. (1993) '10^{12}: a check on the Earth-carrying capacity from man', *Global Bioethics*, vol 6, pp131–142

Potter, R. van (1992) 'Global bioethics as a secular source of moral authority for long-term human survival', *Global Bioethics*, vol 5, pp69–76

Soleri, P. (1969) *Arcology: The City in the Image of Man*, MIT Press, Cambridge, MA

Teilhard de Chardin, P. (1956) *La place de l'homme dans la nature*, Seuil, Paris, France

26 Introducing the rule of ecological law

Geoffrey Garver

The Greek god Apollo empowered Cassandra to know the future in exchange for her love for him, but when she rejected him, he cursed her by making it so nobody would believe her. Those revealing 'inconvenient truths' (Gore, 2006) about the growing global ecological crisis often face Cassandra's dilemma (AtKisson, 1999). Scientists are constantly buttressing their consensus (Oreskes and Conway, 2010) that uncompromising ecological boundaries constrain the human economy. Beyond these limits, the climate changes, nutrients overwhelm ecosystems or biodiversity is lost to such an extreme that the ecological context for the human enterprise irreversibly and catastrophically moves into a new systemic state (Rockström *et al.*, 2009). According to many metrics, human society is already crossing these boundaries (Speth, 2008; Rockström *et al.*, 2009; Hails, 2008). Yet these narratives are routinely ignored, resisted or drowned out in public and political discourse, such that legal and other normative regimes that would confront these dangerous trends either fail to emerge or are rejected. Consequently, the global community's de facto governance structure (Brown and Garver, 2009, p19) lacks legal and policy regimes that would allow hard ecological truths to carry determinative weight.

What is missing is the rule of ecological law. Environmental economics[1] attempts to correct environmental market failures by internalizing environmental costs into the prices of goods and services. However, it is incapable of respecting aggregate ecological boundaries in a systemic manner. The still tractionless field of ecological economics[2] (Heinzerling and Ackerman, 2007) responds to this deficiency by positing the functioning of the global ecosystem as the overarching constraint on the human economy. In law, an analogous deficiency is apparent (Boutelet and Fritz, 2005). The envelope of contemporary environmental law is deficient as a means to enclose and regulate the human enterprise within systemic ecological constraints (Percival, 2007). Just as ecological economics emerged to address limitations of environmental economics, the rule of ecological law is needed to transcend limitations of contemporary environmental law.

Systemic ecological boundaries that promote the enhancement of life systems provide the base of a structure of ecological law (in the legal sense) that must be respected and enforced to fend off catastrophe and enhance the capacity for life. The looming prospect of transgressing critical ecological points of no return requires the global community to fashion a systems-based legal and institutional structure that is built on the foundation of ecological law under an expanded notion of the rule of law.

What is the rule of ecological law?

The rule of ecological law combines the notion of ecological law with the notion of the rule of law. The term 'ecological law' is rarely used.[3] Here, it is akin to the ecologically imbued notion of law described by Berry (1999):

> To achieve a viable human–Earth situation, a new jurisprudence must envisage its primary task as that of articulating the conditions for the integral functioning of the Earth process, with special reference to a mutually enhancing human–Earth relationship … [T]he land, the water, the air, and the complex of life systems … would constitute the integral expression of the Great Commons of the planet Earth to be shared in proportion to need among all members of the Earth community. (Berry, 1999, p61)

From Thomas Berry's perspective, '[e]cology is not a part of law; law is an extension of ecology' (Berry, 1999, p61).

David Boyd's notion of 'sustainability law' (D. R. Boyd, 2004) and Klaus Bosselmann's similar 'principle of sustainability' (Bosselmann, 2008) encapsulate well Berry's ecological conception of law. Boyd characterizes sustainability law as 'a system of laws and policies that facilitate processes, products, and patterns of behaviour which are good for the planet' (D. R. Boyd, 2004, p365). For Boyd, 'sustainability law would focus on *transforming* the relationship between humans and the natural environment from one based on minimizing harm to one based on maximizing harmony' (D. R. Boyd, 2004, pp364–365). It 'would be firmly rooted in science and the laws of nature, beginning with a clear understanding of the laws of thermodynamics and explicit recognition of the biophysical limits of the planet Earth' (D. R. Boyd, 2004, pp364–365).

Bosselmann insists that respecting and maintaining the Earth's ecological integrity are at the core of sustainability (Bosselmann, 2008; Westra, 2008). Emphasizing ecological integrity is consistent with its treatment as a fundamental ethical principle (Westra, 1994). With this grounding, 'sustainability has the historical, conceptual and ethical quality typical for a fundamental principle of law,' (Bosselmann, 2008, p4) on the same order as foundational principles like equality, justice and freedom. In Bosselmann's view, the Earth Charter, with its emphasis on the interdependence of all life forms, the value of all living things regardless of their value to humans, and the dignity and potential of human beings, is the most profound current expression of the principle of sustainability (Bosselmann, 2008, pp73–75).

Boyd's sustainability law and Bosselmann's principle of sustainability both recognize the essential primacy of ecological integrity. The term 'ecological law' emphasizes this primacy by making clear that global ecological limits constrain the economic and social spheres that are usually associated, along with environmental concerns, with 'sustainability' – often in a confusing way. Unlike some notions of sustainability,[4] the rule of ecological law calls into question the current insistence on economic growth.

Ecological law derives from a fundamental normative choice to manage the human enterprise so as to sustain circumstances to which ecology, thermodynamics and the other sciences will apply in ways that keep the human–Earth relationship thriving. An international team of researchers has proposed planetary boundaries (Rockström *et al.*, 2009) that, along with related ecological indicators, help describe those circumstances, providing a key part of the basis for the normative decisions inherent in ecological law. Planetary boundaries are systemic global ecological limits of 'safe operating space' for humanity, beyond which humans face an unacceptable 'risk of deleterious or even catastrophic environmental change at continental to global scales' (Rockström *et al.*, 2009, p2). The nine proposed boundaries are based on climate change, ocean acidification, stratospheric ozone depletion, atmospheric aerosol loading, land use, freshwater use, chemical pollution, biodiversity loss and nutrient cycles. These boundaries are 'non-negotiable' (Rockström *et al.*, 2009, p4), such that '[t]he thresholds in key Earth system processes exist irrespective of peoples' preferences, values or compromises based on political and socioeconomic feasibility, such as expectations of technological breakthroughs and fluctuations in economic growth' (Rockström *et al.*, 2009, p7). The primacy of the boundaries is therefore essential.

Social, political or cultural concerns, grounded in ethics and justice that transcend the notions of safety and survival inherent in the planetary boundaries concept, provide additional grounds for making these normative decisions. The notion of 'right relationship' reflects these other concerns (Brown and Garver, 2009). Right relationship derives from Aldo Leopold's land ethic: 'A thing is right when it tends to preserve the integrity, stability, and beauty of the biotic community' (Leopold, 1949).[5] It serves as a 'guidance system for functioning in harmony with scientific reality and enduring ethical traditions' (Brown and Garver, 2009, p4). Right relationship reflects ecological limits but also 'include[s] the fair sharing of the earth's life support capacities with all of life's commonwealth' (Brown and Garver, 2009, p17). Thus, right relationship seeks a positive, life-enhancing human–Earth relationship, not merely a safe and survivable one.

The 'rule of law' as used here conveys dual notions: first, a coherent set of legal institutions and norms, from the global to the local level, should provide a coherent, reliable, fair and just framework for managing human affairs

(United Nations Security Council, 2004); and second, this legal architecture is bounded by the science that governs Earth systems. The first entrains the notion that no person is above the law. The second is inherent in emphasizing the rule of *ecological* law, which clarifies that the norms and laws of concern are founded not only in legal principles but also in planetary boundaries and other expressions of the uncompromising ecological limits of the life support capacity of the Earth. In this vein, 'the 'rule of law' means that global regulatory limits required to meet ecological limits and ensure fair sharing of the earth's bounty must be respected' (Brown and Garver, 2009, p135).

With these foundations, the rule of ecological law should include at least the ten following mutually reinforcing features:

1. the rule of ecological law recognizes that humans are part of Earth's life systems, not separate from it.
2. Legal regimes must be constrained by ecological considerations necessary to avoid catastrophic outcomes and promote the enhancement of life, with the socio-economic spheres fully contained within these ecological constraints.
3. The rule of ecological law must permeate legal regimes and other disciplines like economics in a systemic, integrated way, and not be seen as a specialty area of the law that applies to isolated problems.
4. Because the human enterprise has already transgressed global ecological limits, the legal regime should support a radical re-focusing of the economy on reduction of its throughput of material and energy.
5. The rule of ecological law must be global, but distributed fairly using principles of proportionality and subsidiarity, with protection of the global commons and public goods paramount, and with constraints on property rights and individual choice as needed to keep the economy within ecological limits.
6. The rule of ecological law must ensure fair sharing of resources among present and future generations of humans and other life forms.
7. The rule of ecological law must be binding (*de jure* or *de facto*) and supranational, with supremacy over sub-global legal regimes as necessary.
8. A greatly expanded program of research and monitoring for improved understanding and continual adjustment of ecological boundaries and means for respecting them is needed to support the rule of ecological law, globally, regionally and locally.
9. The rule of ecological law requires precaution about crossing planetary boundaries, with margins of safety to ensure both that the boundaries are respected from the global to the local level, and that Earth's life systems have the capacity to thrive.
10. Ecological law must be adaptive, because ecosystems evolve constantly and because a comprehensive effort to constrain the economy within ecological limits must start forthwith, despite uncertainty.

The shortcomings of contemporary environmental law

A key flaw of contemporary environmental law is its reductionist tendency to focus on environmental problems as discrete and isolated, which impedes the full integration of a systemic ecological approach into the entire legal infrastructure (D. R. Boyd, 2004). Most environmental laws and regulations adopted in the United States and elsewhere since the 1970s miss the forest of aggregate systemic impacts for the trees of smokestacks and sewage pipes (Percival, 2007; Heinzerling, 2005). They have reduced some of the most patent environmental pollutants in light of known harmful effects (albeit too often allowing pollution despite serious uncertainty as to risks), but they have not evolved to address effectively the cumulative impacts and scale effects tied to the growing material and energy throughput that has accompanied economic growth (Victor, 2008).

A second flaw is the tendency in environmental law, as with environmental economics, to favour monetization as the way to normalize social preferences and to regulate the relationship between environmental problems and the development pressures that create them. Environmental law relies too heavily on assessments of monetized costs and benefits and an enduring allegiance to a reactive, non-precautionary approach that gives primacy to economic constraints instead of ecological ones (Percival, 2007; Heinzerling, 2005). Compared to contemporary environmental law, ecological law would place ecological constraints on property and cordon off the sphere of market exchanges based on abstract monetary units to a considerably greater extent (Brown and Garver, 2009).

A holistic approach has not been entirely absent from contemporary environmental law. As the environmental awakening emerged in the 1960s and 1970s, holistic thinkers helped bring an ecological perspective into the law (Tarlock, 2000). Kenneth Boulding offered the powerful notion of Earth as a finite spaceship; Aldo Leopold's land ethic was revived; and Joseph Sax's public trust theory of environmental protection had wide influence on environmental policy (Delgado, 1991). However, the 'deep ecology' (Naess, 1984), public trust and Leopoldian elements of the environmental awakening gave way to the economically driven ideology of the 1980s, and the economic glaze over environmental law has only hardened since (Heinzerling, 2005; Westra, 2008).

The few system-based mechanisms in contemporary environmental law are generally weak, limited or subservient to economic and political interests. For example, environmental impact assessment laws requiring analysis of the effects of economic activity on ecosystems are, by and large, procedural only,[6] promoting awareness, but rarely if ever binding, concrete action to protect ecosystems (Kass, 2009).[7] Three more specific examples illustrate additional shortcomings: total maximum daily loads (TMDLs) under the United States' Clean Water Act;[8] critical loads and levels for air pollutants under the 1979 Convention on Long-range Transboundary Air

Pollution (LRTAP); and the successful, but exceptional, regime to control ozone-depleting substances under the Montreal Protocol.

The Clean Water Act requires States to establish water quality standards for ambient water quality, taking into consideration different uses and, to an extent, the ecological impacts of pollutants on aquatic ecosystems.[9] States must identify waters in which any applicable water quality standard is not being met, and then calculate the total maximum daily loads of problem pollutants to those waters from point, non-point and natural sources.[10] TMDLs provide a non-binding basis for tightening point-source permits and exploring ways to control non-point-sources like urban or agricultural runoff, which the Clean Water Act regulates weakly—although they are often the most important (Adler, 2009; Caudill and Curley, 2008).

Because TMDLs establish the aggregate loadings needed to maintain water quality at levels established in part according to ecological criteria,[11] they are a possible proxy for a systemic ecological boundary. They have at least an indirect relationship to the planetary boundaries for chemical pollution and nutrient fluxes (Rockström *et al.*, 2009).

State and federal regulators essentially ignored the mandate to establish TMDLs for almost twenty years, until spurred by litigation to do so in the 1990s (Karr and Yoder, 2004; J. Boyd, 2000). Now that the TMDL program has slowly come to life, its functional limitations are becoming apparent. Most critically, States are not required to implement TMDLs or to apply them in a binding manner to non-point sources (United States Environmental Protection Agency, n.d.). In 2003, the Bush Administration withdrew a Clinton Administration TMDL rule that required States to develop detailed implementation plans and schedules for actions to reduce point and non-point pollutant loadings of impaired waters (United States Environmental Protection Agency, 2003). Not surprisingly, many water bodies in the United States still fail to meet water quality standards, often because of non-point-source pollution (United States Environmental Protection Agency, 2009).

The European critical loads and levels approach (Rockström *et al.*, 2009, supplemental information; Umweltbundesamt, 2004; Cresser, 2000) was developed under the United Nations Economic Commission for the LRTAP. Critical levels are 'concentrations of pollutants in the atmosphere above which direct adverse effects on receptors, such as human beings, plants, ecosystems or materials, may occur according to present knowledge' (Umweltbundesamt, 2004, pIII-1). Critical load is a 'quantitative estimate of an exposure to one or more pollutants below which significant harmful effects on specified sensitive elements of the environment do not occur according to present knowledge' (Umweltbundesamt, 2004, pV-1). Systemic modelling and mapping are used to estimate the emissions reductions and allocations that are needed to keep levels of individual pollutants, or pollutants in combination, below systemic thresholds reflected in critical loads and levels (Umweltbundesamt, 2004).

Because technological and economic factors dominate, exceedances of critical loads and levels are still widespread in Europe, even if decreasing (Pelletier, 2010; Spranger *et al.*, 2008). The initial levels of emissions reductions required under the LRTAP were based solely on technical and economic considerations, without taking into account the connection between exceedances and loads (Umweltbundesamt, 2004). In the next set of protocols, environmental considerations carried more weight, but attaining critical loads for all ecosystems in Europe was considered infeasible because of technical and economic considerations (Umweltbundesamt, 2004). Gradual attainment of critical loads and levels remains only a long-term objective; complete elimination of exceedances is not necessarily anticipated, and in some cases is considered impossible.[12]

The equivalent program in the United States is the cap-and-trade mechanism under 1990 amendments to the United States Clean Air Act.[13] A gradually diminishing cap on emissions of sulfur dioxide from all electric utilities and other sources was established, an initial set of emissions quotas was allocated to the sources, and a market was created to allow sources to buy and sell the right to emit sulfur dioxide within the overall cap. Although Congress recognized the ecosystem harm that acid rain caused both nationally and internationally,[14] the acid rain program does not link pollutant reductions to an ecological objective for the affected ecosystems. The program's parameters derive primarily from political and economic considerations (Reitze, 1999; Heinzerling, 1995), and ecosystem damage from acid rain persists (Doremus and Haneman, 2008; Jenkins *et al.*, 2005).

The most prominent example of mostly successful ecosystem-based regulation is the international regime for controlling substances that deplete stratospheric ozone. The Montreal Protocol was adopted in 1987, two years after the ozone hole over Antarctica was discovered (United Nations Environment Programme, 2008). The agreement sets forth a mandatory schedule of reductions for the production and consumption of ozone-depleting substances, along with a process for ongoing monitoring and adjustments. The signatory parties have tightened restrictions six times, both by decreasing the allowable production and consumption of ozone-depleting substances and by bringing additional substances under the Protocol, with exceptions for 'essential uses' and attenuated control schedules for developing countries.[15]

The Montreal Protocol has dramatically reduced the production and consumption of ozone-depleting substances (Steiner, 2007; United Nations Environment Programme, 1999). A 2007 report indicated that, if compliance with the Protocol continued, the levels of ozone in the stratosphere would return to their pre-1980 levels, when no hole in the ozone layer existed, by 2050 at mid-latitudes and a decade or two later at the poles (United Nations Environment Programme, 2007). Because of this apparent progress, protection of stratospheric ozone is considered to be 'a good example where concerted human effort and wise decision making seem to have enabled us to stay within a planetary boundary' (Rockström *et al.*, 2009, p15).[16]

Although scientific consensus on the impacts of ozone-depleting substances was quite strong, it was not absolute, and the Montreal Protocol is therefore a relatively successful application of the precautionary principle to avoid catastrophic systemic effects on human health and the global environment (Sunstein, 2007). The Protocol's relative success has also been attributed to the elaboration of separate tracks for developed and developing countries (Plein, 2007), and to funding capacity building and technology transfer in developing countries (Roberts, 2009). For several reasons, however, the success of the Montreal Protocol has not been repeated with other global problems like climate change. Compared to other problems, the science on the impacts of ozone-depleting substances was relatively uncontroversial, the public was largely in favour of action, the number of producers of ozone-depleting substances was small, and substitutes were feasible (Victor, 2008; Winchester, 2009).

Applying lessons from existing mechanisms in formulating ecological law

The TMDL programme, the critical loads and levels approach under the LRTAP, and the Montreal Protocol are among the most promising of existing environmental mechanisms in that they pay at least some attention to systemic limits. The Montreal Protocol has been successful in ways that other system-based mechanisms have not. Although at least some of those other mechanisms have identified thresholds on the tolerance of receptor systems to the effects of pollutants, they have not yielded effective controls on the industrial and other processes that cause those effects because of the primacy of technological and economic factors.

The context and necessity for weighing the aggregate impact of economic activities against unyielding global ecological limits under the rule of ecological law is becoming increasingly clear. A 2008 study on nitrogen-based pollutants under the LRTAP noted that abatement of emissions should ultimately address global problems like climate change and biodiversity loss (Spranger *et al.*, 2008). In other words, the backdrop for a review of international, national or regional pollution control policy regimes is the planetary boundaries (or like indicators), and particularly the ones that Rockström and colleagues (2009) warn we have already crossed: nitrogen fluxes, climate change and biodiversity.

The example of the Montreal Protocol demonstrates the possibility of collectively tackling a global, systemic environmental problem, with a differentiated system of responsibility for countries at different stages of economic development and well-being, and an adherence to the precautionary principle. This record of performance provides lessons for a more generalized approach, particularly in regard to precaution, fairness and supranationality. The rule of ecological law offers a framework for allowing these lessons to take root with respect to a full spectrum of planetary boundaries.

Closing: the emergence of the rule of ecological law

The call for the rule of ecological law emerges from the tension between opposing narratives of impossibility. On the one hand is the seeming impossibility of ending the current intransigent commitment to infinite economic growth and the primacy of short-term economic interests. On the other hand are the systemic impossibilities and long-term catastrophic socio-ecological consequences if the economy grows infinitely, and economic and political trade-offs continue to outweigh non-negotiable ecological limits. The growing tension between these opposing narratives creates an opportunity for transformation. If the researchers who developed the uncompromising planetary boundaries framework are right, the first set of impossibilities must give way to the second—and the rule of ecological law should emerge as a solution that will break Cassandra's curse.

Notes

1 Environmental economics is '[t]he branch of neoclassical economics that addresses environmental problems such as pollution, negative externalities, and valuation of nonmarket environmental services[,] focuses almost exclusively on efficient allocation, and accepts the pre-analytic vision ... that the economic system is the whole, and not a subsystem of the containing and sustaining global ecosystem' (Daly and Farley, 2004, p432).
2 Ecological economics is '[t]he union of economics and ecology, with the economy conceived as a subsystem of the earth ecosystem that is sustained by a metabolic flow or 'throughput' from and back to the larger system' (Daly and Farley, 2004, p431).
3 For rare examples, see Howarth (2006) and Kolbasov (1989).
4 E.g. Rio Declaration on Environment and Development, Principle 12.
5 Because ecosystems constantly evolve, it would be more consistent with current understandings of ecology to refer to the resilience, rather than stability, of the biotic community (Brown and Garver, 2009, p5).
6 See *Robertson v. Methow Valley Citizens Council*, 490 United States 332 (1989).
7 See *Norton v. Southern Utah Wilderness Alliance,* 542 United States 55 (2004).
8 Consistent with the TMDL approach, the Great Lakes Water Quality Agreement of 1978 aims 'to restore and maintain the chemical, physical, and biological integrity of the waters of the Great Lakes Basin Ecosystem' (Article II) and calls upon the United States and Canada to consult regarding '[t]he control of pollutant loading rates for each lake basin to protect the integrity of the ecosystem over the long term' (Article IV(3)(b)). The agreement relies on implementation through the national and subnational laws of the signatories (Article V), along with state-to-state consultations regarding implementation (Article X).
9 *Clean Water Act* §§303(c)(2)(A), 304(a)(1).
10 *Clean Water Act* §§303(d)(1)(C), 304(a)(2); 40 CFR §130.2(i).

11 The TMDL methodology has been criticized for inadequately reflecting ecological criteria (Karr and Yoder, 2004).
12 See, e.g., Gothenburg Protocol to the 1979 Convention on Long-range Transboundary Air Pollution to Abate Acidification, Eutrophication and Ground-level Ozone (30 November 1999) European Union, Directive of the European Parliament and of the Council 2001/81/EC of 23 October 2001 on national emission ceilings for certain atmospheric pollutants [2001] OJL 309/22.
13 *Clean Air Act* Title IV, 42 USC §§7651–7651o (2006).
14 *Clean Air Act* §401(a), 42 USC §7651(a) (2006).
15 Adjustments to the Montreal Protocol agreed by the Second, Fourth, Seventh, Ninth, Eleventh and Nineteenth Meetings of the Parties; London Amendment to the Montreal Protocol, 29 June 1990 (entered into force 10 August 1992); Copenhagen Amendment to the Montreal Protocol, 25 November 1992 (entered into force 14 June 1994); Montreal Amendment to the Montreal Protocol, 17 September 1997 (entered into force 10 November 1999); Beijing Amendment to the Montreal Protocol, 3 December 1999 (entered into force 12 February 2002).
16 See also Roberts (2009); Winchester (2009); Sunstein (2007). However, Reeves (2005) expresses concern that global warming could impede recovery of the ozone layer.

References

Adler, R.W. (2009) 'Freshwater: sustaining use by protecting ecosystems', *Environmental Law Reporter News and Analysis,* vol 39, pp10,309–10,315

AtKisson, A. (1999) *Believing Cassandra: An Optimist Looks at a Pessimist's World,* Chelsea Green, White River Junction, VT

Berry, T. (1999) *The Great Work: Our Way Into the Future,* Three Rivers Press, New York, NY

Bosselmann, K. (2008) *The Principle of Sustainability: Transforming Law and Governance,* Ashgate Publishing Co., Burlington VT

Boutelet, M. and Fritz, J.-C. (eds) (2005) *L'ordre public écologique/Towards an Ecological Public Order,* Bruylant, Brussels, Belgium

Boyd, D. R. (2004) 'Sustainability law: (r)evolutionary directions for the future of environmental law', *Journal of Environmental Law and Practice,* vol 14, pp357–385

Boyd, J. (2000) *The New Face of the Clean Water Act: A Critical Review of EPA's Proposed TMDL Rule,* Discussion Paper 00-12, Resources for the Future, Washington, DC

Brown, P. G. and Garver, G. (2009) *Right Relationship: Building a Whole Earth Economy,* Berrett Koehler, San Francisco, CA

Caudill, D. S. and Curley, D. E. (2008) 'Strategic idealizations of science to oppose environmental regulation: a case study of five TMDL controversies', *University of Kansas Law Review,* vol 57, pp251–312

Cresser, M. S. (2000) 'The critical loads concept: milestone or millstone for the new millenium?', *The Science of the Total Environment,* vol 249, pp51–62

Daly, H. E. and Farley, J. (2004) *Ecological Economics: Principles and Applications,* Island Press, Washington, DC

Delgado, R. (1991) 'Our better natures: a revisionist view of Joseph Sax's public trust theory of environmental protection, and some dark thoughts on the possibility of law reform', *Vanderbilt Law Review,* vol 44, pp1,209–1,227

Doremus, H. and Hanemann, W. M. (2008) 'Of babies and bathwater: why the clean air act's cooperative federalism framework is useful for addressing global warming', *Arizona Law Review*, vol 50, pp799–834

Gore, A. (2006) *An Inconvenient Truth: The Planetary Emergency of Global Warming and What We Can Do About It*, Rodale, Rodale, NY

Hails, C. (ed.) (2008) *The Living Planet Report*, WWF International, Gland, Switzerland

Heinzerling, L. (2005) 'Risking it all', *Alabama Law Review*, vol 57, no 1, pp155–169

Heinzerling, L. (1995) 'Selling pollution, forcing democracy', *Stanford Environmental Law Journal*, vol 14, pp300–344

Heinzerling, L. and Ackerman, F. (2007) 'Law and economics for a warming world', *Harvard Law and Policy Review*, vol 1, pp332–362

Howarth, W. (2006) 'The progression towards ecological quality standards', *Journal of Environmental Law*, vol 18, pp3–35

Jenkins, J., Roy, K., Driscoll, C. and Buerkett, C. (2005) *Acid Rain and the Adirondacks: A Research Summary*, Adirondacks Lakes Survey Corporation, Ray Brook, NY

Karr, J. R. and Yoder, C. O. (2004) 'Biological assessment and criteria improve total maximum daily load decision making', *Journal of Environmental Engineering*, June, pp594–604.

Kass, M. J. (2009) 'A NEPA climate paradox: taking greenhouse gases into account in threshold significance determinations', *Indiana Law Review*, vol 42, pp47–96

Kolbasov, O. S. (1989) 'The concept of ecological law', *Connecticut Journal of International Law*, vol 4, pp267–277

Leopold, A. (1949) *A Sand County Almanac*, Oxford University Press, New York, NY

Naess, A. (1984) 'A defence of the deep ecology movement', *Environmental Ethics*, vol 6, pp265–270

Oreskes, N. and Conway, E. M. (2010) *Merchants of Doubt*, Bloomsbury Press, New York, NY

Pelletier, N. (2010) 'Of laws and limits: an ecological economic perspective on redressing the failure of contemporary global environmental governance', *Global Environmental Change*, vol 20, pp220–228

Percival, R. V. (2007) 'Environmental law in the twenty-first century', *Virginia Environmental Law Journal*, vol 25, pp1–35

Plein, A. L. (2007) 'A story between success and challenge: 20th anniversary of the Montreal Protocol' *New Zealand Journal of Environmental Law*, vol 11, pp67–98

Reeves, H. (2005) *Mal de Terre*, Éditions du Seuil, Paris, France

Reitze, Jr., A. W. (1999) 'The legislative history of United States air pollution control', *Houston Law Review*, vol 36, pp679–741

Roberts, M. W. (2009) 'The Montreal Protocol must act to prevent global climate change while restoring the ozone layer', *Sustainable Development Law and Policy*, vol 9, pp33–67

Rockström, J., Steffen, W., Noone, K., Persson, Å. F., Chapin III, F. S., Lambin, E. F., Lenton, T. M., Scheffer, M., Folke, C., Schellnhuber, H. J., Nykvist, B., de Wit, C. A., Hughes, T., van der Leeuw, S., Rodhe, H., Sörlin, S., Snyder, P. K., Costanza, R., Svedin, U., Falkenmark, M., Karlberg, L., Corell, R. W., Fabry, V. J., Hansen, J., Walker, B., Liverman, D., Richardson, K., Crutzen, P. and Foley, J. A. (2009) 'Planetary boundaries: exploring the safe operating space for humanity', *Ecology and Society*, vol 14, no 2, article 32, www.ecologyandsociety.org/vol14/iss2/art32/, (accessed 29 August 2011)

Speth, J. G. (2008) *The Bridge at the Edge of the World,* Yale University Press, New Haven, CT

Spranger, T., Hettelingh, J. P., Slootweg, J. and Posch, M. (2008) 'Modelling and mapping long-term risks due to reactive nitrogen effects: an overview of LRTAP Convention activities', *Environmental Pollution,* vol 154, pp482–487

Steiner, A. (2007) '20th anniversary of the Protocol and International Day for the Preservation of the Ozone Layer', speech at the opening of the 19th Meeting of the Parties to the Montreal Protocol on Substances that Deplete the Ozone Layer, Montreal, 16 September

Sunstein, C. R. (2007) *Worst-Case Scenarios,* Harvard University Press, Cambridge, MA

Tarlock, A. D. (2000) 'The future of environmental "rule of law" litigation', *Pace Environmental Law Review,* vol 17, pp237–272

Umweltbundesamt (2004) *Manual on Methodologies and Criteria for Modelling and Mapping Critical Loads and Levels and Air Pollution Effects, Risks and Trends,* Umweltbundesamt, Dessau-Roßlau, Germany

United Nations Environment Programme (1999) *Report of the Eleventh Meeting of the Parties to the Montreal Protocol on Substances that Deplete the Ozone Layer,* Ozone Secretariat, United Nations Environment Programme, Nairobi, Kenya, http://ozone.unep.org/Meeting_Documents/mop/11mop/11mop-10.e.pdf, accessed 29 August 2011

United Nations Environment Programme (2007) *Synthesis Report of the 2006 Assessments of the Scientific Assessment Panel, the Environmental Effects Assessment Panel and the Technology and Economic Assessment Panel,* No. UNEP/OzL.Pro. WG.1/27/3, June, Ozone Secretariat, United Nations Environment Programme, Nairobi, Kenya

United Nations Environment Programme (2008) *Backgrounder: Basic Facts and Data on the Science and Politics of Ozone Protection,* Ozone Secretariat, United Nations Environment Programme, Nairobi, Kenya, http://ozone.unep.org/Events/ozone_day_2008/press_backgrounder.pdf, accessed 29 August 2011

United Nations Security Council (2004) *The Rule of Law and Transitional Justice in Conflict and Post-conflict Societies: Report of the Secretary General,* Document No. S/2004/616, United Nations, New York, NY

United States Environmental Protection Agency (n.d.), *Impaired Waters and Total Maximum Daily Loads?,* http://water.epa.gov/lawsregs/lawsguidance/cwa/tmdl (accessed 29 August 2011)

United States Environmental Protection Agency (2003) *Withdrawal of Revisions to the Water Quality Planning and Management Regulation and Revisions to the National Pollutant Discharge Elimination System Program in Support of Revisions to the Water Quality Planning and Management Regulation,* 68 Fed. Reg. 13608, United States Environmental Protection Agency, Washington, DC

United States Environmental Protection Agency (2009) *National Water Quality Inventory: Report to Congress, 2004 Reporting Cycle,* United States Environmental Protection Agency, Washington, DC

Victor, P. A. (2008) *Managing Without Growth: Smaller By Design, Not Disaster,* Edgar Elgar, Cheltenham, UK

Westra, L. (1994) *An Environmental Proposal for Ethics: The Principle of Ecological Integrity,* Rowman & Littlefield Publishers, Lanham, MD

Westra, L. (2008) 'Ecological integrity: its history, its future and the development of the Global Ecological Integrity Group' in L. Westra, K. Bosselmann and R. Westra (eds) *Reconciling Human Existence with Ecological Integrity*, Earthscan, London

Winchester, N. B. (2009) 'Emerging global environmental governance' *Indiana Journal of Global Legal Studies*, vol 16, no 1, pp7–23

Conclusion

Intersecting governance impacting health: an afterword on climate change, food security, and related legal regimes

Lawrence O. Gostin

> The core concern is succinctly stated: climate change endangers human health. The warming of the planet will be gradual, but the effects of extreme weather events – more storms, floods, droughts and heat waves – will be abrupt and acutely felt. Both trends can affect some of the most fundamental determinants of health: air, water, food, shelter and freedom from disease. (Margaret Chan, quoted in WHO, 2008)

This wonderful book – edited by Laura Westra, Colin Soskolne and Donald Spady – commemorates the 20th anniversary of the Global Ecological Integrity Group (GEIG), dedicated to the compelling idea that ecological integrity is not only a transcending value in its own right, but also that the world in which we live deeply impacts our collective health and well-being. The book showcases the inextricable intersections between ethics, human rights, the environment and public health.

In my forthcoming book I define and systematically probe the field of global health law (Gostin, 2013). In doing so, I have come to learn from the admirable teachings of the GEIG that human health extends well beyond the health sector, to also include the multiple linking strands of ecological governance.

International law can profoundly affect global governance for health – for better or worse. Human rights hold vast potential to improve global health, through the right to health itself, as well as socioeconomic rights, such as education, housing, employment and social support. World trade and intellectual property legal regimes can either fuel prosperity needed for better health, or deeply undermine access to essential medicines and domestic health and safety regulation.

Beyond human rights and trade lie multiple intersecting legal regimes that significantly impact health, including climate change, armed conflict, refugees and food security. If international law in these realms could be expanded, strengthened and faithfully implemented as part of coherent global governance, with health placed nearer the centre of their mandates, considerable improvements in health and well-being would become a reality.

The 2011 famine in the Horn of Africa exemplifies how these intersecting legal regimes influence health – all playing a role in how people have been faring during the worst drought in 60 years. The 20-year-long civil war in Somalia and concomitant breakdown in infrastructure dramatically worsened the drought's impact, leaving millions malnourished and starving, with mass migrations to refugee camps in Kenya and Ethiopia. Extreme weather events similarly can lead to armed conflict, further exacerbating food shortages and mass migration. 'There can be little doubt', said United Nations Environment Programme director Achim Steiner (2011), that 'climate change has potentially far-reaching implications for global stability and security in economic, social and environmental terms.'

Climate change, food security, armed conflicts and migration are key determinants of health – an integral part of global governance for health. Their importance to health is increasing with the rapid growth in urbanization, population, and globalization. Unfortunately, the driving forces behind these regimes – commercial, economic and geostrategic – are often in tension with public health. These and other intersecting regimes must be strengthened so that they protect and promote, rather than detract from, major health goals. Without higher standards and more effective compliance, international law will fail to realize its full potential to safeguard the world's population, particularly for the most vulnerable people.

A global health treaty: making the ideals of ecological integrity work for human kind

From Roger Brownsword's eloquent exploration of individual and common goods in his Foreword to Laura Westra's sweeping examination of life, health and the environment in Chapter 1, and through the rich chapters on how ecosystems impact human well-being, this book is a treasure of ideas, creativity and knowledge. But is it possible to make these ideals a reality for the world's population and the planet on which we live?

One perhaps unlikely place to look is international law and governance. It is unlikely because, after all, so much of international law is vague, and even vague standards seem near impossible to enforce. And the international community has tried repeatedly to negotiate better agreements ranging from the failure of the Doha Round of Trade negotiations through to the stalled negotiations for the next phase of the Kyoto Protocol.

Even with all these hurdles, a major Southern-led campaign is proposing a Framework Convention on Global Health (Gostin, 2008, pp331–392). The campaign, called the Joint Action and Learning Initiative (JALI) on National and Global Responsibilities for Health, seeks a broadly imagined global governance regime that embraces the potential synergies of intersecting regimes, such as fair trade, access to essential medicines, human rights and climate change. JALI advocates for essential human needs, including hygiene, sanitation, clean water, safe and nutritious food, and vector control. JALI's four major questions for research and action mesh seamlessly with the ideals of GEIG (Gostin *et al.*, 2011):

- What are the services and goods guaranteed to every person under the human right to health?
- What responsibilities do all states have for the health of their own populations?
- What duties do states owe to people beyond their borders in securing the right to health?
- What kind of global governance for health is needed to ensure that all states live up to their mutual responsibilities?

This is a moment of rare opportunity. The post-MDG global health framework has yet to be developed. Demand for accountability is growing. The right to health is increasingly motivating not only civil society, but also governments. The World Health Assembly is considering the most far-reaching reform in the WHO's 60-year history. Universal coverage, primary health care, climate change, and socioeconomic determinants are receiving renewed focus.

A Framework Convention on Global Health that harnesses the creativity and ideals of multiple GEIG and health advocacy communities could become a powerful force. Rather than working in our silos, civil society and the academy must realize the power of collective action and the synergies among our ideals. This magnificent book and the 20-year history of GEIG can provide the intellectual foundations for broadly imagined fundamental change to benefit Earth and all its inhabitants.

References

Gostin, L. O. (2008) 'Meeting basic survival needs of the world's least healthy people: toward a framework convention on global health', *Georgetown Law Journal*, vol 96, pp331–392

Gostin, L. O. (2013) *Global Health Law: International Law, Global Institutions, and World Health*, Harvard University Press, Cambridge, MA (forthcoming)

Gostin, L. O., Friedman, E. A., Ooms, G., Gebauer, T., Gupta, N., Sridhar, D., Chenguang, W., Røttingen, J.-A., and Sanders, D. (2011) 'The Joint Action and Learning Initiative: towards a global agreement on national and global responsibilities for health', *PLoS Medicine*, vol 8, no 5, pe1001031, available at www.plosmedicine.org/article/info%3Adoi%2F10.1371%2Fjournal.pmed.1001031

Steiner, A. (2011) 'Warning of climate change's threat to global security, Ban urges concerted action', news release, 20 July, News Centre, United Nations, New York, NY, available at www.unep.org/cpi/briefs/2011Jul21.doc

WHO (2008) 'Climate change will erode foundations of health', news release (quoting the director-general of WHO, Dr Margaret Chan), 7 April, World Health Organization, Geneva, Switzerland, available at www.who.int/mediacentre/news/releases/2008/pr11/en

Index